Degeneration, decadence and disease in the Russian *fin de siècle*

Manchester University Press

Durham Modern Languages Series
Series editor: Michael Thompson

Degeneration, decadence and disease in the Russian *fin de siècle*

Neurasthenia in the life and work of Leonid Andreev

Frederick H. White

Manchester University Press

Manchester and New York

*distributed in the United States exclusively
by Palgrave Macmillan*

The right of Frederick H. White to be identified as the author of this work has been asserted by him in accordance with the Copyright, Designs and Patents Act 1988.

Published by Manchester University Press
Oxford Road, Manchester M13 9NR, UK
and Room 400, 175 Fifth Avenue, New York, NY 10010, USA
www.manchesteruniversitypress.co.uk

Distributed in the United States exclusively by
Palgrave Macmillan, 175 Fifth Avenue, New York,
NY 10010, USA

Distributed in Canada exclusively by
UBC Press, University of British Columbia, 2029 West Mall,
Vancouver, BC, Canada V6T 1Z2

British Library Cataloguing-in-Publication Data
A catalogue record for this book is available from the British Library

Library of Congress Cataloging-in-Publication Data applied for

ISBN 978 0 7190 9164 3 hardback

First published 2014

The publisher has no responsibility for the persistence or accuracy of URLs for any external or third-party internet websites referred to in this book, and does not guarantee that any content on such websites is, or will remain, accurate or appropriate.

Typeset
by Action Publishing Technology Ltd, Gloucester
Printed in Great Britain
by CPI Group (UK) Ltd, Croydon, CR0 4YY

This book is dedicated to my wife
Jaclyn

Contents

Contents

Figures

Acknowledgements

After publishing two articles on Leonid Andreev and mental illness in the Russian academic journals *Novoe literaturnoe obozrenie* and *Voprosy literatury*, six Soviet-trained scholars decided that they would publish a polemic against my scholarly work in yet a third academic journal (*Russkaia Literatura*), breaking the usual code of scholarly conduct. At no point did these scholars attempt to dialogue with me and must have thought that their harsh rebuke would silence the 'young Canadian' (sic) on this topic. The first to offer me their assistance with this polemic were Natal'ia Gronskaia and Yuri Leving. For this and their continued friendship and scholarly support, I am deeply indebted. My response to the polemic was finally published months later by *Russkaia Literatura*, but only after several sharp exchanges with the editor and the threat of publishing my response in *NLO* or *Voprosy literatury*. At this point, I had two options: either I could leave the topic to those Soviet-trained scholars and their ilk who wished to maintain the sanitized biography of the author, or I could commit to research and write a book about mental illness in Russia at the beginning of the twentieth century. The book in your hands is the final result of that initial exchange.

Just as significant, I must thank the Canadian Social Sciences and Humanities Research Council (SSHRC) for their generous funding of my project. Noreen Golfman aided me greatly in this application process and deserves recognition for this and other acts of kindness for a junior colleague. This SSHRC grant allowed me to conduct research at archives in Russia, England and the United States. I would especially like to thank Richard Davies and Liia Zatulovskaia for their assistance and advice in archives in Leeds, UK and Orel, Russia. Thank you also to the staff at the Hoover Institute Archive. Nina Grigor'eva led me to the remains of Andreev's home near the Black rivulet one summer and provided me with relevant information that furthered my research. Ben Hellman, Mikhail Koz'menko, Thomas Seifrid and Andrei Rogatchevski all provided penetrating questions that made me reposition my arguments again and again, until I could negotiate all of the different facets of the issue. Theresa Heath read and edited the first full draft, which greatly improved the manuscript. Dennis Ioffe has provided sound advice and enduring friendship throughout this process, even leading me to my present publisher. For all of them, I extend a heartfelt thank you.

I worked through many of the issues in this book first in scholarly articles and I want to thank in particular the editors (especially Evgeny Pavlov) and peer-review readers of the following journals who helped me to sharpen my argumentation: *Canadian Slavonic Papers, New Zealand Slavonic Journal, Novoe literaturnoe obozrenie, The Russian Review, Slavic and East European Journal,* and *Voprosy literatury.* The specific articles and numbers are listed in the bibliography.

Ten years after the initial confrontation, I feel indebted to so many more people than I can name individually here. For friends and colleagues who endured my constant conversations about Andreev, who gave me a place to stay while on research trips and sabbatical, who provided unstinting support and friendship during this decade of academic work – thank you very much.

Notes on Russian terms, images and abbreviations

Russian terms and images

I have retained Russian names in their transliterated forms (Gor'kii as opposed to Gorky) throughout the manuscript. I have also incorporated as many English translations of the referenced texts as I was able to locate. It is my hope that interested individuals who are unable to read in Russian may still engage this study and the primary texts in translation. For the most part, I have relied on the translated texts in quotes, unless there were clear inaccuracies. All other translations from Russian are my own. Both the Hoover Institute Archive and the United State Literary Museum of I.S. Turgenev were very generous in providing copies of rare photographs of Leonid Andreev for publication in this book.

Abbreviations

IRLI	Institute of Russian Literature, Pushkin House, St Petersburg
LRA	Leeds Russian Archive, Leeds University, UK
OGLMT	United State Literary Museum of I.S. Turgenev, Orel
RGALI	Russian State Archive of Literature and Art, Moscow

1

Introduction

Agonizing health, an agonizing mental condition. Painful. Again I
think about suicide. I think [about it] or does it think about me?
But the ocean is splendid.

Leonid Andreev[1]

Interpretations

Leonid Andreev (1871–1919) was Russia's leading literary and cultural
figure from roughly 1902 to 1914. He and Feodor Sologub
(1863–1927) were the best selling authors during much of that time,
and Andreev was equal to Maksim Gor'kii (1868–1936) in terms of
topical relevance. His name was spoken in the same breath as Lev
Tolstoi (1828–1910), Feodor Dostoevskii (1821–1881) and Anton
Chekhov (1860–1904) during his lifetime. Yet, because he had both
supported revolution in his early years and reviled the Bolsheviks at
the end of his life, Andreev found no defenders among Russian
émigrés living abroad or literary scholars in the Soviet Union. Within
a decade after his death, and for roughly thirty years thereafter, his
literary works were largely ignored.

This book invites reconsideration of one of the leading authors of the
Russian *fin de siècle*, concentrating on a neglected area of his life and
work. Andreev was diagnosed as an acute neurasthenic and struggled
with various illnesses. He gained a reputation in the popular press for
being mentally imbalanced, and a recurring theme of psychopathology
in his creative works seemed to support this contention. Although
Andreev publicly defended his mental health, he could not escape the
popular discourse that constantly conflated his life and literary works. In
fact, Andreev's personal struggle with *neurasthenia*[2] gave him a unique
perspective on the discourse of degeneration theory, which was
prevalent in contemporary Russian culture, making his works particularly timely and appealing for readers. Arguably, it may have been this

1.1 Leonid Andreev from February 1901, while a patient at the Imperial clinic for nervous disorders.

concentration on the decadent issues of devolution, decline and deviance that made Andreev so successful.

In this study, attention will be given to the way in which the discourse of a private body articulated the general anxiety around the mental and physical health of the Russian nation at the beginning of the twentieth century, providing an opportunity for a broad discussion of a medical and scientific type, which became interwoven in the fabric of Russian culture and society. Although the present study is limited to one author's experience and the reaction of critics, medical personages and the public alike, it is meant to bring attention to some of the larger issues, around the popularization of scientific discourse at this time in Russia, issues that deserve further investigation. As such, questions will be raised concerning Russian decadence, degeneration theory, the emergence of psychiatry as a new science and the circular nature that art played in proving science correct. These questions cannot be answered completely by looking at the life and works of Leonid Andreev, but they should promote further discussion and scholarly work.

More specifically, this study examines Andreev within the context of neurasthenia, a double-edged sword that informed his literary works and impacted his personal life. This is not intended as an introduction to, nor an exhaustive biography of the author. Such works, although dated, already exist. English biographies of Andreev include those by Alexander Kaun (1924), James B. Woodward (1969) and Josephine Newcome (1973), and in Russian by Nikolai Fatov (1924) and Leonid Afonin (1959).[3] Arguably, these studies do not fully reflect the possible reasons for Andreev's immense literary success during his lifetime and certainly do not give much attention to his mental health, although Fatov here is the exception. Since the 1960s, scholars have mainly offered what might be called the sentimentalized (or sanitized) version of Andreev's biography. Instead, this study aims to (re)establish what may be called the fourth line of medical discourse, which concentrates on the author's life and works in the light of degeneration theory, and offers a new interpretation of Andreev's place in Russian literary and cultural discourse within the larger context of science in Russia at the beginning of the twentieth century. Previous biographies do not satisfactorily situate Andreev within the larger popular concerns of the era, thereby ostracizing him from the period for which he was an important representative.

The approach employed in this study, illness narrative theory and medical anthropology, offers an explanation for Andreev's perceived literary *greatness* during his lifetime while also allowing contemporary readers to reassess him as a talented and yet misunderstood cultural figure. Examining Andreev's illness experience (this includes the reactions of critics, psychiatrists and the reading public) leads one to certain suppositions, not previously considered. Andreev was immensely popular because his own medical experiences permitted him to tap into the prevailing *hot topic* of the day – Russia's decadent decline. The stigma of mental illness, however, seemed to tarnish his literary reputation and was denied by both Andreev and, especially later, Soviet literary scholars. In denying this, however, the contemporary reader loses all perspective on why the author was such an enormous literary success. Lost is a sense of his social timeliness, the synchronicity of his own battle with neurasthenia and Russia's mounting anxiety about social devolution. Lost is the author's personal struggle to maintain legitimacy and avoid the stigma of mental illness. Lost is most of the public discourse around the author and his works, which often resulted in heated public debates. Lost is the way in which his literary works were utilized by the scientific community to prove their own theories valid. Lost is much of what made Andreev a literary sensation. Remaining today is a sanitized version of the author that was mainly created to satisfy the Soviet literary market, thereby denying him his cultural relevance.[4] In order to reintroduce Andreev in the 1960s, a Soviet biography was created that would focus on his revolutionary activities and concern for the common man. This version of Andreev not only distorted the author's political views, but it obscured most of the popular discourse that made him relevant at the beginning of the twentieth century. This study attempts to recapture the discourse of mental illness that surrounded Andreev during his lifetime in order to restore to him (and for readers) a bit of that excitement and controversy that made this author *the* leading literary figure of his time.

After the thaw

A decade after his death, Andreev and his literary works were largely ignored, until the 1960s when Nikita Khrushchev's (1894–1971) comparatively liberal social and political policies permitted scholars to return to forgotten authors. Once Andreev was rediscovered, concentration was directed at recovering his published and unpublished literary and journalistic works. Only recently has the scholarly gaze turned its attention once again to Andreev's life history as a means to interpret these recovered texts. Scholars have attempted to explain the volatile emotional behavior and gloomy pessimism in the author's literary works, diaries, letters and in memoirs dedicated to him. Logically, they have returned to many of the explanations of Andreev's contemporaries and critics in order to gain insights.

Vatslav Vorovskii (1871–1923) and Anatolii Lunacharskii (1875–1933) offered the opinion in 1908 that Andreev simply reflected the historical milieu in which he lived.[5] Georgii Chulkov (1879–1939) and Gor'kii argued after his death that Andreev's pessimism was caused by his reading of Arthur Schopenhauer (1788–1860) when he was a teenager.[6] Andreev's younger brother, Pavel (1878–1923), cited socio-economic factors – poverty and the stress of supporting the family after their father's death when Andreev was only eighteen years old.[7] These three lines of discourse can be used to describe one or two periods, but they fail to explain the entirety of Andreev's life and literary output. A fourth line of critical discourse argues for an investigation of the author's life and works in light of his medical history.[8]

Each one of these lines can be seen in the biographies of Andreev mentioned above. Kaun gives special concentration to the influence of German pessimistic philosophy. Afonin, Newcombe and most Soviet scholars give preference to the socio-economic pressures that they believe shaped the author. Woodward attempts to give equal time to the first three lines of critical discourse. Fatov alone gives special attention to Andreev's medical history.

The real issue may be found, however, in the popular Andreev that existed until the 1930s and the Andreev that was resurrected in the Soviet Union in the 1960s. It is this later version that is the most sanitized and, arguably, the dullest. In order to make Andreev palatable for literary and political power brokers in the Soviet Union, much of the author's biography was ignored or refashioned so that Andreev could be seen as a defender of the toiling masses (or, more realistic, as a representative of the radical intelligentsia). As such, scholars tended to pay attention to elements of criticism that most satisfied Marxist-Leninist theories. Consequently, controversial elements of the author's life and works, including his battle with ill health, were repressed. Andreev's works that could be read in a positive Soviet way were given special attention, while the author's life was made to fit a uniform pattern, which eliminated much relevant biographical information.

Following the demise of the Soviet Union, scholars were still wary to stigmatize the author as mentally ill and, instead, refashioned once again a version of Andreev to fit the times. He was now a voice of the impending chaos and destruction of Imperial Russia. Such a scholarly position was thought to resonate with readers caught in the similarly chaotic post-Soviet 1990s. The unpleasant aspects of his character (rumors of mental illness included) were part of this *zeitgeist*. Specifically, concentration was given once again to the influence of German pessimistic thought as many of these philosophers were also being rehabilitated within post-Soviet intellectual society. As a result, readers and students of Andreev were left with a version of the author that was initially created for Soviet authorities and then refined to counter the overtly (and incorrect) pro-Soviet elements of this created biography. Resistance to reopening Andreev's biography completely for discussion remains even today among scholars educated in the Soviet school, seemingly because this might tarnish once again the author's literary reputation and diminish the work of Soviet scholars. The concern is that this version of Andreev is both dull and incomplete (not to mention inaccurate).[9] An examination of Andreev's struggle with neurasthenia asks scholars to relinquish this Soviet-like version of the author and reengage the discussion around his life and works.

From his early diaries, we learn that Andreev experienced severe depression, abused alcohol as a type of self-medication, and fixated on his relationships with various women in hopes that he could be saved from his condition. During his university years, due to the bouts of depression, Andreev tried to commit suicide at least three times and engaged in what one friend called 'pathological drunkenness.'[10] When Andreev finally began to experience literary and financial success, he was still tormented by self-doubt and depression. He sought treatment in 1901 and was diagnosed as an acute neurasthenic as attested to by his sister Rimma (1881–1941) and friend Vladimir Azov (1873–c. 1941).[11] Neurasthenia, depression caused by extreme exhaustion, was included within a broad diagnostic classification for mental illness and was associated with various other illnesses of degeneration. It was this diagnosis that most influenced Andreev's self-perception and artistic production.

To elucidate this point further, one might offer the following scenario to underscore the importance of a medical diagnosis on the life of an individual: A man visits his doctor due to a backache. After examining him, the doctor tells the man that he possibly has cancer, but would like to run more tests to be sure. For two weeks, while tests are being run, the patient's life is completely consumed by the possibility that he will soon die of cancer. It influences his relationships with his wife and children. He begins to look at his job and the demands of his profession in a different light. He commits to exercise regularly and buys books on alternative medicine. In short, the specter of cancer influences everything that he does. After two weeks, the man learns that he is absolutely healthy and that it was just a benign tumor causing the pain that can easily be removed. But the incident serves as a wakeup call and he vows to live a more healthy life. Important here is the understanding that the man's perception of his life was gravely influenced by the doctor's initial diagnosis. Unfortunately, after Andreev was diagnosed, no doctor ever told him that he was healthy. Therefore, he lived as an acute neurasthenic, complicated by a variety of other health issues and, like the man who was told that he was dying of cancer, every aspect of Andreev's life was affected by his medical diagnosis. Additionally, because of his fame, each of his illnesses was reported in the popular press as a sign of madness, forcing the author to constantly contextualize his life in these terms of mental illnesses and defend himself publicly as sane.

In this study, therefore, I concentrate on how Andreev's life and works were influenced by the medical theories of degeneration that were gaining currency in Russian popular culture. I suggest that Andreev's personal experience with mental illness and Russia's growing fascination and anxiety with degeneration contributed in large part to his rapid rise to literary stardom. In turn, a circular argument was created. That is, Andreev's personal conception of illness was informed by science, these concepts were realized in his literary works, and his works were then used as evidence that Russian society was degenerate, with Andreev serving as a prime example, thereby reinforcing the 'legitimacy' of the science as well as Andreev's understanding of his own condition. This approach provides a new interpretation of Andreev's impact on the Russian *fin de siècle* and addresses the role of degeneration theory in Russia at the beginning of the twentieth century. It asks that Andreev's life and literary works be viewed within the cultural discourse of pathology, bringing to the fore once again that which was lost in Soviet scholarship, the influence of literary decadence and the development of Russian psychiatry.

The first part of this study examines degeneration theory and its impact in Europe and Russia around the turn of the twentieth century. Psychiatry, the latest medical discipline at this time, attempted to claim the irrational for science. In so doing, a net was cast widely to capture both the mentally and morally ill. As a result, there was talk of an epidemic that negatively impacted not only the individual, but society as a whole. This study also reexamines the Russian decadent movement as more than just the proclamations and manifestos of certain individuals. If we look beyond personal friendships and literary allegiances, Andreev's works are concerned with issues (many relating to mental illness) consistent with European literary decadence. Such a reading provides a richer and more nuanced understanding of his works. The next five sections explore Andreev's life and works with a specific focus on his illness experience and its expression in his fiction, as the two were read and discussed in conjunction with his reported mental illness by critics, psychiatrists and the general public. This served to promote his literary fame but simultaneously dogged his personal reputation. The final section places Andreev within the larger decadent literary movement of the *fin de siècle* and suggests why he was so immensely popular during his lifetime, but has been largely ignored in recent scholarly discussions of the period.

By reexamining Andreev's life and literary works through the popular discourse of pathology, we see the combined influence of European medical discourse, the development of Russian psychiatry, the role that it had in shaping the popular dialogue on social deviance, and the way Andreev's personal illness experience and his literary works interacted with these issues. This concentration on psychiatric pathology in popular discourse will also augment scholarship on philosophical, religious and political influences of the Russian Silver Age and open the topic for broader discussion.

Illness narrative

In this study, the working definition of *narrative* and, specifically, *illness narrative,* is broad in order to account for Andreev's fictional works and personal texts (letters, diaries, etc.). This is done so as to understand how the author perceived his own illness experience and then articulated it in his literary works and personal behavior. Illness narrative theory recognizes that an individual's perception is mediated by his personal experience, therefore, a line between what is fictional and what is factual cannot be so clearly drawn. In order to understand Andreev's criminally insane and morally corrupt characters, one must explore the lived experience that informed the creation of those characters and, in turn, gives us insight into how the author interacted with his illness.

Hayden White asserts that in any historical narrative created by an individual there is an ordering process by which some events are highlighted and others are repressed to develop a sequence of *cause and effect.*[12] He argues that individuals need to stabilize the chaos of *real* life, placing events in a recognizable context so that the narrative gains meaning. By establishing a narrative progression we attempt to *make sense* out of the world around us, assign classifications such as *good times, bad times, the best time of my life, a difficult time in my life.* In creating a personal narrative, we employ elements often associated with fiction – storytelling. Therefore any narrative, fictional or not, will follow an individual ordering process to tell a particular story.

White calls this 'emplotment' – when life events are organized by the individual in order to create a coherent narrative. *We won the battle because of certain events, as well as the courage and valor of specific soldiers.* The chaos of war is turned into a coherent series of meaningful events, highlighted by the efforts of several noteworthy characters that led to a perceived outcome. The author selects certain elements of the experience to emphasize, while repressing others, and assigns motivations and actions to some individuals while ignoring others, in order to support a specific conclusion. Drawn from real life, the author of the narrative provides his own meaning for the lived experience that may be a tale he tells to his family, a portion of his memoir or a novel about war.

Similarly, the author draws from life events in order to create fictional narratives that rely on similar literary archetypes that are employed when telling a tale, writing a memoir or penning a novel. White argues that human beings are predisposed to organize factual details into coherent narrative wholes in order to structure their life experience. Consequently, we can examine a similar process of emplotment in which the life events of a particular author are organized in order to create a narrative, whether autobiographical or fictional. The author's experience allows the autobiographical imagination to reformulate and restructure experience as a conscious act of interpretation. Arguably, Andreev's depiction of illness originates from personal experiences and is depicted as meaningful events with remarkable characters. Andreev selected elements of his experience and assigned motivations and actions to his characters in order to provide a specific interpretation of that experience. In this way, Andreev provided meaning for his lived experiences in conversations with his family, in comments to the press and in his stories and dramas.

When examining Andreev's works, scholars have noted the close parallels between his fiction and his own life.[13] In stories like 'In the Spring' (Vesnoi) and 'Youth' (Mladost'), Andreev revisits the death of his father and his difficult adolescence. 'Little Angel' (Angelochek) is a fictionalized account of an event that occurred during the Christmas holidays when he was eight years old. The suicide of a priest's daughter in his hometown of Orel was Andreev's inspiration for 'Silence' (Molchanie). After meeting the terrorist Pinkhus Rutenberg (1878–1942), Andreev distorted Rutenberg's activities in a bordello in his story 'Darkness' (T'ma). Andreev used his one experience as a trial lawyer in November 1897 to write 'The First Fee' (Pervyi gonorar) some three years later. *Days of our Life* (Dni nashi zhizni) and *Gaudeamus* describe Andreev's student life in 1890s Moscow, while many have read his play *Life of Man* (Zhizn' cheloveka) as a foreshadowing of his final years in Finland. 'The Yoke of War' (Igo voiny) reads like Andreev's adolescent diary, and 'Two Letters' (Dva pis'ma) may be a fictional response to his unrequited love for Liudmila Chirikova (1896–1995), his neighbor and the daughter of a literary colleague.

In works like 'In the Fog' (V tumane), 'The Governor' (Gubernator), *Savva*, 'The Flight' (Polet) and many others, Andreev took events directly from the pages of newspapers and created a fictional narrative to amplify the bare facts. He mined the rich soil of his own life and the events of the day to create fiction. As a result, we can confidently suggest that Andreev's life experiences, or at least how he perceived them, were transformed and presented to the public as fiction. Kaun argues, 'Andreyev's life and work are so interwoven, so inter-reflective, that neither can be adequately understood without a complementary study of the other.'[14] One might suggest that in the same way that individuals organize events to create narratives about life, Andreev seemed to organize his life to produce fictional narratives.[15]

The close relationship between Andreev's life and literary works prompts the question: Why was Andreev so interested in madness as a literary theme? We return to our four lines of critical discourse to answer this question. First, Andreev was interested in the theme of madness because he was reflecting the turmoil and chaos of historical events during the revolutions of 1905 and 1917, as well as the upheavals of the Russo-Japanese War and World War I. This explanation applies to some of his works, but not all. For example, it helps to explain 'Red Laugh' (Krasnyi smekh), but not 'The Thought' (Mysl'). Second, the theme recurs because the adolescent Andreev read and was greatly influenced by the pessimistic philosophy of Schopenhauer and Eduard von Hartmann (1842–1906). Andreev may have understood this as an explanation for his melancholy but it provides little insight into the theme of madness in his literary works. After all, Andreev read this philosophy as a teenager. Are we to believe it remained such a significant part of his self-identification for the next thirty years? Third, we can suggest that madness resurfaces due to the extreme poverty and stress that Andreev felt in supporting his family following his father's death. This theory can definitely be applied to Andreev's early works, but how do we account for the persistence of this theme even in the years when he had enough money to build a large villa in Vammelsuu?

What if we accept that Andreev suffered from some form of illness that psychiatrists and other medical personages associated with moral and mental degeneration? What if he had spent time in hospitals at different times during his life for severe depression, fatigue and attacks of anxiety? What if due to periods of depression, and possible mania, Andreev had been a binge drinker, had tried to commit suicide several times as a youth, and was well-known among family and friends for his chaotic behavior? Added to these personal experiences, what if he lived in a place and time when it was believed that mental illness was linked to deviance and that contemporary society was regressing into a state of primitive bestiality? This might explain why so many mentally disturbed characters and references to lunatic asylums populate the works of an author who drew his fictional narratives from his own life experience.

After all, too many of Andreev's literary works contain references to madness, insane asylums and related issues to be ignored.[16] Add to this that during his lifetime, there were critics and pathologists who felt that Andreev's stories captured mental illness with such clinical accuracy that they could be used as medical examples of supposedly real psychological conditions.[17] This returns us to the circular argument noted above that is specific to Andreev's own illness experience.

After his death, a majority of the memoir literature dedicated to Andreev addressed his chaotic behavior, his drinking, his pessimistic moods and much more unflattering conduct. Clearly, his friends and colleagues felt that they must comment on such abnormal behavior. A story, letter or memoir examined individually might not support the notion that Andreev suffered from a persistent illness, but the accumulation of these documents clearly attests to a life of distress and pain.

In this context, we can learn about Andreev and his literary works by examining the theme of madness. To do so, we first have to return to his narrative of madness and examine what it says about being ill. *Disease* is the clinical explanation for or diagnosis of a medical condition: cancer and leukemia are diseases. *Illness*, however, is the experience of being sick – what happens to a body and mind during a period of sickness.[18] Arthur Kleinman suggests that illness is the lived experience of certain ailments. This experience includes categorizing and explaining for others the forms of distress caused by a particular ailment.[19] Based on this distinction we can talk about an illness narrative as the explication of how it feels to be ill: what one experiences physically, emotionally and psychologically when suffering from a disease such as cancer or, as in Andreev's case, neurasthenia.

Arthur W. Frank argues that the contemporary illness narrative makes a private experience public, competes for the suffering voice in opposition to a medical voice, and balances the illness experience against the life as a whole.[20] Frank located the genre of the illness narrative within contemporary literary practice, but the explication of illness in written form is not limited to the period since the 1960s.[21] The public's acceptance of or even demand for *real life* narratives has led to modes of literary discourse which were not acceptable at the beginning of the twentieth century.[22] This does not mean, however, that elements of the contemporary illness narrative did not exist formerly. Instead, such narratives were often presented as *literature* (the accepted mode of Russian social discourse in the early 1900s) rather than as memoir, autobiography or self-help advice. The issue of madness further complicates the matter, as mental illness has been more highly stigmatized than other medical conditions and therefore fewer narrative accounts of this experience have been produced. Catherine Prendergast perceptively suggests that '[t]o be disabled mentally is to be disabled rhetorically.'[23]

The use of the term *illness narrative* is in some ways a more developed reiteration of pathography. Contemporary Russian scholars such as Konstantin Bogdanov, Vadim Rudnev and Igor' Smirnov have expanded and developed the term pathography in fields such as history, philosophy and cultural studies.[24] Bogdanov uses it in its widest context so that he can critically engage any relevant text involved in the representation of illness or death.[25] I employ a similar critical position, allowing for the possibility that both Andreev's autobiographical and fictional illness narratives reflect the cultural construct of madness at the turn of the century and represent his own sense of self in this dynamic construct.

Andreev most certainly embedded his own illness experience in his fictional narratives about madness. The idea is not to select one paragraph or one story and suggest that this was Andreev's exact illness experience, but to examine the entire six volumes of Andreev's collected works, in parallel with his life, to identify recurring patterns and modes of expressing mental illness. From these narratives we learn more about Andreev, both as a writer of fiction and as a man who suffered from chronic illness. As a result, it is then possible to replace the Soviet Andreev and to reevaluate his place in *fin de siècle* cultural discourse. In turn, we also gain some perspective on mental health issues at the beginning of the twentieth century, particularly in Russia.

Andreev's illness experience was quite complex, but certain themes were consistently exhibited throughout the author's life and works. Andreev was plagued by feelings of solitude and the seeming meaninglessness of life, which in turn were exacerbated by bouts of depression and anxiety. These bouts were remedied in various ways, most often through self-medication (usually alcohol) and the belief that the right female companion could save him from himself. These two 'remedies' are a recurrent leitmotif in his narratives.

Andreev's growing literary fame forced him to negotiate his illness experience in the public sphere. As a result, we find narratives about institutional spaces which purported to treat the ill, but actually were used to isolate the sick from the healthy. Institutionalized social control took the form of hospitals, asylums and prisons where illness, madness and criminality were all met with the same response – incarceration. Andreev was of a generation that understood the irrational within the context of atavistic characteristics and degenerate criminal types. This clearly influenced the author's understanding of the diagnosis, treatment and public reaction to mental illness.

In this context, it is not surprising that Andreev tried to avoid the public stigma of moral and mental depravity. Therefore, we find the theme of *performance* as a way of masking the effects of illness in his life and literary works. The creative performance confuses, replicates and disguises madness, bringing into doubt what is in/sane behavior. Verisimilitude, as one of Andreev's characters defines it, is allowing people to see the 'truth' that they *want* to see. Andreev did not want to be stigmatized as mentally ill so he performed in order to seem healthy – because he knew that science and society were calling him a degenerate. Whether or not Andreev was completely sane, society perceived him as pathological, if not mad. Some said that Andreev was sane; some said that he was a neurasthenic; some said that he was insane and Andreev had this debate with himself, but he certainly wanted to *appear* mentally healthy. For Andreev, periods of ill health meant isolation from family and friends – either locked away in his own room or resident in various hospitals in Moscow and Petrograd. Assuredly, Andreev understood that if his condition were to grow worse, that isolation might not be self-imposed, but mandated by the state. The real possibility of incarceration for the mentally ill meant that he needed to seem healthy. This influenced Andreev's relationship with the media, critics and psychiatrists who wanted to use his life and works as evidence of deviance and degeneration within Russian society.

These are very large themes, but they help to organize, in part, this examination of Andreev's illness experience as expressed in his life and works. It is important to remember that Andreev's works were not written in a vacuum, but within the larger discourse of doctors, psychiatrists and literary critics. Andreev's diagnosis of acute neurasthenia had specific scientific meaning and this influenced his perception of his life, from which he then drew ideas for his works of fiction.

As a result, it is not the focus of this study to fall into the trap of previous scholarship, to try to classify Andreev as a realist or an expressionist, to argue that he wrote in a certain style. It can be left to other scholars to decide if we may now perceive Andreev's literary style as psychological or psychiatric realism, just as long as we finally accept that the author was a human being who reflected in his literary works the complexities of living in a society that misunderstood much about mental health. Illness narrative theory is utilized by medical professionals to gain an understanding of the realities of their patients' lives with certain diseases and, in this same way, it provides a means of access for us into Andreev's life with neurasthenia.

The codification of illness

Sander Gilman argues that there are at least two different levels in the codification of illness. One level is the social construction of the disease. The other is the internalization of these social constructions by those labeled as being at risk.[26] In Andreev's case, we are considering the social construction of neurasthenia within the context of degeneration theory and the ways in which he negotiated these constructions in his autobiographical and fictional narratives of mental illness. Gilman suggests that signs of illness are read within the conventions of an interpretive community informed by the medical profession, artists and others. Symbolic meaning is, therefore, provided for signs of pathology within a community's cultural and social context.[27] Consequently, this study explores how Andreev's self-perception and diagnosed illness is negotiated and depicted for his various audiences, within his community's context.

Soviet critics have examined Andreev's life and works within the context of historical materialism, ignoring the author's individual illness experience. In this framework, Andreev's suicide attempts, his drinking, pessimism and depression can be explained by historical, social and economic factors. Yet, if a person is only a sum total of such pressures, why recreate the biographical and artistic record of a lone author? Archival collections of diaries, letters, photographs, literary works, clothes and medical records suggest that there is value in the individual experience.

One might argue that the only elements of Andreev's biography still worth considering are those that past scholars have ignored as a *sign of the times*. Andreev's narratives that address illness may be the one element of his literary works that separate him from other Russian authors of the early twentieth century, which warrants further discussion of literary genres and philosophical influences. Specifically in this case, we gain an understanding of why Andreev was perceived as a weathervane of Russian society, how we might better understand his relationship with the decadent/symbolist movement and why his works were used as part of the medical and legal discourse on Russian degeneration.

Once we accept that Andreev suffered from what was perceived as mental illness in Russia, it is important to understand the ramifications of such a diagnosis. We can assert that Andreev's protests were influenced by his desire to avoid being associated with deviant behavior and classified as a psychopath. His neighbor Vera Beklemisheva (1881–1944) attests that he collected and read everything that was written about him.[28] This interest in his personal and literary image, as well as other instances of Andreev's 'public relations,' lends insight to speak about in the following chapters of an ill, private Andreev and a healthy, public Andreev. This binary opposition will juxtapose the author's public pronouncements of perfect health with his letters and diary entries describing severe periods of melancholy, fatigue, constant headaches as well as a heart condition.

Such a complicated personal relationship with illness then finds its way into Andreev's works of fiction. If people prefer verisimilitude (the appearance of truth, rather than truth itself), what does this add to our understanding of Andreev's characters who try to disguise their insanity in works such as *Black Maskers*, 'My Notes,' *He Who Gets Slapped* (Tot, kto poluchaet poshchechiny), 'The Thought,' 'Sacrifice' (Zhertva) and others? Is the stigma of mental illness so great that it is better to hide its effects? For whom is this performance of sanity intended or necessary?

Given the state of psychiatry at the beginning of the twentieth century, what is Andreev saying about the treatment of the mentally ill in works such as 'The Thought,' 'Red Laugh,' 'Phantoms,' 'Ipatov,' 'He' (On) and others? If Andreev's perception of treatment is mediated through his own experience then what were his expectations for a cure as he was enduring electric shock therapy, rest therapy and a strict diet of semolina and no more than four cups of weak tea a day in hospitals in Moscow and Petrograd? Although this is not an exhaustive list of the questions to be discussed in the following study, it does set the tone of inquiry and ask that the reader explore the ways in which life and literature might inform each other.

As a result, a distinction is made regarding Andreev's *diagnosis* and his *perception* of mental illness. It is of little importance whether or not Andreev would be considered clinically ill based on contemporary diagnostic criteria. Neurasthenia is no longer considered a legitimate diagnosis, but has been reassessed as three separate diagnoses: severe depression, fatigue syndrome or free-floating anxiety.[29] For Andreev, however, neurasthenia was all three of these diagnoses united in one symptomology. It is relevant in this case to note that mental illness is a reality insofar as it reflects the social forces and psychological models of a particular time and place. Unlike in America where neurasthenia was simply the exhaustion of one's nerve forces, in Russia it was considered an early indication of moral and mental depravity.[30] The fact that

Andreev was diagnosed as an acute neurasthenic allows a critical investigation of the complex system that informed his reality. In a previous work, I suggested that Andreev's condition replicates symptoms of current understandings of manic depression or bipolar disorder.[31] It is not necessary to repeat these arguments, as the present study is concerned with narratives of mental illness by and about Andreev as mediated by the medical profession, popular science, the artistic community, and Russian society at the beginning of the twentieth century. Those who suffer from mental illness, and commit this experience to artistic expression, provide an illness narrative of a self-perceived experience but at the same time reflect the cultural construction of mental illness by a particular community.[32]

Rather than accepting universal explanations for Andreev's actions, this study views his fictional and autobiographical narratives as individualistic expressions of mental illness within a specific scientific and popular discourse. The difference between this approach and that of previous scholarship on Andreev is the way in which the explanation is constructed. For example, one might argue that Andreev did not experience depression because he read pessimistic philosophy, but that he read pessimistic philosophy in a personalized way because of his own bouts of depression. In a cultural context where mental instability was associated with the degenerate psychopath rather than the Romantic tormented genius, Andreev defended his sanity in the press not because he was perfectly healthy, but because he wished to avoid the stigma associated with mental illness. Andreev's alcoholic behavior was a method of self-medication rather than an aspect of his youthful bohemian revelry and, while he refrained from drinking at certain points of his life, he never completely gained control of his dependence on alcohol. Thus, my approach is not to dismiss unsavory elements of Andreev's biography with widespread economic, philosophic or cultural trends as Soviet scholars have done, but to address how Andreev perceived and reacted to these trends in an individual way. His literary works are a reflection of the world in which he lived; therefore thematic threads are examined in order to understand Andreev's construction of madness and the way in which popular medical discourse shaped that perception.

The fourth line of criticism

In 1924 Fatov provided the first biography of Andreev, concentrating on his early years, offering a psychiatric explanation for the behavior of an author who since childhood was afflicted with severe depression and emotional instability – 'the frequent and unexpected transitions from a convivial to a melancholic attitude are especially demonstrative in distinguishing the hysteria of his psyche.'[33] According to Fatov, these emotional problems 'spilled from the 'psyche' of the writer into his works.'[34] Parallel with these observations, the biographer also wished to settle the hereditary issues around Andreev's 'alcoholism and the implicit pathology.'[35] The critical methods and overall knowledge of mental illness at this time were limited, and Fatov offered no definitive answers.

Andreev's exclusion from Soviet literary discussions meant that few critical works followed Fatov's analysis and the question of Andreev's mental health remained unanswered. Many of Andreev's works had been read within the context of psychological pathology during his lifetime and shortly after his death. Once he was rediscovered the first three lines of critical discourse were reanimated by scholars, but the fourth remained dormant. Only recently has Avram Brown's biographical entry in *Russian Writers of the Silver Age, 1890–1925* reflected this new and necessary evaluation of Andreev (warts and all) that has been missing from Soviet and post-Soviet scholarship.[36]

In reaction to this confused biographical legacy, my initial research focused on the memoirs dedicated to Andreev. This literature created a posthumous legacy for the author and defined how his literary works would be interpreted to the present day. My monograph, *Memoirs and Madness: Leonid Andreev through the Prism of the Literary Portrait*, explored the first collection of memoirs dedicated to Andreev and how his mental health was described by his literary contemporaries. Given that Andreev was known for his extreme mood swings, suicidal tendencies and abuse of alcohol, an examination of his mental health seemed vital to further study. My ensuing findings suggested that Andreev suffered from a form of mental illness for which he sought treatment, but about which he was also loath to speak in public spheres. The memoir literature, therefore, often skirted this part of Andreev's biography and attempted to contextualize his mental illness in vague phrases like 'creative energy' or 'inner turmoil.'

In suggesting that Andreev suffered from mental illness, questions arise as to the validity of diagnostic classifications and the reliability of a modern diagnosis influenced by the social and cultural milieu of today. The options are to continue using the diagnosis of acute neurasthenia which Andreev was given; to ignore and not 'name' his condition (which has contributed to ongoing confusion); or to give a contemporary diagnosis to clarify why he 'was broken and carried his life in pain.'[37] Andreev's granddaughter states in her memoirs that Leonid Nikolaevich probably suffered from manic depression.[38] The diagnosis of acute neurasthenia, however, will be referenced in this study, as the main focus is on the cultural discourse around mental illness at the beginning of the twentieth century, a discourse that was greatly influenced by degeneration theory.

In a 'Letter to the Editor,' published in the *Literary Gazette* (Literaturnaia gazeta) in 1964, Andreev's son Vadim (1902–1976) attested to the fact that his father was not insane.[39] Although Andreev certainly was not insane, it is probable that he did suffer bouts of mania and depression at a level that would be classified as 'clinical' – meaning outside the range of normally acceptable high and low moods. Many people suffer from mental illness, but still conduct the functions of daily life quite adequately. Even during a manic or depressive episode, then, Andreev could still answer correspondence, attend the theater and create literary works. It is only at the upper and lower edges of these psychological episodes that one might become disenfranchised from society for periods of time. Individuals can also go through long periods without symptoms or even with milder (almost unnoticeable) expressions of illness.

The primary focus of this study is the cultural construction of madness and the stigma attached to this designation which informs the illness experience. Important to this discussion is the emergence of psychiatry in Russia, a new medical science, as it stakes its claim to the irrational at the beginning of the twentieth century. The development of degeneration theory articulated social anxieties about the mentally ill, which quickly became part of popular culture. This medical discourse subverted romantic notions of madness and promoted a strictly *scientific* approach, exercising moral and social authority over the insane. I argue that this cultural construct influenced Andreev's own narratives of mental illness as well as informed the reactions of his friends and critics. It gave further ammunition to scientists and psychiatrists of the day, proving that Russia was in a state of national decline and that the author himself was ill and a purveyor of this sickness.

This book attempts to revive the fourth line of critical discourse, examining Andreev's diaries and creative works to illustrate his struggle with neurasthenia; his illness experience; his creation of a public 'healthy' self and a private 'ill' self. Within the critical framework of *illness narrative*, the study explores Andreev's personal and fictional narratives about mental illness. Investigating this relationship provides insight into mental illness issues as well as Andreev's own coping mechanisms. His un/published diaries contain candid descriptions of a personal relationship with mental illness, unlike his published materials, where his reaction is always mediated for a particular audience. To his reading public, Andreev denied his condition and defended his mental health. For family and close friends, he often complained of various illnesses (heart problems, toothaches, migraines, fatigue etc.), but only occasionally within the context of mental illness. In his literary works, however, madness and abnormal behavior are prevalent themes. Only in his diaries do we find a relatively unmediated personal narrative of his insomnia, drinking binges, depression, anxiety and much more. Here, Andreev reflects on how his condition influenced his relationships and shaped his life.

This study attempts, therefore, to reflect the various scientific and popular lines of discourse that influenced and informed Andreev's sense of self and his relationship with neurasthenia. Of equal importance is the impact that Andreev had as a major contributor to the popular discourse of pathology in the Russian *fin de siècle*. His illness experience as an acute neurasthenic was informed by numerous medical and popular factors that were ultimately distilled into his literary works, leading to his unprecedented success and popularity. By reexamining Andreev and a nation's anxiety over its own perceived moral corruption and physical devolution, Andreev will once again come into focus as one of the leading literary voices of his age.

Notes

1 Andreev, Leonid. *SOS: Dnevnik (1914–1919), Pis'ma (1917–1919), Stat'i i interv'iu (1919), Vospominaniia sovremennikov (1918–1919)*. Edited by Richard Davies and Ben Hellman (Moscow, St Petersburg: Atheneum/ Feniks, 1994)149. Diary entry for 27 September 1918.

2 Even though neurasthenia is no longer considered a legitimate diagnosis, I will use the language offered by experts of the time.

3 Kaun, Alexander. *Leonid Andreyev: A Critical Study* (New York: AMS Press, 1970); Woodward, James B. *Leonid Andreyev: A Study* (Oxford: Clarendon Press, 1969); Newcombe, Josephine M. *Leonid Andreyev* (New York: Frederick Ungar, 1973); Fatov, N. *Molodye gody Leonida Andreeva* (Moscow: Zemlia i Fabrika, 1924); Afonin, L. *Leonid Andreev* (Orel: Knizhnoe iz-vo, 1959).

4 For a discussion of certain factors surrounding the creation of a sanitized Soviet version of Andreev's biography see White, Frederick H. 'Marketing Strategies: Vadim Andreev in Dialogue with the Soviet Union.' *The Russian Review*, 70, 2 (April 2011): 185–97.

5 Orlovskii, P. [V. Vorovskii]. 'V noch' posle bitvy: L. Andreev, F. Sologub.' In *O veianiiakh vremeni* (St Petersburg: Tvorchestvo, 1908) 3–17; Lunacharskii, A. 'T'ma.' In *Literaturnyi raspad: Kriticheskii sbornik*, 1 (St Petersburg: Zerno, 1908) 153–78.

6 Chulkov, Georgii. *Kniga o Leonide Andreeve,* Vospominaniia M. Gor'kogo, K. Chukovskogo, A. Bloka, Georgiia Chulkova, Bor[isa] Zaitseva, N.

Teleshova, Evg[eniia] Zamiatina and A. Belogo. 2nd edn. (Berlin, St Petersburg, Moscow: Izdatel'stvo Z.I. Grzhebin, 1922)105–24. For Chulkov's memoir in English see White, Frederick H. *Memoirs and Madness: Leonid Andreev through the Prism of the Literary Portrait* (Montreal: McGill-Queen's University Press, 2006)79–89; Andreyev, Leonid. *Sashka Jigouleff*. Translated by Luba Hicks. Edited and introduced by Maxim Gorky (New York: Robert McBride & Company, 1925) v–xi.

7 Andreev, Pavel. 'Vospominaniia o Leonide Andreeve.' *Literaturnaia mysl'*: *Al'manakh*, 3, Leningrad: Mysl' (1925): 140–207.

8 Galant, I. 'Psikhopatologicheskii obraz Leonida Andreeva. Leonid Andreev isteronevrastenicheskii genii.' *Klinicheskii arkhiv genial'nosti i odarennosti*, 3, 2 (1927): 147–65; Galant, I. 'Evroendokrinologiia velikikh russkikh pisatelei i poetov. L. N. Andreev.' *Klinicheskii arkhiv genial'nosti i odarennosti*, 3, 3 (1927): 223–38; Ivanov, I. 'Leonid Andreev na sude psikhiatrov.' *Birzhevye vedomosti*, 90 (20 February 1903): 3; Ivanov, I. 'G-n' Leonid Andreev kak khudozhnik-psikhopatolog.' *Voprosy nervno-psikhiatricheskoi meditsiny*, 10, 1, Kiev (January–March 1905): 72–103; White, *Memoirs and Madness*.

9 This argument is offered in greater detail in White, Frederick H. 'The Role of the Scholar in the Consecration of Leonid Andreev (1950s to Present).' *New Zealand Slavonic Journal*, 44 (2010): 85–110.

10 Fatov, *Molodye gody Leonida Andreeva*, 87.

11 Andreeva, Rimma. 'Trudnye gody.' *Orlovskaia pravda*, no. 275 (21 November 1971): 3; Azov, V. [V.A. Ashkinazi]. 'Otryvki ob Andreeve.' *Vestnik literatury*, 9 (1920): 5.

12 See White, Hayden. 'The Historical Text as Literary Artifact.' In *Tropics of Discourse, Essays in Cultural Criticism* (Baltimore: Johns Hopkins University Press, 1978) 81–100, and the introduction to *Metahistory: The Historical Imagination in 19th Century Europe* (Baltimore: Johns Hopkins University Press, 1973) 1–42.

13 Afonin makes direct references to Andreev's literary and journalistic works in his biography of the author, combining his life and literature as though they were one and the same. See Afonin, *Leonid Andreev*, 14; 18; 20; 35–6; 40–1. Fatov also makes direct connections between Andreev's life and fictional works. See Fatov, *Molodye gody Leonida Andreeva*, 22; 31; 40; 70–2; 88–90; 166–7. Brusianin intertwines interviews with Andreev and quotes from his literary works to talk about Andreev's life. See Brusianin, V. *Leonid Andreev. Zhizn' i tvorchestvo* (Moscow: K.F. Nekrasov, 1912)35–43; 47–9, 54–8. Chukovskii notes that Andreev, as a former reporter, reflected the immediate events around him in his literary works. See Chukovskii, Kornei. *Leonid Andreev: Bol'shoi i malen'kii* (St Petersburg: Izdatel'skoe biuro, 1908)34–44. Kaufman, in his memoir of Andreev, explains that the key to the author's literary and artistic works is found in his biography. He provides his own gloss of Andreev's life and the literary works which were directly produced from these experiences. See Kaufman, A. 'Andreev v zhizni i v svoikh proizvedeniiakh.' *Vestnik literatury*, 9 (1920): 2–4.

14 Kaun, *Leonid Andreyev: A Critical Study*, 21.

15 This is one of the central ideas of Chukovskii's literary portrait of Andreev.

See Chukovskii, *Kniga o Leonide Andreeve*, 73–92. In English see White, *Memoirs and Madness*, 59–70.

16 A partial list includes: 'The Grand Slam' (Bol'shoi shlem), 'The Alarm-Bell' (Nabat), 'The Thought,' 'The Life of Vasilii Fiveiskii' (Zhizn' Vasiliia Fiveiskogo), 'The Abyss' (Bezdna), 'Red Laugh,' 'Phantoms' (Prizraki), *To the Stars* (K zvezdam), 'The Story of the Seven Who Were Hanged' (Rasskaz o semi poveshennykh), 'My Notes' (Moi zapiski), *Tsar Hunger* (Tsar' Golod), *Black Maskers* (Chernye maski), 'Day of Anger' (Den' gneva), *Gaudeamus, Sashka Zhegulev, The Thought* (Mysl') and many others.

17 Amenitskii, D. *Analiz geroia «Mysli»: K voprosu o paranoidnoi psikhopatii* (Moscow: MVO, 1915); Galant, 'Psikhopatologicheskii obraz Leonida Andreeva'; Galant, 'Evroendokrinologiia velikikh russkikh pisatelei i poetov. L. N. Andreev'; Ianishevskii, A. 'Geroi rasskaza L. Andreeva «Mysl'» s tochki zreniia vracha-psikhiatra: Publichnaia lektsiia, chitannaia v aktovom zale Kazanskogo universiteta 12 aprelia 1903 g. V pol'zu pansionata Obshchestva vzaimopomoshchi sel'skikh i gorodskikh uchitelei i uchitel'nits.' *Nevrologicheskii vestnik*, 11, 2, Kazan (Supplement 1903): 1–31; Ivanov, 'Leonid Andreev na sude psikhiatrov'; Ivanov, 'G-n' Leonid Andreev kak khudozhnik-psikhopatolog'; Mumortsev, Aleksandr. *Psikhopaticheskie cherty v geroiakh Leonida Andreeva* (St Petersburg: Otedl'nye ottiski 'Literaturno-meditsinskogo zhurnala,' 1910); Shaikevich, M. *Psikhopatologiia i literatura* (St Petersburg, 1910); Tkachev, T. *Patologicheskoe tvorchestvo: (Leonid Andreev)*(Kharkov: Mirnyi trud, 1913).

18 Kleinman, Arthur. *The Illness Narratives: Suffering, Healing and the Human Condition* (New York: Basic Books, 1988) 3–6. Also see Frank, Arthur W. *At the Will of the Body: Reflections on Illness* (Boston: Houghton Mifflin Company, 1991) 13. Frank writes: 'Illness is the experience of living through disease. If disease talk measures the body, illness talk tells of the fear and frustration of being inside a body that is breaking down. Illness begins where medicine leaves off, where I recognize that what is happening to my body is not some set of measures. [...] Disease talk charts the progression of certain measures. Illness talk is a story about moving from a perfectly comfortable body to one that forces me to ask: What's happening to me? Not it, but me.'

19 Ibid., 3.

20 Frank, Arthur W. 'Reclaiming an Orphan Genre: The First-Person Narrative of Illness.' *Literature and Medicine* (Narrative and Medical Knowledge), 13, 1 (Spring 1994): 2.

21 Frank designates Stewart Alsop's *Stay of Execution: A Sort of Memoir* (Philadelphia: Lippincott, 1973) as 'the first book of the new genre.' Frank, 'Reclaiming an Orphan Genre,' 3.

22 Morris makes a distinction between Modern and Postmodern narrative within the biocultural model. In the Modern period the biological process is reduced to the language of chemistry and physics, while in the Postmodern period the biomedical model 'encompasses a recognition that disease and illness are often inseparably linked with culture.' I contend that this suggests that during the Modern period, individuals were forced to find other modes for the expression of illness and this usually came out in the

form of literature. See Morris, David B. 'Narrative, Ethics, and Pain: Thinking *With* Stories.' *Narrative*, 9, 1 (January 2001): 58. For a discussion of some of the issues involved in contemporary life writing and the seeming requirement for intellectualized tabloid material see Eakin, Paul. *How Our Lives Become Stories: Making Selves* (Ithaca; London: Cornell University Press, 1999) 142–86.

23 Prendergast, Catherine. 'On the Rhetorics of Mental Disability.' In *Embodied Rhetorics. Disability in Language and Culture*. Edited by James C. Wilson and Cynthia Lewiecki-Wilson (Carbondale: Southern Illinois University Press, 2001) 57. Roy Porter explores how mental illness can lead to rhetorical isolation in his article, 'Madness and Creativity: Communication and Excommunication.' In *Madness and Creativity in Literature and Culture*. Edited by Corinne Saunders and Jane Macnaughton (New York: Palgrave Macmillan, 2005) 19–34.

24 Bogdanov, Konstantin. *Vrachi, patsienty, chitateli: Patograficheskie teksty russkoi kul'tury XVIII–XIX vekov* (Moscow: O.G.I., 2005); Rudnev, V. *Kharaktery i rasstroistva lichnosti. Patografiia i metapsikhologiia* (Moscow: Klass, 2002); Smirnov, Igor'. *Psikhodiakhronologika. Psikhoistoriia russkoi literatury ot ronantizma do nashikh dnei* (Moscow: Novoe literaturnoe obozrenie, 1994).

25 Bogdanov, *Vrachi, patsienty, chitateli*, 11.

26 Gilman, Sander L. *Disease and Representation. Images of Illness from Madness to AIDS* (Ithaca: Cornell University Press, 1988) 3–4.

27 Ibid., 7.

28 Andreev, Daniil and V. Beklemisheva, eds. *Rekviem: Sbornik pamiati Leonida Andreeva* (Moscow: Federatsiia, 1930) 207.

29 *The Diagnostic and Statistical Manual of Mental Disorders* that is published by the American Psychiatric Association now maintains three separate classifications for these diagnoses. As will be discussed in Chapter 3, Aleksei Kozhevnikov's classification of neurasthenia included all three symptoms as elements of a singular, dynamic and evolving symptomatology.

30 Porter, Roy. *Madness: A Brief History* (Oxford: Oxford University Press, 2002) 149–53; Beer, Daniel. *Renovating Russia: The Human Sciences and the Fate of Liberal Modernity 1880–1930* (Ithaca: Cornell University Press, 2008) 68–70.

31 White, *Memoirs and Madness*.

32 Gilman, *Disease and Representation*, 99.

33 Fatov, *Molodye gody Leonida Andreeva*, 17.

34 Ibid.

35 Ibid.

36 Brown, Avram. 'Leonid Nikolaevich Andreev.' In *Dictionary of Literary Biography, Volume 295: Russian Writers of the Silver Age, 1890–1925*. Edited by Judith E. Kalb and J. Alexander Ogden (Detroit: Thomas Gale, 2004) 21–33.

37 Zaitsev, Boris. 'Molodost' Leonida Andreeva.' *Vozrozhdenie*, 1362 (24 February 1929): 3.

38 Carlisle, Olga Andreyev. *Far from Russia: A Memoir* (New York: St Martin's Press, 2000) 147.

39 Leeds Russian Archive (LRA), MS. 1350 / 1677. Draft letter to the editor of *Literaturnaia gazeta* from 1964. Vadim's letter was in response to a review of his childhood memoirs recently published (1963) in the Soviet Union. His 'Letter to the Editor' was published on 4 May 1964 (no. 66, page 2) under the headline 'About My Father' (O moem ottse).

2

Degeneration and decadence

One issue in the study of mental illness labeling is how the features of mental illness labels are related to labels of disease and of crime and deviance. Psychiatrists typically consider mental illness to share the major characteristics of disease, while sociologists are more likely to regard mental illness as behavior that violates social norms. While mental illness labeling is related in certain ways to labels of both disease and deviance, it is greatly different from both of these categories. It is most appropriate to regard characterizations of mental illness as a distinctive type of reaction to undesirable behavior.

Allan Horwitz[1]

In order to understand Andreev's illness experience, we must first gain insights into what it meant to be an acute neurasthenic in Russia at the beginning of the twentieth century. Medical science believed that neurasthenia was just one of the early indications of a much larger problem negatively impacting civilized society. This new science was concerned with degeneration theory, which argued that if a species could evolve, then it could also devolve. Simply stated neurasthenia was one of the signs of an individual's physical, moral and psychological devolution. The majority of this chapter explores the development of this scientific discourse in order to better understand the context for Andreev's diagnosis.

Following a discussion of the science of degeneration, attention will be given to literary decadence. Degeneration emerged as scientific theory, but was soon incorporated into legal, political and literary discourse. The idea of a nation in a state of decline coincided with other cultural trends which viewed the end of the nineteenth century in apocalyptic terms. The final few sections of this chapter concentrate on the broad outlines of literary decadence in order to support the assertion that Andreev and his works share similarities with European decadence. In many respects this study is an invitation to reexamine our understanding of Russian literary decadence and its resulting influences on Russian culture. By briefly discussing decadence and degeneration theory in Russian and European national literatures as well as making allusions to other *decadent* figures such as Oscar Wilde (1854–1900), I am attempting the first tentative steps towards an evaluation of Andreev's role in this cultural discourse. After all, a comprehensive reexamination of Russian decadence would necessitate an entire monograph of its own. Nonetheless, just as Wilde came to represent English decadence and social mores, Andreev could be similarly understood as a representative of Russian national concerns at the beginning of the twentieth century. Unfortunately, Soviet scholarship did not embrace a Russian decadent period, while Western scholars have mainly accepted the literary classifications offered by the cultural figures themselves, often determined by class allegiances and personal friendships.[2] An exhaustive scholarly discussion concerning Russian decadence, therefore, remains to be had in Slavic scholarship.

Madness: art and science

The Enlightenment attempted to create a new society based on rationalism. However, its mechanistic principles gave way to disillusionment at the beginning of the nineteenth century, followed by a retrogressive movement away from reason and toward emotion. This was captured in the 'Byronic heroes' of Lord Byron (1788–1824) and reproduced in a Russian version – Evgenii Onegin – by Aleksandr Pushkin (1799–1837). During the Romantic era literary characters reflected this psychological withdrawal and struggled more with their internal strife than with their external world.

With such a heavy focus on the self it is little wonder that art and science in the Romantic period concentrated on and so strongly shaped present-day conceptions of madness. Philosophers, doctors and artists of the Romantic period described, depicted and defined concepts of normal and abnormal behavior. Allen Thiher writes:

> The world of German romanticism was the last time, in our history, where doctors and poets, philosophers and scientists – often one and the same person – shared a unity of thought. Virtually all of the themes found in the romantic psychiatrists and their views of madness are embodied in the literature of the romantics. What is most striking about psychiatry and literature is their representation of the self. For both it is a space described by allegory. Allegory is the standard literary and psychiatric technique for the romantic exploration of madness, and, through madness, a description of the psyche.[3]

Russia's cultural and scientific understanding of madness was influenced by German writers such as Joseph Eichendorff (1788–1857), Ludwig Tieck (1773–1853), Novalis (1772–1801) and E.T.A. Hoffmann (1772–1822); philosophers such as Schopenhauer and Friedrich Nietzsche (1844–1900); and psychiatrists such as Emil Kraepelin (1856–1926) and Sigmund Freud (1856–1939). By 1875, 83 percent of professors in Russia had received a degree in Germany.[4]

The first systematic treatise of psychotherapy was published by a German physician in 1803. Johann Christian Reil (1759–1813) formulated the principles and techniques of psychological treatment – for example, exposing silent patients to loud noises or securing an excited patient in a dark, quiet room.[5] In France, Jean-Étienne Dominique Esquirol (1772–1840) provided precise descriptions for many clinical syndromes – idiocy, hallucinations, monomania and lypemania. Esquirol's followers continued to contribute new and basic definitions to clinical psychiatry, thereby laying the foundation for a new medical discipline that would use a methodological approach for classifying and describing mental symptoms.[6]

A fundamental shift in medicine occurred at this time, altering the way in which madness (and all other illnesses) would be conceptualized and discussed. German somatic medicine and French positivism suggested that illnesses have a pathology – medicine was no longer about symptoms as much as about causal agents and organic forms.[7] In psychiatry, this shift resulted in an evolution of thought on madness. No longer would doctors take a binary approach of either normal or abnormal behavior. There would now be one conceptual norm with deviations or variations from that norm. Known as materialist monism, the idea was that psychiatrists thought that they might be able to provide a reductive model for explaining mental illness.

This new direction in psychiatry had a direct influence on literature. Jacques-Joseph Moreau (1804–1884) explored the mind–body connection with the first drug-oriented psychological experiments. Using hashish he induced euphoric states in individuals (and himself) that he associated with poetic experience – still identifying madness with revelation (a Romantic notion). Moreau believed that revelatory states of consciousness could be identified with poetry or madness. This supposition was accepted by Moreau's literary friends, French Symbolist poets, some of whom may have been mentally ill.[8] Moreau is representative of the Romantic trend in psychiatry to move beyond the mere classification and description of madness in an attempt to understand the irrational and hidden forces of the personality.

Despite Moreau's theories, there was an uncomfortable struggle between doctors and poets for the right to describe madness, which soon led to an ideological split. In an attempt to carve out a place for psychiatry within medicine, doctors denied literature its epistemological function by claiming madness for science. In response, artists rejected scientific medicine in favor of the irrational – championing madness over reason. It was at this point, according to Thiher, that literary modernity was born; at the same moment that medical modernity exerted its independence.[9]

Thiher makes an important distinction. One of the main themes of this critical study is the tension that existed between artistic and scientific understandings of madness. Literary, mythical and biblical representations of madness informed artistic notions of the tormented genius – notions that allowed artists to embrace abnormal and decadent behavior as part of their creative posturing. The competing discourse offered by science suggested that mental illness was morally deviant and physically degenerative – calling for institutionalization, shock-therapy and physical restraints. Madness was caught in this struggle between art and science – placing the mentally ill artist, in this case Leonid Andreev, in an uncomfortable position between creative posturing and illness; between a sanatorium and a mental asylum; between the sacred and the criminal.

Devolution

In the 1830s the English physician James Cowles Prichard (1786–1848) formulated the concept of moral insanity, arguing that derangement could occur in an individual's mental and moral faculties.[10] In the second half of the nineteenth century, this idea was widely used by Russian psychiatrists to mean not only madness but also amorality and deviance.[11] Under the influence of Jean-Baptiste Lamarck's (1744–1829) theories on the inheritance of acquired traits and Charles Darwin's (1809–1882) theory of evolution, the Austrian-French physician Bénédict Augustin Morel (1809–1873) developed the idea of mental degeneration. Although theories about degeneracy had existed previously, Morel convinced various intellectual communities that certain elements of society were devolving, becoming genetically weaker with each generation, which would result in imbecility and sterility. The afflicted family might first show signs of neurasthenia or nervous hysteria, then alcohol and opiate addiction, leading to prostitution and criminal behavior and finally resulting in insanity and utter idiocy.[12] Roy Porter claims that this pessimism was a byproduct of failures in the asylum system to deal with various diseases, including tertiary syphilis.

As we will explore in the following chapters, Andreev was diagnosed as an acute neurasthenic and was also known to be a heavy drinker, if not an alcoholic. Significant also was that one of his brothers died from tertiary syphilis so the taint of degeneration was quite real for Andreev and his family. Unfortunately for them, the trend in psychiatry was moving away from moral therapy and effective treatment and towards long-stay cases and inherited psychopathic taints.[13]

Morel's theories on degeneration were particularly influential around 1857 when Professor Ivan Balinskii (1827–1902) was establishing the first independent department of psychiatry in St Petersburg.[14] A decade later, Balinskii organized a psychiatric clinic, which graduated some of Russia's first psychiatrists. The most promising of these students were given stipends to complete their studies in European laboratories and clinics with eminent scientists such as Moreau and Jean-Martin Charcot (1823–1893).[15] Therefore, degeneration found a place in the early curriculum and practice of Russian psychiatry.

Magnus Huss (1807–1890) and Valentin Magnan (1835–1916) continued to develop the theory of degeneration in Europe. Huss, a Swede, was the first to systematically classify the damage caused by alcohol ab/use, noting the moral and physical problems associated with what would later be called alcoholism. This work influenced the Russian psychiatrist Sergei Korsakov (1854–1900) who studied the nutritional deficiencies and disorientation (memory-gaps) associated with chronic alcohol ab/use. Magnan became one of the leaders of the French school of organic psychiatry, arguing that alcohol and absinthe were leading to the degeneration of France. His work influenced the Russian psychiatrist Ivan Merzheevskii (1838–1908), who investigated idiotism, alcoholism and dementia paralytica.[16] National borders did not limit the flow of knowledge in the area of psychiatry at the turn of the century, thus we do not speak solely about European or Russian psychiatric concepts of madness.

In Europe, the leading psychiatrists associated mental degeneration with sexual perversion and psychopathology (Richard von Krafft-Ebing, 1854–1902), genius and abnormal aptitude (Paul Möbius, 1853–1907), and criminality (Cesare Lombroso, 1836–1909). Max Nordau (1849–1923) expanded the concept beyond psychiatry, recognizing degeneration in the decadence and willful rejection of moral boundaries in *fin de siècle* Europe. Nordau continued to classify it as an illness and associated it with psychological conditions such as hysteria and neurasthenia. In each case, issues of heredity, moral insanity and deviance were at the core of these psychiatric hypotheses – all issues that Andreev, himself, confronted in his works.

In America, George Beard (1839–1883) popularized the diagnosis of neurasthenia, which was supposedly caused by the frantic pressures of an advanced civilization, and was often treated with bed rest, strict isolation, fattening-up with milk puddings, and passive massage.[17] Russian psychiatrists like Pavel Kovalevskii (1849–1923) echoed many of these same concerns, suggesting that Russia's new secular culture of materialism and individualism was having a negative impact on members of the *raznochintsy*, the children of priests, bureaucrats, merchants and traders. Kovalevskii argued that a thirst for money had pushed these individuals to make extreme demands on their bodies and that their limited capacity to adjust to their changing environment could trigger the onset of the degenerative syndrome.[18]

Daniel Pick convincingly argues that the sheer volume of medical and scientific writings on social evolution, degeneration, morbidity and perversion during the second half of the nineteenth century seemingly legitimized the claims of Morel, Lombroso, Nordau and many others.

> Degeneration moves from its place as occasional sub-current of wider philosophies and political or economic theories, or homilies about the horrors of the French and the Industrial Revolutions, to become the centre of scientific and medical investigation. This can be understood in both a sociological sense (the names of the authors of the key works on degeneration are often qualified with titles as doctors, anthropologists and zoologists) and in a discursive sense: the texts appeal to the authority of naturalist theory. The potential degeneration of European society was thus not discussed as though it constituted primarily a religious, philosophical or ethical problem but as an empirically demonstrable medical, biological or physical anthropological fact.[19]

Degeneration was increasingly seen as more than just a social condition of the poor, but a biological force that was the cause of crime, destitution and disease. In Germany and Russia, where G.W.F. Hegel's (1770–1831) philosophy of history had caused much hand-wringing about national identity, the notion that both societies were now quickly deteriorating into psychopaths, perverts and criminals caused great consternation.[20] Degeneration was not associated with treatment but with the identification of deviance and immoral behavior.

Daniel Beer argues that by the 1880s, degeneration theory was no longer limited to isolated medical treaties. Following the First Congress of Russian Psychiatrists in 1887, it became accepted among the wider public that the degeneration of the Russian people 'was a demonstrable fact and an issue of pressing medical concern.' However, with this acceptance, there arose a paradox. Although it was acknowledged that degeneration was a demonstrable medical, biological and physical anthropological fact, its causes and trajectory remained contested. Beer suggests that this created an 'interpretive vacuum into which subsequent commentators rushed with their own explanations of the precise mechanisms involved.'[21]

In Russia, this opening was filled by, among others, the next wave of psychiatrists. Issak Orshanskii (1851–1923) published and lectured extensively on physiognomy and pathology, supporting the scientific ideas of Morel, Magnan and Lombroso in publications such as *Our Criminals and the Studies of Lombroso* (Nashi prestupniki i uchenie Lombrozo, 1890) and *The Role of Heredity in the Transfer of Illness* (Rol' nasledstvennosti v peredache boleznei, 1894). After completing his dissertation in St Petersburg in 1876, Orshanskii spent a year and a half studying nervous disorders in Berlin, Leipzig and Paris, before becoming a professor of psychiatry at Kharkov University.[22] Nikolai Bazhenov (1856–1923) worked with Charcot and Magnan in Europe where he studied the skulls and busts of criminals. After a time working as a psychiatrist at an asylum in Riazan', Bazhenov ran a private clinic in Moscow and was appointed medical director of the Moscow City Psychiatric Hospital (Preobrazhenskaia) in 1904.[23] At Kharkov University, Kovalevskii was editor of the first Russian psychiatric journal (1883–96) and author of the first Russian psychiatric textbook (1880). He conducted psychological and anatomical research on famous people and studied the effects of syphilis on the nervous system.[24] The theories of degeneration especially influenced the work of Russian psychiatrists such as Bazhenov, Vladimir Chizh (1855–1922), Merzheevskii, V.V. Vorob'ev (1865–1905), Nikolai Osipov (1877–1934), Viktor Kandinskii (1849–1889), Petr Obninskii (1867–1917), Petr Kapterev (1849–1922), Nikolai Mikhailovskii (1842–1904) and many others.[25] As a result, the degeneration and the devolution of Russian society seemed to be a demonstrable, scientific fact.

A decadent context

Degeneration theory developed in a Darwinian world in which the upper class felt uneasy about poverty, crime, public health issues and numerous crises in national identity. Decadent artists, including Andreev, reflected these anxieties in their syphilitic, criminal, depraved and insane characters. Empirical science offered an explanation for normal and abnormal behavior that took on binary oppositions such as civilized or primitive, healthy or depraved, contented or melancholic. As a result, degeneration became a medium by which the respectable classes could articulate their hostility for culturally subversive elements of society, and science could claim the abnormal and irrational from art.

Following the disappointments of the 1860s, degeneration theory seemed to provide plausible answers for Russia's unresolved problem over heredity and the environment. The reform era had described change as intentional and rationally structured, therefore the hereditary component of degeneration offered an explanation for the problems of a society plagued by a legacy of serfdom, economic backwardness and social stratification. These problems were further exacerbated by the environmental factors of industrial modernization that brought a perceived social and moral disorder to Russia.[26]

Rapid industrialization in Europe and the emancipation of the serfs in Russia resulted in economic, social and cultural changes – especially in the urban areas where socio-economic extremes were more closely concentrated. Cultural and social concepts of religion, morals, class and sexuality were interrupted. Degeneration theory provided an explanation for the seemingly palpable regression of society. The Darwinian revolution spread to psychology, the social sciences, art and literature, and each tried to gain a handle on the irrational that was threatening the orderly progress of civilized society. Medicine and science were the first to find proof that this enormous problem was systemic.

Disease was evidence of poor cultural health during the final decades of the nineteenth century, and science supplied confirmation that abnormal and pathological states negatively impacted society. It was believed that urban living was leaving men and women vulnerable to fatigue and disease, while heredity was the ticking genetic time bomb hidden from reason. The urban environment exacerbated inherited conditions like neurasthenia and hysteria, contributing to the generalized deviance and regression of society. William Greenslade argues that the upper echelons of the social order had much to gain from reasserting control, order, clarity and reason by use of scientific surveillance.[27]

For Russian readers these ideas were not incomprehensible, as Dostoevskii's characters had been victims of urbanization (*Crime and Punishment*), heredity (*Brothers Karamazov*) and mental illness (*Idiot*). Tolstoi's *Anna Karenina* explored marital infidelity, the collapse of the family, the negative effects of capitalism, and the failure of legal reforms. The author himself ultimately rejected modern society and advocated a return to rural living, manual labor and moral fortitude. According to Olga Matich, Tolstoi's *What Is Art?* (Chto takoe issusstvo) reflects the influence of 'the epoch's preoccupation with medical pathology' and especially degeneration theory.[28] By the mid-nineteenth century, educated Russian society was experiencing an unprecedented enthusiasm for science, which most certainly broadened the audience for scientific ideas, practices, and potential applications.[29]

In Russia as well as Europe, classifying abnormal behavior as deviant and ascribing a pathology in effect allowed the purveyors of the social order to lump the anarchist, mentally ill, hooligan, prostitute, syphilitic, homosexual and mad genius into one category. Science seemed to gain the upper hand by offering a name for this category (degenerate), for providing an explanation (evolutionary regression), and for promoting hope for a cure from the newest medical science (psychiatry). After all, this was an epidemic of massive proportion – a disease with no rigid symptomatology that could manifest itself as hysteria, madness, melancholia, epilepsy, or numerous other degenerate illnesses.

The notion of progress and the possibility that Russia was headed in the wrong direction had long been an obsession of the nineteenth century. Degeneration theory was an expression of this concern, and biological development proposed that modernization might propel the population of the Empire into an abyss of moral and physical illness, crime, vice, and sedition. Ivan Sikorskii (1845–1919), in his speech to the First Congress of Russian Psychiatrists in 1887, underscored the contradictory nature of a technologically advanced society with steam engines and telegraphs, that simultaneously experiences a physical, mental and moral decline. The cost of modernization, claimed the professor of nervous and mental diseases at the University of Kiev, was seen in the increasing instances of suicide, insanity and nervous illnesses, which were all indicators of the poor mental health of a population suffering from degeneration. This pessimistic mood pervaded all areas of educated Russian society.[30]

Neurasthenia became the classic illness of the late nineteenth century. In *American Nervousness* (1881) Beard details the symptoms:

Insomnia, flushing, drowsiness, bad dreams, cerebral irritation, dilated pupils, pain, pressure and heaviness in the head, changes in the expression of the eye, neurasthenic asthenopia, noises in the ears, atonic voice, mental irritability, tenderness of the teeth and gums, nervous dyspepsia, desire for stimulants and narcotics, abnormal dryness of the skin, joints and mucous membranes, sweating hands and feet with redness, fear of lightening, or fear of responsibility, of open places or of closed places, fear of society, fear of being alone, fear of fears, fear of contamination, fear of everything, deficient thirst and capacity for assimilating fluids, abnormalities of secretion, salivation, tenderness of the spine, and of the whole body, sensitiveness to cold or hot water, sensitiveness to changes in the weather, coccyodynia, pains in the back, heaviness of the loins and limbs, shooting pains simulating those of ataxia, cold hands and feet, pain in the feet, localized peripheral numbness and hyperaestasia, tremulous and variable pulse and palpitation of the heart, special idiosyncrasies in regard to food, medicines, and external irritants, local spasms of muscles, difficulty swallowing [... and it goes on and on].[31]

It is easy to be dismissive of Beard's overly inclusive catalogue of symptoms, but degeneration seemingly posed a real threat to individual and collective health and livelihood in Russia at the beginning of the twentieth century. Unfortunately, this wide range of symptoms was a disservice to those who actually did suffer from mental illness or numerous other illnesses, as the broad cast of the degenerate net caught the ill and the healthy alike. For someone like Andreev, real symptoms seemed to lead to very unattractive outcomes. The point is not to dismiss these diagnoses as simple hocus-pocus, but to understand them in their cultural context and the personalized anxiety they caused.

Irina Sirotkina argues that the Russian diagnosis of neurasthenia was different from the Western diagnosis in which the rapid pace of industrial life supposedly sapped the individual's life-force. 'The archetypal Russian neurasthenic was hard-working, intelligent, often poor and a physically unfit person, oppressed by a lack of freedom and suffering from unfulfilled desires to serve the people.'[32] Accordingly, after the failed 1905 Revolution, unfavorable political conditions were identified by Russian psychiatrists as the cause of rising rates of hysteria and neurasthenia; thereby degeneration in Russia took on political rather than biological connotations.[33] Less politically motivated psychiatrists believed that neurasthenia was a product of overwork, malnutrition and ignorance. 'Both groups, however, identified in literature an index of mental health, a representation of what was healthy and what was harmful for the nation. Literature provided illustrations of decline, degeneration, mental instability, and lack of ideals, but it also inspired hopes for regaining national strength.'[34]

Laura Goering notes that while Beard's version of neurasthenia – involving depleted nerve forces – could be relatively easily treated, the European and Russian versions were enmeshed with Morel's theories on hereditary transmission, and implied that sufferers' families were possibly only a few generations away from extinction. Kovalevskii further confused the various medical theories on degeneration with neurasthenia by replacing Beard's theory of technological stress due to an advanced society with Nordau's belief in moral stress due to a deviant social order. This equated the health of the individual with the health of the nation and made neurasthenia a sign of Russia's declining national wellness.[35]

Nordau's confirmation of the connections between creative genius and degenerate madness was undoubtedly very influential for the young

Andreev. In 1892, Nordau seemed to legitimize all of the scientific theories of atavism, disease and deviance in his denunciation of modern art – particularly in literature. His book, *Degeneration* (Russian translation 1893), was concerned with the pathology of artistic production, whereby the very act of creation results in the release of vapors that are both the source of creative fantasy and the result of physical illness. Henrik Ibsen (1828–1906), Oscar Wilde, Paul-Marie Verlaine (1844–1896), Charles Baudelaire (1821–1867), Richard Wagner (1813–1883) and many others fell into his purview. Nordau referenced the scientific theories of Lombroso and depicted the authors listed above as dangerous, at times criminal, spokesmen for the world of the debauched *fin de siècle*, nourishing a neurotic audience with artistic delusions.[36]

Greenslade argues that Nordau's polemic stance actually helped to undermine degeneration as a serious diagnostic category, especially in the area of mental pathology. However, as the diagnostic value of the concept diminished for specialists, it gained cultural currency among the general public. By the early 1900s, it was a catch-all *buzz* word for *mentally unstable* and doggedly remained an element of the cultural dialogue on art and modernity even through the 1930s.[37]

Andreev was aware of degeneration theory from his early adolescence. His diary references to Lombroso,[38] Nordau[39] and Krafft-Ebing[40] show that these scientific theorists influenced the way Andreev constructed his sense of self and how he perceived the world around him.[41] Philosophical pessimism and scientific degeneration informed a belief that genius was found in the abnormal mind. Andreev was diagnosed as an acute neurasthenic according to Korsakov's diagnostic criteria. This diagnosis seemed to be a double-edged sword: a sign of possible genius that could also be used to stigmatize an individual as insane. Indeed, a biographical document written after 1912 by an unidentified member of Andreev's inner circle, notes that the author's stay in the clinic for nervous disorders in 1901 'armed [Andreev's] literary enemies,' allowing them to discredit his literary works and spread rumors about his illness.[42]

Just as syphilis was one of the terrors of the nineteenth century, degeneration caused a similar type of angst at the beginning of the twentieth.[43] This anxiety clearly found its way into Andreev's early literary works and was magnified later in his life as he was plagued by constant migraines, a heart condition and bouts of depression. This suggests that degeneration theory provided a backdrop for Andreev's life and literary career. The assertion is that the discourse of degeneration persisted even when pessimistic philosophy and childhood hardships receded in the author's autobiographical narrative.

Genius and madness

The modern understanding of genius, an individual with a peculiar or extraordinary creative energy, comes from the eighteenth century. The Enlightenment was particularly interested in the science of human nature and the rational process of genius. George Becker explains that the Enlightenment concept of genius recognized the creative imagination, juxtaposed with reason as a counterweight. Judgment, it was believed, was capable of averting *caprice* and *extravagance*, making madness a virtual impossibility for genius.[44]

At the end of the eighteenth century, the pre-Romantics made no distinction between genius in science and genius in art. However, the Romantics disassociated the two, elevating the artist to a predominant position and reformulating the notion of genius to include intuition, fantasy and inspiration. The Romantics conceptualized the artistic genius whose powers were organic and natural, not mechanical and artificial; a Promethean figure, an intuitive creator, rather than a learned man-of-letters.

In 1836, Louis-François Lélut (1804–1877) wrote the first pathography, arguing that Socrates (470–377 BC) experienced hallucinations and took inspiration from these moments of madness. Ten years later Lélut made a similar argument about Blaise Pascal (1623–1662).[45] It was not until the *fin de siècle*, however, that the Romantic genius was reinterpreted as a morbid and pathological figure. It was partially under the influence of degeneration theory that mental illness, disease (syphilis and tuberculosis) and decadent behavior (drug and alcohol ab/use) became associated with the tormented artist.[46]

In *Genius and Madness* (1864) Lombroso characterized the spontaneous act of painting among his mental patients with the impulsive act of painting among savages. This study resulted in two clear lines of scientific investigation: one follows the psychopathological origins of *greatness* in certain individuals while the other follows the aesthetic production of the mentally ill to discover *greatness* in their illness.[47] Francis Schiller argues that degeneration and decadence preoccupied nineteenth-century thought about human failings because '[i]t was the complement as well as the antithesis to eighteenth-century "perfectibility" and nineteenth-century evolutionary optimism. It functioned as a psychiatrist's crutch for "explaining" the underdevelopment, the defective, and the progressively deteriorating minds. [...] In the twentieth century, degeneration progressively lost its hold once more on the psychiatric and the anthropological vocabulary, while establishing itself, curiously, as a major diagnostic category in pathology, especially neuropathology.'[48]

Paul Möbius was inspired by the work of Magnan, especially by his ideas on *dégénérés supérieurs* (higher degenerates) – individuals who showed deviations from the norm in thought, feeling and social behavior without intellectual impairment. Magnan concentrated on patients who displayed immorality, a lack of empathy for others, hyper or perverted sexuality and superior abilities.[49] Möbius was further influenced by Lombroso's argument that genius and madness were closely connected manifestations of an underlying degenerate neurological disorder. Lombroso and his students studied the best-known geniuses, examining their life, works, appearance, heredity, illnesses and idiosyncrasies, and noted that the subjects had suffered from epileptic spells. Schiller states: 'No major figure in history, art or the sciences escaped Lombroso's systematic search aimed at reducing the uncanny side of genius to one or more significant personality flaws.'[50]

That Andreev was influenced by Lombroso's theories on madness and genius is evidenced in his claim to Gor'kii: 'I, brother, am a decadent, a degenerate, a sick person. But Dostoevskii was also sick, like all great people. There is a little book – I do not remember whose – about genius and madness, in which it is proven, that genius is a psychological disease![51] That book ruined me. If I had not read it, I would be simpler. But now I know that I am almost a genius, but I am not sure if I am crazy enough. Do you understand, I am pretending to myself that I am crazy to persuade myself that I am talented – do you understand?'[52]

Motivated by Lombroso and Magnan, Möbius turned his attention to pathography to educate the public about psychiatry. His first subject was Jean Jacques Rousseau (1712–1778) who, according to Möbius, suffered from paranoia and an undiagnosed urinary disorder.[53] In his study of Johann Wolfgang Goethe (1749–1832), Möbius was concerned with Goethe's interest in insanity. 'Möbius also provides a detailed analysis of Goethe's personality, coupled with a phrenological interpretation; and he examines the poet's persistent and quite successful efforts to alleviate his excessive sensitivity, his cyclic mood disorder, and other, mostly acute pulmonary, illnesses.'[54] In his study of Schopenhauer, Möbius refuted many of Lombroso's vicious claims about the philosopher. He did, however, pay attention to certain pathological traits – the suicide of the philosopher's father (hereditary taint), Schopenhauer's extraordinary mental capacity and his extreme negativity.[55] In his pathography of Nietzsche, Möbius was constrained by several factors and, therefore, did not specify venereal disease when discussing the philosopher's struggle with mental illness. According to Möbius, secondary illnesses included a lifelong struggle with headaches, eyestrain and stomach problems.[56] Möbius attempted to provide a medical, psychological and psychiatric biography for each of these men. He conducted a holistic analysis of each individual's heredity, biological development, personality, life history and mental and physical pathology to evaluate his achievements and show that mental illness does not always separate the afflicted individual from the rest of humankind.

In contrast, Becker argues that pathographies were used to stigmatize, labeling the artist as deviant, although he also notes that Romantics often *victimized* themselves with the madness label.[57] Sirotkina concentrates on the moral overtones of the genre and physicians who wanted to 'express a world-view, make moral as well as professional claims, and thereby integrate their special interests with[in] a wider culture.'[58] Sirotkina notes that Kovalevskii wrote the first Russian pathography for Ivan the Terrible (1530–1584) and that the role of pathography was different in Russia than in the West. In Russia, where censorship had driven political and social discourse into the pages of *fiction* and where literature was meant to uplift society, not just reflect it, the psychiatrist identified with the writer in that both aimed to explore the human psyche and the psychological ailments of their time.[59]

At the beginning of the twentieth century, Swiss psychiatrist Eugene Bleuler (1857–1939) popularized the concept of schizophrenia in which patients no longer suffered from a disease of the mind, but from a disorder of the psyche. An altered sense of self meant that the art of a schizophrenic could provide insight into this dynamic psychopathology. Bleuler's theories greatly influenced students in the university clinics in Heidelberg, and in 1922 Hans Prinzhorn (1886–1933) published *Artistry of the Mentally Ill* in which he argued that the artistic works of schizophrenics contained hidden expressions of their psychological disruption. Sander Gilman suggests that this study is remarkable not only for its results, but for the ideological implications of the insane as artist. The patients were ill (not oracles or Romantic poets) and their artistic expressions reflected their personal pain and anguish.[60] As an artist himself, Andreev was caught in this madness-genius dilemma, especially as he attempted to define for himself how a diagnosis of acute neurasthenia impacted his own creative production.

Pathography

In 1927 two pathographies concerning Andreev's mental condition were published by Dr Ivan Galant. In his first article, the doctor suggested that Andreev suffered from hysteric-neurasthenia.[61] This diagnosis accounted for Andreev's manic and depressive episodes. The purpose of the article was less about diagnosing Andreev's mental condition, and more about exploring a perceived connection between madness and genius. Galant stated in his first paragraph that he was not as concerned with the psychological diagnosis as he was with what could be learned about the mental state of the person, thereby increasing his understanding of an already well-known condition. In effect, Galant was exploring the illness experience that, in his opinion, led to Andreev's literary genius.

Galant believed that Andreev's condition was innate, rather than caused by any one external event, which accounted for his behavior as a child – overly serious and gloomy – and, in turn, shaped his adult character. This caused Andreev to fear both life and death; convincing him that everything was in a state of prolonged decay. Andreev withdrew into a world of solitude and fantasy as a defense against this undefined anxiety. His need for solitude led to a love of nature and a desire to escape the activities of everyday life. However, the solitude he craved also had negative consequences when Andreev experienced bouts of depression – when he felt isolated and alone.

The public paid attention to the fact that Andreev was a literary decadent, a degenerate and an alcoholic, but Galant argued that this behavior was the result of Andreev's feelings of loneliness. As a defense against his self-imposed solitude, Andreev developed his talent as a writer and used this imaginative process as a type of catharsis. Galant understood Andreev's alcoholic behavior and attempts at suicide as reactions to his mental illness, but he also believed that these same negative factors led to Andreev's literary genius. It was Andreev's personal experience with mental illness that was then transferred to his literary works, which seemingly delighted his literary audience.

Galant saw evidence of this illness experience in Andreev's habit of rushing the completion of his stories, resulting in underdeveloped heroes and/or ideas, due to his 'lack of persistence and stubbornness when it came to reworking a topic to its logical end.'[62] Gor'kii's claim that Andreev did not understand reality also seemed to Galant to be a sign that the author lived in a world of fantasy – thereby protecting him from his anxiety and also providing him with the ability to create great works of imaginative art. However, what made Andreev's brand of hysteric-neurasthenia particularly his own, and therefore defined his literary persona, was his 'gloominess.' Galant suggested that the further Andreev moved from the influence of writers like Chekhov and Gor'kii, the more depressing his stories became – expressing his true nature. According to the doctor, neurasthenia influenced every aspect of Andreev's decision-making process and actions: 'Hysteric-neurasthenia forever remains an inseparable part of the whole that we call the life of L.

Andreev, Leonid-Andreev-esque art, and the part in Leonid Andreev which resulted in a hysteric-neurasthenic genius.'[63]

Although the notion that madness results in genius betrays the sway of degeneration theory, there remains a kernel of truth in Galant's argument – that Andreev's mental condition, which appeared early in his childhood, influenced his development as a human being and an artist. Loneliness and the seeming meaninglessness of life were core concerns for Andreev and influenced how he perceived the world around him.

In his second article, Galant was interested in hereditary factors contributing to Andreev's hysteric-neurasthenia. Relying heavily on Fatov's biography of Andreev's early years, Galant came to the conclusion that although Andreev's father was prone to drinking and violence, he was not a neurasthenic. Galant also could not find any obvious signs of neurasthenia on the maternal side of Andreev's family. He did note Andreev's claim that his talent for drawing and literature came from his mother's family. Here Galant was still concerned with the connection between mental illness and genius. He also paid special attention to the fact that Andreev's mother was extremely attached to her son and lived with him for most of his adult life. Galant concluded that his mother's love caused Andreev's obsessive love for his first wife and that with her death in 1906, he was driven to repeat the alcoholic behavior of his father.

As in his first article, Galant concentrated on Andreev's 'gloomy moods' which began in early childhood. He focused on the various attempts at suicide as proof that Andreev suffered from neurasthenia, and suggested that the untimely death of Andreev's father as well as his difficult romantic relationship with Zinaida Nikolaevna Sibeleva, his first adolescent love, contributed to this condition. However, Galant stated: 'The main disease of L. Andreev during his student years was his excessive alcoholism.[64] [...] The main symptoms of Andreev's neurasthenia were headaches, chest pains, a fear of death and, at this time, a lack of will to live. Andreev had lost the instinct of self-preservation and did not value life; he had a lack of energy, resulting in exhaustion, apathy, an aversion to work and life in general, a misanthropic attitude, etc.'[65] Galant concluded by suggesting that both parents contributed to Andreev's condition. He found signs of most of the resulting problems (alcoholism, attempted suicide, headaches, etc.) in Andreev's youth and argued that these factors were important in both the author's development into adulthood and in his literary production.

Although Sirotkina is dismissive of these early Russian pathographies, it is realistic to assert that the noted symptoms contributed to Andreev's adult behavior and literary works. One can take issue with Galant's diagnosis and the way in which he connects this to literary genius. However, most critics accept that Andreev's childhood depression and pessimism were important factors in his artistic development. Yet, these same Soviet-trained critics are unwilling to accept that bouts of depression, attempts at suicide and alcoholic behavior are clinical (above or below the norm) in nature and suggest some form of mental illness. In the following chapters, I hope to disprove this notion.

Heredity: the criminal and the genius

The theory of hereditary insanity, a fundamental law of degeneration, was one of Morel's legacies. The law of double fertilization referred to the impact of heredity from both parents, while the law of progressivity indicated that there could be hereditary transmission of destructive biological material within a family that eventually resulted, over the course of three or four generations, in idiocy and insanity.

Morel included criminals in his description of degenerates, which ultimately influenced Lombroso and led to the development of criminal anthropology. The belief was that criminals were born that way, primitive savages living in the midst of modern civilization. A significant amount of time and research energy was consequently spent on trying to establish anatomical and physiological stigmata that would make the criminal *visible*. How could one detect moral insanity in someone who appeared perfectly normal? This issue was further confused as 'newer versions of the doctrine found that the intellect could remain essentially intact while there were emotional and behavioral disturbances.'[66]

Russian researchers compounded the problem by suggesting that there were no stable criteria for predicting or anticipating hereditary transmission of degeneration. Kovalevskii identified two different forms of heredity: homogeneous heredity suggested that epileptic parents would have epileptic children; heterogeneous heredity resulted in unpredictable transmission of illness (alcoholic parents might have one melancholic child and one deaf child) or it could completely skip a generation. This meant that degeneration was transformative and capricious. According to Beer, such uncertainty 'heightened anxieties concerning the power of medicine and psychiatry to identify, categorize, and ultimately control it. The degenerative syndrome was thus in part engaged in a guerilla war against moral and physical health, delivering deadly blows before melting away into the psychophysical constitution of subsequent generations, only to reappear subsequently without warning in their offspring.'[67] This issue of hereditary taints dogged Andreev throughout his life (and after his death) with references to his father's alcoholism and violent behavior. It also found expression in his literary works, suggesting Andreev's own awareness of the scientific theories on hereditary transmission of degenerate traits.

Matters were further complicated when some degenerates showed evidence of superior abilities. Both Francis Galton (1822–1911) and Lombroso argued that genius was an inherited trait, consistent with degeneration theory. As noted previously, the perceived connection between genius and insanity had a long history prior to degeneration and subsequently remained a popular notion. For scientists the problem seemed to be that the overexcited sensibilities of the genius could lead to 'a lowered sensory threshold, retarded moral development, and a tendency to manic-like excitement.'[68]

Concepts of genius and criminality in the context of moral insanity were thus combined and explored by Russian and European theorists. In many of these studies, identification was a key goal. How could one pick out the criminal or the genius from among the common masses? How could they be identified, especially if they were potentially one in the same person? We find at times in Andreev's works a reaction against the prying eyes of science to determine what is sane or even moral. Given this cultural background, we must explore Andreev's reactions from another side – not the healthy Andreev defending his literary reputation, but the neurasthenic author trying to avoid the stigma of degeneration.

Criminal typology

Sander Gilman argues that the social construction of aggressive madness developed out of general anxiety over the tenuousness of life. Societies selected a number of groups such as Jews, homosexuals, gypsies and the insane onto which to project general anxieties such as the fear of theft, bodily harm and rape. In essence, they created bogymen to justify their uncertainties around personal safety. As a result, the insane were perceived as dangerous to the status quo, thereby necessitating that they be held in check. An institutional response to the perceived aggressive-ness of a deranged homeless person reassures society and provides comfort that there are controls in place to protect individuals. This sense of security is disrupted if the madman turns out to be a respected member of the community – a lawyer or doctor – thereby not typically identifiable as a psychopath.[69] Degeneration theory was an early attempt to identify physical traits which would make madness overtly *visible*, while also providing scientific evidence that the insane should be incar-cerated, thereby easing social anxieties.

In 1870, Lombroso was given the opportunity to perform a post-mortem on the body of a famous criminal. Cutting open the skull, he found what he considered to be regressive anomalies characteristically found in rodents. The professor of psychiatry theorized that atavistic qualities in certain individuals reproduce the behavior and instincts of primitive humanity and inferior animals. Lombroso's ideas shifted attention away from a discussion about criminal justice, a scale of punishment for similar transgressions, and redirected it toward the personality, biology and life history of the criminal.[70]

The degenerate criminal *typology* extended beyond thieves and murderers to anyone considered to be a social '*other*.'[71] Charles Bernheimer writes, 'In each of his books, Lombroso traces the analogous manifestations of the subversive influence, which is the agency of decadence itself. His awareness of the analogies between his descriptions of, say, the hysteric, the epileptic, the alcoholic, the prostitute, the morally insane, the inspired genius, the born criminal (whether male or female), repeatedly defeats his attempts to establish satisfactory taxonomies of deviant types and behaviors.'[72] All-inclusive scientific claims establishing a multitude of deviant typologies, once generally accepted, forced governments to create mechanisms for social order – institutions to house those designated as *other*.

Russian criminologists and psychiatrists accepted the supposed link between the moral and physical deformity of the born criminal. Dmitrii Dril' (1846–1910) and Orshanskii paid particular attention to environmental factors, while Susanna Ukshe (1885–?) and Kovalevskii argued the existence of a criminal predisposition. Russian scientists pondered the notion that social forces were possibly the genesis of criminal impulses. Under the influence of the German law professor Franz von Liszt (1851–1919), who argued that punishment should fit the criminal rather than the crime, Russian psychiatrists began to advocate that deviants be removed from unhealthy environments as a preventative measure, as well as to maintain public safety.[73]

In 1900, Pavel Iakobii (1842–1913) published a book entitled *The Principles of Administrative Psychiatry* (Printsipy administrativnoi psikhiatrii) in Orel, Andreev's hometown. Iakobii, who had spent many years as a physician in Europe and practiced psychiatry in Moscow, presented a radical argument that class fears were to blame for the mistreatment of the insane in Russia. The ruling social classes built asylums to remove from society perceived enemies and competitors as well as anyone who displayed uncontrolled passions or incomprehensible behavior. Therefore asylums and hospitals were not designed to treat the ill, but to detain them, thereby turning psychiatrists into wardens in charge of a captive population.[74] According to Iakobii, Russian psychiatrists practiced *police* psychiatry by insisting on the dangers of the mentally ill; simultaneously occupying two incompatible roles – physician and policeman. Iakobii argues that by emphasizing their role as defenders against the perils of the insane, Russian psychiatrists eliminated the possibility that they might help their ailing patients.[75]

The infusion of scientific and political discourse in popular culture is significant in this process – affirming the *acceptance* of social anxiety about mental illness. Andreev provides evidence of just this type of cultural practice. In his early works, hospitals and asylums are associated with isolation of the sick from the general public. In later works, mental illness is allied with punishment and incarceration. In both cases, Andreev accurately reflects the realities of the practice and popular discourse on madness in early twentieth-century Russia. After all, the asylum system in Russia was established and expanded on the notion that undesirables should be separated from the general population and housed in facilities similar to prisons. In many cases, little distinction was made between the criminal population and the mentally ill.

The great confinement

Until the eighteenth century, responsibility for the insane was the domain of monasteries in Russia. The problem was that the mentally ill were only a portion of the general population of 'unfortunates' and in many cases were left to roam about towns and forests. This changed with the legalization of serfdom in 1649, which restricted freedom of movement by the peasantry, and the religious schism within the Russian Orthodox Church, which classified religious dissenters and deviants together as hostile enemies of the established order. Martin A. Miller notes, 'This important historical development was to haunt the "healers of the soul," as the physicians in the era before psychiatry have been called. Immorality as defined by the church, deviance as defined by the state, and insanity as defined by the medical community were no longer distinct.'[76]

As Peter the Great (1672–1725) organized Russian society, he instituted state service requirements with specific demands for productivity. Correctional institutions were therefore established for those who were unproductive and idle. This transferred responsibility for the insane from the monasteries to workhouses and hospitals. Peter was not concerned with the rehabilitation of the ill, but was more interested in creating clear criteria for state service. Peter did not actually establish an asylum system, but he introduced the mandate that would move the insane from monastic to secular care.

According to Miller, the origins of the asylum system can be traced to a 1762 government decree by Emperor Peter III (1728–1762) that the insane were to be placed in special madhouses, based on the German *Tolhaus* model. Epileptics, lunatics, melancholics and maniacs were housed and treated in these facilities. Although asylums were established under Catherine the Great's (1729–1796) provincial reforms, they became dumping grounds for criminals and other undesirables of society. The facilities were overcrowded and the inmates were often mistreated. These problems were compounded by a general lack of funding.[77] The first asylums were built to protect society from dangerous elements and, therefore, were constructed so that inmates could never escape.[78] Therapy regularly consisted of physical restraint, as well as hot and cold water treatments. It is clear that these spaces were designed and perceived, like prisons, as a way to institutionally control undesirable elements of society.

Asylum populations rapidly expanded as a result of the 'Great Reforms' of the 1860s. Serfdom was abolished and all of the institutions of the empire were restructured. A system of limited local self-government was established and responsibility for education, public health (including madhouses), roads, insurance and famine relief were given to the zemstvos (regional governing bodies). In the mid-1870s, the government ordered the zemstvos to expand the asylums to accommodate the influx of patients. Julie V. Brown argues, 'The government's justification for placing this heavy weight on the backs of the zemstvos was the need to remove "dangerous" madmen from society quickly.'[79] She argues that when the Russian winter set in and families began to run out of food, they were forced to go to the larger urban centers. 'The greatest proportion of new admissions to the asylum came from those groups which had left the village to work or to beg, and subsequently proved unable or unwilling to adjust to the requirements of the urban environment.'[80] Young men were admitted to asylums for alcohol abuse, begging, brawling, and consorting with prostitutes – offenses that would normally demand prison space. 'A request by the police was interpreted to mean that the individual was potentially dangerous, and the institution was obligated by law to accept him. [...] Russian psychiatrists complained vociferously about the role of the police in asylum admissions.'[81]

Psychiatry emerged as a distinct specialization in Russia only during the nineteenth century. As noted, in 1857 the first department of psychiatry was established at the Medical Surgical Academy in St Petersburg. Students received both clinical and theoretical training and many studied or had contacts with leading European psychiatrists and neurologists. Under Nicholas I (1796–1855) oversight of the country's almshouses, orphanages and hospitals was assigned to a government department. Diagnostic criteria were established to distinguish between the curable and incurable with attention to diet, lifestyle and family background. Even with these improvements, hospitals dedicated to the mentally ill in St Petersburg and Moscow had inadequate funding, poorly trained staff and suffered from overpopulation.

It was only in the last third of the century that the terrible condition of the asylum system was publicly acknowledged and the level of financial support increased. This coincided with the maturation of Russian physicians who had completed doctoral dissertations in psychiatry in collaboration with colleagues abroad. Although psychiatry was growing in sophistication, hospital and asylum care once again began to deteriorate at the end of the nineteenth century. Miller explains: 'By 1911, the year the first congress of the Union of Russian Psychiatrists and Neuropathologists was held, it was generally recognized that conditions for the insane had not improved since the alarms had been sounded at the 1887 congress. In spite of Korsakov's efforts to have all mental patients removed from restraints, psychiatrists continued to complain that shackles remained at most institutions. [...] By 1914, there were only 350 psychiatrists and neurologists in an empire of 160 million people.'[82]

A brief discussion of the Russian asylum system confirms many of the issues raised by Michel Foucault (1926–1984) in *Madness and Civilization*, which compares the emergence of a new class of madmen in eighteenth-century society with institutions once occupied by lepers. He concentrates on the 1657 establishment of the Hôpital Général in Paris, which he understands to be a semi-judicial and administrative structure, rather than a medical institution to help the sick and poor. Almost twenty years later, an edict was passed by the king to enlarge the *hôpital général* to each city in the kingdom, thereby expanding the reach of bourgeois and monarchical control.[83] Foucault argues that this network began a period of confinement in which those who had once been driven from city limits (beggars, indigents, and the insane) were now contained and housed apart from the general population.[84] In these hospitals, labor was instituted as exercise and combined with moral rehabilitation to justify the site constraints and administrative enforcement. In this equation, there are both economic (putting the idle to work) and moral (maintaining the city for the virtuous) factors at play in herding undesirables into institutional spaces. The insane were grouped together with other unfortunates and little was done to treat, much less cure, their ills. Foucault argues that during the eighteenth century madness was equated with the bestial and this is why patients were treated inhumanely; often caged, chained and restrained.[85] 'Unchained animality could be mastered only by *discipline* and *brutalizing*.'[86]

Although *Madness and Civilization* created controversy, it also proved to be highly influential in inciting a reexamination of the history of madness and psychiatry.[87] This new approach reoriented the critical discourse regarding asylum culture, institutional control and professional imperialism. Each one of these issues is significant to the discussion of Andreev's relationship with mental illness, medical treatment and social stigmatization, especially given Russia's *great confinement* of the mentally ill. Insight may be gained into how Andreev perceived and depicted institutional spaces in his life and works – that at their basis hospitals and asylums were built to separate 'undesirables' from society, therefore limiting their contact with the general population. The term undesirables included the criminal along with the mentally ill. In these institutional spaces, patients were restrained with leather straps, shackles and strait-jackets in lieu of treatment. As Russia experienced political upheaval, political activists were added to the category of *dangers to society* and also housed in mental asylums, further uniting the association of asylums with prisons and punishment, thereby blurring the distinction between criminality and mental illness.

National fitness and wellbeing

In his 1869 book *Russia and Europe* (Rossiia i Evropa), the Russian naturalist and historian Nikolai Danilevskii (1822–1885) compared nations to species, arguing that each nation goes through periods of development in an evolutionary, biological process. In his opinion, the Slavic world was in its youth, while Europe had reached a period of cultural degeneration. When his theories were translated into French in 1871, Danilevskii's assertion caused much anxiety in Europe. By the end of the nineteenth century, however, rapid urbanization, social stratification, and political upheaval cast into doubt the resilience and *youth* of the Slavic world.[88]

By the first decade of the twentieth century, Russia was experiencing its own decadent period of cultural degeneration. Some, like Valerii Briusov (1873–1924), Konstantin Bal'mont (1867–1942), and Sologub, willingly depicted the perceived despair, perversity and degradation of contemporary Russian society in poetry and literature. Matich argues that it was in reaction to degeneration theory that some Russian cultural figures explored radical ways to cheat death; they rejected the impulses of the body, and embraced an apocalyptic mythos of the end of the world.[89]

Simultaneous with this cultural response, science was developing ways to identify and classify medical conditions which supposedly reflected the health of the whole society. Theories about disease and pathology, nurture or nature, and social change became the main subjects of both scientific and cultural discourse. Cultural pathologies were explained by way of scientific analogies, which often included references to either development or decline.[90] This captured the popular imagination regarding the rise and fall of entire civilizations and led to sweeping generalizations about the health of the Russian nation.

The notion that an individual's mental health was dependent on national fitness and wellbeing is seen in Andreev's ironic explanation for his own ill health. He claimed that he had Russian, Polish, Ukrainian and Finnish ancestry. This was compounded by bourgeois bloodlines on his father's side, and peasant ancestry on his mother's. 'It turns out that the reason for my being a bit screwy results from Russian separatism, splintering my hitherto singular personality much like the splitting of Russia: the separation of Poland, of the Ukraine, of Finland, and others gave rise in me to a corresponding separation.' Ivan Belousov (1863–1930) claims that although the tone of the comments was jocular, it betrayed a deeper truth about Andreev's variable moods and personality.[91]

As a result of the perceived link between individual and national health, the medical professional became the healer of not only physical ailments, but also social and national ills. Following from the supposition that disease was hereditary, it was projected that moral and physical conduct could influence successive generations and lead to constitutional deterioration. Once again, biological issues had ramifications for the moral health of a nation. Degeneration theory provided an explanation for sexual inequalities and class distinctions in the context of social disease.[92]

The problem was that degeneration remained a shifting and evolving term, despite efforts by various theorists to fix meaning to it. Decline, decay, excessive passion and many more concepts were used interchangeably and, because these were so pervasive in the arts, sciences, medicine and politics during the late nineteenth and early twentieth centuries, elicited very different intellectual responses.[93] The important thread was that degeneration was understood as a self-producing biological force; it was not the result of poor social conditions, but the *cause* of crime, destitution and disease.[94]

As a matter of fact, the public discourse about mental illness, national pandemics and the devolution of civilized society was much more widespread than many of the philosophical and literary issues that have concerned scholars of the Russian *fin de siècle*. This medical discourse found its way into legal arguments, political debates and social experiments. One could read about it daily in newspapers and journals of all types. More so than many of the ideas that circulated in small intellectual circles and literary salons, this was the popular discourse of an entire society – rich and poor; intellectual and uneducated; liberal and conservative.

It is within this context that Andreev lived as a neurasthenic. This perception of illness found its way, not unexpectedly, into his literary texts, and soon critics were discussing Andreev's latest works about psychopaths in parallel with popular gossip about his own mental health. His works were then used as instructive medical texts by psychiatrists, and Andreev's mental health was further entangled in discourse about degeneration theory. Rather than straying from these topics in his creative works, Andreev developed elements of the popular discourse surrounding genius and madness, the deviant criminal, confinement and more. After all, this was the 'hot topic' among all layers of Russian society and it was a factor in his literary success. Even as he defended his sanity in the press, Andreev, as I shall argue, further explored these ideas in his writing, and began to see his own life within this social construct of illness. It is therefore important to examine Andreev's biographical and fictional texts as one illness narrative, as the author's perception of illness informed by degeneration theory. After all, previous studies have bestowed great importance on the influence of German pessimism in the life and works of Andreev and yet, the ideas of Schopenhauer and Hartmann were certainly no more widespread or personally relevant to the author than the popular discourse concerning mental illness and the devolution of Russian society.

Literary movements

The influence of degeneration theory on cultural and artistic production, particularly literature, was quite widespread at the beginning of the twentieth century. A partial list of leading authors and important works of the time gives a sense of its scope: Joseph Conrad's (1857–1924) *Heart of Darkness* (1899 serialized/1902 book), George Gissing's (1857–1903) *In the Year of the Jubilee* (1894), Gerhard Hauptmann's (1862–1946) *Before Dawn* (1889), Jack London's (1876–1916) *People of the Abyss* (1903), Robert Louis Stevenson's (1850–1894) *The Strange Case of Dr Jekyll and Mr Hyde* (1886), Bram Stoker's (1847–1912) *Dracula* (1897), Thomas Hardy's (1840–1928) *Tess of the d'Urbervilles* (1891), H.G. Wells' (1866–1946) *The Island of Doctor Moreau* (1896), Virginia Woolf's (1882–1941) *Mrs Dalloway* (1925), Emile Zola's (1840–1902) *Les Rougon-Macquart* novels (1871–1893) and many more. Degeneration theory clearly found its way into the discourse of popular culture and became a fundamental pillar upon which *decadence* was constructed as an artistic movement.

French decadence traces its aesthetic roots to Charles Baudelaire's *The Flowers of Evil* (1857); Théophile Gautier's (1811–1872) *Mademoiselle de Maupin* (1835) and his poems of the 1850s; the 1860s novels of Edmond (1822–96) and Jules de Goncourt (1830–70); Gustave Flaubert's (1821–1880) *Salambô* (1862), *The Temptation of Saint Anthony* (1874), and *Three Tales* (1877). However, it did not become a movement until the 1880s, insisting on the autonomy of art, displaying disgust for philistinism and utilitarianism, and an interest in arcane and elaborate language. There was also a fascination with the perverse, morbid and artificial as well as a desire to escape from the *ennui* of everyday existence. Zola was one of the leaders of this new movement with a focus on the sordid aspects of life.[95]

British decadence was influenced greatly by Joris-Karl Huysman's (1848–1907) *Against the Grain* (1884), which dealt with perversion, morbidity, ennui and spiritual malaise. In this novel, the British found a happy medium between naturalism and aestheticism. However, due to a cautious publishing industry, writers such as George Moore (1852–1933), Havelock Ellis (1859–1939), Arthur Symonds (1865–1945) and Lionel Johnson (1867–1902) introduced decadence to the British public in the late 1880s in critical essays. Oscar Wilde's *The Picture of Dorian Gray* (1890) was the first British attempt to garner mass public attention, as well as a harsh critical rebuke.

Kirsten MacLeod writes, 'Decadence was used loosely by critics to describe everything from Naturalism and Impressionism to Realism and New Woman fiction. At the same time, with the advent of medical discourse that associated artistic genius with criminality and degeneracy, Decadent writers and artists were increasingly subject to *ad hominem* attacks in which their art was represented as a direct reflection of their own pathological condition.' British decadence came to a boiling point with the 1895 arrest and trial of Wilde for acts of gross indecency. Wilde's crimes of homosexuality were linked with the entire movement, making many artists disassociate themselves from it. In England, decadence soon was renamed symbolism.[96]

Russian symbolism and decadence were beholden to the neo-romantic movement of the French decadent movement. Adrian Wanner argues, 'The period was characterized by a general sense of crisis, malaise, and *bezvremen'e* (stagnation, literally timelessness), exacerbated by the fierce political reaction to the killing of Tsar Alexander II in 1881 and by the death or silence of virtually all of the great Russian novelists around 1880.'[97] An early Russian strain, influenced by the pessimistic philosophy of Arthur Schopenhauer, was associated with the works of Bal'mont, Briusov and Sologub. A second wave of poets concentrated on philosophical religiosity, which changed the tenor of the movement for a time. This positivism diminished however, after the failed revolution of 1905, and a decadent strain was soon found among poets of this second wave such as Aleksandr Blok (1880–1921), Andrei Belyi (1880–1934) and Viacheslav Ivanov (1866–1949).

Russian literary scholarship has tended to divide writers of the period into either (neo-)realists or decadents/symbolists. This approach excludes a writer like Andreev from Russian decadence as he was not a member of the symbolist artistic circles. In this sense, there is a concentration on literary camps, personal allegiances and social class, rather than thematic concerns. This issue of literary allegiances is captured in Chulkov's memoir:

> At this time in Moscow, a group of new poets had already made a name for themselves, uniting under the sign of the *Scorpion*.[98] These individuals, 'founders of a new art,' to a certain extent were true decadents, giving voice to the 'fin-de-siècle.' It was as if their works heralded a turning point in cultural life. Leonid Nikolaevich Andreev never belonged to this circle and never could have. He was too 'provincial,' not 'refined' enough for them, and he did not like or respect them. However, in his unconscious essence, which was belied by his externalities, he and the *Scorpion* group were 'birds of the feather.'[99]

Recent scholarship by Olga Matich has begun to shift that focus. In *Erotic Utopia* she examines the ways in which degeneration theory influenced the ideas of such Russian cultural figures as Lev Tolstoi (1828–1910), Vladimir Soloviev (1853–1900), Blok, Zinaida Gippius (1869–1945), and Vasilii Rozanov (1856–1919). Matich argues that degeneration theory can be seen in the public disquiet about the blood taint of the Romanov dynasty (hemophilia), the sexual questions raised by Tolstoi and others, and the anti-Semitic behaviors around the 'Jewish question.' However, she mainly focuses on how degeneration influenced the Russian spiritual renaissance of the time and its resulting challenge to notions of individualism, procreation and genealogy. This line of discourse once again eliminates Andreev from the discussion.

Andreev has typically been identified in scholarship as a neo-realist writer, associated with the publishing house *Znanie* (Knowledge) and the political radicalism of many of its authors. Andreev is grouped with, among others, Gor'kii, Aleksandr Kuprin (1870–1938) and Skitalets (1869–1941). As a result, Andreev's themes of depravity and criminality are understood as social commentary and revolutionary realism. Woodward takes note of this specific issue: 'This failure of criticism would seem to be due, at least in part, to an incorrect understanding of Andreyev's position *vis-à-vis* Gorky and the writers associated with *Znanie* and [the literary circle] *Sreda*, and to the resultant tendency to judge him by the same yardstick.'[100] Again, this classification is partially reliant on literary and personal friendships as well as class distinctions. This is why the issue of Andreev's literary allegiance to both Russian realism and symbolism befuddled his contemporaries as well as literary scholars. One only has to remember the often quoted statement that Andreev made to Gor'kii, 'Who am I? For the noble-born decadents I am a contemptible realist. For the hereditary realists I am a suspicious symbolist.'[101] Yet, for David Weir it is just this inability to adhere to aesthetic definitions that results in decadence: 'the epithet *decadent* comes to be applied to certain novels for their "failure" to adhere to the aesthetic dictates of realism or to the conventions of some established genre.'[102]

If we discard literary camps and allegiances, however, Andreev would be considered a decadent writer. For example, in discussing one of his first unsuccessful attempts at fiction, Andreev recalled that the story was 'characteristically decadent, and curiously enough, it was written before Russian decadence had manifested itself in any noticeable way.'[103] In 1903, Platon Krasnov already associated Andreev's first collection of stories with the 'decadent style' and, more importantly, with foreign writers such as Edgar Allan Poe (1809–1849) and Baudelaire.[104]

When Andreev was offered the editorship of the *Znanie* almanac in 1907, he immediately planned to include the works of both Blok and Sologub. Gor'kii reacted negatively to this suggestion, claiming that Blok was a poor substitute for Verlaine and that Sologub was in love with death and addicted to sadism. Undoubtedly, Gor'kii was reacting to the decadent strains in their poetic and literary works, strains which he felt were in opposition to the more politically democratic leanings of his publishing house and its journal. Andreev thus declined the editorship, stating that he shared Gor'kii's opinion about Sologub, Blok and the other decadents (Andreev refers to them as such), but that if *Znanie* was publishing only democratic writers, then he himself should not be included in this group as he was not a democratic writer. Andreev did not go so far as to label himself a decadent writer in this exchange, but certainly placed himself somewhere between the two literary classifications.[105] Andreev eventually became the editor of the *Shipovnik* (Sweetbriar) almanacs which did publish writers from the different literary camps, bringing him closer to the decadents.

Woodward points to this problem of literary classifications noting that, during his lifetime, Andreev was more often associated with literary decadence. 'It was obvious to most contemporary writers that he had far more in common with [the symbolists] than with the realists, and for Kleynbort and Veresaev the failure of any alliance to materialize was an insoluble mystery. Brusyanin states that there was a marked tendency to associate him with the "decadents." "Leonid Nikolaevich himself understood," writes Beklemisheva, "that in the literary sphere he was closer to Blok, Belyi, and Sologub than to Gusev-Orenburgsky and Chirikov." [...] At the same time, all of the symbolists were conscious of the cultural gap between Andreyev and themselves, of this lack of "refinement," of the fact that they belonged to a different strata of the intelligentsia.' As a result, many of these symbolist critics classified Andreev's works as 'pseudo-decadence,' eliminating him based on social status, educational background and literary friendships.[106]

Even so, shortly after his death, Chulkov identified Andreev as a decadent. He does not associate him with the Russian decadent poets, but with the larger cultural pessimism in European decadence and Russian society.

> I write these lines in January, 1920. The future of Russia is dark and unpredictable. But now we know that many events of Russian cultural life, on the eve of revolution, had a special meaning, prophetic and significant. We loved to repeat that Russia, cultural Russia, was still young; exhausted by the political reaction of the last Tsarist reigns, somehow we failed to notice that the spiritual culture of our country, despite the decrepitude of its form of government, had reached its peak; that the appearance of the so-called Decadents was by no means accidental – they were authentic harbingers of a cultural turning point. Such fragrant but poisonous flowers can only grow on the soil of a great culture that has outlived itself. The Decadents worked quite a bit on the minds and hearts of their contemporaries: 'Absolute values do not exist. Everything is relative. You could laugh at anything. Besides, there is nothing sacred. It would not be a bad idea to say, to hell with everything.' All of this was said with wit and subtlety, and some even infused this thought with a certain demonic profundity. Leonid Andreev repeated this same thing, but mixed with distress and grief: he felt pity for man. He rebelled like a Decadent, but his rebellion was somehow feminine, hysterical and sentimental. Less subtle than the Decadent poets, he was probably more typical and definitive for our cultural dark age than they were. As a personality, Andreev always represents for me not so much a poisoner of his contemporaries, as a victim. He himself was poisoned and tortured by the strange, dark forces that invisibly penetrated our life and corrupted it.

Leonid Andreev had a specific spiritual experience; let us call it 'mystical,' (I say this not based on his writings, but on personal impressions), but religiously, Andreev was *blind* and he did not know what to do with that experience. He bore not a trace of the cold cynicism typical of Decadents. He was a genuinely good person, but a person tortured by premonitions, confused and lost.[107]

So was Andreev a decadent or realist? Valerii Bezzubov examined Andreev's personal and literary relationships with realists Dostoevskii, Tolstoi, Chekhov and Gor'kii as well as with the symbolist Blok. He argues that Andreev was not a realist in the tradition of nineteenth-century realism, but also disliked most symbolist works, except for those of Blok and Sologub. At various times, Andreev had imitated the works of both Tolstoi and Dostoevskii, but claimed the literary influence of Vsevolod Garshin (1855–1888) and Chekov. Even if Andreev had wanted to become a member of the symbolist movement, he was deemed by its members to be too uncultured and out of tune with symbolist (not decadent) ideology to become one of its affiliates.[108]

Keeping in mind that the critic was limited by Soviet groupthink, Bezzubov reasons that Andreev came out of the classical nineteenth-century realist, democratic and humanistic traditions and did not migrate to the decadent-symbolist movement.[109] Andreev's literary roots grew in the soil of Gor'kii's *Znanie* publishing house, but he continually struggled against dogmatism, employing the newest literary forms that confused those who wanted to assign him to a literary camp. Bezzubov views Andreev's work in the spirit of neo-realism or fantastical realism, but suggests that as a result of bold artistic experiments, Andreev produced an expressionistic style that would later be realized in part in the existentialist and other avant-garde movements.[110]

I offer the alternative suggestion that Andreev was, in fact, a Russian decadent – relying on the medical discourse and science of degeneration theory. He was not a 'noble-born decadent' poet with the proper aesthetic vocabulary, but certainly he was employing many of the thematic strains of European decadence – degeneration and decline, malaise and pessimism, perversity and deviance. That Andreev should be considered a representative of this movement is supported by Kirsten Lodge's recent publication, *The Dedalus Book of Russian Decadence*, in which 'The Abyss' (Bezdna), 'In the Fog' and 'The Story of Sergei Petrovich' (Rasskaz o Sergee Petroviche) are included along with works by Briusov, Gippius, Sologub and others.[111] We might also recall that Vasilii L'vov-Rogachevskii (1873–1930) argued that Andreev was decadent before it was fashionable to be a decadent. He was the antidote to Gor'kii's positive escapism found among many of the *Znanie* writers.[112] By accepting this premise, we can offer a compromise in the realist-symbolist debate as well as reexamine our understanding of Russian decadence and Andreev's role in it.

The Russian *fin de siècle*

Russian decadence was not simply a reaction to the French and English literary movements. It reflected Russia's own national trajectory during a time of mourning, after the assassination of the Tsar, but also during a period of rapid industrialization under the guidance of Sergei Witte (1849–1915). By the last decade of the nineteenth century, Russian industry, mining and oil production was expanding rapidly, garnering a huge influx of foreign capital. Wages and working conditions, however, were still quite dismal and the threat of disease and death were daily concerns among the lower class. At the same time, the Russian middle class was rapidly expanding and major Russian cities were beginning to resemble their European neighbors in the areas of manufacturing, commerce, banking and public transportation. One result of a burgeoning middle class was a growing rate of literacy, even in the countryside. As a result, there was greater access to higher education as thousands of Russians also took advantage of opportunities to study abroad, mostly in Germany, Switzerland and France. This resulted in the free exchange of ideas between Russia and Europe.

The age of the Russian realist novel had come to an end and the short story was the preferred genre of Garshin, Chekhov and Vladimir Korolenko (1853–1921). Poetry flourished too under the influence of French decadence and German pessimism. In 1891, *The Northern Messenger* (Severnyi vestnik) became one of the first outlets for Russian decadents such as Bal'mont, Sologub and Gippius. This artistic rebellion was made possible in part by wealthy patrons of the arts, exemplified in the industrialist Savva Mamontov (1841–1918), the Duchess Maria Tenisheva (1867–1928), and the banker Nikolai Riabushinskii (1876–1951).[113]

The Russian decadent/symbolist movement, generally speaking, reflected the essence of the *fin de siècle*, which was predominantly pessimistic and rife with an impending sense of apocalyptic doom. The Russian revolutionary movement heightened the natural tendency to see the end of a century in revelatory terms, in particular that human existence was fragile and near extinction. One reaction was to believe that individuals were living in an unreal shadow world full of masks, doubles and devils. Satanism and the demonic as well as searches for a new godhead were pervasive during this period. In this searching, we might find the basis for the perceived difference between Russian decadence and symbolism, a seeming division between good and evil. The *evil* elements of Russian decadence were further associated with brazen asceticism, sensuality, cruelty and an attraction to death and destruction. This negative impulse was solidified, if not realized, following the disappointment of the failed revolt of 1905 and, eventually, the death and destruction of world war and revolution in the coming years. As such, it is no surprise that in the works of Andreev, as well as those of Blok and Sologub, are found devils, doppelgängers, madmen and murderers.

As one might expect, there were many critics of this literary trend, those who believed that Russian decadents were 'feeble individuals who, unable to sustain the pace of contemporary development, preferred to distort it, and who embodied the undesirable traits of Western man, such as vacuity, in their most extreme forms.'[114] Others, as will be a main focus of this study, believed that decadence was an early sign that Russian civilized society was in a state of rapid decline, that these literary offerings were much like a dead canary in the coal mine, a visible warning of a silent killer.

The symptoms were many even though the killer of Russian society was unknown. Rapid industrialization had increased the natural pace of life and the average person could no longer keep up. It was believed that machines were outpacing mankind, placing an enormous physical and psychological strain on the body. A disruption of traditional social classes along economic and educational lines meant that social barriers, long maintained to ensure what many believed was a natural balance between the classes, were being destroyed. Most also thought that the comingling of dangerous ideas on religion, gender, sex, class and politics were feeding the revolutionary fervor in Russia. Significantly, apprehensions about the end of the century had given way to disappointment following the first decade of the twentieth century, a period of regicide, labor strikes, political terrorism and murder. Russian decadents captured these feelings in their petty demons, their prostitutes in ostrich feathers and their half-mad insomniacs, in dimly-lit back allies, at masquerades and in taverns on the edge of town.

There was certainly a decadent literary movement as constructed and self-identified by Briusov and others, but there was also a decadent literature, created outside of certain literary salons, that reflected the zeitgeist of the era. It is this larger understanding of Russian decadence that will guide this study. As such, the argument that Andreev should be considered a decadent writer does not suggest a belated invitation for him into the social and artistic circles of Gippius and Briusov, but that his works should be read within the context of the larger social, political, literary and scientific trends that informed this decadent period in Russia. Andreev's texts describe the perceived devolution of Imperial Russia and might again be read within this context of Russia's degeneration.

It is significant that authors and their literary works were nearly inseparable in modernist discourse at the turn of the century. For example, Wilde played a cat-and-mouse game in his works, including vague reference to his sexual proclivities, from which many passages were then quoted during his trial as evidence against him. In the Russian context, Vladislav Khodasevich (1886–1939) viewed Nina Petrovskaia (1884–1928) as a victim of decadence in her relationship with Belyi and Briusov, a relationship realized as *art* in Briusov's *The Fiery Angel* (Ognennyi angel). Arguably then, Andreev conducted his own game of hide and seek regarding his mental health; he too was a *victim* of degeneration discourse, which is captured in his fictional and autobiographical illness narratives. It is to his life and works, therefore, that we shall now turn.

Notes

1 Horwitz, Allan V. *The Social Control of Mental Illness* (New York: Academic Press, 1982) 25.

2 A detailed discussion of many relevant issues is provided by Rylkova, Galina. *The Archeology of Anxiety: The Russian Silver Age and Its Legacy* (Pittsburgh: University of Pittsburgh Press, 2008). Rylokva, however, is not concerned with the role of scientific discourse. For a standard understanding of the symbolist movement see Pyman, Avril. *A History of Russian Symbolism* (New York: Cambridge University Press, 1996).

3 Thiher, Allen. *Revels in Madness: Insanity in Medicine and Literature* (Ann Arbor: University of Michigan Press, 1999) 182.

4 McClelland, James C. *Autocrats and Academics: Education, Culture and Society in Tsarist Russia* (Chicago: University of Chicago Press, 1979) 61–2.

5 Alexander, Franz G. and Sheldon T. Selesnick. *The History of Psychiatry: An Evaluation of Psychiatric Thought and Practice from Prehistoric Times to the Present* (New York: Harper & Row, 1966) 135–6.

6 Thiher, *Revels in Madness*, 137–8.

7 Ibid., 196.

8 Thiher discusses how the poets Gerard de Nerval (1808–1855), Baudelaire, Lauréamont (Isidore Dicasse, 1846–1870) and Arthur Rimbaud (1854–1891) expressed their struggles with mental illness in poetry. See Thiher, *Revels in Madness*, 204–23. These poets were influential in Russian literary circles, especially among the first generation of Russian Symbolists.

9 Ibid., 223.

10 For more on the development of Prichard's theory of moral insanity see Augustein, Hannah Franziska. 'J C Prichard's Concept of Moral Insanity: A Medical Theory of the Corruption of Human Nature.' *Medical History*, 40 (1996): 311–43.

11 Bogdanov, *Vrachi, patsienty, chitateli*, 256.

12 Thiher writes: 'In Morel's work a version of Lamarckian biological determinism dovetails with bourgeois self-justification: like giraffes who cannot help having long necks because their ancestors preferred the leaves on the tops of trees, the degenerates of society are predestined to their alcoholism, crime, and insanity because their fathers were unhealthy. Inheritance offered a drama that writers utilized, with a sense of Greek tragedy, to show that fathers could bequeath a curse on their children. Naturalists, like Ibsen and Zola, welcomed scientific variation of their visions of destiny. Morel presents the interesting case in which a mediocre scientist was able to influence great writers.' See Thiher, *Revels in Madness*, 204.

13 Porter, *Madness: A Brief History*, 147–8.

14 Iudin, T. *Ocherki istorii otechestvennoi psikhiatrii* (Moscow: Medgiz, 1951) 108–9.

15 Sirotkina, Irina. *Diagnosing Literary Genius: A Cultural History of Psychiatry in Russia, 1880–1930* (Baltimore: Johns Hopkins University Press, 2002) 26.

16 Iudin, *Ocherki istorii otechestvenoi psikhiatrii*, 113–14; Alexander and Selesnick, *The History of Psychiatry*, 158.

17 Porter, *Madness: A Brief History*, 149–53.

18 Beer, *Renovating Russia*, 68–70.

19 Pick, Daniel. *Faces of Degeneration. A European Disorder, c. 1848–c. 1918* (Cambridge: Cambridge University Press, 1989) 20.

20 Ibid., 19–21.

21 Beer, *Renovating Russia*, 40–1.

22 Biographical information on Orshanskii can be found on many websites including the online Russian biographical encyclopedia, see: www.biografija.ru/show_bio.aspx?id=101640, accessed on 24 November 2007.

23 Sirotkina, *Diagnosing Literary Genius*, 61; 65.

24 Iudin, *Ocherki istorii otechestvenoi psikhiatrii*, 138.

25 Bogdanov, *Vrachi, patsienty, chitateli*, 262–3; Sirotkina, *Diagnosing Literary Genius*, 23–35; 57–65; 79–82; Beer, Daniel. 'The Medicalization of Religious Deviance in the Russian Orthodox Church(1880–1905).' *Kritika: Explorations in Russian and Eurasian History*, 5, 3 (Summer 2004): 468.

26 Beer, *Renovating Russia*, 33.

27 Greenslade, William. *Degeneration, Culture and the Novel, 1880–1940* (Cambridge: Cambridge University Press, 1994) 17.

28 Matich, Olga. *Erotic Utopia: The Decadent Imagination in Russia's* Fin de Siècle (Madison: University of Wisconsin Press, 2005) 29–30.

29 Hachten, Elizabeth A. 'In Service to Science and Society: Scientists and the Public in Late-Nineteenth-Century Russia.' *Osiris* (Science and Civil Society, 2nd Series) 17 (2002): 182.

30 Beer, Daniel. '"Microbes of the Mind": Moral Contagion in Late Imperial Russia.' *Journal of Modern History*, 79, 3 (September 2007): 538–9; Beer, *Renovating Russia*, 31–2.

31 Beard, George M. *American Nervousness: Its Causes and Consequences* (New York: G.P. Putnam, 1881) 7–8.
32 Sirotkina, *Diagnosing Literary Genius*, 134.
33 Ibid., 126–7.
34 Ibid., 143–4.
35 Goering, Laura. '"Russian Nervousness": Neurasthenia and National Identity in Nineteenth-Century Russia.' *Medical History*, 47, 1 (2003): 26–8; 31; 38.
36 Greenslade, *Degeneration, Culture and the Novel*, 120–4.
37 Ibid., 128–9.
38 LRA, MS. 606 / E. 6 *26 September 1892–4 January 1893; 04 January*; Entry for 20 November 1892.
39 LRA, MS. 606 / E. 1 *12 March–30 June 1890; 21 September 1898*; Entry for 16 March 1890.
40 LRA, MS. 606 / E.4 *15 May–17 August 1891*; Entry for 2 August 1891.
41 There is no evidence that Andreev knew or read Freud, as there is for Nordau, Kraft-Ebbing and Lombroso. Karanchi supports this claim and states that if there is anything Freudian in Andreev's works, then it must be attributed to the general discussion around psychology at the turn of the century. See Karanchi, L. 'Leonid Andreev o psikhologicheskom izobrazhenii.' *Studia Slavica Hungarica*, 12 (1972): 98–9. Also, Andreev was seemingly never treated with psychoanalysis, but rather with electro-shock and water treatments prescribed by medical professionals who attempted to remedy mental illness in a physical way.
42 LRA, MS. 606 / G.1.i.c.
43 Gilman, Sander L. *Difference and Pathology: Stereotypes of Sexuality, Race, and Madness* (Ithaca: Cornell University Press, 1985) 231.
44 Becker, George. *The Mad Genius Controversy: A Study in the Sociology of Deviance* (Beverly Hills: Sage Publications, 1978) 25–6.
45 Ibid., 28.
46 Porter, *Madness: A Brief History*, 80–1.
47 Gilman, *Difference and Pathology*, 221–2.
48 Schiller, Francis. *A Möbius Strip: Fin-de-Siècle Neuropsychiatry and Paul Möbius* (Berkeley: University of California Press, 1982) 74–5.
49 Ibid., 75.
50 Ibid., 78.
51 Andreev is probably referring to Lombroso's *Genius and Madness: Parallels between Great and Mad People*, which was published in several editions in St Petersburg.
52 White, *Memoirs and Madness*, 29.
53 Schiller, *A Möbius Strip*, 81.
54 Ibid., 82.
55 Ibid., 83.
56 Ibid., 86.
57 Becker, *The Mad Genius Controversy*, 127.
58 Sirotkina, *Diagnosing Literary Genius*, 4.
59 Ibid., 4–7.
60 Gilman, *Difference and Pathology*, 225–7; 230–1.

61 This is not necessarily a new diagnosis. Other doctors had diagnosed Andreev as a neurasthenic, and Fatov suggests that people knew of Andreev's 'hysterical-nervous' condition. See Fatov, *Molodye gody Leonida Andreeva*, 65. The awareness and understanding of mental illness at the turn of the twentieth century was very limited. Conditions such as depression were considered to be the result of nervous exhaustion. It was believed that the expenditure of and/or the depletion of bodily energies (neurasthenia) as a result of excessive living caused emotional problems. 'Neurasthenia involved pervasive feelings of low mood, lack of energy, and physical symptoms that were considered to be, in part, related to "life style" problems brought on by the demands of civilization.' See 'Nineteenth Century Views of the Causation and Treatment of Mental Disorders' in *Abnormal Psychology and Modern Life, 1998 Update*, 47. Today neurasthenia has no formal clinical status and is not a diagnostic category in the American Psychiatric Association's *Diagnostic and Statistical Manual of Mental Disorders*.

62 Galant, 'Psikhopatologicheskii obraz Leonida Andreeva. Leonid Andreev isteronevrastenicheskii genii,' 161.

63 Ibid., 165.

64 Galant, 'Evroendokrinologiia velikikh russkikh pisatelei i poetov. L. N. Andreev,' 233.

65 Ibid., 236.

66 Carlson, Eric T. 'Degeneration and Medicine: Theory and Praxis.' In *Degeneration: The Dark Side of Progress*. Edited by J. Edward Chamberlin and Sander L. Gilman (New York: Columbia University Press, 1985) 136.

67 Beer, *Renovating Russia*, 53–4.

68 Carlson, 'Medicine and Degeneration,' 137.

69 Gilman, *Disease and Representation*, 11–13.

70 Bernheimer, Charles. *Decadent Subjects: The Idea of Decadence in Art, Literature, Philosophy, and Culture of the* Fin de Siècle *in Europe*. Edited by T. Jefferson Kline and Naomi Schor (Baltimore: Johns Hopkins University Press, 2002) 144.

71 Greenslade, *Degeneration, Culture and the Novel*, 92.

72 Bernheimer, *Decadent Subjects*, 150.

73 Beer, Daniel. 'Blueprints for Change: The Human Sciences and the Coercive Transformation of Deviants in Russia, 1890–1930.' *Osiris*, 22 (2008): 30–6.

74 Iakobii's text is discussed in Miller, Martin A., *Freud and the Bolsheviks. Psychoanalysis in Imperial Russia and the Soviet Union* (New Haven: Yale University Press, 1998) 13–14. Miller provides the following publication information: P.I. Iakobii, *Printsipy administrativnoi psikhiatrii*. Orel: Tip. gib. pravleniia, 1900. For more on Iakobii see Iudin, *Ocherki istorii otechestvennoi psikhiatrii*, 196–200.

75 Brown, Julie V. 'Psychiatrists and the State in Tsarist Russia.' In *Social Control and the State*. Edited by Stanley Cohen and Andrew Scull (Oxford: Basil Blackwell, 1986) 278–9.

76 Miller, *Freud and the Bolsheviks*, 4.

77 Ibid., 5–6.

78 Brown, Julie V. 'Peasant Survival Strategies in Late Imperial Russia: The

Social Uses of the Mental Hospital.' *Social Problems*, 34, 4 (October 1987): 314.

79 Ibid.

80 Ibid., 318.

81 Ibid., 319.

82 Miller, *Freud and the Bolsheviks*, 14.

83 Foucault, Michel. *Madness and Civilization: A History of Madness in the Age of Reason*. Translated by Richard Howard (London: Routledge Classics, 2001) 36–8.

84 Ibid., 44–5.

85 Ibid., 68.

86 Ibid., 70.

87 Porter provides a concise summary of the way in which Foucault's text has been received. See Porter, Roy. 'Introduction.' In Porter, Roy and David Wright. *The Confinement of the Insane. International Perspectives, 1800–1965* (Cambridge: Cambridge University Press, 2003)3–5; Porter, Roy. *Madmen: A Social History of Madhouses, Mad-Doctors & Lunatics* (Stroud: Tempus, 2004) 17–21. Also see Still, Arthur and Irving Velody, eds. *Rewriting the History of Madness: Studies in Foucault's Histoire de la folie* (London: Routledge, 1992) for detailed critiques on Foucault's ideas about madness.

88 Eksteins, Modris. 'History and Degeneration: Of Birds and Cages.' In *Degeneration: The Dark Side of Progress*. Edited by J. Edward Chamberlin and Sander L. Gilman, 10–11; Vucinich, Alexander. *Science in Russian Culture, 1861–1917* (Stanford: Stanford University Press, 1970) 30–4.

89 Matich, *Erotic Utopia*.

90 Chamberlin, J.E. 'An Anatomy of Cultural Melancholy.' *Journal of the History of Ideas*, 42, 4 (October–December 1981): 687–99.

91 Belousov, Ivan. *Ushedshaia Moskva: Vospominaniia* (Moscow: Russkaia kniga, 2002) 257–8; 433–4.

92 Gilman, Stuart C. 'Political Theory and Degeneration.' In *Degeneration. The Dark Side of Progress*. Edited by J. Edward Chamberlin and Sander L. Gilman, 170–3.

93 Pick, *Faces of Degeneration*, 8.

94 Ibid., 21.

95 MacLeod, Kirsten. *Fictions of British Decadence: High Art, Popular Writing, and the* Fin de Siècle (New York: Palgrave MacMillan, 2006)1–2.

96 Ibid., 2–7; quote 6.

97 Wanner, Adrian. *Baudelaire in Russia* (Gainesville: University Press of Florida, 1996) 58.

98 *Scorpion* was a publishing house mainly for Symbolist poets.

99 Chulkov, *Kniga o Leonide Andreeve*, 108; in English, see White, *Memoirs and Madness*, 80.

100 Woodward, *Leonid Andreyev: A Study*, 276.

101 Anisimov, I., ed. *Literaturnoe nasledstvo. Gor'kii i Leonid Andreev: Neizdannaia perepiska*, vol. 72 (Moscow: Nauka, 1965) 351.

102 Weir, David. *Decadence and the Making of Modernism* (Amherst: University of Massachusetts Press, 1995) 15.

103 Kaun, *Leonid Andreyev: A Critical Study*, 27.

104 Krasnov, Pl. 'Koshmarnyi pisatel'. Literaturnaia kharakteristika Leonida Andreeva.' In *Literaturnye vechera* Novogo Mira. *1903 god* (St Petersburg: M.O. Vol'f, 1903) 43–4.

105 Anisimov, *Literaturnoe nasledstvo*, 284–96.

106 Woodward, *Leonid Andreyev: A Study,* 121–2.

107 Chulkov, *Kniga o Leonide Andreeve*, 122. In English, see White, *Memoirs and Madness*, 88.

108 White, *Memoirs and Madness,* 181–93.

109 There is evidence of this in his discussion of Russian decadence. For Bezzubov, this movement was represented by writers who criticized the democratic literature of Gor'kii and were 'apolitical' in their aspirations of 'art for art's sake.' See Bezzubov, V. *Leonid Andreev i traditsii russkogo realizma* (Tallin: Esti Raamat, 1984) 121.

110 Ibid., 329–34.

111 Lodge, Kirsten, ed. *The Dedalus Book of Russian Decadence. Peversity, Despair and Collapse* (Cambridge: Dedalus, 2007) 221–35; 239–81; 286–317.

112 L'vov-Rogachevskii, Vasilii. *Dve pravdy. Kniga o Leonide Andreeve* (St Petersburg: Protemei, 1914) 20.

113 For readers not familiar with this period in Russia's cultural history, Terras' *A History of Russian Literature* offers a coherent discussion of the period in question. Terras, Victor, *A History of Russian Literature* (New Haven: Yale University Press, 1991) 379–501.

114 Grossman, Joan Delaney. *Valery Bryusov and the Riddle of Russian Decadence* (Berkeley: University of California Press, 1985) 106.

3

Diaries and diagnosis

> If someone were to glance at me sideways, then there is no way that
> he would think that I was insane. The thing is that I am a cunning
> madman. I sanely speak about everything, about which other
> people speak, giving the appearance that I am interested in every-
> thing that interests others – in a word, in my external appearance
> there is nothing precisely that distinguishes me from my surround-
> ings. I do not distribute by word or suggestion this singular idea,
> which alone composes the contents of my entire internal life, alone
> makes my nerves react, alone evokes suffering and pain.
>
> Leonid Andreev[1]

Typically scholars focus on several main themes when describing Leonid
Andreev's childhood. The death of his father in 1889 meant that
Andreev assumed complete responsibility for his family at an early age.
The author's tumultuous relationship with Zinaida Nikolaevna Sibeleva
exacerbated many of the usual growing pains of adolescence. An intense
interest in the philosophies of Schopenhauer and Hartmann influenced
Andreev's perception of the world around him. Each of these factors are
referenced when discussing, or in some cases avoiding, the young
Andreev's depression, abuse of alcohol and thoughts of suicide.

   As with most scholarly works on Andreev, we will begin with his birth
and childhood, but where this study strikes a different cord is when we
begin to examine Andreev's adolescent diaries, which provide a personalized narrative of illness. Attention is given to Andreev's illness
narrative in order to suggest that melancholic episodes were the impetus
for much of his abnormal behavior. Recognizing the strong impact that
bouts of melancholy had on Andreev's personal life and literary output
opens up nuanced moments of imbedded autobiography in his texts,
which were enacted as a type of creative therapy, and provide a means
for contextualizing the theme of madness in Andreev's literary works.

Childhood

Leonid Andreev was born in Orel, a small provincial town south of Moscow, on 21 August 1871. Andreev's father, the illegitimate son of a land owner and a peasant girl, worked for the railroad as a land tax assessor. Shortly after Andreev's birth he took a job at a bank and built a house on Pushkarnaia Street, a rough area on the outskirts of town. Nikolai Ivanovich Andreev (1847–1889) was respected in this part of town because of his great physical strength and willingness to brawl. There, he and his wife Anastasiia Nikolaevna Patskovskaia (1851–1920) raised another five children – Vsevolod (1873–1916), Pavel (1878–1923), Rimma (1881–1941), Zinaida (1884–1905) and Andrei (1885–1920).[2]

Andreev's father was a stout, tall man who was quite exacting of his family. Although they loved him greatly, they feared his bad temper, which was often exacerbated by heavy drinking. As Fatov notes, Nikolai Ivanovich led the typical life of a provincial bureaucrat – work in the morning, lunch, and then a nap, with a game of cards at home or billiards and drinks at the club in the evening, which at times led to scandalous behavior.[3]

From his father, Andreev developed a love for gardening, but also a propensity for street fighting and heavy drinking. Josephine Newcombe writes: '[Andreev's father] would invite his friends to join him for an evening's drinking at home, and they would get through vast quantities of vodka and beer, usually leading to noisy scenes and fights. Leonid was never able to overcome the tendency to indulge in prolonged drinking bouts, sometimes for two or three days on end, particularly when he was depressed.'[4] In later years, much would be made of Andreev's own alcoholism and emotional intensity with comparisons to his father as evidence of some hereditary taint.

Andreev's mother was a kind, semiliterate woman who showed a particular fondness for her first child and encouraged the artistic side of his personality. Leonid learned to read at an early age and, like his mother, preferred adventure stories. He was also exposed to the theater, drawing and painting at a young age. At one point Leonid thought of becoming a professional visual artist and it remained one of his favorite hobbies even into adulthood. Anastasiia Nikolaevna spent her entire life as her son's faithful companion, living with him in various places in Russia and abroad. More will be said about this enduring relationship, but suffice it to say that she looked after everything for him and 'indulged his every whimsy and caprice.'[5]

Following the end of serfdom in Russia, the 1870s were a period of commercial and cultural development, especially in small provincial towns like Orel. As a result of new responsibilities for local governments, regional centers began to bustle with political, legal and cultural activities. The expanding railroad bridged vast distances, roads were paved and sewage systems were installed. At this time, the Andreevs lived in modest comfort, which provided young Leonid with a relatively carefree childhood. Wide and quiet Pushkarnaia Street gave way to open lush fields, streams and a forest that in summer was full of life. In the winter, these same spaces were silent, covered in snow and looked like the dark side of the moon. Andreev was an avid reader and sometimes played *Indians*, under the influence of Mayne Reid (1818–1883) and James Fenimore Cooper (1789–1851), covering his body in clay.[6] However, even as a young boy, he displayed a 'serious, pensive disposition, his melancholy brooding alternating with outbursts of vivacity.'[7]

On 1 March 1881 Tsar Alexander II (1818–1881) was assassinated as he passed the Catherine Canal in St Petersburg. A month later the conspirators of the assassination were hanged. Alexander's reign had instituted far-reaching reforms, but also spawned uncompromising terrorism. The mood of Russia changed for the worse following the regicide and people had little sympathy for the revolutionaries following their violent excess. Along with the political upheaval, Russia lost most of its leading literary figures: Dostoevskii died in 1881 and Ivan Turgenev (b. 1818) in 1883; Tolstoi also withdrew from literature at this time. Few of these events directly affected Andreev as a young boy, but they would have a significant influence on his life and works as an adult.

In September 1882 Andreev entered the Orel gymnasium. He spent most of his time learning Latin, Greek and mathematics, subjects mandated by the Russian government to discipline the mind and prevent the development of revolutionary ideas. The gymnasium was uninspiring and Andreev's fierce sense of independence chaffed under its rules and regulations. He admittedly did not do well at school mainly due to boredom – he liked only Russian composition – and this resulted in bad conduct. He was forced to repeat grade six, and in grade seven his performance became even worse as he fell in love with Zinaida Nikolaevna Sibeleva.

Pavel Andreev remembers that his elder brother's relationship with Zinaida was never particularly joyous and that Zinaida was overly dramatic and slightly capricious. This ran counter to Andreev's true needs, someone who could reduce his natural anxiety about life. Pavel calls the relationship, which lasted more than three years, 'very unsuccessful and very dramatic.'[8] As such, Andreev was tortured for the last two years of the gymnasium and during his first year at the University of

St Petersburg, further inflaming the author's own emotional excessiveness.

Woodward notes the 'unevenness of [Andreev's] temperament' during his years at the gymnasium.[9] Many who knew him at this time remember that Andreev could be the life of the party at one moment, but then quickly become gloomy and miserable, driving everyone away. At such times he took refuge from his depression in books and painting, as well as alcohol. A friend from the gymnasium, Sergei Blokhin, remembers: 'An inclination for constant self-analysis and self-castigation produced in Andreev a deep pessimism, and the idea that he was incurably ill (as a hereditary alcoholic and afflicted with neurosis of the heart – the latter he, maybe from the words of doctors, called angina pectoris) – an idea that rendered him obsessive and for periods of time reduced Andreev to a gloomy and morose frame of mind (hypochondria).'[10] Andreev's 'bad heart' would continue to plague him for his entire life, but according to his second wife, Anna Il'inichna (1883–1948), Blokhin was correct in suggesting that it was in part a psychological affliction caused by Andreev's hypochondria.[11]

Despite his lack of performance at school, Andreev's interest in books evolved from adventure stories by Reid and Cooper to more serious intellectual expeditions into Tolstoi's *What Is my Faith?* (V chem moia vera?), Schopenhauer's *The World as Will and Representation*, and Hartmann's *Philosophy of the Unconscious*. Maybe under the influence of this pessimistic philosophy, at the age of sixteen Andreev attempted suicide, or at least tried to test the will of providence, by throwing himself under an approaching train. He fell lengthwise between the rails and only his jacket was torn as the heavy ballast passed over him. Andreev, many years later, gave a vivid description to Gor'kii of the sensations of a thirty-five thousand pound load as it passed over him. How he had felt the stream of iron and timber rushing just above his face, the rumble and grinding of the iron wheels screaming in his ears.[12] This was the first of his several attempts to kill himself. Fatov writes that Andreev was instinctually drawn to the precipice by his own 'addiction to hysteria' and an 'unbalanced psyche.'[13] L'vov-Rogachevskii would write much later that Andreev's periods of melancholy were caused by bouts of anxiety and an overactive mind.[14]

Some contemporary scholars, still under the influence of Soviet research, understand Andreev's suicide attempts as a part of a 'widespread epidemic of the times.' They argue that suicide was covered in newspapers and literature at the beginning of the twentieth century and suppose that Andreev was simply following the trend.[15] This seems like an oversimplification of the issues which allows us to avoid a rather unattractive and confusing aspect of the author's character. If someone tries to kill himself several times, questions should be asked. Was Andreev really trying to kill himself or was he seeking attention? If he wanted attention, then to what end? What was the root cause of his depression or his desire to be a victim of this 'epidemic'? It is more fruitful to answer these questions than to discount suicide as a widespread cultural phenomenon – that is, if we are to get to the root of Andreev's character.

Certainly more devastating than popular tales of suicide was the death of Andreev's father from a brain hemorrhage on 19 May 1889 – the same year that Andreev was repeating grade six. Rimma remembers that she had just taken a bath with her mother and then had fallen asleep in the garden. When she awoke, her mother was gone. She went into the house and asked 'Where is mother?' She was told that their father was feeling poorly and that their mother had been called to the bank where he worked. After some time, her father was brought home in a cart. Almost the entire town of Orel attended Nikolai Ivanovich's funeral.[16]

In the highly autobiographical story 'In the Spring,' the main character contemplates suicide due to the meaninglessness of life, but experiences a newfound purpose following his father's unexpected death, understanding that he must support his mother and siblings. Nikolai Ivanovich's death left the Andreev family destitute at a time when there were no social safety nets available to help Anastasiia Nikolaevna and her children. Responsibility for his mother and five siblings fell to Leonid at the age of eighteen and certainly weighed heavily upon him for the rest of his life. Like his fictional character, Andreev accepted this responsibility and worked at various jobs to provide financial support, while remaining in school. 'In the Spring' may be one of the few indications of how Andreev felt about his father's death, as we find little reference to this dramatic turn of events in his diaries.

Diaries and self-perception

Andreev kept a fairly regular diary at two stages in his life: from 1890, when he was at school in Orel, to 1901, when his first collection of stories was published; and from the outbreak of World War I to his death in 1919. Both sets of diaries, from Andreev's 'pre-literary' period on the one hand, and from what was effectively his 'post-literary' period on the other, reveal much about his personality and views, and are impressive documents in their own right. By examining the illness narratives in the diaries we gain access to the ways in which Andreev contemplated and understood his pain.

David B. Morris claims that 'In perceiving our pain, we transform it from a simple sensation into the complex mental-emotional events that psychologists and philosophers call perception.'[17] From these self-produced and recorded perceptions, Andreev created his personal narratives about his mental distress. Andreev's first diary entry was for 12 March 1890, when he was only nineteen.[18] In his second entry (15 March), he wrote that Benedict de Spinoza (1632–1677) was celebrated for his theory that human emotions are like mathematical equations. However, Andreev disagreed, doubting that there was anything new in the mental condition of a man who suddenly experiences painful melancholy upon realizing the inaccessibility of a life that he despises.[19] This is the first recorded expression of Andreev's lifelong struggle with the seeming meaninglessness of life.

Andreev's first recorded illness experience was on 16 March 1890 when he wrote of 'fits' which lasted for a week or two. He described how he would walk around like a madman, not able to think, speak, or experience joy or happiness, as if a gloomy color covered everything.[20] He thought about suicide, but could not bring himself to act upon this idea. Andreev wrote that these fits came in the form of strong emotions and influenced all of his words and actions. He was troubled by the seeming meaninglessness of life which left him feeling as though he had a double.

The issue of the 'double' in Andreev's early diaries is a complex one. In short, the theme of an internal and external 'I' often occurs in the diaries; sometimes Andreev's double taunts him from a distance and sometimes he is inside his head, banging and scraping. The doppelgänger was first used and associated with mental illness by Hoffmann, influencing Dostoevskii and others in Russia. Thiher notes that the romantics gave new meaning to literary doubles like Narcissus, Oedipus, Hamlet and Hoffmann's Sandman in order to explore the psyche. Hoffmann and others implied that 'the literary space of representation is analogous to the space of madness in which representations split themselves into doubles.'[21]

Closer to home, Andreev's interpretation of his own double may well have sprung from Dostoevskii's *The Double*, in which the character Goliadkin develops a doppelgänger as part of his mental illness. The double is a symbol of Goliadkin's madness and may have provided Andreev with a means to describe his own illness experience. Elena Dryzhakova claims that Dostoevskii 'portrayed the "dangerous illness of doubling" not as an "odd madness," but instead as a distorted form of ambition and a timid – and doomed to failure – attempt at *defense of personality* in a pitiless and unjust world, where the strong of this world treat a man like a "dirty old rag."'[22] In 1908, Andreev used the double in his play *Black Maskers* to represent psychological conflict and, in a sense, also as a defense of personality. One might suggest that in an attempt to provide a narrative for his depression, Andreev turned to a plot structure that he knew in order to bring meaning to his experience. The double was a way in which Andreev could conceptualize the normal external (healthy) and abnormal internal (ill) selves.

In an attempt to further reconcile this preoccupation, Andreev turned to the philosophy of pessimism, identifying his double as a pessimist and thoughts of suicide as pessimistic. One element of an illness narrative is its cultural contextualization.[23] Narratives are understood to be constructions, performances, enactments, plots and counterplots, which emphasize action, motive, event and process within a social context.[24] Hayden White argues that events are value neutral, although we organize them into a coherent structure to make a story, assigning value and meaning. In examining Andreev's diaries, one must be aware of the ways in which he creates meaning, perceives 'cause and effect' and attempts to emplot his episodes of depression within the context of his life.

Philosophical pessimism offered Andreev a way to rationalize his depressive episodes. In *The World as Will and Representation*, Schopenhauer suggests that we are not in control of our individual lives. We are all driven by the Will – the force of both the inorganic and organic world. According to Schopenhauer, our wants cannot be satiated: thus suffering, frustration, and a sense of deficiency are always present. Desire, passion, hate, hunger, sleepiness are only manifestations of the Will. Life, therefore, is tragic, full of misery and pain. In the *Philosophy of the Unconscious*, Hartmann locates the Will in suffering and the Idea in order and consciousness. Over time, Idea prevails over Will but, paradoxically, intellectual development increases our capacity for pain. Hence, ultimate happiness is not attainable and we will eventually shed this illusion and commit collective suicide. For both philosophers, the underlying nature of the world is the Will feeding and preying upon itself, a world filled with more pain than pleasure. According to these philosophies, the individual has little if any hope to escape misery – suicide and overcoming the self are the only options.[25]

In the philosophies of Schopenhauer and Hartmann, Andreev found an explanation for his depressive episodes – when life seemed meaningless and full of pain. His illness experience seemed to support the philosophical ideas of pessimism; consequently, he conceptualized his illness within this framework, often contemplating suicide as the only sufficient option.

On 21 March 1890, Andreev wrote that he was experiencing a quickly changing mood of the psyche, feeling more despondency than joy. There did not seem to be any reason for these feelings, so Andreev suggested that possibly they were caused by a 'stimulus' from his internal world. He believed that life's pointlessness was at the heart of all of his problems, and he looked to the pessimistic philosophy of Hartmann for answers. Once he began to feel better, he wrote: 'All of this time there has been a void in my head, an inability to think about anything serious.'[26]

In May 1890, Andreev experienced an episode of depression and thoughts of suicide were present. He believed that a bicycle was the only thing that would free him from this mental lethargy: 'Terribly vile: boring; it would be better if there was some kind of misfortune, rather than this foul mood. There seems to be only one escape – this is a bike.'[27] Andreev also combined his feelings of depression with his feelings of love for Zinaida and his anxiety about school examinations; yet he realized that his depression sprang from within.

For the month of June, Andreev's emotional energy was spent on Zinaida. His high and low moods were attributed to their tumultuous relationship. On 6 June, Andreev felt that his life was quickly leading towards suicide. Although he had just passed exams, was on vacation and planning to buy a bike, he was experiencing boredom and sorrow. Instead of thinking about the positive things in his life, Andreev could only think about shooting himself in the head. 'If this current mood were to continue only a week without relief, I would start drinking and would kill myself – but no, a new day will dawn, not quite as difficult, and the thought of suicide will recede, but then when this sorrow begins again I am forced to start all over again and little by little I become conscious of the necessity of suicide.' Andreev said that this cycle of depression made him feel 'like a squirrel on a wheel.'[28]

A week later, Andreev felt poorly while returning home by train from Smolensk. He noted that with physical pain there are ways to express what one feels, but there are few expressions for mental pain; saying that one is 'bored' is not enough. 'I am not even bored [...] I am sickened; everyone and everything has become hateful; before me I see nothing that is positive [...]'[29] The next day Andreev wrote that he doubted that he could be cured of his condition as others are cured of diseases. This entry shows the young man struggling to understand and express his episodes of depression. Concepts associated with physical ailments were not applicable to what Andreev was experiencing.

In October, after a seemingly final break with Zinaida, Andreev sank into an especially severe period of depression.[30] For most of the month, he self-medicated with alcohol. On 22 October he was drunk and wrote that he felt foul. 'Oh God, how painful; I would like to cry but there are no tears and something oppresses and stands on top of [me].'[31] Yet, Andreev soon found love with Liubov' Nikolaevna Tukhina and this brought him out of his despair. In November, looking back on his behavior of October, Andreev blamed it on poverty.[32] However, on 18 February 1891 he concluded several self-reflective entries with a discussion of his psychological condition, stating that his gloomy mood was organic in nature and not connected to his economic woes. He claimed that he grew just as melancholy when circumstances went his way as when they went against his wishes. These bouts of depression were actually worse when they occurred during moments of success. Suicide seemed the only escape from this cycle of sadness and boredom, but he lacked the will to carry it out.

The death of Andreev's father in 1889, financial difficulties, and academic problems caused Andreev to remain in Orel while his friends went to university in Moscow and St Petersburg. Andreev became the sole breadwinner for his family and it was due to these financial responsibilities, he claimed, that he did not kill himself. In August 1891, Andreev finally went to St Petersburg, where Zinaida was studying, and entered the law faculty. Although reunited with friends, Andreev was still impoverished and very much in love, and his periods of depression often were made worse by these two tensions.

In more sober moments, Andreev knew that Zinaida would not be the kind of companion that he wanted or needed. He believed that she was too proud and self-possessed, that she did not have the instincts of a good homemaker. Even so, Andreev was drawn to her. His mother had pleaded with him to go to university in Moscow, but he had decided to reunite with Zinaida in the capital.[33] Woodward writes of Andreev's time in St Petersburg: 'Almost the entire period appears to have been spent in agonizing and hopeless conflict with the "dark power" which both fascinated and repelled him. The situation was not resolved until Zinaida Nikolaevna finally left him to marry an engineer with whom she subsequently departed for Siberia.'[34]

In a diary entry of 24 September 1891, Andreev wrote that his psychological condition was constantly changing and that he was afraid that it would eventually lead him to the madhouse. Feeling that he had reached a critical stage, Andreev noted: 'symptoms of genuine neurasthenia are appearing in me.'[35] Almost a week later, Andreev wrote that there was something broken in his core, that again he was experiencing melancholy for no apparent reason; a deaf, dull internal pain, which had the potential to become very sharp and tortuous. He thought again about suicide, but felt that he could not leave his mother. The next day he wrote that he felt physically and mentally ill, but did not know why; however, he was beginning to perceive his depression as an internal defect rather than a philosophical state of being. Andreev's remedy was to drink vodka.

On 29 November, he wrote: 'I feel very bad. So bad, that I do not even know of what this badness consists.'[36] Shortly after this, Andreev returned home to Orel, where he began drinking heavily, talking of philosophical pessimism and days without happiness. On 20 December he wrote that his life would end in one of three ways: madness, suicide, or complete moral decline. The possibility of a 'moral decline' underscores Andreev's belief in the effects of degeneracy. Again, boredom and melancholy were alleviated only by vodka.

Yet, Andreev's return to Orel for the Christmas holidays was not completely deleterious. Like most first-year university students, he was glad to be home, among family and friends, where he could indulge in the provincial life of food, drink and constant parties. At one of these parties, he met Evgeniia Nikolaevna Khludeneva.[37] Just imagine Andreev's state of mind having recently left St Petersburg, a place he found cold and oppressive. There, he was a wretched, starving student, tortured by Zinaida, who 'only loved herself.' At home, he was satiated, loved and suddenly fascinated with Evgeniia, who appeared as a possible rival for Andreev's affection.[38]

In February 1892, Andreev returned to St Petersburg where his depression was fueled by his feelings for Zinaida and his loneliness in the capitol. Drunk for several days, Andreev wrote that there was something odd in his head, some kind of strange sensation which made him feel as if he were sitting and looking at himself – his double.[39] During this period of depression, Andreev again attempted suicide and spent several days in the St Mary Magdalene hospital on Vasil'evskii Island. Fatov claims that Andreev used a Finnish knife to stab himself in the chest, believing that Zinaida had cheated on him.[40] Once he was released, his problems with Zinaida and preparations for exams continued to influence his 'abominable life.'[41] Despite these external factors, Andreev still associated his problems with a feeling of emptiness: 'It is not people who are guilty that I am alone, it is I, my emptiness and insipidness.'[42]

The Soviet scholar Leonid Afonin believes that these diary entries reflect the sign of the times and should not be taken out of context – 'the confusion and panic that seized the sensitive Russian people at the beginning of the [18]90s, when the old was irrevocably rejected and the new gleamed faintly through a predawn fog, tormented by uncertainty.'[43] Historical factors most definitely influenced Andreev's psyche and must be considered along with his age, gender, social status, financial position and mental health. The individual experience expressed in these entries cannot be discounted as solely a reflection of the times, but as one of the factors that shaped Andreev's perception and representation of self.

Afonin takes a similar position regarding Andreev's 'pathological inclination toward drinking,' arguing that it was common among students in the 1890s.[44] Afonin does acknowledge that Andreev's father was a heavy drinker and that Andreev, too, drank heavily while at the gymnasium in Orel and at university in St Petersburg. He attributes this to Andreev's poverty and the resulting pressures. However, Andreev maintained this 'pathological inclination' for his entire life, so Afonin's explanation falls short given that Andreev continued his drinking binges after he finished university and was financially secure. Moreover, if extreme drinking was so common among students of the 1890s, then why has it become such a distinctive characteristic of Andreev's posthumous legacy described in memoirs and biographical sketches? Fatov too notes the student life of the time, but says that Andreev's chaotic behavior far exceeded what could be classified as 'bohemian.'[45] Blokhin, the author's classmate and a future psychiatrist, confirms that Andreev was already drinking heavily while at the gymnasium and that these periods of drunkenness led to obsessive self-analysis and self-reproach, brought on by a deep pessimism. This seems to run counter to Afonin's assertions of strictly historical and sociological factors, and again calls into question Andreev's mental health.[46]

At the end of his first academic year, Andreev did surprisingly well on his final exams given the financial and emotional strains under which he had lived. For History of Roman Law, History of Russian Law and Political Economy he received a five (similar to an A). For a Comprehensive Overview of the Law and the History of Legal Philosophy he received a four (similar to a B). Unfortunately, these fours put Andreev's financial support in jeopardy and he returned to Orel for the summer deflated. In July, he went to St Petersburg once again to see Zinaida, but for all intents and purposes the relationship was over, and as such, Andreev returned to Orel two weeks later.[47]

At this point in his life Andreev increasingly expressed the idea that he had some kind of internal defect.[48] He held to philosophical pessimism as the context for his illness experience, but began seeking a cure for this perceived flaw. Suicide was one possibility, but finding a sympathetic companion who could cure him of his problems seemed to emerge as a more desirable option. In an entry of 24 August 1893, Andreev wrote that he felt like an acrobat on a high wire. On one side was suicide and on the other was madness. He suggested that his latest love, Evgeniia Khludeneva,[49] was his balance. 'Where goes the balance, there I go – but drop it and kaput? [...] Kaput means the end.'[50]

In many earlier entries Andreev wrote that his romantic successes and failures were the cause of his high and low moods; however, he finally sensed that his mental health was the underpinning and that his relationships only exacerbated his condition. This might seem a minor distinction, but the illness experiences remained consistent – boredom, loneliness and thoughts of suicide; only the 'balances' (i.e. his romantic interests) changed. We should not discount Andreev's feelings for various women, especially Zinaida, but realizing his belief that these women could stabilize his mental condition must mediate our understanding of Andreev's notions of love and relationships. He once wrote in his diary, 'It pains me, pains me, my old heart ... The truth is spoken by Maupassant and others that it is only worth living for love. Work, success, intellect and heart are only good when they might be placed at the feet of a woman. And to rejoice alone is boring, and to despair.'[51] Andreev's feelings about love were often impulsive and placed great emotional demands on the individual woman. Just as quickly as Andreev fell in love, he could become completely dispassionate, depending on his changing mood.

Andreev's belief that love could cure his condition probably stems from his connection with his mother. Their relationship was extremely close and provided Andreev with comfort during his periods of depression. The importance of Anastasiia Nikolaevna's role in Andreev's life is evident in the fact that she lived with her son almost his entire life.[52] In his 1927 pathography, we might remember that Galant notes Anastasiia Nikolaevna's 'exclusive love for her oldest son Leonid,' suggesting that this exceptional relationship caused Andreev's obsessive love for his first wife.[53]

Throughout his life, Andreev depended on his mother and two wives as emotional stabilizers. They helped to even out his psychological condition, but did not cure or eliminate his periods of depression. After Andreev's death, Gor'kii, his friend and fellow author, wrote about their turbulent relationship and how he could not offer Andreev the emotional support that he demanded. However, Gor'kii noted that Andreev's first wife did, in fact, act as his friend's balance:

She understood perfectly the need for a maternal, supportive attitude towards Andreev; she immediately and profoundly felt the significance of his talent and the agonizing fluctuations of his moods. She was one of those rare women who, at the same time as being a passionate mistress, does not lose the ability to love with a mother's love. This double love armed her with a subtle instinct, so that she was well able to distinguish between the genuine complaints of his soul and the clanging words of capricious passing moods.[54]

Boris Zaitsev (1881–1972), another friend and fellow writer, made a similar observation: 'Th[e] influence [of his first wife] calmed his stormy, passionate and sometimes not too stable nature.'[55] While Andreev may have used philosophical pessimism to rationalize his bouts of depression, as both an adolescent and as an adult, vodka was his medicine and he hoped that love would provide the cure.

In the fall of 1893, Andreev left St Petersburg and enrolled in the law faculty at the university in Moscow. According to Rimma he was actually dismissed from the University of St Petersburg because he could not pay his fees and was forced to re-enroll in Moscow where he was able to get some financial aid.[56] For two years, Andreev lived alone in Moscow, a difficult time dominated by extreme poverty and pathological drinking. During this time there were possibly two more attempts at suicide, caused in one case, so his friends thought, by his love for Nadezhda Aleksandrovna Antonova (1877–1947).[57]

The specific details of Andreev's suicide attempt(s) are not absolutely clear. Multiple sources tell of two attempts, but they always give the same basic details of one particular incident. Each attempt is blamed on Andreev's broken heart and drunkenness. What can be said is that Andreev attempted suicide at least once and possibly twice, both times, so friends and family believed, due to failed relationships and for one of these attempts the details of the suicide were well known.

In November 1893, Andreev was given leave from university lectures so that he could go home to Orel to convalesce from a bad case of the flu and a very high fever. Still quite depressed, Andreev tried to commit suicide. As noted, his friends blamed it on a failed romance and his drunkenness – constant themes in Andreev's struggle with depression.[58] Andreev himself would later write of this experience: 'In 1894, in January, I shot myself; the consequence of this unsuccessful shot was church penance, imposed on me by the authorities, and a sick heart, not dangerous, but obstinate and annoying.'[59]

To compound matters, in April Andreev's mother was arrested for allowing two men, who were not legally registered, to rent a portion of her house. For this, Anastasiia Nikolaevna was sent to prison in St Petersburg and Rimma, 17 at the time, was left in charge of the household. At first, the children were able to keep this news from their eldest brother who had returned to his studies in Moscow, but when Andreev found out, he was completely beside himself. Anastasiia Nikolaevna spent a total of twenty days in prison, but was eventually released and returned to Orel.

That summer, Andreev also returned to Orel. Rimma writes that while home, her brother asked Nadezhda to marry him but she declined his offer because her mother was against it. That evening, Andreev returned home drunk. Pavel, his younger brother, remembers that he argued with his mother about killing himself, leaving again still quite distraught. Rimma remembers that Andreev convinced his mother that he would be alright and kissed her hand as a last parting. At midnight, Andreev's mother and Rimma went out to look for him. His brother Pavel soon joined the search, finding a policeman who said that a student had tried to shoot himself with a revolver, but had only been wounded when the bullet struck a copper button on his double-breasted jacket.[60] It turned out to be Andreev, who had yet again averted death.

Soon after this incident, Andreev's mother and siblings joined him in Moscow, after selling the house in Orel. Woodward writes: 'His life changed radically with the arrival of his family. He became more settled and devoted much of his time to reading and writing. The family lived constantly under the threat of starvation. [...] Nevertheless, his spirits were generally high during this third year in Moscow.'[61] Woodward romanticizes this period but Andreev's life did not drastically improve. The Andreevs lived in drafty attics and damp basements. For a while they even lived above a horse stable. To help feed the family, Andreev took odd jobs – he was a tutor, wrote articles for newspapers, and drew portraits for three to five kopecks. He was drinking heavily, however, and often wasted what little money they had on vodka. Anastasiia Niko-laevna sold used items at a flea market and Andreev's two sisters worked in a corset shop for thirty kopecks a day. In the evenings, the Andreevs often went to the local bakery and asked for donations and when they were desperate they would sell a mirror or pillows, the last remnants of their life in Orel.[62] It has been suggested that Andreev's fierce attachment to his mother crystallized at this time as she seemed to be the only person who believed in her son after he had lost confidence in himself. Anastasiia Nikolaevna alone considered him remarkable and capable of delivering the family out of poverty.[63]

In 1895, Andreev published his first story 'He, She and Vodka' (On, ona i vodka). In this story, the character He hates himself and turns to drink as an alternative to suicide. He thinks that his ideal She will 'save' him from despair. Each time he meets a woman He stops drinking. When he realizes that this woman cannot save him, He returns to drink. Finally, He finds She but they are both married to other people.[64] This drives him nearly mad. He returns to drink and eventually is beaten to death by strangers.[65] The story is naïve but does provide yet another narrative response to Andreev's illness experience.[66] Loneliness and boredom lead to thoughts of suicide, excessive drinking, and the idea that somehow the ideal woman will alleviate internal despair. These themes appear in Andreev's diaries and later in his published works. According to several sources, Andreev drew on his relationship with Nadezhda for this story.[67]

As Andreev would come to find, however, Nadezhda was not the answer to his problems. She was too young (sixteen) and immature. At times she could be gentle and caring, but she could also just as easily be unwittingly cruel. Certainly, Andreev was looking for someone to fulfill his own needs and had, therefore, convinced himself that Nadezhda was the one. As usual, he was greatly disappointed when she did not live up to his expectations. Eventually, Nadezhda and her family moved to Moscow and this extended the duration of their relationship.[68]

Continuing to draw from life, Andreev's next published story was 'The Riddle' (Zagadka), in which the main character kills himself after being rejected by his girlfriend. 'The Riddle' is full of autobiographical details – from the two characters reading works by Arthur Schopenhauer, Max Nordau, Dmitrii Pisarev (1840–1868) and Andreev's childhood friend Mayne Reid, to the way in which the main character, Bolotin, deals with rejection and heartbreak – suicide. When the main characters attend a funeral for a student who has committed suicide, Bolotin argues that the student must have been a deserter, an idiot, or insane to commit suicide. This is one of the riddles in the story – is Bolotin an idiot, or is he insane when he commits suicide? Following his failed romance with Zinaida and others, 'The Riddle' reflects Andreev's struggle to understand his relationships, his constant despair, and his suicide attempts.[69]

In March 1896, Andreev finished his university courses, but asked that he might delay taking his final exams for a year. That summer, he rented a country house in Tsaritsyno and began studying. He also met Aleksandra Mikhailovna Veligorskaia (1881–1906), who would become his wife in 1902. At the time of their first introduction, Aleksandra was only fifteen, ten years younger than Andreev. The young law student did not make a good impression as he was slightly tipsy on one of his first official visits that fall to the Veligorskii home. At this meeting, he declared his love for Aleksandra, but it would be five years of discontinuous courting before he could win her hand, and her family's confidence.

There is a gap of nearly four years in Andreev's diaries (1893–1897), but when his personalized narrative resumes on 27 March 1897, he is in final preparation for his exams. In April, Andreev wrote in one entry: 'Bouts of momentary fear occur, such that a cold sweat appears. But this is not a fear of my exams, failure – all of that is nonsense, but a fear of what is going on in my head.'[70] At the end of May he passed all of his exams, but could not enjoy this accomplishment because his nerves were shattered.[71] One of the reasons for Andreev's lack of joy was that he was again struggling with a new balance, *falling in love*, which was always an emotionally taxing process for him.

In July, Andreev complained of heart palpitations and the feeling that he had gone insane.[72] In August, he returned to the idea of a double and claimed that love might unite this division.[73] He believed that the ideal woman would heal him of his condition. However, far from providing Andreev with peace, romantic adventures agitated him further. At one point, he had three different women in his sights: Zinaida Ivanovna Terpigoreva, Nadezhda Aleksandrovna Antonova and Aleksandra Mikhailovna Veligorskaia.[74] Ever searching for the balance that would allow him to walk the tightrope above his depression, Andreev placed his faith in his romantic relationships. Love and illness were conflated yet again and he was quite often heartbroken. The illness experience in most cases remained the same, suggesting that the external reasons for the depression might have varied, but the actual experience did not. Clearly, one might suggest that Andreev's foul moods were greatly influenced by biochemical factors, more than romantic failures.

The diary was an important medium through which Andreev could explore his illness experience and conceptualize his periods of depression. In these entries he transformed events into stories, providing 'cause and effect' explanations, in order to make sense of his *real world*. However, this narrative was only a *first draft* of the life story that would be presented later in *final draft* form for friends, lovers, relatives, and ultimately would find its way into his literary works. Andreev wrote in one entry: 'It's as if the very nature of the diary is contrary to the introduction of any kind of later amendment, but, in reading it several months later, I am so outraged by the role I play in this diary, that I absolutely cannot remain silent.'[75] The process of revisions and edits of his *first draft* diary entries occurred rather quickly. Therefore, the immediacy of these entries, especially in the context of illness narrative, provide a unique look at the process by which Andreev confronted and dealt with his depression and also how he (re)fashioned himself for his various audiences.

Reading Andreev's early diaries within the critical framework of illness narrative suggests that melancholic episodes were the impetus for much of his 'abnormal' behavior. Andreev's reading of Schopenhauer and Hartmann was a way to rationalize his feelings of futility and boredom, brought on by depression. Pessimism gave meaning to his illness experience, and this underlines the probability that Andreev was susceptible to popular intellectual trends. It is also evident that Andreev's excessive drinking was often caused by depressive episodes. Finally, Andreev acknowledged that he looked to the numerous women in his life to save him from himself, hoping to find the ideal soulmate. Poverty clearly was a factor that exacerbated Andreev's situation; however, it was arguably not the cause of his depression as his episodes of melancholy continued well after he had achieved great wealth and material comfort.

One might look at these conclusions and still question whether philosophical pessimism caused Andreev's depression or depression fueled his interest in Schopenhauer.[76] However, as scholars explore the effects of illness on the individual, there is a greater understanding that perception is mediated through various narratives (social, cultural, philosophical, etc.) in an attempt to contextualize each experience and thereby give meaning to the whole life. As a result, it is important for scholars working on Andreev's life and literary works, and for those interested in how mental illness was negotiated, to understand Andreev's attempt to bring coherence to his illness experience. Andreev gave meaning to, self-medicated, and sought a cure for his depression in philosophical pessimism, vodka and love. As noted, recognizing the strong impact of melancholy on Andreev's personal life and literary output provides a means for contextualizing the theme of madness in Andreev's literary works.

Courier

After graduation Andreev immediately found employment in Moscow as assistant to the lawyer Pavel Nikolaevich Maliantovich (1870–1939). A short time later it was actually Maliantovich who directed Andreev towards his literary career by suggesting that he write short accounts of court cases for the newspaper *The Moscow Herald* (Moskovskii vestnik).[77] Andreev needed the money and readily accepted the offer. He eventually used this experience as a legal assistant and court reporter in writing several of his short stories – 'The First Fee,' 'The Defense' (Zashchita),[78] 'Christians' (Khristiane)[79] and court scenes in longer works such as 'The Story of Seven Who Were Hanged' and *Tsar Hunger*. Due to the success of his first reports, Andreev was offered a regular position at a new, larger and wealthier Moscow daily newspaper *Courier* (Kur'er). For a time he worked as both a reporter and a lawyer's assistant, but he increasingly wrote more and more for the newspaper until finally becoming its feuilletonist under the name of James Lynch.

Andreev was not the paper's first choice, but after a few successful columns, he was given the job. The feuilletonist in pre-revolutionary papers was an important functionary. He engaged the burning questions of the day in politics and art, careful to avoid the censor's wrath while still conveying a message to readers trained to seek meaning between the lines. Andreev was a second rate feuilletonist according to Kaun but, even so, he occupied the lower half of the front page of *Courier* for several years while honing his literary craft.[80]

One such piece was entitled 'Influenza patients, neurasthenics and alcoholics' (Influentiki, neirasteniki, i alkogoliki), which demonstrated the author's dark humor. Andreev describes each affliction and then how three patients climb onto a roof to look out across Moscow. The neurasthenic does not believe that the roof exists, the influenza patient forgets his dose of medicine, and the alcoholic falls off the roof without a word to anyone.

Andreev's description of mental illness in this piece is significant. Unlike diseases that clearly attack the physical body and possibly lead to death, neurasthenia is an illness of the contemporary cultured individual. As a neurasthenic 'you cannot sleep at night, nerves are taut, brain boils and you work like a genius.'[81] Not surprisingly, we find a connection between madness and genius. Here too we get the sense that the mentally ill inhabit a kind of purgatory in that they are neither sick nor well. Andreev's early response to neurasthenia reveals the influence of medical discourse on popular notions of sickness.

Working full-time at the newspaper was a welcome change after many years of odd jobs and near starvation as a poor law student. With this latest position, Andreev's self-confidence grew and he made many new friends. Sergei Goloushev (1855–1920), a practicing doctor who also enjoyed writing theater reviews under the name of Sergei Glagol', would long remain one of Andreev's best friends. Yet, while his professional and personal life improved, Andreev was still under a lot of pressure to support his family. As such he worked long hours, pushing himself to near exhaustion.

In 1898, Andreev was asked to contribute a short story for the Easter edition of *Courier*. This story, 'Bargamot and Garas'ka' (Bargamot i Garas'ka), was a success and Andreev was encouraged to submit more of his stories. That year, Andreev published more than a dozen of them in *Courier, The Moscow Herald* and the *Nizhegorodskii Sheet* (Nizhegorod-skii listok). Most of these early stories came directly from the author's childhood experiences in Orel. A few more came from his recent experiences as a lawyer and a newspaper reporter.

Gor'kii later remembered reading Andreev's first story and how he followed the young author's development:

In the Spring of 1898 I read in the Moscow *Courier* a story called *Bergamot and Garas'ka*[82] an Easter story of the usual type. Written to appeal to the heart of the holiday reader, it reminded him once again that man is still capable, at certain moments and in certain special circumstances, of a feeling of generosity, and that at times, enemies become friends, if only for a short while, if only for a day.

Since the time of Gogol's 'Overcoat,'[83] Russian literati have written, probably, hundreds or even thousands of these intentionally touching stories. Amid the magnificent flowers of genuine Russian literature, such stories are dandelions, intended to decorate the wretched life of the afflicted and coarse Russian soul.[84]

Moreover from *this* story, I caught a distinct whiff of talent, a talent that somehow reminded me of Pomialovskii,[85] besides which the author had snuck into the tone of the story a wise little grin of mistrust toward facts. This little grin easily reconciled one with the obligatory sentimentalism of 'Easter' and 'Christmas' literature.

I wrote the author a few lines about his story and received from Leonid Andreev an amusing reply; a few cheerful and funny remarks in eccentric handwriting, with half-printed letters; amongst them stood out an unpretentious but skeptical aphorism: 'For the well-off, being generous is as pleasant as having coffee after dinner.'

Thus began my literary and epistolary acquaintance with Leonid Nikolaevich Andreev. In the summer, I read some more of his short stories and the satirical feuilletons of James Lynch, while observing how quickly and boldly the distinctive talent of the new writer was developing.[86]

Unfortunately, Andreev's early literary success came at the expense of his health. These artistic endeavors were now added to his responsibilities as court reporter and feuilletonist. The stress from this work and his family obligations weighed heavily upon him. Arkadii Alekseevskii (1871–1942), who worked with Andreev at *Courier* and eventually married his sister Rimma, remembers that during 1900–1901 Andreev's bouts of alcoholism were accompanied by uncontrollable 'delirium tremens.' Andreev would drink so much and so long that he actually would experience 'typical delirium tremens with green imps included.' The medicine that Andreev was given to calm his nerves, a combination of chloral hydrate and sulphers (at levels that Alekseevskii calls 'poisonous'), did not have much effect, still leaving Andreev high-strung and unable to sleep. This chaotic behavior often created further problems for the author. Alekseevskii recalls when a drunken Andreev was beaten by the police, so badly that one could not even make out the features of his face and there was fear that he might lose his sight. Due to instances like this, Alekseevskii opined that Andreev's depression led him to sadistic and self-immolating acts.

When discussing these issues, some contemporary Russian scholars are willing to admit that Andreev was an alcoholic, but still argue that he was mentally sound on the whole. Alekseevskii, however, states that he had known many alcoholics in his time, in all of their different conditions (sober, drunk, angry, sad), but he 'never met a doomed prisoner, sentenced to death by alcoholic poisoning, similar to L.N. Andreev.' If Andreev was not drinking alcohol then he was drinking strong tea and smoking cigarettes. According to Alekseevskii, Andreev could only handle one narcotic at a time.[87] This self-medication with stimulants or depressants was Andreev's way, one might argue, of seeking control over his mental state. Alekseevskii and many others, even Andreev himself, felt that alcohol fanned the flames of his imagination, or liberated him from his deep despair at least long enough to facilitate his creativity. Despite the fights, alcoholic binges, attempts at suicide and much more troubling behavior, it was truly believed that a sober Andreev was a lesser author.[88]

Acute neurasthenia

Even as he began to have literary success and his relationship with Aleksandra Mikhailovna matured, Andreev continued to experience bouts of fatigue and depression.[89] In July 1899, Andreev wrote to the publisher Viktor Miroliubov (1860–1939) that he was delayed in responding due to 'my illness' which prevented him from picking up a pen for three months.[90] Fatov writes that the bouts of melancholy that led him to suicide several times had left their mark on his nervous system. 'The abuse of alcohol, the reckless life of his student years, the excessive fatigue – all of this led, in the end, to the point where L[eonid] N[ikolaevich] fell seriously ill with a severe form of neurasthenia that demanded medical treatment.'[91]

His friend Belousov supported the notion that Andreev's illness was caused by a 'disorderly life' and that his exhausting work for *Courier* had exacerbated his health problems.[92] From 25 January to 22 March 1901, Andreev was hospitalized under the care of Mikhail Cherinov (1833–1905), emeritus professor of Moscow University and director of the clinic.[93] Friends convinced Andreev to check into the university clinic, where he was diagnosed as suffering from acute neurasthenia.[94]

The argument has been made that almost everyone suffered from neurasthenia at the beginning of the twentieth century. Certainly its broadly inclusive criteria caused skepticism as to its authenticity as a medical condition.[95] Beard's work on neurasthenia was translated into German in 1881, resulting in an immediate scholarly reaction among

European scientists. Ensuing scholarship was known and applied in Russia; so much so that by 1889 Pavel Rozenbakh (1858–1918) gave a paper entitled 'On Neurasthenia' at the Third Congress of Russian Physicians, in which he cautioned against overuse of this diagnosis. As already noted, Beard's version of neurasthenia could be relatively easily treated, while the European and Russian versions implied that sufferers' families were possibly only a few generations away from extinction. Kovalevskii replaced Beard's theory of technological stress due to an advanced society with Nordau's belief in moral stress due to a deviant social order making neurasthenia a sign of Russia's declining national wellness.[96]

Even with such murky diagnostic criteria we should not completely disregard Andreev's diagnosis. He was admitted to the Imperial clinic for nervous disorders and was given a diagnosis for presented symptoms, which at the time also carried cultural and social significance. More specifically, for Andreev the diagnosis of acute neurasthenia carried symbolic (if not real) meaning that he was unwell and abnormal.

The Imperial university clinic where Andreev was treated originally opened in January 1887. The director was Aleksei Kozhevnikov (1836–1902), but psychiatric instruction was delegated to Korsakov, the head of the department of psychiatry. For the next twelve years, Korsakov had great influence in the training of psychiatry students and the treatment of patients. In 1893 he published a psychiatric textbook with a second edition posthumously published in 1901, the same year that Andreev was admitted to the clinic.[97]

Korsakov's classification system was likely used in diagnosing Andreev. Neurasthenia and neurasthenic psychosis as well as degenerative-neurasthenic psychosis are in Korsakov's second of three classifications of mental conditions. According to the textbook, neurasthenia results in a combination of physical and psychological hyperactivity, and physical and mental exhaustion. The patient experiences alarm, fear, distress and anxiety, culminating in mental fatigue and an inability to concentrate. Patients worry that they are going insane, usually suffer nightmares, and may experience agitation to such a degree as to affect their sight or hearing.[98]

Especially applicable to Andreev's case, Korsakov says that patients will often complain of back pain that feels as though it is 'in the heart.'[99] Andreev was obsessive about heart pains (possibly to the level of hypochondria) and neurasthenia may have been the underlying cause. After his death, many contemporaries wrote that Andreev died of a heart attack, although his death was believed to be from a brain hemorrhage.[100] Korsakov claims that visceral neurasthenia appears in one of three types: heart, stomach or sexual. Patients with neurasthenia of the

3.1 Leonid Andreev in the Imperial clinic for nervous disorders.

heart may feel as though they suffer from an irregular heartbeat or heaviness in the chest. They may experience an anxiety attack that feels like a heart attack, leading them to a paranoid belief that the next attack will be fatal.[101]

Korsakov is less certain about how neurasthenia is contracted or triggered. He leaves open the possibility that it can either be innate or acquired, but suggests that it appears as either periodic or degenerative. With periodic neurasthenia the nervous system is temporarily 'poisoned,' but returns to a normal state over time, although the patient must recognize the factors which might have caused the condition, such as extreme exhaustion or moral upheaval. Degenerative neurasthenia is a constitutional illness that remains in the body's 'uniting material' and lymphatic apparatus.[102]

Korsakov argues that there are three basic elements underpinning the neurasthenic disorder: (1) The illness is both a psychological and physical condition (neurasthenia psychica or phrenasthenia); (2) The illness can exist without noticeable or with only minor symptoms, but can then be triggered so that the symptoms are extreme in nature and take on the character of other psychological disorders such as hypochondria or obsessive behavior; (3) Neurasthenia can act as a basis for other types of psychosis (melancholy, etc.), thereby resulting in psychosis with a neurasthenic taint.[103]

Due to the physical symptoms, neurasthenic patients often first turn to an internist. The physical symptoms result in one of two states – agitated or listless. The agitated condition manifests itself as hyperactivity, excessive anxiety, a lack of self-control and an obsessive state of alarm which hinders the individual's ability to concentrate on a given task. The patient is cognizant of these symptoms, but cannot regain control over his psychological state. These symptoms can last for months at a time, up to a year, and then disappear for long periods of time with only minor recurrences of certain symptoms.[104] The listless condition manifests itself as an uncomfortable feeling of physical and mental powerlessness. The patient will complain of mental exhaustion, bad memory and an inability to concentrate. He might also complain of physical fatigue and sexual impotence. The listless state, according to Korsakov, is more persistent, and although there are times at which symptoms are more or less extreme, it is rarely completely cured.[105]

In Korsakov's description, we find many of the symptoms which Andreev complained of – anxiety of impeding death, a perceived heart condition, headaches, a fear of going insane, insomnia, and periods of mental and physical exhaustion.[106] These symptoms are prevalent in various biographical texts and memoirs about Andreev and are readily found in his letters and diaries as well. The fact that these ailments are such a consistent and persistent part of Andreev's self-representation suggests that we cannot disregard them as typical physical ailments, but must acknowledge that Andreev perceived himself as ill.

Unfortunately for Andreev and others at the beginning of the twentieth century, the recommendations for treatment were limited and while psychiatrists might be able to identify an illness (to place it within a classification system), they were less equipped to prescribe therapy. Korsakov suggests a regime of rest, but with limits so that the patient does not sleep or eat too much. For the most part, patients are asked to remedy their ailments with willpower – Korsakov warns against prescribing medication as neurasthenics tend to rely too heavily on narcotics. He does suggest a few medications, but argues that water treatments, shock therapy, massage and gymnastics are just as effective.[107]

Andreev wrote to Miroliubov from the clinic that he had suffered a 'complete breakdown' and did not expect to make a full recovery for some time. 'I find myself in a general ward and my days are broken into pieces: water [treatments], electrification, lunches, walks, teas, dinners.'[108] Two months into his treatments, Andreev again wrote to Miroliubov, this time indicating that he has lost weight, has begun to sleep well and is in good spirits, and that the doctors recommended that he take the summer off from work to fully recover. '[My] heart illness is considered unimportant: there is no defect of the heart, but all of the abnormal manifestations, which have currently been reduced to a minimum, are due to my ancestry of neurasthenia.'[109] A friend of Andreev's writes of the author's experience: 'He left the clinic renewed and energetic, got himself a bike and started to exercise. But only a month later the same Andreev was facing me, with the inextinguishable flicker of despair and doubt in his beautiful eyes, with a grimly set mouth.'[110]

Much to his dismay, Andreev continued to be plagued by insomnia and exhaustion. So, he spent the month of July in the quite town of Karlsbad, Riga. There he swam in the ocean, took long hikes and rode a bike. Each time, these rest treatments only seemed to bring temporary relief. Andreev's struggle with various illnesses continued for the rest of his life, an issue that was complicated by his growing literary success and personal celebrity. The newspaper *Courier*, for example, reported that Andreev again spent time in the clinic for nervous disorders in November 1902, treated for extreme exhaustion and anxiety.[111] Unlike the literary decadents who wished to invoke the romantic notion of the *mad genius*, Andreev did not want to be stigmatized as *insane* or *a degen-*

erate, as was the growing tendency. He wanted his struggle with mental illness to remain private.

Andreev's adolescent melancholy cannot be connected solely to his father's death, to his failed relationships or to his attraction to pessimistic philosophy. Instead, all of these external factors amplified and sometimes exacerbated what was going on inside of the young man. The results of both the internal and external pressures are found in the author's severe mood swings, his use of alcohol, black tea and cigarettes to try to find some emotional equilibrium and to ward off thoughts of suicide. His perception was also drastically influenced by his belief that life was meaningless, even as he searched desperately for the woman who would deliver him from his deep feelings of despair. In these personal traits of the early Andreev are already found many of the themes that are embedded in his later literary works, those that propelled him to literary success. In the following chapters, we will examine the author's developing illness narrative and its relationship with his artistic growth.

Notes

1 An entry from Andreev's diary on 3 June 1892. See Generalova, N., ed., 'Dnevnik Leonida Andreeva.' In *Literaturnyi arkhiv: Materialy po istorii russkoi literatury i obshchestvennoi mysli*. Edited by K. Grigor'ian (St Petersburg: Nauka, 1994) 272.

2 Four more children died soon after birth – Nikolai, Vladimir, Larissa and Zoia. Rimma Andreeva does not note the dates of birth and death for these siblings. See OGLMT, f. 12, op. 1, no. 165 (KP 5693 of). Rimma (Andreeva) Vereshchagina, *Moi vospominaniia*, 2.

3 Fatov, *Molodye gody Leonida Andreeva*, 24.

4 Newcombe, *Leonid Andreyev*, 4.

5 Fatov, *Molodye gody Leonida Andreeva*, 27.

6 Ibid., 38–9.

7 Kaun, *Leonid Andreyev: A Critical Study*, 23.

8 Pavel Andreev, 'Vospominaniia o Leonide Andreeve,' 151.

9 Woodward, *Leonid Andreyev: A Study*, 5.

10 Fatov, *Molodye gody Leonida Andreeva*, 241–2.

11 Kaun, *Leonid Andreyev: A Critical Study*, 28, footnote 18. L'vov-Rogachevskii argues that Andreev blamed his heart problems on a failed suicide attempt in 1894; however, this perceived condition was evident well before that date and can be attributed to anxiety attacks and feelings of deep despair. See L'vov-Rogachevskii, *Dve pravdy. Kniga o Leonide Andreeve*, 17.

12 Gor'kii, *Kniga o Leonide Andreeve*, 10–11. In English, see White, *Memoirs and Madness*, 13.

13 Fatov, *Molodye gody Leonida Andreeva*, 66.

14 L'vov-Rogachevskii, *Dve pravdy. Kniga o Leonide Andreeve*, 16.

15 Aingori, L.E., O.V. Vologina, V.Ia. Grechnev, L.A. Iezuitova, L.N. Ken and L.I. Shishkina. 'Zabluzhdenie ili obman: o tak nazyvaemom sumasshestvii Leonida Andreeva.' *Russkaia literatura*, 4 (2005): 109.

16 OGLMT, f. 12, op. 1, no. 165 (KP 5693 of), 3–5.

17 Morris, *The Culture of Pain*, 29.

18 It is believed that Andreev irregularly kept a diary on loose sheets of paper when he was sixteen, but these have seemingly been lost.

19 LRA, MS. 606 \ E. 1 *12 March–30 June 1890; 21 September 1898*.

20 Ibid., 16 March.

21 Thiher, *Revels in Madness*, 189–94; quote is on pages 193–4.

22 Dryzhakova, Elena. 'Madness as an Act of Defense of Personality in Dosto-evsky's *The Double*.' In *Madness and the Mad in Russian Culture*. Edited by Angela Brintlinger and Ilya Vinitsky (Toronto: University of Toronto Press, 2007) 59–74; quote is on page 70 and italics are Dryzhakova's.

23 Fee, Dwight. 'The Broken Dialogue: Mental Illness as Discourse and Experi-ence.' In *Pathology and the Postmodern: Mental Illness as Discourse and Experience* (London: Sage Publications, 2000) 3.

24 Garro, Linda C. and Cheryl Mattingly. 'Narrative as Construct and Construction.' In *Narrative and the Cultural Construction of Illness and Healing*. Edited by Linda C. Garro and Cheryl Mattingly (Berkeley: Univer-sity of California Press, 2000) 17.

25 Scholars agree that the philosophies of Schopenhauer and Hartmann played an important role in Andreev's philosophical and intellectual under-standing of life. See Afonin, *Leonid Andreev*, 23–5; Fatov, *Molodye gody Leonida Andreeva*, 64–5; Brusianin, *Leonid Andreev. Zhizn' i tvorchestvo*, 29; 53. Andreev states as much himself in a 1908 letter to L'vov-Rogachevskii, which in turn was quoted by the critic; see L'vov-Rogachenskii, *Dve pravdy. Kniga o Leonide Andreeve*, 24.

26 LRA, MS. 606 \ E. 1; 26 March.

27 Ibid., 10 May.

28 Ibid., 6 June.

29 Ibid., 13 July.

30 LRA, MS. 606 \ E. 2 *3 July 1890–18 February 1891; 05 October*.

31 Ibid., 22 October.

32 Ibid., 13 November.

33 Ken, Liudmila and Leonid Rogov. *Zhizn' Leonida Andreeva, rasskazanna im samim i ego sovremenikami* (St Petersburg: OOO 'Izdatel'sko-poligrafich-eskaia kompaniia 'KOSTA', 2010) 27; 31–2.

34 Woodward, *Leonid Andreyev: A Study*, 9.

35 Generalova, N. 'Leonid Andreev, Dnevnik 1891–1892.' In *Ezhegodnik rukopisnogo otdela Pushkinskogo doma na 1991 god*. Edited by T. Tsar'kova (St Petersburg: Akademicheskii proekt, 1994) 98.

36 Ibid., 120.

37 This was the surname of the family who raised her. Her legal surname was Strezheletskaia. See Fatov, *Molodye gody Leonida Andreeva*, 70; Generalova, 'Dnevnik Leonida Andreeva,' 293, footnote 22.

38 Ken and Rogov, *Zhizn' Leonida Andreeva*, 39.

39 Generalova, 'Leonid Andreev, Dnevnik 1891–1892,' 132.

40 Fatov, *Molodye gody Leonida Andreeva*, 75–6.

41 Generalova, 'Dnevnik Leonida Andreeva,' 257.

42 Ibid., 267.

43 Afonin, *Leonid Andreev*, 32–3.

44 Ibid., 38.

45 Fatov, *Molodye gody Leonida Andreeva*, 87.

46 Ibid., 68–9.

47 Ken and Rogov, *Zhizn' Leonida Andreeva*, 45–6.

48 Generalova, 'Dnevnik Leonida Andreeva,' 289; LRA, MS. 606 \ E. 6 *26 September 1892–4 January 1893; 4 January*; LRA, MS. 606 \ E. 7 *5 March–9 September 1893; 19 March.*

49 Andreev simply refers to 'Evgeniia' in his diary, but it is my assumption that he is referring to E.N. Khludeneva.

50 LRA, MS. 606 \ E. 7; 24 August.

51 LRA, MS. 606 \ E. 8 *27 March 1897–23 April 1901; 1 January 1903; 9 October 1907; 28 April.*

52 Leonid Andreev died in 1919 and Anastasiia Nikolaevna Andreeva died in 1920.

53 Galant, 'Evroendokrinologiia velikikh russkikh pisatelei i poetov. L. N. Andreev,' 226; 228.

54 Gor'kii, *Kniga o Leonide Andreeve*, 53. In English, see White, *Memoirs and Madness*, 40.

55 Zaitsev, *Kniga o Leonide Andreeve*, 129. In English, see White, *Memoirs and Madness*, 94.

56 OGLMT, f. 12, op. 1, no. 165 (KP 5693 of), 8.

57 Fatov, *Molodye gody Leonida Andreeva*, 85; 87–9. Also see Brusianin, *Leonid Andreev. Zhizn' i tvorchestvo*, 51–4.

58 Fatov, *Molodye gody Leonida Andreeva*, 85.

59 Quoted from Andreev's 1903 autobiography in Ken and Rogov, *Zhizn' Leonida Andreeva*, 54.

60 Pavel Andreev, 'Vospominaniia o Leonide Andreeve,' 165–6; OGLMT, f. 12, op. 1, no. 165 (KP 5693 of), 14.

61 Woodward, *Leonid Andreyev: A Study*, 11.

62 Afonin, *Leonid Andreev*, 37.

63 Andreev, Vadim. *Detstvo: Povest'* (Moscow: Sovetskii pisatel', 1963) 67–8. In English, see Andreyev, Vadim. *Childhood*. Translated and adapted by Neil Roper (London: Cromwell Publishers, 2003) 47.

64 It is actually not clear if She is married or simply 'in love' with another man. Either way, He is driven mad by the thought that She loves another man.

65 Andreev, Leonid. 'On, ona i vodka.' *Orlovskii vestnik*, no. 240 (9 September 1895): 1. Andreev's first published story of 1892, 'In the Cold and Gold' (V kholode i zolote), was about an impoverished student who briefly seems to have a job as a tutor in a rich family, only to be turned away by the master of the house. The sentimental story questions whether the rich and pampered are really any happier than the poor and unlucky. Andreev, Leonid. 'V kholode i zolote.' *Zvezda*, 16 (19 April 1892): 418–22.

66 Alekseevskii suggests that the story is written about Nadezhda Aleksandrovna Antonova. Rimma remembers that Andreev three times asked her

to marry him and three times was refused. See OGLMT, f. 12, op. 1, no. 144 (KP 5692). Alekseevskii, Arkdaii Pavlovich. *'Gertsog Lorentso'* = <*Dni dalekie*>. *(Iz vospominanii zhurnalista).* *Vospominaniia ob Andreeve, Leonide Nikolaeviche*, OGLMT, f. 12, op. 1, no. 165 (KP 5693 of), 14.

67 For example, see the biographical reference of N.A. Chukmaldina (born Antonova, 1877–1947). OGLMT, f. 12, op. 1, no. 356 (KP 8759), 2; Alekseevskii's memoir. OGLMT, f. 12, op. 1, no. 144 (KP 5692), 17–18.

68 Ken and Rogov, *Zhizn' Leonida Andreeva*, 57; 62–3.

69 Andreev, Leonid. 'Zagadka.' *Orlovskii vestnik*, 312 (21 November); 314 (24 November); 316 (26 November 1895): 1.

70 LRA, MS. 606 \ E. 8 *27 March 1897–23 April 1901; 1 January 1903; 9 October 1907; 28 April.*

71 Ibid., 28 May. Also see Fatov, *Molodye gody Leonida Andreeva*, 141–3.

72 Ibid., 12 July.

73 Ibid., 25 August.

74 MS. 606 \ E. 8; 15 October.

75 LRA, MS. 606 \ E.3 *27 February–13 April 1891; 5 October 1891; 26 September 1892; 5 October.*

76 Brusianin argues that Andreev's early attempts at suicide are directly linked to the philosophical ideas of Schopenhauer, Hartmann, Nietzsche and Tolstoi. See Brusianin, *Leonid Andreev. Zhizn' i tvorchestvo*, 51–4.

77 Woodward, *Leonid Andreyev: A Study*, 13.

78 Andreev, Leonid. 'Zashchita,' vol. 1. In *Sobranie sochinenii v 6 tomakh.* 6 vols. (Moscow: Khudozhestvennaia literatura, 1990–1996) 61–8.

79 Andreev, 'Khrestiane,' vol. 2, *Sobranie sochinenii v 6 tomakh*, 175–91.

80 Kaun, *Leonid Andreyev: A Critical Study*, 37–8.

81 Andreev, Leonid. 'Influentiki, neirasteniki, i alkogoliki,' vol. 1. In *Leonid Andreev: Sobranie sochinenii s portretom avtora i vstupitel'noi stat'ei professora M.A. Reisnera.* 13 vols. (St Petersburg: Prosveshchenie, 1911) 91. This was originally published on 12 November 1900.

82 'Bargamont and Garas'ka' was first published in *Courier*, 94 (5 April 1898).

83 Nikolai Vasilievich Gogol' (1809–1852) published 'The Overcoat' in 1842.

84 *Gor'kii writes*: It is highly probable that now I do not perceive events the way I did then, and my old perceptions are not as interesting to recall.

85 Nikolai Gerasimovich Pomialovskii (1833–1863), author.

86 Gor'kii, *Kniga o Leonide Andreeve*, 7–8. In English, see White, *Memoirs and Madness*, 11–12.

87 OGLMT, f. 12, op. 1, no. 144 (KP 5692), 38–41.

88 Ibid., 49.

89 MS. 606 \ E. 8; *3 January 1899; 25 December; 14 April 1900; 1 November.*

90 Andreev, Leonid. 'Pis'ma V.S. Miroliubovu.' In *Literaturnyi arkhiv. Materialy po istorii literatury i obshchestvennogo dvizheniia.* Edited by K. Muratova, Institut russkoi literatury (Pushkinskii Dom), issue 5 (Moscow: AN SSSR, 1960) 72.

91 Fatov, *Molodye gody Leonida Andreeva*, 166.

92 Belousov, *Ushedshaia Moskva*, 246.

93 Andreeva, 'Trudnye gody,' 3.

94 Azov, 'Otryvki ob Andreeve,' 5.

95 For information about neurasthenia see Costa e Silva, Jorge Alberto and Giovanni DeGirolamo. 'Neurasthenia: History of a Concept.' In *Psychological Disorders in General Medical Settings*. Edited by Norman Sartoriua et al. (Toronto: Hogrefe & Huber, 1990) 69–81; Goering, 'Russian Nervousness,' 23–46.

96 Goering, 'Russian Nervousness,' 26–8; 31; 38.

97 Iudin, *Ocherki istorii otechestvennoi psikhiatrii*, 140–52; Kannabikh, Iu. *Istoriia psikhiatrii* (Moscow: Gosudarstvennoe meditsinskoe izdatel'stvo, 1929) 384–5; Brown, Julie V. 'Heroes and Non-Heroes: Recurring Themes in the Historiography of Russian-Soviet Psychiatry.' In *Discovering the History of Psychiatry*. Edited by Mark S. Micale and Roy Porter (Oxford: Oxford University Press, 1994) 299.

98 Korsakov, Sergei. *Kurs psikhiatrii*. 2nd edn. Vol. 2 (Moscow: I. Rikhter, 1901) 1008.

99 Ibid., 1008.

100 LRA MS. 606 \ G.1.xi.a** Andreev's death certificate. Published in Andreev, *SOS*, 522, footnote 31. Mariia Iordanskaia claims that Andreev's death was due to a brain hemorrhage. See Andreev, *SOS*, 386.

101 Korsakov, *Kurs psikhiatrii*, vol. 2, 1008–9.

102 Ibid., 1010–11.

103 Ibid., 1011–12.

104 Ibid., 1012–13.

105 Ibid., 1014.

106 For a representative description of many of these physical and psychological ailments, see White, *Memoirs and Madness*, 230–8.

107 Korsakov, *Kurs psikhiatrii*, vol. 2, 1015.

108 Andreev, 'Pis'ma V.S. Miroliubovu,' 83.

109 Ibid., 85.

110 Iudin, *Ocherki istorii otechestvennoi psikhiatrii*, 140–52. Also see Kannabikh, *Istoriia psikhiatrii*, 384–5.

111 N/A, *Kur'er*, 304 (8 November 1902), 2.

4

Controversy and success

Hence the hubbub that at times turned into a howl that surrounded
Andreev from the very beginning. He somehow immediately
amazed everyone, arousing admiration and irritation; and only
three or four years after our acquaintance his name became known
all over Russia. Fame yielded to him immediately. But it did him a
disservice at the same time – dragged him roughly onto the market
square and began to push and pull, to taunt and poison him in
every way.

Boris Zaitsev[1]

Andreev's rise to literary fame reached dizzying heights in a short
amount of time. There were, unquestionably, many factors that
contributed to his success. Yet, this chapter will mainly concentrate on
the development of Andreev's particular illness narrative and how it
contributed to the author's cultural relevancy. Stories about sexual
deviance and criminal madness propelled Andreev beyond literary
discussions and into larger debates about the health of the Russian
nation. His works were used by scientists, journalists and scholars alike
to support arguments of all colors and stripes, but the most important
being that Andreev was representative of a society under duress,
suffering from the rapid and disorienting pace of modernization.

INSTITUTIONAL SPACES: HOSPITALS

As noted in the previous chapter, Andreev first came to the attention of
Gor'kii after publishing the sentimental short story 'Bargamot and
Garas'ka' in *Courier* in 1898. Bargamot is a tough policeman, patrolling
a rough area of town. Garas'ka is a drunkard who is constantly in
trouble. The two meet on Easter morning and Bargamot shows kindness
to Garas'ka, inviting him to his home and giving him an Easter egg.
Gor'kii was so impressed with the story that he befriended the young
writer and soon began to offer him literary advice.

Along with introducing Andreev to critics and publishers, Gor'kii also invited the young writer to participate in the literary circle *Sreda* (The Wednesday Circle), which meant that Andreev was soon a part of the new, young Moscow artistic scene. The purpose of the circle was to provide an environment in which young authors could read their latest works and receive constructive criticism. This is where Andreev also made some of his closest friendships that sustained him throughout his life. It was through *Sreda* that he met Belousov, Ivan Bunin (1870–1920), Evgenii Chirikov (1864–1932), Kuprin, Miroliubov, Feodor Shaliapin (1873–1924), Skitalets (Stepan Petrov), Nikolai Timkovskii (1863–1922), Vinkentii Veresaev (1867–1945), Zaitsev and others.

Nikolai Teleshov (1867–1957), the organizer of *Sreda*, remembers Andreev's introduction to the group:

A year or two before Andreev's first book of stories came out – it came out in 1901 – Gor'kii wrote to me once from Nizhnii Novgorod, that he liked our friendly gatherings, our so-called 'Wednesdays,'[2] where authors read unpublished works in progress in an intimate circle of their colleagues, primarily young at the time. The comrades expressed frank opinions about the new work. And Gor'kii, when he was next in Moscow, definitely wanted to visit these Wednesday circles. Besides, Gor'kii wrote that he recommended and asked us to look after and be kind to a young beginning writer named Andreev, an unknown, but very nice and talented.

Shortly afterwards, Gor'kii came to Moscow and brought Andreev with him to the next meeting of the Wednesday circle. He was a young man, a student type, with a handsome face, very quiet and shy, dressed in a tobacco colored dress jacket. At ten o'clock, when our meetings usually began, Gor'kii suggested that we listen to a short story by the young author.

'I heard it yesterday,' said Gor'kii. 'I confess that I had tears in my eyes.'

'Go ahead, Leonid Nikolaevich,' they suggested to Andreev. But he started by saying that his throat was sore and he would be unable to read. In a word, he was shy and embarrassed.

'Then give it to me, I will read it,' volunteered Gor'kii.

He took the thin notebook, sat down by the lamp and began, 'The story is called "Silence" ...'

The reading lasted under half an hour. Andreev was sitting next to Gor'kii and never stirred the entire time, his legs crossed and his eyes staring at one fixed point in a dark corner at the far end of the room. Of course, he could feel that everyone looked at him. But it was doubtful that he could feel that every new page turned brought him closer to these men he knew, yet did not know, sitting among them like a new boy at school.

The reading came to an end ... Gor'kii lifted his eyes, tenderly smiling at Andreev and said,

'The Devil take it, it has moved me again to tears!'

Aleksei Maksimovich was not the only one who had been 'moved.' It immediately became clear that in this new boy the Wednesday circle had gained a good comrade. Miroliubov, publisher of the popular *Journal for Everyone*, was there that night, went up to Andreev, took the notebook and put it in his pocket. Andreev's eyes gleamed. To be published by Miroliubov, in his journal, with his great reputation and huge number of subscribers and readers, was quite another thing from appearing in *Courier*, the modest Moscow newspaper where he worked at the time. This was his first step forward and a good one.

Soon after, the story was published.

From that first time at the Wednesday circle, Andreev was one of us. After 'Silence,' other stories followed and they all passed through the Wednesday circle. 'Once There Was,' 'Sergei Petrovich,' 'The Wall,' and the famous 'The Abyss' – all of them were read to the Wednesday circle by the author himself while still in rough draft. The author listened to the most frank comments, to both praise and objections. Once he read a story called 'The Little Ruffian' and received such a unanimous rebuff that to this day the story has not been published anywhere.[3]

Andreev's first real literary success came with the publication of 'Once There Was' (Zhili-byli) in 1901. Dmitrii Merezhkovskii (1865–1941) asked whether it was Chekhov or Gor'kii who was hiding behind the name of Leonid Andreev. 'Once There Was' had been written during the two months that the author spent in the Imperial university clinic for nervous disorders. In this story the merchant Kosheverov and the Deacon Speranskii are in the university clinic and we learn that both will die of unspecified illnesses. For Kosheverov this means a terrible end to a life that was devoid of meaning. For Speranskii death represents the great price of a meaningful life. He pays less attention to his own illness and more to other patients, the doctors and students. The Soviet critic Liudmila Iezuitova suggests that Andreev is interested in describing how life can be meaningless and joyless for one person while for another it is eternal and dear. Andreev views impending death as a time to assess the path of one's life as either a confirmation of that life or as a series of lost opportunities.[4]

Upon arrival at the clinic, all of Kosheverov's personal belongings are taken and he is given 'a government-issued grey robe, clean underwear with a black mark "Ward No. 8" and shoes.'[5] His illness is described as 'relentless,' an illness which devours his strength and causes feelings of loneliness, especially in the company of his greedy relatives. Finding himself in an atmosphere of lies, hatred and fear, Kosheverov came to Moscow where the illness changed to something dull within his psyche, described as a fading pain. Kosheverov is weighed and then examined by the doctors and their students. During this process it is explained that Kosheverov is overweight and has not lived a healthy life.

Although he is probed and prodded, Kosheverov is not relieved of 'a gloomy feeling of deep loneliness.'[6] 'The more they were occupied with the body the deeper and more terrible became the loneliness of the psyche.'[7] The white walls and high ceilings of the clinic exacerbate these feelings of 'cold alienation.'[8] In the evenings, he cannot sleep, but instead thinks about his life. During the day Kosheverov takes his medicine and does all that is prescribed, but his body continues to weaken and soon he becomes silent and unmoving. In the final days he is very nervous and the doctor notes in his file: 'The patient complains of boredom.'[9] Kosheverov dies in bed early in the morning.[10]

In contrast to Kosheverov, Deacon Speranskii is thin and, although very sick, he never feels lonely because he has made friends with everyone in the clinic. He is very positive and the clinic's cleanliness and the attention of the doctors bring him happiness. As he grows weaker, his faith continues to give him emotional strength. He takes comfort in the doctors' promise that he will live – even though this is probably not the truth.

Belousov remembers that in the spring of 1901, he went with Timkovskii to meet the young Andreev, who was being treated by Doctor Savei-Mogilevich. Timkovskii told Belousov that the young author was quite sick due to a 'desultory life.' At the hospital they found Andreev playing checkers with a deacon. Andreev would later tell Belousov that the deacon in the story was the same person, with whom he had played checkers on the day of their visit.[11]

A third patient is the student Torbetskii, who remains in bed and receives a female visitor each day. They are in love. Torbetskii seems to be the only person in the clinic who gets better although he suffers when his girlfriend does not visit for several days. Vadim Chuvakov suggests that Torbetskii represents Andreev himself.[12] This is supported by a note that Andreev wrote to his wife in 1902 in which he states: 'The best tales in this book were inspired by you. Are you no longer the girl who came to me in the hospital and gave me the strength to do my work?'[13]

At six o'clock in the morning the day begins with tea, a check of each patient's temperature as well as individual treatment. An hour later, the sun comes pouring in through an enormous window. At eleven o'clock the doctors and students arrive for lengthy consultations. The patients are given lunch, again tea and then dinner. At nine o'clock in the evening the lights are turned off and by eleven everything is silent.

Andreev makes a distinction between an outside world bustling with activity and the isolation of the clinic, 'where sick people laid in bed, with hardly enough strength to turn their weakened heads to the light; dressed in grey robes limply they drag along the smooth floor; here they grew sick and died.'[14] The outside world is animated with rain, wind and snow, while the hospital ward 'with its high ceilings, seems like [...] a narrow and stuffy alley in which it is impossible to stretch one's arms without striking the wall.'[15] Through a large window sunlight pours in, contrasted with the sickly electric light of a lamp within the clinic. No sound reaches the patients through the window except the song of some sparrows, which is only briefly heard until the *fortka* is closed.[16] The window is a false portal to the outside world as death is the only way of leaving the clinic.[17]

'Once There Was' is an accurate depiction of the author's own experience in the clinic. Andreev later revealed that while a patient, he befriended a merchant with whom he discussed important philosophical questions concerning life, death and God. One night the merchant knocked on his door, but Andreev sent him away as he was busy with work for *Courier*. That night the merchant died. Long after this, Andreev regretted that he had not taken the time for one more conversation with the man.[18]

A month after 'Once There Was' appeared in print Andreev published 'The Present' (Gostinets). In this story Senista, an apprentice tailor, pleads with Sazonka, a 'respectable craftsman and a drunk,'[19] to visit him again in the hospital. Sazonka dreads returning to the hospital that smells of medicine and is full of despair. When he finally returns, Sazonka finds that Senista died the previous day. As in 'Once There Was,' the loneliness and boredom of the hospital represent separation from the outside, real world.

In this story, the reason Senista is in the hospital and the nature of the characters' relationship is ambiguous. It begins as Sazonka promises for the third time not to abandon Senista to the 'loneliness, suffering and fear' of the hospital.[20] The only thing we know for sure is that both characters find the hospital an uncomfortable place. Senista does not want to be abandoned and Sazonka can only think about leaving. Sazonka is there out of pity and a mix of emotions influenced by the 'tight row of beds with pale, gloomy people; the air, that is completely spoiled by the smell of medicine and the vapor of a sick person's body; the feeling of one's own strength and good-health.'[21] Sazonka promises a fourth time to return and then leaves the hospital although 'for a long time the smell of medicine and the departing voice: "Come again!" pursued him.'[22]

Sazonka, however, does not visit Senista right away. The Easter holidays are approaching and as a tailor he is quite busy. There is a clear contrast between the restrictive and sickly conditions in the hospital and the fresh air, the scent of manure, the flies and voices that enter the open window of Sazonka's shop. The town is full of activity and on the street Sazonka sees some children and tells them that Senista is still in the hospital. He suggests that they should give him a present, and one of the boys recommends giving Senista a ten kopeck piece. Again Sazonka is consumed by his work but the thought of Senista and the present, now to be wrapped in a handkerchief, stays in his mind. To everyone he meets, he says that he will visit Senista on the first day of Easter.

However, Sazonka is drunk for the first two days of the holiday. He is beaten by other drunkards and sleeps in a field. Only on the fourth day does he set off to see Senista. Along the way, there is a description of the bright sunshine and various sights and sounds of nature and the town. Sazonka is recovering from the drinking binge and is ashamed of his appearance, but the closer he gets to the hospital, the better he feels. And yet, when Sazonka sees the hospital, he describes it as an enormous yellow building with black windows that look like dark sullen eyes, 'long corridors and the smell of medicine and the vague sense of terror and despair.'[23] In the hospital he finds a rude nurse who tells him that Senista died the day before. Sazonka goes to the morgue and finds his friend's dead body. He experiences a terrible coldness, notices the moldy blotches on the walls and looks out a window that never lets in any sunlight.

The hospital sits on the edge of town so, upon leaving, Sazonka goes out into a field where he is struck by the wide-open expanse and the wind that seems to him like 'a free and warm breath.'[24] He walks to a river and lies down in a grassy hollow, feels the warmth of the sun and listens to a lark. As he turns over he feels in his pocket the present that he had brought for Senista. Sazonka thinks about how Senista had waited for him to return and how he had died 'alone and forgotten.'[25] Sazonka rolls on the ground in grief and hears church bells in the distance.

The story is full of symbolic meaning, but it is important to focus on the not so subtle contrast between the hospital and the outside world. The hospital is not a place where doctors heal the sick, but where ill people are housed until they die. We never confront a doctor, only a rude nurse, and the lasting impression is the smell of medicine and the stench of the sick. The color gray is predominant inside the hospital with dark windows that do not allow in sunlight, blocking the vibrance of the outdoors.

The two stories, 'Once There Was' and 'The Present,' provide a negative commentary on illness and medical treatment. The illnesses are never defined and treatment, if any exists, does not result in improvement or recovery. The hospitals, sterile and alienating, are segregated from the outside natural world, which is associated with the living. The hospitals house the sick, separating them from the public, and none of Andreev's characters except Torbetskii, representing the author himself, actually leave the hospital alive.

Having just spent time in the Imperial university clinic, Andreev depicted for readers his perception of this institutional space. Over time, hospitals would give way to asylums and, eventually, to prisons in his literary works – all of which were meant to separate 'undesirables' from society. In these literary works the mentally ill are equated with the criminal and treatment evolves into punishment. Andreev's depiction of institutional spaces is emblematic of a time when Russian society made little distinction between therapy and incarceration.

Literary life

By the spring of 1901 several of Andreev's stories had been published in *Courier* and *A Journal for Everyone* (Zhurnal dlia vsekh). The author was interested in publishing a separate volume of his stories and hastily sold the collection to a publisher, Ivan Sytin (1851–1934), who placed it on reserve as Andreev was little known at this time outside of a few literary circles. Gor'kii, however, had recently formed a co-operative publishing house *Znanie* and was now able to publish Andreev's volume. With the help of his friends from *Sreda*, Andreev bought back this collection and sent it directly to Gor'kii's publishing house in St Petersburg. On 17 September 1901 the first volume of Andreev's short stories was released and was met with unexpected popular success. Within a year, it went through four editions. Literary critics praised Andreev's stories, highlighted by a favorable article by the well-respected dean of critics Nikolai Mikhailovskii (1842–1904).

The book originally cost eighty kopecks and contained ten stories: 'The Grand Slam,' 'Little Angel,' 'Silence,' 'Valia,' 'The Story of Sergei Petrovich,' 'On the River' (Na reke), 'The Lie' (Lozh'), 'At the Window' (U okna), 'Once There Was' and 'Into the Dark Distance' (V temnuiu dal'). Andreev received over 6,000 roubles in royalties this first year, a very large sum for the formerly impoverished journalist. He also was offered by Miroliubov the position of co-editor of the St Petersburg *A Journal for Everyone*, but was forced to decline because of his family commitments in Moscow.[26]

Not everyone, however, was completely overwhelmed by Andreev's literary talents. One of the most often quoted accounts is Tolstoi's response to Andreev's first collection of short stories. It would later be reported in a negative light that Tolstoi was unimpressed with Andreev's stories and said: 'Andreev tries to scare me, but I am not scared.' According to Gor'kii, however, this was not the case or the proper tone of the comment. Gor'kii was discussing the collection with Tolstoi when the elder writer stated that he particularly liked 'Once There Was,' 'The Grand Slam,' 'At the Window,' and 'The Story of Sergei Petrovich.' Tolstoi then said: 'There is this anecdote about a young boy, who told a tale to his friend in this way: "It was a dark night – Are you scared? In the woods there was a wolf – Are you scared? Suddenly beyond the window – Are you scared?" Here, Andreev is the exact same: He writes as if asking me – "Are you scared? Are you scared?" But, I am not scared! Disappointed?' Gor'kii then remembered that Tolstoi greatly praised Andreev's use of language and the power of his imagery. Undoubtedly, this *'I am not scared'* was a criticism of Andreev's work, but not with the negative intentions that would be later attributed to this exchange. Even so, the young Andreev was stung by Tolstoi's anecdote.[27]

A second edition included six new stories that thrust Andreev into a higher realm of literary celebrity. The first press run had been of 4,000 copies and had sold out in two months. The second edition of 8,000 copies sold out in two weeks. Altogether, there were nine press runs of 47,000 copies. Afonin identifies the main theme of this first volume of stories as the tragic destruction of the individual. Characters unsuccessfully attempt to break out of a feeling of cursed isolation and the sense that there is no meaning in their wretched existence.[28] Understanding the close connection between Andreev's diaries and early stories, Afonin finds parallels in the narratives of personal seclusion. Behind the literary persona *Leonid Andreev* – nervous, lyrically enthusiastic and rebellious – is a co-author who is broken and marginalized.[29]

It might also be argued that in the additional stories in the second edition – 'The Alarm-Bell', 'The Abyss,' 'In the Basement' (V podvale), 'The Wall' (Stena), 'Pet'ka at the Dacha' (Pet'ka na dache) and 'Laughter' (Smekh) – is found the first tangible evidence of degeneration theory. 'The Wall' tells the story of lepers who repeatedly dash themselves against an immense wall. They want to penetrate the wall to see what is on the other side, but their efforts are futile and the dead bodies simply pile up. In this story some critics saw a depiction of Nordau's degenerate modernity and the description of mental illness. Andeev suggested that the story illustrated the imperfection and sickness of human nature, its animal instincts, maliciousness and avarice.[30]

Although 'The Wall' disturbed critics and readers alike, an explosive public debate erupted in the daily newspapers and journals due to 'The Abyss' and 'In the Fog.' The characters' deviant sexual behavior leads to rape and murder, expressing various strains of Darwinism, the erotic sensibilities of the French decadents and late Victorian repression. Many of the sexual paradigms in these stories can be connected to psychiatry and its medical discourse, and they portrayed the complexity of the ego. However, Andreev's tales of evil were interpreted as advocacy, for which he was attacked by many in the press.

However harsh were the critics, Andreev found defenders as well, especially among the younger generation. University students wrote to newspapers suggesting that Andreev benefited the reader by showing, without adornment, the brute which exists in mankind. Andreev was also defended by such literary figures as Chekhov and Gor'kii who congratulated the author on presenting the moral agonies of sexual life to the reading public. For better or worse, this firestorm of controversy propelled Andreev into the forefront of Russia's literary and cultural scene. It also indicates how Andreev's works were perceived as a bellwether of contemporary debates in Russian society.

Kreutzer Sonata and 'The Abyss'

'The Abyss' caused a controversy due to the sexual subject matter and depiction of an adolescent boy engaged in a depraved act with a young girl. The merits, or lack thereof, of this story were debated on the pages of newspapers all across Russia. Twelve years earlier, a similar story by Tolstoi sparked comparable public debate, and only through the intervention of Tsar Alexander III (1845–1894) was his novella *Kreutzer Sonata* (Kreitserova Sonata) legally published.

By 1902, Tolstoi was the last remaining of Russia's great novelists. Both Turgenev and Dostoevskii had died in the 1880s. Tolstoi too had disappeared for a time due to a crisis of faith, but when he returned to the literary scene he abandoned the novel in favor of short stories and religious tracts. As a result, Tolstoi's short stories were highly didactic and reflected his rather unorthodox religious views. Peter Ulf Møller states that *Kreutzer Sonata* had been designed to provoke a strong reaction – and from the early 1890s onward, any discussion of the sexual question in Russia used this text as a reference point.[31] Bezzubov argues that Andreev intentionally wrote stories in the style of other authors and that Tolstoi's themes are particularly evident in his first collection of stories.[32]

More specifically, 'The Abyss' and *Kreutzer Sonata* were compared in literary discussions of the time due to their scandalous sexual subject matter; although Tolstoi's story eluded the classification of *pornographic* given his stance on the woman issue, marriage and morality, while Andreev's was pigeonholed as vulgar boulevard literature.[33] 'The Abyss,' however, was meant as a rejoinder to *Kreutzer Sonata*, rather than as a slavish imitation.

Andreev was responding to Tolstoi's attempt in *Kreutzer Sonata* to confront with religious asceticism the pervasive notions of sexual degeneracy which equated most sex acts with immoral and criminal behavior. The main difference between the two was that Andreev was interested in the psychological motivation for sexual aggression and did not offer the moral rejection so desired by Tolstoi and a portion of the reading public.

Pessimism

Andreev's story was constructed out of building blocks provided by Schopenhauer's concept of the Will and crafted in the shadow of Tolstoi's story of sexual aggression. The abyss that serves as the title of the story and represents the final irrational state of sexual debauchery for both writers is most clearly a fictionalized representation of Schopenhauer's Will to Life (Wille zum Leben). Pessimistic philosophy offered a theoretical underpinning for the scientific discourse on degeneration, and a way for Andreev to interpret and eventually respond to Tolstoi's demonization of sexual desire.

The philosophy of Schopenhauer was very influential at the turn of the century, read and discussed in conjunction with other European and Russian thinkers. Belyi states that the pessimistic philosophy of Schopenhauer and Hartmann profoundly informed Russian decadence.[34] Therefore, the connections between Tolstoi's literary text and Schopenhauer's philosophical ideas would have been readily understandable to a large part of educated society. For Schopenhauer, the Will is found in the blind force of nature and manifests itself in the deliberate action of man. All striving, loving, hating is nothing but an affection of the Will. The intellect is secondary, at best, and can temporarily restrain the Will, but never completely conquers it. The Will to Life, according to Schopenhauer, can result in violent sexual aggression when one consciously resists or blocks the sexual impulse, be it for moral, logical, or other reasons.[35] As noted earlier, Andreev read *The World as Will and Representation* and was greatly influenced by it. Philosophical pessimism, therefore, provided Andreev a unifying thread of continuity between the work of Tolstoi and the cultural discourse on sexual deviance.

Andreev introduces readers to the students Nemovetskii and Zina Nikolaevna while they are taking a walk in the countryside. When Nemovetskii helps Zina over a puddle, he sees her dainty foot and it becomes the sexual impetus for the events that follow. Nemovetskii contemplates the image of Zina's foot, but forces himself to suppress his sexual impulse. In his attempt to quiet the image, Nemovetskii turns to his intellect and enters into an artificially distanced literary world.

Andreev's reference to a literary reality is not arbitrary. In Schopenhauer's system, the individual can suppress the Will by two methods. The first is through contemplation of the suffering of others. The second is through art and contemplation of the aesthetic. Nemovetskii's attempt to suppress his Will to Life through contemplation of literary models, which portray idealized life, develops in the rest of the story. This use of the intellect as a buffer is not a foolproof defense. Schopenhauer uses a metaphor to explain the role of the Will and the intellect. He offers the image of a hulking giant who is blind (the Will), guided by a lame sighted man (the intellect), seated on the giant's shoulders. The intellect can quiet the Will to a significant extent, but the intellect is powerless to restrain the Will once the giant becomes determined to act.

Zina and Nemovetskii's stroll continues and they talk about literature and the noble thought of dying for love. At one point, Zina reaches up and pulls a string from Nemovetskii's jacket and then asks why he is so pale and thin. She suggests that maybe he studies too much – a reference to the intellect. He ignores this comment and notices the physical in Zina, that she has blue eyes. Then Zina begins to comment on Nemovetskii's eyes but is too embarrassed to finish her sentence.

Although he realizes that they are lost and the night is coming, Nemovetskii is not willing to admit this to Zina. Metaphorically, the blind giant has already shrugged off the intellect and begins his descent into the darkness of the approaching evening and the abyss of his human desire. This begins to strip Zina and Nemovetskii of the artificial social and intellectual elements, the quieters, which buffer them from the blind passions of the real world. As darkness deepens, the comfort of home, a safe haven where they read books in which heroes die for their maidens, is rendered irrelevant.

The young couple encounters the disenfranchised, degenerate people who live on the edge of town. A gang of men beat Nemovetskii senseless and rape Zina. The tension to this point has been between Nemovetskii's Will to possess Zina and his intellect's attempt to quiet his Will through the social conventions indicated in books and polite society. Suddenly, he finds himself in a primitive environment where these social conventions do not apply. Schopenhauer is very clear that the same Will and a similar intellect drive man and beast. Man is separated from animal, however, by his degree of perception and his ability to conceive ideas. Schopenhauer emphasizes the distinction between the man restrained by the intellect and the brute restrained by fear.[36]

Andreev depicts the distinction between brute and man at Zina's expense. Nemovetskii is a man until he tumbles into the abyss, which represents the dissolution of the rational ego into the primordial unconscious and willful impulses of the brute. In one of his defenses of 'The Abyss' Andreev wrote, 'The horror of our false and deceptive life lies precisely in the fact that we do not notice the brute.'[37] The men who rape Zina are not thinkers or knowers, but brutes. They have nothing to fear once they have disposed of Nemovetskii and are carried away by their Will to Life to possess this young girl who has been dropped into their midst to satisfy their Will. 'Me too! Me too!' ('И я ! И я!')[38] is their only concern.

When Nemovetskii revives, he crawls out of one abyss, in which he has lain, beaten and unconscious, only to fall into a second more dangerous abyss of unconscious sexual impulse. When he finds Zina he begins to kiss and fondle her naked body. Eventually, he screams 'This is me! Me!' ('Это я ! Я !'),[39] which sounds very similar to the brutes' call of 'Me too! Me too!' ('И я ! И я !'). No longer is Nemovetskii a man who can ignore the object of his desire by means of his intellect, by contemplation of the aesthetic. Possessed by his brutal Will, he violates the comatose Zina.

Parallels in sexual aggression

The similarities between Andreev's 'The Abyss' and Tolstoi's *Kreutzer Sonata* were not limited to their *cause celebre* status. *Kreutzer Sonata* circulated widely in manuscript form until the author's wife, Sofia Tolstaia (1844–1919), received special permission from the Tsar for publication of the story in a limited quantity.[40] The issue created such a scandal in Russian society that Tolstoi published a postface to the story to clarify and reiterate his main ideas. 'The Abyss' was published with greater ease but caused a similar reaction. In response to the public outcry, Andreev also published an 'addition' to his story; not as Andreev, the author, but in the voice of his main character Nemovetskii, in a 'Letter to the Editor.' When we examine 'The Abyss' and Nemovetskii's letter as a whole, the substantial connections between 'The Abyss' and *Kreutzer Sonata* become more visible and enhance our understanding of their continuity.[41]

Nemovetskii's letter appeared in the 6 March 1903 issue of *Courier*, in which he made no attempt to deny the events that had occurred, but offered this explanation for his actions:

Are we really not jealous of our wives for all of their earlier infatuations, and can you ever really come to some sort of peace with this fact, if you know that your glowing, innocent, pure bride, at some time, loved and belonged to another? Will not this memory spoil for you every moment of pleasure, while you worry once again about her? And, while loving her, won't you despise and hate her at the same time?[42]

The letter is meant to explain Nemovetskii's rape of Zina but repositions Nemovetskii's deviant behavior within the context of marriage, which is clearly pointed at Tolstoi and his *Kreutzer Sonata*, a point that would have been readily apparent to the Russian reading audience.

In Tolstoi's story, sexual aggression drives the husband Pozdnyshev to kill his wife. The reader first meets Pozdnyshev in a train compartment with three other passengers. The discussion turns to marriage and, after two of the passengers express their opinions and leave, Pozdnyshev tells of his debauched adolescence, his marriage and his antagonistic relationship with his wife, which was only briefly quelled by their sexual interludes. Eventually, a musician becomes a frequent visitor to their apartment on the premise that Pozdnyshev's wife shares an interest in music with this man. Pozdnyshev becomes suspicious while away on business and returns early to find them together in the music room. He threatens the man and kills his wife in a fit of rage. Pozdnyshev is not legally punished as his act is deemed a 'crime of passion.' Significantly, his remorse is not solely for his dead wife, but largely for their sexual transgressions, and this ultimately leads him to advocate celibacy, even in marriage.

Tolstoi began reading Schopenhauer as early as 1868 and within a few years he was consumed by the idea that a tension existed between natural freedom (the absence of law or reason) and morality. Schopenhauer argued that man is naturally sinful and lives entirely for himself; therefore, the only way to maintain order is to hold the individual responsible for his actions. To avoid the selfish desire for happiness, the individual must yearn for death. Tolstoi selectively accepted those portions of Schopenhauer's philosophical system which allowed him to construct his own brand of idealism on a stronger theoretical footing.[43] Consequently, Tolstoi's Anna Karenina commits suicide seemingly as punishment for her moral transgressions.[44]

After more than a decade, Tolstoi began to replace Schopenhauer's metaphysical Will with notions of God, love and nonresistance to evil. Moral self-perfection for both thinkers meant asceticism, abstinence and empathy for others. In parallel, Tolstoi's ascetic negativism towards sex became increasingly extreme from the late 1880s onward. In *Anna Karenina*, the transgression was having sex outside of legal marriage. By the time Tolstoi wrote *Kreutzer Sonata*, he believed that any form of passion, especially sexual intercourse, should be rejected. Such was not lost on Andreev, who wrote to Gor'kii in 1904: 'I can see that it wasn't for nothing that Tolstoi appreciated Schopenhauer, his *Anna Karenina* ... is an artistic embodiment of the world as will and idea.'[45] In *Kreutzer Sonata* Pozdnyshev refers to Schopenhauer and Hartmann and then suggests that sexual passion is the most unyielding of impulses, that only by eliminating this malignancy will goodness and happiness reign among mankind.[46]

In August of 1902, Andreev openly stated the connection between his and Tolstoi's two works in a letter to the literary critic Aleksandr Izmailov (1873–1921): 'Have they not read, of course, how Tolstoi criticized me for "The Abyss?" He does this in vain – "The Abyss" is the biological daughter of his "Kreutzer Sonata," albeit illegitimate.'[47] In Nemovetskii's 'letter to the editor,' Andreev explicitly emphasizes the link between these two stories with references to the violent jealousy of a husband. This could have been a conscious decision on the author's part, given that Tolstoi's wife had a month earlier initiated the controversy over the 'The Abyss' by publishing a letter in the newspaper *New Time* (Novoe vremia) claiming that Andreev wanted to examine the corpse of human degradation rather than the beauty of nature.

Degeneration theory

Tolstoi was familiar with the literature on degeneration and psychopathology as early as 1860. He corresponded with the noted psychiatrist Kovalevskii, read case studies on sexual behavior, and employed the names of the leading theorists on degeneration in his literary works.[48] As noted, Andreev was also aware of degeneration theory from his early adolescence. Therefore, it is very probable that Andreev recognized the parallels between science and art in Krafft-Ebing's *Psychopathia Sexualis* (1886; Russian translation 1887) and Tolstoi's *Kreutzer Sonata* (1889).[49] Andreev might also have been aware of Nordau's argument that '[t]he way to happiness is, according to Tolstoi, the turning away from science, the renunciation of reason.' Nordau deemed Tolstoi's moral doctrine in *Kreutzer Sonata* insane and suggested that he saw science as the enemy.[50] Unlike Tolstoi, however, Andreev was not making moral pronouncements. His approach was more in keeping with the popular discourse on psychopathology which had moved morality out of the hands of the church and into the realm of science. In public forums, psychiatrists were lumping together criminals, syphilitics, homosexuals, prostitutes and other social deviants, all under the rubric of moral insanity.[51] Andreev, consequently, was interested in understanding the complexity of the ego, which supposedly contained brute elements that could unexpectedly emerge in a seemingly otherwise civilized and healthy individual. According to Bezzubov, Tolstoi disliked 'The Abyss' because Andreev was interested in depicting the psychological motivation for deviant behavior rather than establishing a moral opposition to it.[52]

Andreev's focus was evidently reflective of Lombroso's theory that atavistic characteristics in certain individuals reproduce the behavior and instincts of primitive humanity and inferior animals, which could cause 'an irresistible craving for evil for its own sake, the desire to not only extinguish life in the victim, but to mutilate the corpse, tear its flesh, and drink its blood.'[53] In most *fin de siècle* scientific studies on degeneration, identification was a common goal. 'The Abyss' must be read within this context because Andreev was influenced by a medicalized understanding of immoral behavior as an indication of degeneracy. The boundaries separating civilized man from savage throw-back were still undefined, stimulating Andreev's fascination with scientific investigation. In essence, Andreev's literary endeavor was no different from *The Strange Case of Dr Jekyll and Mr Hyde* or *Dracula*. Simply put, Andreev sought to grasp and explain what drives people to sometimes behave in monstrous ways.

It was logical then for Andreev to create a character that was in most ways exactly like Tolstoi's, drive him to commit an equally vicious act of sexual aggression and then underline the fact that he felt no remorse. Tolstoi believed in the religious conscience; that through celibacy and mortification of the flesh, the individual could ward off the impulse of the Will and also gain control over the deviant physical body. Andreev answered this assertion by countering that the Will was more powerful than the intellect, that atavistic regression could result in sexual aggression, trumping the thin veneer of civilization (and moral indignation). For Nemovetskii, there was no divine intervention following Zina's rape. Once his sexual urge was satisfied, the romantic emotions (and notions) disappeared. His criminal act was consistent with degeneration theory in which the seemingly healthy individual regresses to a latent, primitive self. In Andreev's understanding of sexual aggression, the realities of scientific theory triumphed over moral doctrine. Andreev's response to Tolstoi's suggestion that celibacy could overcome these animal urges was to reassert the scientific and philosophical claims of the day – man can revert to the savage that resides within, throwing himself into the abyss of sexual desire with no remorse for his bestial actions.

'In the Fog'

Krafft-Ebing and many other scientists had viewed the rising tide of crime, alcoholism and sexual perversion as behaviors indicative of nervous exhaustion. Physical stigmata were signs of moral corruption, while moral weaknesses were symptoms of bodily disease. Krafft-Ebing wrote in *Psychopathia Sexualis*, 'Exaggerated tension of the nervous system stimulates sensuality, leads the individual as well as the masses to excesses, and undermines the very foundation of society, and the morality and the purity of family life.'[54] For these theorists, sexual excess led not only to moral ruin, but was psychopathological in nature and revealed the decadence and degeneration of individuals, communities and nations.

This scientific discourse can be found in Andreev's 'In the Fog,' which was published in the December 1902 issue of *A Journal for Everyone*. Miroliubov took a great risk in publishing this story as the journal had already received a warning from the censor that it was to publish only 'items suitable for family reading.'[55] The story tells of the young schoolboy Pavel, who has contracted a venereal disease from a prostitute. Pavel is ashamed and feels that he is unworthy of human contact, tortured by his desire for lofty love with his sister's friend. Further tension is created by the inability of Pavel and his father to connect personally, denying Pavel an emotional catharsis and driving him out into the street late one evening. He is propositioned by an inebriated prostitute and goes with her to her room. Pavel's guilt and the prostitute's drunkenness cloud their interaction, leading to a fight in which Pavel stabs and kills the prostitute and then himself.

Andreev worked on this story during the previous summer, while at a dacha in Tsaritsyno, just outside Moscow. He had originally been inspired by a short news item, which appeared in the 21 June edition of *Courier*, about a young boy who had killed two prostitutes. Intrigued by the story, Andreev wanted to explore the possible psychological motivation for such behavior. In creating a psychological portrait that might explain such conduct, Andreev clearly relied on degeneration theory in both Pavel's illness experience and his father's advice.

And [Pavel] could feel the filth that enveloped and permeated him. He had been feeling it ever since he was infected. Every Friday Pavel went to the bathhouse, twice a week he changed his underclothes, and everything he wore was new, fresh and expensive; but it seemed as if he were completely immersed in some kind of foul-smelling swill, and wherever he went he left a foul smelling trace in the air. [...] His thoughts were equally dirty, and it seemed that if you opened his skull and took out his brains, they would be as dirty as rags, as the brains of an animal's splayed out in the slaughterhouse among the filth and manure. [...] When he was asleep and powerless to regulate his feelings and desires, they arose like flaming ghosts from the depths of his being; when he stayed awake, a strange, terrifying force took him in its iron hands and threw him – blinded, changed, unrecognizable, as himself – into the filthy embrace of a filthy woman. 'It's all because I'm debauched,' thought Pavel with calm despair.[56]

This passage emphasizes signs of contagion, physical traces in the brain and uncontrollable base urges. Pavel recognizes that he is deviant, more than just infected with a venereal disease. His fears are then confirmed in a conversation with his father in which degeneration is directly offered as a diagnosis for the ills of society (and Pavel).

> Yes, it is a terrible problem, and I am convinced, Pavel, that the fate of all civilized humanity depends on how it is resolved. Really ... the degeneration of whole generations, even whole countries; psychological disturbances with all the horrors of insanity and enervation ... So there you are ... And finally, innumerable diseases that destroy the body and even the soul.[57]

Andreev was shocked by the public furor that arose once the story was published. As noted, Tolstoi's wife had seemed to add fuel to the already volatile public debate. Her rhetoric must have seemed to Andreev like similar aspersions cast by Nordau at Nietzsche, Ibsen and Wilde. In such attacks, there was little distinction made between the perceived deviance of the author and his literary works. This was the first such experience for Andreev, but an accusation by critics that would become ever more frequent as his literary fame grew. For example, in January 1903 Platon Krasnov wrote a review, 'Nightmarish Writer' (Koshmarnyi pisatel'), of Andreev's first collection of stories. 'This critic, prone to paradox, in the manner of Max Nordau, would accuse Mr. Leonid Andreev of a particular mania-necrophilia.'[58] This reference to Nordau clearly stigmatizes Andreev and his literary works as *degenerate*. Krasnov continued by suggesting that Andreev's 'decadent-morose' works had an overall negative impact on Russian society and reflected the decadent trend of both Russian and European literature.

Other critics supported Andreev's depiction, and discussed similar crimes that had occurred in Moscow and Kiev. They did not read the story as pornographic, but as a snapshot of the state of society.[59] Certainly, Andreev had relied on the latest medical theories to find a psychological explanation for such gruesome criminal behavior. Dr M.P. Manasein's response, in which he points to the prevalence of syphilis and gonorrhea in contemporary (1903) Russian society, evidences how seriously the medical profession took Andreev's assertions.[60]

The public scandal resulted in enormous sales of Andreev's collected works, especially those that included the scandalous sex stories. For an author who had experienced such severe poverty in his youth and adolescence, this rapid rise to literary stardom with the resulting financial rewards was unprecedented. Andreev quickly learned, however, that literary success also included intrusive media attention and speculation about his personal life.

Marriage

As his literary fame grew, Andreev also found fulfillment in his personal life. In January 1902, Aleksandra agreed to marry the young author, although, she asked that Andreev first confront Nadezhda Antonova to confirm that he was no longer in love with her. Even though Nadezhda had been married for some time, the marriage was going badly and she remained in contact. On the eve of the wedding, Andreev went to see Nadhezha while Aleksandra and the author's sister, Rimma, waited at home. After some time, Andreev returned and announced that he was no longer in love with Nadezhda, that he loved only Aleksandra.[61]

On 7 January, Andreev wrote to Konstantin Piatnitskii, 'Sickness has overwhelmed me – [my] neurasthenia has become acute from overwork – and I have taken a week's vacation from *Courier.*' The same day, Andreev wrote to Gor'kii, 'I have gone to complete ruin, driven to the edge, I've begun water treatments and the like – for a week I received permission from *Courier* not to work.'[62] Unquestionably, exhaustion and the stress of his personal life complicated the author's already compromised health.

Yet, on 10 February 1902 the couple was married in The Church of Nikola Iavlenyi on the Arbat. The organizer of the *Sreda* literary circle, Nikolai Teleshov, stood in place of Andreev's father and Sergei Goloushev was his bestman. Andreev's brother Pavel was originally to stand as bestman, but he had been arrested for political activities just before the wedding.[63] Teleshov would later write of the wedding:

> And his father I was ... The wedding was very joyous. Leonid Nikolaevich was somehow internally happy and unusually humble. Whatever they said to him, he did without objection, without a second thought, as they say, and with pleasure.
>
> There was dancing. They taught Andreev how to dance beforehand. He danced the waltz, the polka and the quadrille. By the way, he came up to me and, glancing at the dancing couples with a smile, said, 'Well, Father, what if we taught our whole Wednesday circle to dance? Imagine, there they'd all be suddenly dancing – Veresaev, Belousov, Vanechka Bunin ...

There would be the gloomy Skitalets waltzing in a whirl ... or Mamin-Sibiriak with his pipe and his smoke ... What a sight! Just imagine ...'[64]

Andreev's young wife brought a measure of stability to his daily existence and, as Teleshov claims, Andreev 'worked hard and well, and consolidated his literary reputation' during this period.[65] Andreev's friend and fellow writer, Veresaev would later write of the couple:

> [They] were inseparable. If invited anywhere, he would not go unless she too was invited. Aleksandra Mikhailovna jealously guarded him from life's minutia and squabbles and placed him in the best situation for work. Her influence on him was enormous. Andreev went on drinking binges. After marriage he completely stopped drinking and while Aleksandra Mikhailovna was alive, as far as I know, he stuck to this firmly.[66] [...] I never met a better writer's wife and friend. In general theoretical 'smart' conversations Aleksandra Mikhailovna did not stand out at all and gave the impression of an ordinary intelligent young woman. Yet, she had an enormous intuitive understanding of what her husband-artist wanted and what she could give, and in this relationship she was the living embodiment of his artistic conscience.[67]

It has been noted by most contemporaries that Andreev needed such a calming influence in his life to negotiate the variable mood swings of his neurasthenic condition. This element of Andreev's life is evident whether discussing the unconditional love of his mother; the anguish caused by the loss of his first love, Zinaida Sibeleva; or the short-lived peace that he finally found with Aleksandra Mikhailovna. Andreev's problems did not disappear with love, but the presence of a *balance* in his life did allow Andreev to better negotiate his illness experience. Yet, the underlying mental condition always weighed heavily on the author.

In July 1902, Andreev and his wife took a cruise along the Volga River. Andreev wrote to Miroliubov of their vacation and his persistent ill health: 'I still have the nerves to such a degree that in September I am going to again check into the clinic.'[68] Almost a month later, Andreev wrote to the editor of *Russian Riches* (Russkoe bogatstvo), 'My health is wretched and in October I want to check into the clinic.'[69] He wrote to Izmailov at the end of August 1902, 'I sit and am in despair about something invisible. Either it is because I am sick (without an abrupt attack) all of the time and my nerves are like that of a hysterical woman's, or because somewhere, sometime, by some strange turn of events, I have lost and cannot seem to find myself.'[70] Finally in November he went to the clinic for treatment. He quit smoking and did not work while taking water treatments.[71] In the 3 November number of *Courier* was published a note from the editor:

Today we announce, that the belletrist L.N. Andreev has once again succumbed to illness, [who] not more than a year ago, spent about two months in the clinic. Then as now, the illness of the young writer has its origins in the strong overall fatigue and aggregate nervousness [inherent in] his work. We wish him a speedy recovery and resumption of his work at our paper.[72]

In reality, Andreev did not quickly resume his work at *Courier*. Upon the recommendation of his doctors, Andreev decided to take a ten-month hiatus from the draining work of the newspaper and try to support himself and his family with his literary endeavors.[73] Yet, even with such health problems, Andreev experienced the first joys of family life. On 25 December 1902 (according to the Russian calendar) at 11:20 in the evening, the couple welcomed their first child, Vadim.[74]

The performance of madness

Kornei Chukovskii (1882–1969) created a literary portrait of Leonid Andreev shortly after the author's premature death in 1919.[75] In this memoir, Chukovskii identified Andreev as an actor who played various roles in life, on the basis of which he invented characters for his stories. Chukovskii associates this acting with Andreev's creative energy or, more specifically, with his periods of mania. Even though Andreev had been diagnosed as an acute neurasthenic and sought treatment several times, he vigorously defended his sanity in the public sphere. Therefore, Chukovskii situates issues concerning Andreev's mental health within the context of the creative performance.

In Andreev's life and literary work, the creative performance confuses, replicates and disguises mental illness, bringing into doubt what is in/sane behavior. The performance becomes the means for inter-action with mental illness and contextualizes the illness experience. For Andreev, however, the performance is an exercise in deception rather than a means of healing. Through the performance, the audience is to believe that the mentally ill are in fact well. Arguably, Andreev deceived his reading public about his mental health, and yet explored the notion that mental illness is bound with the performance in many works, most clearly in his story and play of the same name, 'The Thought' – although we will discuss several other works for which this is an important motif.

Published in the seventh number of *God's World* (Mir Bozhii) in 1902, 'The Thought' is written as the confession of Anton Kerzhentsev, a medical doctor, after he has killed his childhood friend – Aleksei Savelov. Kerzhentsev, now in an asylum, explains for doctors how he wished to simulate madness so that he could commit the crime without punishment. His crime is presented as a performance in which he convinced those around him that he was mentally ill. After killing Savelov, he begins to doubt his sanity and whether he successfully played the role of the criminally insane. The boundaries between sanity and madness are confused, as are the issues involving the performance – was Kerzhentsev acting or was he actually mad?

In examining 'The Thought' in the context of the illness experience, there are certain motifs (heredity, performance and creativity) that offer insights into Andreev's literary work and how he conceptualized the illness experience. Most significant is the issue of heredity and the idea that mental illness is passed down through the generations. Another is the theatrical aspect of Kerzhentsev's madness – the notion that one can act in/sane. In Chukovskii's memoir and in Andreev's own behavior there is an affinity for presenting mental illness in the context of the performance. In this way, there is an attempt to avoid the stigma of madness. In the performance the individual is only *acting* or, at least, the margins are confounded between the performance and the real, the actor and the 'I.' Andreev suggests in this story that the performance does not negate the effects of mental illness, but only masks the symptoms. Finally, 'The Thought' questions the idea that madness and creativity are connected, such that abnormal behavior is not only acceptable but to be expected from the artist. Here we see the shift in perception away from the artistic and toward the scientific in the area of the irrational. For Andreev, madness is a disease, not the impetus for artistic creation: 'Madness is a fire that is dangerous to play with. A bonfire in a powder magazine is less threatening than the first inkling of madness.'[76]

At first, Kerzhentsev feels confident that he can play the role of a madman, confusing those around him and hiding his true intentions. When planning his crime, Kerzhentsev realizes that his family history of mental illness provides a perfect alibi. He writes:

> The first thing the experts will have to address themselves to is heredity. To my great joy mine turned out to be completely suitable. My father was an alcoholic; his brother, my uncle, ended his days in an insane asylum; while my only sister, now dead, suffered from epilepsy. It is true that everyone on my mother's side was bursting with health. But then, one drop of insanity is enough to poison many generations.[77]

Later, as Kerzhenstev begins to realize that he might in fact be ill, he returns to the issue of heredity:

> I *am insane*. Shall I tell you why?
> First of all, I am condemned by my heredity, the very heredity that pleased

me so when I was conceiving my plan. [...] My heredity and my attacks testify to my predisposition to psychic illness. And, unnoticed by me, it began a long time before I contrived the plan of murder. But, possessing, *like all madmen,* an unconscious cunning and an ability to accommodate my insane actions to the norms of various modes of thinking, I began to deceive not others, as I had thought, but myself.[78]

Heredity is the basis for Kerzhentsev's illness, reflecting Morel's theory that degeneration led to imbecility after several generations. Kerzhentsev echoes popularized medical discourse on the hereditary taint, while also displaying general anxiety that mental illness is not readily identifiable. This leads to the possibility of deception which is carried out via the performance: 'At one time I even considered going on stage, but I abandoned this silly idea: deception, when everyone knows it's deception, loses its value.'[79] Deception is created when the audience does not realize that the actor is playing a role. A problem arises, however, when the performance merges with the real – when the actor can no longer distinguish himself from the theatrical role. Kerzhentsev thinks he is playing the role of a madman, but later discovers that he might have only been pretending to be sane.

As Chukovskii described Andreev's manic behavior in the context of the theatrical performance, Andreev presents Kerzhentsev as a great actor disguised to commit a crime: 'I saw then that I would be able to enact my role. An inclination toward dissimulation has always been part of my character and was one of the forms whereby I strove for inner freedom.'[80] Chukovskii maintained that Andreev did not just play a role, but actually became the character. Andreev describes a similar situation for Kerzhentsev: 'Altogether it seemed to me that an exceptional actor was hidden within me, one capable of combining a naturalness of performance, which at times led to a complete identification with the character portrayed, with a relentless, cold control of the mind.'[81]

The murder is constructed as a type of play with several acts leading to a final outcome. To establish his insanity, Kerzhentsev stages two public attacks. In the first attack he becomes agitated and then falls into deep meditation during a dinner party. Once he has gained his audience's attention, Kerzhentsev swats a wineglass out of his neighbor's hand and smashes his own plate. He is finally subdued by the guests after a struggle. Kerzhentsev writes later in his confession: 'All in all there was nothing accidental about any of this. On the contrary, every detail, no matter how small, had been carefully thought through.'[82] The second attack occurs a month later and Kerzhentsev tells us: 'This time it all had not been so well thought out, but such care was unnecessary since there was an overall plan.'[83] During this performance, he screams obscenities at his friends and fights with them when they try to bring him under control. After these two attacks, still within the context of his performance, Kerzhentsev decides to get a medical certificate for his illness: 'This was perhaps an excessive refinement in the perfecting of my role.'[84] Once diagnosed as ill, he sends a book to his friend, the future victim: 'I even disregarded the fact that from the standpoint of the artistic perfection of my performance, the sending of this gift was excessive.'[85]

A few days later, Kerzhentsev visits Savelov and his wife Tatiana Nikolaevna. He engages them in conversation and then takes a paperweight and bludgeons Savelov to death. After the murder, Kerzhentsev returns home and decides to take a nap in his office: 'My entire body was weary; I felt like an actor who has just performed his role brilliantly.'[86] He now realizes that he might be insane – that while thinking he was only simulating madness, he is actually insane. Later, in explaining to his doctors what happened, Kerzhentsev writes: 'Like a true artist I went too far in my role. I for a time identified myself with an imaginary character, and briefly I lost my sense of who I am.'[87] The role is an expression of his mental illness. The danger is losing oneself and never recovering – from the role or the disease.

In reading 'The Thought' it is important to focus on the illness experience. Kerzhentsev loses the distinction between the role of madman and his own 'I'. Sanity and madness are also conflated and boundaries are confused. The illusion for the actor is that he can create, control and manipulate the role, but Kerzhentsev is not in control: 'One thought splintered into a thousand thoughts, and each of them was strong, and all were hostile.'[88] He is frightened by this lack of restraint, the fact that he cannot manipulate the role to regulate his own mental faculties: 'The most frightening thing that I experienced was the realization that I do not know myself, and never did.'[89] Mental illness has taken away Kerzhentsev's understanding of his own self and therefore the performative act must be reexamined as a mechanism to mask his insanity. Kerzhentsev explains:

> As long as my 'I' was to be found within my brightly lighted head, where everything moves and lives in regulated order, I understood and knew myself, and reflecting on my character and plans, it seemed to me that I was the master. Now I saw that I was not the master but the slave, wretched and powerless.[90]

The mentally ill must deal with the fact that they are not in command of themselves and must thereby devise ways in which to hide the effects of illness if they are to escape detection. The actor is a productive persona engaged in developing various roles, masking the variable mental condition of the individual. Further, as noted in a previous chapter, romantic cultural associations with the artist, genius and madness were turned into romantic philosophy by German intellectuals whereby the artist was vested with a special intuitive connection to nature and an ability to discern a higher truth. Violence, madness and destruction became entwined with notions of artistic rebirth and creation. This line of discourse is found in 'The Thought' when Kerzhentsev suggests that Savelov, who also seems to suffer from some sort of mental illness, is allowed bizarre behavior because he is an artist:

> People close to him, often suffering from his outbursts, and who because of the illogic of human nature loved him very much, tried to find a justification for his defects and for their own feeling and declared him an 'artist.' Indeed it appeared that this meaningless word explained him perfectly and that what to a normal person would appear objectionable thus became tolerable or even good. [...] Moreover, he was unwell. Frequent headaches, insomnia, and these indispositions caused him distress.[91]

The same idea reappears when Kerzhentsev writes about his father:

> He drank heavily, and his intoxication expressed itself only in that his whole behavior became manic and accelerated and then showed abruptly as he dropped off to sleep. Everyone considered him exceptionally gifted, while he simply declared that had he not become a famous lawyer, he would have been a famous artist or writer. Unfortunately, this was true.[92]

These two statements reference the cultural belief that abnormal behavior is acceptable in the context of creativity. The fact that Kerzhentsev believes that he is a great actor is a further extension of this construct. However, Andreev suggests that this is a fallacy. At the time, popular discourse was replacing the idea of the Romantic artist tormented by his muse, with the syphilitic artist whose literary production was a byproduct of deviant behavior. Kerzhentsev does not believe that Savelov's oddities or his father's behavior should be excused. He also realizes that he may have been mad long before he decided to play the role of a madman. Andreev, therefore, discounts the connection between creativity and madness. For Andreev, mental illness is a debilitating disease that causes great suffering for its victims. He also accurately reflects popular perceptions of his time about the artist, the irrational and medical discourse.

In 'The Thought' Andreev explores madness within the framework of the performance. Kerzhentsev fashions himself as an actor, playing the role of a madman in order to commit murder. Although he is successful, he realizes that the role was an expression of his mental illness, that his performance was a lie and that he is insane. Examined as a type of illness narrative, we can infer Andreev's position on several points. Heredity plays a role in mental health and an artistic temperament is not a legitimate diagnosis. The individual engages in a performance to interact with the illness experience, possibly to try and gain control of it. By gaining control of the illness, the actor can then convey his own sense of *self* to his audience. The performative act, therefore, becomes an act of deception, an attempt to mask mental illness from the audience. These suppositions are relevant for an author who had gained rapid fortune and fame and was now the talk of literary criticism and gossip columns alike.

Mental illness and the media

From the very beginning of Andreev's literary career, critics noted the theme of madness in his works. Comments such as '[I]t seems that Mr Andreev needs not a critic but a clinic' became quite common along with reports of the author's recurring illness.[93] Much of this original discourse was generated by the publication of 'The Thought' shortly after his stay in the Imperial university clinic for nervous disorders. It was probably just such gossip that led Andreev to write to the literary critic Izmailov in August 1902, 'By the way, I don't understand a thing about psychiatry and did not read anything for "The Thought."'[94]

Yet, Andreev was designated as a writer who captured the 'psychology of horror' and was compared to Dostoevskii and Poe. The critic, V. Podarskii [N.S. Pusanov], argued that literary reviewers might not be appropriate judges of 'The Thought' and anxiously awaited the opinion of Russian psychiatrists.[95] Nevertheless, after discussing Pierre Janet's (1859–1947) *Obsessions and Psychasthenia*, Podarskii provided his own psychological diagnosis of Andreev's main character, and stated that the story could be situated somewhere between a fantasy and an intellectual work on the disharmony of the human organism.[96]

As noted, at this time there was an uneasy relationship between art and science in their attempt to define the irrational. Psychiatry claimed the abnormal for science as a medicine of the mind. This new medical science, however, was still beholden to its artistic roots, utilizing the literary text to demonstrate psychological conditions. Andreev and his literary works satisfied the needs of psychiatrists because he wrote about the insane and was rumored to be mentally ill himself. These two issues contributed to a large amount of psychiatric literature dedicated to Andreev's literary works.

In 1903, Dr Aleksei Ianishevskii (1873–1936) published *The hero of Leonid Andreev's 'The Thought' from the perspective of a doctor-psychiatrist*.[97] The article developed out of a public lecture at Kazan University, where he was attending physician in the psychiatric clinic from 1897 to 1901. Ianishevskii defended his dissertation on commissural systems in the brain's core in 1903 and the following year became a professor of mental and nervous diseases at Novorossiiskii University in Odessa.[98]

Ianishevskii's article begins as a primer for psychiatry, taking several pages to explain the new science of degeneration theory. Turning to literature because 'it draws material from real life,' he admits that he cannot speak to the literary value of a story, but does 'note that in many types of our contemporary literature one may distinguish sickly traits.'[99] Ianishevskii determines that Kerzhentsev is insane, suffering from defective moral faculties and an elevated sense of self. He believes that the character is a 'complete degenerate' and underscores his heredity.[100]

Following the prevailing scientific theory, Ianishevskii argues that degeneration is caused by the demands of a fast-paced modern society and that Kerzhentsev exemplifies the worst case scenario in the development of the genius-madman. He poses the idea that for every madman there is also a bona fide genius produced from these psychological pressures, and that the benefit to Russia in the arts and sciences outweighs the detriment.

On 18 February 1903, Dr I. Ivanov read a lecture entitled 'Leonid Andreev as artist-psychotherapist,' which was subsequently covered in the *Stock Exchange News* (Birzhevye vedomosti).[101] According to this article, the lecture hall was full to overflow capacity, with people sitting in the aisles, and well-respected psychiatrists, including Vladimir Bekhterev (1857–1927), were in attendance. The aim of the lecture was to address to what extent Andreev's story was an accurate portrayal of madness. Ivanov argued that the symptoms presented in the story fit the requirements of what was then modern-day psychiatry. He further believed that Andreev was the closest to Dostoevskii and Guy de Maupassant (1850–1893) in providing stories worth psychiatric study. Ivanov stated that this was due to Andreev's firsthand knowledge of such matters after spending time in a 'special clinic.'

Andreev promptly wrote an open letter to the *Stock Exchange News* in response to reports of Ivanov's lecture. He stated that his stay in the hospital was not for psychiatric treatment, but for an internal illness – implying some sort of heart condition associated with fatigue. He wrote that he was willing to ignore gossip about his madness, but once it had been reported in a scientific publication and connected to his literary works, he wanted to state for the record that he was not mentally ill.[102] This was the second time, following 'The Abyss' and 'In the Fog,' that Andreev's life and literary works were intertwined and his fiction was used as evidence of his own sickness.

Author Nadezhda Lukhmanova (1840–1907) immediately wrote in Andreev's defense, stating that critics had no right to delve into a person's family history and that there was no reason not to believe Andreev's assertions of mental health.[103] The literary spat was satirized in *News of the Day* (Novosti dnia) in the form of two women gossiping:

— [...] Yes, do you know the news? Your vaunted Leonid Andreev ... Oh, no, he is simply a beauty this one ... Your Andreev ...
— Well what, my dear? Did he go to Egypt?
— Worse ...
— He wrote a drama?
— Worse ...
— My dear, you are terrorizing me ... What is it?
— He's been committed to a madhouse!
— It's not possible my dear!
— I assure you, Kasatochka ...
— I myself, read it with my own eyes. There was even a report about this ...
— You said a 'lecture' my dear.
— Merci! C'est à dire thank you, Kasatochka ... A lecture at the St Petersburg Medical Society ... The lecture of doctor Ivanov.
— But this is terrible my dear!
— Oh, Kasatochka, it ought to have been expected. Even before this he had been in a madhouse ... Every summer he was in a madhouse ... Everybody knows this already.
— My dear, you astonish me!
— Kasatochka, mais je vous jure ... Oh my soul! And you know, I anticipated this long ago ... I saw him at an exhibit. He had, you know, this swagger, comme cher les aliénés ... Just like a madman.
— My dear, but this is nonsense! I recollect, I encountered him last night on the street ...
— Kasatochka, this does not prove anything.[104]

Ivanov responded to both Andreev and Lukhmanova on 1 March 1903 in a letter to the editor of the *Stock Exchange News* stating that he had based his comments about Andreev's medical condition on what he had read in the newspapers as well as what he had heard from others. We must keep in mind that the doctor probably knew some of the psychiatrists who treated Andreev. However, Ivanov retreated from his position since he was unable to substantiate the rumors. He wrote that he respected Andreev's artistic talent and noted his 'indiscretions' in insinuating that Andreev was mentally ill.[105]

The issue would have ended there, if Ivanov had not published his lecture two years later while an attending physician in the psychiatric division of the Uiazdovskaia military hospital in Warsaw.[106] In this version, Ivanov skirted the issue of Andreev's hospitalization by stating that Andreev must have thoroughly studied the primary literature dealing with the mind, deleting the sentence that mentioned Andreev's own psychiatric treatment. Even this would not be enough, Ivanov claimed, if it were not for Andreev's enormous artistic talent, which allowed the author to penetrate 'the secret and hidden corners of the sickly functioning psyche.'[107] It is left to the reader to interpret whether Ivanov meant this ironically, but there is no doubt that the psychiatrist read Andreev's story as an accurate depiction of degeneration. In 1908, Chukovskii raised the issue again, but claimed that the 'benign and even enthusiastic aspersion of Mr Ivanov – [was] a mendacious aspersion based on nothing at all.'[108]

Despite Ivanov's 1903 retreat from making a direct connection between Andreev's literary works and his mental health, critics could not ignore the psychological aspects of Andreev's texts and the public narrative of illness surrounding the author. As examples, the critic Naum Gekker (1861–1920) divided Andreev's stories into three categories: children's, symbolic and psycho-pathological. The first two groupings only contained six stories, while the vast majority of Andreev's works fell into the third category. The stories of childhood included 'Pet'ka at the Dacha,' 'Little Angel' and 'Valia.' The symbolic stories were 'The Lie,' 'Laughter' and 'The Wall.' All of the remaining stories were considered by Gekker to be psycho-pathological. In these, the critic saw a depiction of contemporary society in which people had lost their moral compass, having fallen into the 'black abyss' of individualism and decadence.[109] Prince Aleksandr Urusov (1843–1900) suggested that Andreev reflected the 'sick soul of our generation.'[110] His characters were either feeble individuals fighting against their own human frailty or they were mentally ill and powerless to gain control over themselves.[111] As noted, this discourse was only further enhanced by reports of Andreev's own illness. For example, in 1907 it was reported in *Our Monday* (Nash ponedel'nik): 'L.N. Andreev, arriving in Moscow in order to complete his new play *Love of a Student*, fell seriously ill. Upon advice of a doctor, he must check into the clinic.'[112]

Controversies over 'The Abyss,' 'In the Fog' and 'The Thought' only made Andreev more popular at home and abroad. As a result, he signed an agreement with a German publisher (lasting through 1 January 1910), giving the publishing house exclusive rights to sell Andreev's works in Germany and other countries outside of Russia. This, in actual fact, established Andreev's copyright as his works would be published in Russian in Germany (a country that recognized copyright law) before they were to be published at home (a country that did not). In this contract it was also stipulated that translations of Andreev's works would be published no later than two years after their original publication.[113] Andreev was now an international literary figure and this success would bring the author great riches, but also significant media attention at home and abroad concerning his mental health.

Apologies

Although Andreev had begun to enjoy a certain level of personal comfort, many of the same demons continued to plague him. One can find countless stories which underline that Andreev's former poverty and loneliness, once addressed with money and marriage, did not lighten the burden on his soul. As a result, it was those who cared most about him, who also suffered the greatest. The following story is only one such example.

On 14 February 1903, Andreev went to Nizhnii Novgorod to see his friend Gor'kii and to help raise money for local school children. For the organized program Andreev read from two of his works – 'The Alarm-Bell' and 'Laughter'. The benefit raised a large amount of money, 600 roubles, for Nizhegorodskii schools and afterward, Gor'kii, Andreev, the singer Mikhail Malinin (1853–1919) and a doctor from Yalta Aleksandr Aleksin (1863–1925) all went back to their host's house for dinner. Andreev proceeded to get extremely drunk and decided that he wanted to return to Moscow. As it was four o'clock in the morning, Gor'kii hid his friend's boots so that he could not leave. Enraged, Andreev grabbed a knife and nearly stabbed Aleksin, driving the blade into a door. At this point, Andreev was allowed to leave. Seven months later, Andreev wrote to Gor'kii of his drunken behavior in this and other instances:

> An unbearable idea – that over us, rational people, might triumph nonsense, that we, good people, giving [our] strength for fine objectives, might clash because one of us, I, in the course of several hours, even days, was insane. If I became psychiatrically sick and committed murder or some sort of beastliness, you would not attach, of course, any particular meaning to this insane behavior. But when I drink, I become a genuine madman. Strange ideas seize me, by which reality disappears, as if in a crooked mirror. I pass through a series of formal manias, beginning with common megalomania [and] finishing with persecution mania; the last lingers for a long time, especially while hungover. I break things, get into fights; often my companions, friends beat me up; they beat me up in the street, on [their] property; once almost four years ago, they practically

knocked out my eye. I remain on my feet, but completely lose consciousness and [my] memory.

Andreev asks for Gor'kii's forgiveness and states that he has sought help
from the psychiatrist Ardalion Tokarskii (1859–1901) and, through the
help of hypnosis, has stopped drinking.[114] In this instance and many,
many others, Andreev's psychological problems are addressed and self-
medicated with alcohol. Once again, Andreev himself connects this
behavior with madness and seeks treatment from a professional psychiatrist. In this continuing pattern of psychological pain, drunkenness and
guilt, we find the true Andreev, not the image of an insane deviant
fomented by journalists and critics, but a man struggling with his own,
real problems.

Institutional spaces: asylums

Boris Zaitsev first met Andreev in 1901 when he was living in Moscow
on Vladimir Dolgorukii Street in a little apartment on one of the top
floors. Andreev then worked in a tiny office with a small window looking
onto a filthy courtyard, furnished with only a leather couch and a simple
desk. Following his marriage and literary success, 'the Andreevs lived
bigger – they had given up their little apartment on Vladimir Dolgorukii
Street long ago, but they still stayed in the area. They lived near the
public garden in Gruziny then on some little street nearby and then only
once on Presnia. The apartments kept getting better and there appeared
a level of prosperity. Often guests appeared; there were literary readings.
At this time the literary group, the Wednesday circle bloomed, on
Wednesdays they gathered at Nikolai Dmitrievich Teleshov's, at Sergei
Sergeevich Goloushev's and at Andreev's.'[115]

Zaitsev often visited Andreev in the mornings. The two talked about
God, death, literature, revolution and war, all of the pressing issues of
the day. Andreev drank tea and paced from corner to corner, extinguish-
ing and then lighting a new cigarette, as he held forth on various topics.
At three Andreev would eat lunch and then take a nap until around
eight, when he again drank strong tea, smoked, and sat down to write all
night. Zaitsev suggests that the process of writing was intoxicating for
Andreev. The night, tea and cigarettes were the fuel that ignited this
process.

This daily routine was facilitated by Aleksandra, who brought a
degree of stability to her husband's life. As early as 1898, Andreev had
written to her that he did not consider a work complete until she had
commented on it.[116] Her role only increased once they were married.

Much like his mother had done, Andreev's wife seemed to buffer him
from the outside world and his emotional turmoil, and this helped him
to function with a greater level of 'normalcy.' Happily married and while
an active member of *Sreda*, Andreev published mainly short stories.[117]
Richard Davies suggests: 'The works Andreev wrote between 1903 and
1906 reflect his new personal and professional fulfillment in their greater
artistic mastery, philosophical range and psychological penetration,
without losing anything of the urgency and ambiguity of earlier
stories.'[118]

In 1904 Andreev published in the eleventh number of the journal
Truth (Pravda) 'Phantoms' about life in an insane asylum. Although
there are fourteen patients in the asylum, the story is mainly concerned
with Georgii Timofeevich Pomerantsev, Petrov and an unnamed patient
who incessantly knocks on closed doors. Pomerantsev in many ways
seems quite sane, helping the staff and other patients, but he is delusional – talking regularly to St Nicholas; believing that he can shed his
earthly body and fly all over the world – and on rare occasions aggressive, the first noticeable sign of his illness. Petrov is afraid of being
murdered and always carries a rock or some other object to fend off the
inevitable attack.

As in 'Once There Was' and 'The Present,' stories that depict life in a
hospital, life in the asylum is juxtaposed with the world outside. 'The
asylum was right on the edge of town, and as seen from the high-road
looked like an ordinary country house lying on the fringe of a small
forest of pine and birch.'[119] It is separated from the neighboring village,
'where dogs barked, cocks crowed and children shouted. There are no
children or dogs here, but a high blank wall instead.'[120] As with the two
stories just noted, the outside world is dynamic, while the hospitals and
asylum are limiting spaces.

The hospital physician Dr Shevyrev spends his free time at the
Babylon, a countryside restaurant, from ten in the evening until early the
next morning. Here the doctor drinks champagne, listens to the gypsy
and Russian choirs and acts as an intermediary between the management of the restaurant and the drunken customers. The outside world of
the *Babylon* is, as we have seen before, full of sounds, smells and energy
that are not found in the asylum:

> Until about midnight he would sit in the large room at one of the
> numerous little tables, amid a colorful sea of faces, voices, dresses, turned
> sideways to the stage where singers – men and women – followed one
> another and occasionally gave way to jugglers and acrobats. Wineglasses
> and tumblers rang, voices merged into a steady lively murmur; perfume
> mingled with the aroma of wine, and beautiful, painted women, tripping

about between the small tables, smiled at Dr Shevyrev, while electric bulbs flooded everything with dazzling, festive light.[121]

The *Babylon* is a whirl of lights, people and voices. At one or two in the morning Dr Shevyrev's friends arrive and he moves to a private room. At first it is cool in the room but soon everything becomes stuffy and less orderly. 'People drank, laughed, all speaking at once and listening to their own voices; they made love, kissed and sometimes fought.'[122] A changing parade of people attends these parties and soon they are entertained by gypsy singers. At five o'clock in the morning, Dr Shevyrev finishes his third bottle of champagne and returns to the asylum.

Iezuitova sees little difference in the *phantoms* that populate the asylum and the *Babylon*. She suggests that for Dr Shevyrev madness is 'great passion, deep emotions, strong desires, efficacious ideas,' and people in both the restaurant and the asylum demonstrate the destructive results of civilization on individuality.[123] She echoes Petrov's brother, who 'has his own views on his brother's illness, something very clever, partly based on science and partly attributing Sasha's illness to the general unsatisfactory conditions of life.'[124] Iezuitova's opinion reflects the influence of degeneration theory in contemporary ideas on mental illness – the belief that the rigors of modern industrialized life sapped the individual's life-force and caused mental illness.

Indeed, Dr Shevyrev does not distinguish between the patrons in the *Babylon* and the patients in the asylum. Iezuitova notes that his reaction is the same for both – he listens and gives the impression that he is wise, but does nothing.[125] Also, the restaurant patrons are phantasmagorical and quite grotesque – a student commits suicide, a merchant is robbed and killed, a gypsy girl possibly dies after an abortion. Again, all signs of a deviant society in the process of devolution.

The name of the restaurant is significant, as are other biblical references to Babylon, the Tower of Babel and the madness of Nebuchadnezzar. Certainly Andreev is referencing the pride and vanity of mankind and the subsequent punishment inflicted upon them. The asylum, however, is a very different place and in many ways is more benign than the restaurant. Therefore, these two spaces are not to be understood as one in the same, nor the activities at the *Babylon* confused with the affective illnesses found in the asylum.

It must be remembered that degeneration was supposedly spreading rapidly in large urban areas, and the fall of Rome was referenced in scientific publications as historical evidence of the results of decadent behavior. Krafft-Ebing wrote in *Psychopathia Sexualis*, 'Large cities are hotbeds in which neuroses and low morality are bred, as is evidence in the history of Babylon, Nineveh, Rome and the mysteries of modern metropolitan life.'[126] Babylon was certainly chosen by Andreev for its symbolic representation of deviance (both biblical and scientific), which makes the contrast with the serene conditions in the insane asylum all the more compelling.

In the asylum, there is a different set of religious references. Pomerantsev has a relationship with St Nicholas, who is one of the most revered Russian Orthodox saints and, among other things, is known for his defense of the falsely accused. In the final chapter, St Nicholas appears alongside Pomerantsev and says to him, 'One can't live in a madhouse and not feel lonely occasionally.'[127] Pomerantsev admits that he feels alone and asks if they can leave, and so they fly away together.

Andreev underlines this difference between the physical spaces with yet another biblical reference. Dr Shevyrev's name and patronymic is Nikolai Nikolaevich, associating him with St Nicholas, though Pomerantsev says that Dr Shevyrev is more like St Erasmus.[128] The Monk Erasmus of the Kiev Caves, after giving his entire fortune to the Orthodox Church, succumbed to temptation, fell into despair and lived an aimless and lawless life until he repented three days before his death. Pomerantsev associates Dr Shevyrev's trips to the *Babylon* with the aimless life of St Erasmus and maintains the sanctity of St Nicholas for the asylum alone.

In viewing the two physical spaces differently, the madness of the *Babylon* is associated with the vanity and pride of Nebuchadnezzar,[129] and the patients in the asylum with the patron saint of the falsely accused. As in Andreev's other stories, institutional spaces separate patients from the outside world and, therefore, the incessant knocking by the unnamed patient, the need to open all locked doors, takes on added relevance. 'Phantoms' ends: 'The night wore on, and he continued knocking. The lights at the "Babylon" were going out, one by one, but he went on knocking, madly-insistent, tireless, well-nigh deathless.'[130] In light of the literary works to come, it can be argued that Andreev was beginning to depict mental illness as a prison sentence. After all, none of the patients recover and the only escape is death.

In a letter to his friend, Andreev asserts that Gor'kii is like Pomerantsev and Andreev himself is the madman continually knocking.[131]

The only noise that perpetually disturbed the silence, day and night, for ten years – ever since the home was first opened – was so regular, muffled and unvarying that no one paid any attention to it, just as people no longer notice the ticking of a clock or the beating of their own hearts. It was one of the patients locked in his room knocking at his door; wherever he was he always found a locked or closed door and began to knock at it; if this door were opened he promptly found another which was shut and began to knock at that: he wanted all doors to be open. He knocked day and night – numb with weariness. Probably the intensity of his crazy desire had enabled him to train himself to knock while he slept; otherwise he would have died long ago from lack of sleep; for the knocking never ceased and no one ever saw him asleep.[132]

Scholars have used Andreev's comparison to examine the relationship between the two authors, suggesting that it represents Gor'kii's optimism and Andreev's continual questioning of the status quo. But these scholars have not explored what this might mean in the context of Andreev's literary works.[133]

In 'Phantoms,' Pomerantsev flies away with St Nicholas, while the unnamed patient is left endlessly knocking in the asylum – metaphorically abandoned and imprisoned. One might argue that having defended his sanity in the press, Andreev was knocking to open the doors of the metaphorical asylum in which the press had placed him. Certainly, patients committed to a mental asylum by friends and relatives, as is the case in 'Phantoms,' would feel falsely accused, especially while other unstable individuals live in the outside world inhabiting places like the *Babylon*. The problem with this interpretation is that the patients in the asylum *are* mentally ill. There does not seem to be any doubt about this. We might look at the reference in another way, given that Andreev wrote two stories involving prisons tinged with madness: Andreev equated mental illness with a prison sentence from which there was no escape. The doctors can provide no cure and the only relief is through complete insanity or death.

The Wednesday circle

Teleshov remembers one evening around this time, the autumn of 1904, when Gor'kii, Miroliubov and Shaliapin were all in Moscow and planned to come to the Sreda meeting. The place was packed when Shaliapin arrived and told everyone that he just had to sing:

> [Shaliapin] went over to the telephone and called up [Sergei] Rakhmaninov and said: 'Serezha, get yourself a likhach [horse-drawn cab] and hop round to Sreda quick. I'm bursting to sing. We'll sing all night!'
>
> Rakhmaninov was soon there. Shaliapin did not even give him time for a cup of tea. He sat him down at the piano, and something very wonderful began. This was at the very height of Shaliapin's fame and powers; he was in a great mood, and sang literally without end. There was no reading *that* evening, nor could there be. He was inspired, possessed. Never anywhere at any time was there so much magic as he

was that night. He himself said, several times: 'This is me – not at the
Bolshoi!'

Shaliapin fired Rakhmaninov, and Rakhmaninov set Shaliapin on fire;
and these two, urging each other on, achieved a miracle. This was not
music nor singing as anyone had ever known it – it was the inspired
ecstasy of two great artists.[134]

It is difficult to imagine the collective success that the participants of
Sreda were experiencing at this time. Many of them had come from such
humble beginnings that this newfound celebrity must have been
absolutely intoxicating. It was certainly the case for Andreev. After all,
these meetings were not always centered on literary discussions. Food,
drink and song were just as often the main attraction. Sometimes
Skitalets would bring his gusli (a multi-string lyre-type instrument) and
sing Volga songs. Most meetings consisted of twenty to twenty-five
people. However, on special nights, there might be as many as fifty. For
example when Andreev or Gor'kii read one of their new stories, or if
Shaliapin planned to make an appearance, this was considered a *special
occasion*.

Along with the regular meetings, there were also special *Sreda* events,
to which people from other literary movements were invited. Many of the
decadent writers such as Bal'mont, Briusov, Belyi and Sologub attended
these events, which were usually held at either Andreev's or Goloushev's.
Belyi would later write of his attendance at the literary circle:

I remember him standing before me in the middle of an empty, illumi-
nated, square room uncrowded by objects – his apartment on Presnia
street. It is obvious that people were sitting in this room moments ago.
Chairs are variously placed about in intricate patterns – in groups of twos
and threes, half turned to one another. They describe the arrangement of
the guests only just seated. Everyone has moved on. There in the doorway
to the neighboring room, they move about – and they seem to be absurd
silhouettes. The honking of human voices resounds indistinctly. It might
be that they are eating appetizers and probably Teleshov, Aleksei Evgen'e-
vich Gruzinskii,[135] the late Sergei Sergeevich Goloushev, the artist
Pervukhin,[136] Ivan Belousov, Timkovskii and Chirikov, and other participants of the Wednesday circle are there. I do not remember who is there.
Before me in the empty room is Boris Konstantinovich Zaitsev, asking me
about something. He seems undersized to me only due to the fact that the
really quite large and stout figure of Leonid Nikolaevich [Andreev] is
leaning heavily on Boris Zaitsev's shoulder, half-embracing him, resting
one foot on an empty chair. Leonid Nikolaevich is staring at me with a
sharp, piercing glance; his black eyes quite astonishing, setting off the
whiteness of a calmly hardened face, with a loose black strand of somehow
disheveled hair, cutting his forehead in two.

The entire scene of memories is like a flash.

I do not remember what I said to Boris Konstantinovich Zaitsev. I do not remember what followed. What did Leonid Nikolaevich and I talk about? I do remember that a decidedly trivial conversation occurred between us, producing the impression that we had both made every effort to talk only of things that scarcely mattered to us. Meanwhile, the black gaze of Leonid Nikolaevich, sharply and curiously fixed on me from behind his white face, said:

'Yes, yes, – no use trying to wriggle out of it, brother mine.'

'It doesn't matter what is said. What matters is what is *behind* it. '

'Come on, come on, show me what is going on inside of you.'

'How do you look at things when you are all alone?'

That is what I heard said by the unblinking glance slicing through the conversation about art that transpired between us. His very pale cheeks and nose, very pale, a small beard, tufts of unmoving hair – this all seemed to have absolutely nothing to do with the discourse that was taking place between us.

It was then that I sensed that Leonid Nikolaevich had become close and dear to me; and yet during these years we were in opposite camps. We *Scorpion* writers regarded the writers of *Knowledge* as opponents, while the writers of *Knowledge* regarded us at best as 'eccentrics, at worst – as something like traitors to the traditions of the public good.'[137] Earlier, the creative works of 'Leonid Andreev' to a large degree seemed to me profoundly congenial. I made an effort, mixed with a kind of annoyance at the fact that Leonid Nikolaevich 'did not see' us, to be restrained. I tried to be cordial with this celebrated writer, towards whom newspaper columnists acted subserviently, while victimizing and insulting us. Finally, I practically did not know Leonid Nikolaevich personally – all of this raised a fence between us, but finally through the 'fence' an attentive, curious glance suddenly penetrated my soul, encouraging me, as if saying: 'Literary schools and their opinions about one another are such nonsense. We are all equally lonely in the ultimate things, in our nocturnal existence.'

All of this lasted an instant (a flash of magnesium in the darkness) and the glance from behind the words remained with me – a little sad, sympathetic 'through it all.' No, I do not even remember what year this was – maybe 1905 or maybe 1906? I do not remember whether this was the same evening we first met, or whether the meeting took place at Sergei Sergeevich Goloushev's, at one of those delightfully cozy *Wednesday* meetings. I used to go then to these Wednesday gatherings and there I argued with writers remote from ourselves in terms of style and tastes. Sergei Sergeevich Goloushev usually started the arguments, about Symbolism, which I defended and which were attacked by this or that writer from *Knowledge*. (By the way, the arguments were conducted in a completely friendly manner. A wonderful atmosphere at the Andreev-Goloushev Wednesday meetings did not allow things to degenerate into tabloid tones.) Then we ate dinner.

For that matter, I do not remember when I met Leonid Andreev. How we met, what was said between us, again I cannot recall. I was familiar with the massive and seemingly motionless figure of the writer before we met personally. I remember Leonid Nikolaevich, his head rising above the public in the foyer of the Moscow Art Theater. He seemed to be frozen in conversation. I recall him leaning against the wall and around him is a small circle of young ladies, a small circle of students – gazing at the writer with amorous eyes. I recall the black velvet shirt, the high black glossy boots and the silver belt, restraining an expanding girth. That evening on Presnia, in just such a shirt, he stood before me, girded in the same silver belt. He was already close to me. I do not know why.

He was very affectionate and a hospitable host. Every movement of his ample body reminded me by its rhythm of his strange hieratic phrases. It seemed that everything he did, he did in front of himself; he observed himself in sharp focus among us, separated by spaces: from himself; and he was looking: *from there to here*; his experiences were *over there*, while his learning took place here; his knowledge was never overlaid upon his experiences; his knowledge was ordinary; his experiences were prodigious; regarding himself through his knowledge, he saw emptiness (instead of images of the other world); feeling and probing the texture of life through his experience, he saw: incoherence, to which he tried to lash himself so as not to plummet into a reality about which he consciously knew nothing: a split, and enormous loneliness; you could be sitting next to him: a man like any other; yet – no, no: not like any other; you could sit next to him, but you cannot touch him. Like a traveler leaning against a window where a group of friends is having a banquet, he convinces himself that he, too, is actually here – *with everyone*. Hence his 'theatricality,' which was an effort to coordinate the rhythm of his emotions from *over there to here*, so as to reach for a glass; for anyone else, that would be natural, but for Andreev, any gesture was the result of a great many efforts: to will from *over there* (from the constellation Canis Major, perhaps) so that the exertion of his will enters an *apparatus* representing the temporal and spatial shell of the 'Andreev' sitting next to Bunin – just imagine – in Presnia.

The spatial shell tries to be like everyone else: a gesture of effort seems a pose. In his liveliness he is *too lively*; in silence, too slow-moving. A sudden sharp glance, a flash of magnesium that bridges spaces: from over there; a flash that abolishes the representation of 'Leonid Andreev,' hence the shell is incapable at any time of assuming the pose of Doctor Kerzhentsev: – quickly dropping to all fours.

That evening I understood all of this. It seemed that he understood that I understood. The words did not seem interesting. I kept casting my glance at him 'from over there.' He felt that I was looking. Twice I caught a quick glance – goodhearted and a little ironical – cast at me, catching me, and I understood from where it was that he set his Kerzhentsev 'on all fours.' And he understood what dictated to me the phrase, 'There is no hope for a person who has sat down on the floor.'[138]

And that is how he remained for me; in the realm of infrequent meetings; I met him, but I did so *from there – to there*. In everyday life he could scold me and I could be indignant with the *Knowledge* writers for their inability to understand.[139]

The literary circle played a very important role in Andreev's life. More than just a boost to his career, *Sreda* provided him with lasting friendships. For the most part, these men were like Andreev and had experienced significant material hardship before finding themselves the toast of Moscow's cultural scene. These were undoubtedly heady times, shared with close friends. Not surprisingly, Andreev felt that he had finally come out on top – personally and professionally. Yet, as Belyi notes and as will be discussed in more detail in coming chapters, there was a theatricality about Andreev. He performed a role, the part of a successful literary personage, even as there was an internal truth about himself that he did not wish to share with the public.

Andreev's literary success was established, in part, by the controversy that surrounded 'The Abyss' and 'In the Fog.' 'The Thought' and the public spat over his mental health further solidified Andreev's position as a leading literary figure in the eyes of the public. This celebrity was then confirmed with the positive reception from all sides of 'The Life of Vasilii Fiveiskii', published in the first *Znanie* collection, which will be discussed later in this book. One could say that by 1904, Andreev had arrived as both a writer and personality both in Russia and abroad. His personal life was settled with his marriage to Aleksandra and the birth of their first son and by the fact that he could finally provide financially for his mother and siblings. Andreev also enjoyed the friendship and camaraderie of *Sreda* and the respect of those in other literary camps.

The unifying theme of many of the works upon which his fame was based was the tenuous nature of the human psyche and the horrific results that occur once the civilized mind gives way to the bestial or irrational. His celebrity grew, partly, as it was revealed that his characters' maladies were reflections of Andreev's own frailties. He soon was considered a bellwether for Russia and this perceived responsibility would eventually draw Andreev further into the political and social debates that were soon to dominate the social discourse.

Notes

1 Zaitsev, *Kniga o Leonide Andreeve*, 128–9 / 94.
2 The meetings originally took place on Wednesdays.

3 Teleshov, *Kniga o Leonide Andreeve*, 149–51; In English, see White, *Memoirs and Madness*, 109–10.

4 Iezuitova, L. *Tvorchestvo Leonida Andreeva (1892–1906)* (Leningrad: Izdatel'stvo Leningradskogo universiteta, 1976) 81–2.

5 Andreev, 'Zhili-byli,' vol. 1, *Sobranie sochinenii v 6 tomakh*, 277.

6 Ibid., 279.

7 Ibid., 280.

8 Ibid., 279.

9 Ibid., 288.

10 Ibid., 295.

11 Belousov, *Ushedshaia Moskva*, 246.

12 This assertion is made by Vadim Chuvakov in the commentary to vol. 1, *Sobranie sochinenii v 6 tomakh*, 605.

13 Vadim Andreev, *Detstvo*, 158; in English, see Vadim Andreyev, *Childhood*, 109.

14 Andreev, 'Zhili-byli,' 283.

15 Ibid., 286.

16 A 'fortochka' is a small paned window within the frame of a larger window. This allows for a breeze without opening the entire window.

17 Andreev, 'Zhili-byli,' 286–7.

18 Pavel Andreev, 'Vospominaniia o Leonide Andreeve,' 195.

19 Andreev, 'Gostinets,' vol. 1, *Sobranie sochinenii v 6 tomakh*, 296.

20 Ibid., 295.

21 Ibid., 296.

22 Ibid., 297.

23 Ibid., 300.

24 Ibid., 301.

25 Ibid., 302.

26 Woodward, *Leonid Andreyev: A Study*, 22.

27 As quoted in Ken and Rogov, *Zhizn' Leonida Andreeva*, 96.

28 Afonin, *Leonid Andreev*, 107.

29 Ibid., 126–7.

30 Ibid., 66; Avram Brown, 'Leonid Nikolaevich Andreev,' 25.

31 Møller, Peter Ulf. *Postlude To The Kreutzer Sonata: Tolstoj and the Debate on Sexual Morality in Russian Literature in the 1890s*. Translated by John Kendal (Leiden: E.J. Brill, 1988) 210.

32 Bezzubov, *Leonid Andreev i traditsii russkogo realizma*, 13; 20–3.

33 Engelstein, Laura. *The Keys to Happiness: Sex and the Search for Modernity in* Fin-de-Siècle *Russia* (Ithaca: Cornell University Press, 1992) 368–9; 371–2.

34 Belyi, Andrei. 'Vospominaniia ob Aleksandre Aleksandroviche Bloke.' In *Aleksandr Blok v vospominaniiakh sovremennikov v dvukh tomakh*, vol. 1. Edited by V. Orlov (Moscow: Khudozhestvennaia literatura, 1980) 205–7.

35 Schopenhauer, Arthur. *The Philosophy of Schopenhauer*. Edited by Irwin Edman (New York: Modern Library, 1956) 278; 343.

36 Ibid., 34.

37 As quoted in Kaun, *Leonid Andreyev: A Critical Study*, 73.

38 Andreev, 'Bezdna,' vol. 1, *Sobranie sochinenii v 6 tomakh*, 363. In English, I

use the translation of 'The Abyss' and page reference for: Andreyev, Leonid. *Visions: Stories and Photographs by Leonid Andreyev*. Edited and Introduced by Olga Andreyev Carlisle (San Diego: Harcourt, Brace, Jovanovich, 1987) 180.

39 Ibid., 366 / 182.

40 The history of *Kreutzer Sonata* is in Møller, *Postlude to The Kreutzer Sonata*.

41 This assertion is strenghtened by a 1903 publication of 'The Abyss,' which included Nemovetskii's 'letter to the editor' as well as two other letters to the editor written in the name of Zina and a peasant – Feodor. Also, a literary critique by Tolstoi on pornographic literature was included in this publication. See Andreev, Leonid. *Bezdna. S stat'ei L'va Tolstogo i polemicheskoi literaturoi* (Berlin: Ioanna Rede, 1903).

42 Andreev, 'Bezdna,' commentary, 615.

43 Orwin, Donna. *Tolstoy's Art and Thought 1847–1880* (New Jersey: Princeton University Press, 1993) 154. Also see Greenwood, E.B. 'Tolstoy, Wittgenstein, Schopenhauer: Some Connections.' In *Tolstoi and Britain*. Edited by W. Gareth Jones (Oxford: Berg, 1995) 243–8.

44 Eichenbaum, Boris. 'Tolstoi i Shopengauer' (K voprosu o sozdanii «Anny Kareninoi»). *Literaturnyi sovremenik*, no. 11 (1935): 134–49. Also see Baer, Joachim T. 'Anregungen Schopenhauers in eineigen Werken von Tolstoj.' In *Die Welt Der Slaven. Halbjahresschriften für Slavistik*. Edited by Peter Rehder (Munich: Verlag Otto Sagner, 1979) 225–47.

45 Anisimov, *Gor'kii i Leonid Andreev neizdannaia perepiska*, 218–19. Also see Silard, Lena. 'K voprosu o tolstovskikh traditsiiakh v russkoi proze nachala XX. veka.' *Acta Litteraria Academiae Scientiarrum Hungaricae*, 20 (1978): 215–30.

46 Tolstoi, Lev. 'Kreitserova sonata.' In *Sobranie sochinenii v dvadtsati dvukh tomakh*, vol. 12 (Moscow: Khudozhestvennaia literatura, 1982) 146–7.

47 Anisimov, *Literaturnoe nasledstvo*, 616.

48 Tolstoi, 'Kreitserova sonata,' 152–3. Also see Matich, *Erotic Utopia*, 52–3; Rancour-Laferriere, Daniel. *Tolstoy on the Couch: Misogyny, Masochism and the Absent Mother* (New York: New York University Press, 1998) 80; 197.

49 The literary critic Botsianovskii felt that Andreev captured the animalistic quality of his characters with particular clarity and that this bestial excess was at the root of a majority of his works. Botsianovskii makes specific reference to Krafft-Ebing in his discussion of Andreev's 'The Abyss' and 'In the Fog.' See Botsianovskii, V. *Leonid Andreev* (St Petersburg: Gerol'd', 1903) 32; 46–7.

50 Nordau, Max. *Degeneration*. Translated and with an introduction by George L. Mosse (New York: Howard Fertig, 1968) 160–3.

51 Pozdnyshev claims that he was a fornicator; behavior he associates with morphine addicts, alcoholics and opium smokers – the seeming connection being a lack of moral fortitude (similar to degeneration theory). Tolstoi, 'Kreitserova sonata,' 135. Ruddick argues that 'both writers are suggesting that gynecide is only one symptom of a degenerative pandemic precipitated by modern social conditions.' See Ruddick, Nicholas. 'The Ripper Naturalized: Gynecidal Mania in Tolstoy's *The Kreutzer Sonata* and Zola's *La Bête Humaine*.' *Excavatio*, 14, 1–2 (2001): 181–93.

52 Bezzubov, *Leonid Andreev i traditsii russkogo realizma*, 26.
53 As quoted in Greenslade, *Degeneration, Culture and the Novel*, 92: Lombroso, Cesare. Introduction to Gina Lombroso-Ferrero, *Criminal Man According to the Classification of Cesare Lombroso* (New York and London: G.P. Putnam & Sons, 1911) xiv–xv.
54 Krafft-Ebing, Richard von. *Psychopathia Sexualis*. Translated by Franklin Flaf (New York: Stein and Day, 1965) 3–4.
55 Woodward, *Leonid Andreyev: A Study*, 68, footnote 2.
56 Andreev, 'V tumane,' vol. 1, *Sobranie sochinenii v 6 tomakh*, 451–52. In English, I used the translation of 'In the Fog' by Margo Shohl Rosen and page references for: Lodge, *The Dedalus Book of Russian Decadence*, 259.
57 Ibid., 456 / 265.
58 Krasnov, 'Koshmarnyi pisatel', 39.
59 Andreev, 'V tumane,' vol. 1, commentary, 624–8.
60 Manasein, M.P. 'V meditsinskom tumane. ('V tumane', rasskaz Leonida Andreeva).' *Novyi put'*, 8 (1903): 227.
61 Ken and Rogov, *Zhizn' Leonida Andreeva*, 102–3.
62 Anisimov, *Literaturnoe nasledstvo*, 132 footnote 1; 129.
63 OGLMT, f. 12, op. 1, no. 144 (KP 5692), 89.
64 Teleshov, *Kniga o Leonide Andreeve*, 157 / 114.
65 Ibid.
66 According to the author's brother, Andreev curtailed his drinking once married but never stopped completely. See Pavel Andreev, 'Vospominaniia o Leonide Andreeve,' 152. Gor'kii writes of Andreev: 'He suffered from hereditary alcoholism; his malady would manifest itself at comparatively rare intervals, but nearly always in a very aggravated form. He fought against it, the struggle cost him enormous efforts, but at times, falling into despair he scoffed at his efforts.' See Gor'kii, *Kniga o Leonide Andreeve*, 45. In English, see White, *Memoirs and Madness*, 35.
67 Veresaev, V. 'Leonid Andreev.' In *Sobranie sochinenii v piati tomakh*, vol. 5 (Moscow: Pravda, 1961) 401.
68 Andreev, 'Pis'ma V.S. Miroliubovu,' 95.
69 Andreev, Leonid. 'Pis'ma k N.K. Mikhailovskomu.' In *Literaturnyi arkhiv*. Edited by K. Muratova, 57.
70 RGALI, f. 11, op. 1, ed. kh. 34, l. 3. Letter of 30–31 August 1902 from Andreev to A. Izmailov.
71 Andreev, 'Pis'ma k N.K. Mikhailovskomu,' 60.
72 Anisimov, *Literaturnoe nasledstvo*, 160 footnote 2.
73 Ibid., 165 footnote 3.
74 OGLMT, f. 49, no. 7903/5 of. Letter of 20 January 1972 from Vadim Andreev to Leonid Afonin.
75 Chukovskii, Kornei. 'Iz vospominanii o L.N. Andreeve.' *Vestnik literatury*, 11 (1919): 2–5. This literary portrait was revised and republished in *Kniga o Leonide Andreeve* in 1922.
76 Andreev, 'Mysl',' vol. 1, *Sobranie sochinenii v 6 tomakh*, 392. In English, I use the translation of 'The Thought' and page reference for: Andreyev, *Visions: Stories and Photographs by Leonid Andreyev*, 44.
77 Ibid., 389 / 42.

78 Ibid., 411 / 67.
79 Ibid., 391 / 43.
80 Ibid., 390 / 42.
81 Ibid., 391 / 43.
82 Ibid., 393 / 46.
83 Ibid., 395 / 48.
84 Ibid., 403 / 57.
85 Ibid., 405 / 59.
86 Ibid., 408 / 63.
87 Ibid., 413 / 69.
88 Ibid., 409 / 65.
89 Ibid., 410 / 65.
90 Ibid.
91 Ibid., 383; 385 / 34; 36.
92 Ibid., 399 / 52.
93 Burenin, V. 'Kriticheskie ocherki.' *Novoe vremia*, 9666 (31 January 1903): 2. Also see for example N/A, *Birzhevye vedomosti*, 10234, morning edition (4 December 1907), 2.
94 Grechnev, V. 'Pis'ma L.N. Andreeva k A.A. Izmailovu.' *Russkaia literatura*, 3 (1962): 198.
95 Podarskii, V. [N.S. Rusanov]. 'Nash tekushchaia zhizn': («Mysl'»).' *Russkoe bogatstvo*, 9 (September 1902): 137.
96 Ibid., 142.
97 Ianishevskii, *Geroi rasskaza Leonida Andreeva 'Mysl'' s tochki zreniia vracha-psikhiatra.*
98 Information on Ianishevskii was found on the following websites on 31 July 2007: www.mochola.org/russiaabroad/encyclopaedia/data/28/29014009 025006003018011009010_01012006011018006010_2701700101801901500 3009024.html; www.ihst.ru/projects/emigrants/janishevskii.htm.
99 Ianishevskii, *Geroi rasskaza Leonida Andreeva 'Mysl'' s tochki zreniia vracha-psikhiatra*, 5.
100 Ibid., 29.
101 N/A. 'Leonid Andreev na sude psikhitatrov.' *Birzhevye vedomosti*, 90, morning edition (20 February 1903): 3.
102 *Birzhevye vedomosti*, 103 (27 February 1903): 2.
103 Lukhmanova, Nadezhda. 'Iz chustva spravedlivosti.' *Birzhevye vedomosti*, 105, morning edition (28 February 1903): 2.
104 Pek [V.A. Ashkinnazi]. 'Kstati.' *Novosti dnia*, 7088 (2 March 1903): 4.
105 Ivanov, I. 'O g. Leonide Andreeve i ego kritikakh: Pis'mo v redaktsiiu.' *Birzhevye vedomosti*, 107, morning edition (1 March 1903): 2.
106 Ivanov, "G-n' Leonid Andreev kak khudozhnik-psikhopatolog,' 72–103.
107 Ibid., 101.
108 Chukovskii, *Leonid Andreev: Bol'shoi i malen'kii*, 9–10.
109 Gekker, N. *Leonid Andreev i ego proizvedenie* (Odessa: M.S. Kozman, 1903).
110 Urusov, [A.I.] *Bezsil'nye liudi v izobrazhenii Leonida Andreeva (Kriticheskii etiud)* (St Petersburg: Obshchestvennaia pol'za, 1903) 11.
111 Ibid., 54.
112 N/A. 'Bolezn' pisatelia.' *Nash ponedel'nik*, 3 (3 December 1907): 3.

113 Ken and Rogov, *Zhizn' Leonida Andreeva*, 115.

114 Anisimov, *Literaturnoe nasledstvo*, 178.

115 Zaitsev, *Kniga o Leonide Andreeve*, 129 / 94.

116 LRA, MS 606\G. 8. ii. Letter of 20 November 1898.

117 His works of this time include: 'At the Station' (Na stantsii), 'Spring Promises' (Vesennie obshchaniia), 'The Life of Vasilii Fiveiskii,' 'There is no Forgiveness' (Net proshcheniia), 'Phantoms,' 'Red Laugh,' 'The Thief' (Vor), 'Ben-Tovit', 'Marseillaise' (Marsel'eza), 'The Christians,' 'Lazarus' (Eleazar), 'The Governor', *To the Stars*, *Savva*, 'So It Was' (Tak bylo) and *The Life of Man*. See Chuvakov, V., comp. *Leonid Nikolaevich Andreev: Bibliografiia, vypusk 1; Sochineniia i teksty*. Edited by M. Koz'menko (Moscow: Nasledie, 1995) 40–6.

118 Davies, Richard. *Leonid Andreyev: Photographs by a Russian Writer. An Undiscovered Portrait of Pre-Revolutionary Russia* (London: Thames and Hudson, 1989) 13.

119 Andreev, 'Prizraki,' vol. 2, *Sobranie sochinenii v 6 tomakh*, 74. In English, I use the translation of 'The Phantoms' and page references for: Andreyev, Leonid. *Judas Iscariot and Other stories*. Translated by Walter Morison and E.M. Walton (London: John Westhouse, 1947) 145.

120 Ibid., 74 / 146.

121 Ibid., 86 / 166–7.

122 Ibid., 87 / 169.

123 Iezuitova, *Tvorchestvo Leonida Andreeva (1892–1906)*, 103.

124 Andreev, 'Prizraki,' 95 / 181.

125 Iezuitova, *Tvorchestvo Leonida Andreeva (1892–1906)*, 103.

126 Krafft-Ebing, *Psychopathia Sexualis*, 4.

127 Andreev, 'Prizraki,' 98 / 188.

128 Ibid., 81 / 158.

129 Daniel 4:1–37.

130 Andreev, 'Prizraki,' 99 / 189.

131 Anisimov, *Literaturnoe nasledstvo*, 382.

132 Andreev, 'Prizraki,' 75 / 147.

133 Iezuitova, *Tvorchestvo Leonida Andreeva (1892–1906)*, 101–2; Kaun, *Leonid Andreyev: A Critical Study*, 62; Grechnev, V. 'Rasskaz L. Andreeva «Prizraki».' *Russkaia literatura*, 2 (1997): 69–77.

134 Teleshov, Nikolai. *Zapiski pisatelia: Vospominaniia i rasskazy o proshlom* (Moscow: Moskovskii rabochi, 1966) 64–5. In English, Teleshov, Nikolai. *A Writer Remembers: Reminiscences*. Translated by Lionel Erskine Britton (London: Hutchinson, c. 1945) 46.

135 Aleksei Evgen'evich Gruzinskii (1858–1930), literary critic and pedagogue.

136 Konstantin Konstantinovich Pervukhin (1863–1915), painter and member of the *Wanderers* artistic group.

137 *Belyi's footnote:* 'The Words of Gor'kii.'

138 *Belyi's footnote:* 'First Symphony.'

139 Belyi, *Kniga o Leonide Andreeve*, 178–83. In English see White, *Memoirs and Madness*, 130–3.

5

Loss and rebellion

It began in the morning. Her hand trembled, and she broke a cup; then it all came over her with a sickening shock, and she forgot what she was about, ran from one thing to another, and repeated foolishly. 'Oh God, what am I doing?' … Then finally she was quite silent! And dumb, with stealthy tread, she slid from corner to corner, taking things up and putting them down – moving them from place to place – and even, in the beginning of her madness, hardly able to tear herself away from the stove. The children were in the garden flying their kites, and when little Petjka ran in for a piece of bread he found his mother stealthily hiding all sorts of things in the oven – a pair of shoes, an old coat, and his cap! At first the boy laughs, but when he caught sight of his mother's face he ran shrieking into the street. 'A-a-ai!' he screamed as he ran and set the lane in wild alarm.

Leonid Andreev, 'The Governor'[1]

In June 1904, *Courier* ceased to exist after a prolonged period of financial difficulties. This meant that Andreev now had to earn his livelihood solely as a creative writer. The heady times of his initial success gave way to a period of significant political upheaval and personal loss. Andreev's life was turned upside down by the deaths of both his youngest sister and his wife, while his works began to reflect his own political ruminations, if not vacillations. This chapter concentrates on the ways in which madness interacts with Andreev's personal and fictional narratives of loss and rebellion. The central focus is the period 1904–8, although many of the sections in this chapter are organized thematically rather than in strict chronological order.

Survival of the Fittest

At the beginning of 1904 Nicholas II (1868–1918) declared war on Japan, hoping to gain territory and establish a sphere of influence in the Far East. He had been encouraged in this endeavor by government ministers who wanted to divert the public's attention from their growing dissatisfaction with the Tsar's government. Nicholas and his ministers expected an easy victory even though they only had a single-track railroad to transport supplies to their troops and intended to conduct the war from St Petersburg.

As a result of these blunders and many others, the Russo-Japanese War had significant and long-lasting political and cultural ramifications for Russia. A surprise attack on Port Arthur by the Japanese was only the first blow to Russia's national pride. The eventual loss of political influence in Korea and Manchuria to what was, at the time, considered an inferior nation, raised questions about Russian national fitness and signaled the obvious decline of its imperial power. After all, this was the first major military victory of an Eastern country over a Western one in the modern era. Russia was left practically without a navy and was humiliated in the eyes of its European allies – France and Germany. The ensuing lack of faith in the Romanov dynasty led to the 1905 Revolution and eventually to the Revolutions of 1917.

An underlying issue in this crisis of national faith was the emergence of social Darwinism, concentrating on the fitness of individuals, races and nations. Science was used to legitimate social and cultural practices in an attempt to identify strains of the 'struggle for survival,' especially the 'unfit' elements in this equation. Degeneration clearly played into these discussions as scientific proof of the possibility of individual and national regression and devolution.[2]

The alarm had been raised in 1883 by Francis Galton, but seemed more relevant to Russians after their defeat at the hands of the Japanese; it fueled the fear that the social organism could no longer eliminate the weak from the herd and that the *unfit* had gained differential reproductive success, making the entire Russian nation *unfit*. The British biologist Ray Lankester (1847–1929) noted the devolution of ship barnacles which, over time, went through an atrophy of their physical structure in order to find a less austere environment where food could be more easily obtained. This degenerate crustacean became a symbolic warning light that other species (read: races or nations) could also quit the struggle for survival and move toward parasitism. Russian psychiatrists like Bekhterev provided an explanation for Russia's military defeat in just such language. They suggested that despite its overwhelming numerical advantage, Russia was comprised of weakly developed and degenerate individuals, leading to military defeat at the hands of a healthy Japan.[3]

Andreev was repulsed by this war and took his family mid-March to a Crimean resort in Yalta to escape the never ending public debate. Even there, however, he could not avoid reading daily reports of the staggering losses in Manchuria as the Japanese continually outmaneuvered the larger and less efficient Russian army. At this same time, an explosion due to a welding accident killed a Turkish tradesperson and injured another outside of Andreev's cottage. As the dead body was being carried away, Andreev saw the man's mangled face and, on it, what he called a 'red smile.'[4] This seems to be the initial inspiration for his eventual story 'Red Laugh.'

This, along with one other event, may have influenced Andreev's writing of this story. The weather in Yalta transitioned from a cold and wet spring to an absolutely scorching early summer. A friend of Andreev's was to visit the Crimea for the first time from Siberia. The friend had no sooner arrived, when he went completely insane. After an examination, the doctors claimed that this psychological breakdown was brought on by the abrupt and extreme change in climate.[5]

In October, Andreev finished 'Phantoms,' his story about patients in an insane asylum, in which one of the patients suffers from night visions that are 'warlike and disturbing.' Every night he is attacked by evil creatures and he fights them off with a fiery sword. The battles leave him exhausted, but the patient knows that he will have to fight again the next evening.[6] Here is an early instance where battle is used as a metaphor for mental illness. Following 'Phantoms,' Andreev planned to write a new story called 'War.'[7] The red smile, madness brought on by searing heat, insane asylums and war eventually came together for Andreev at the beginning of November and he wrote 'Red Laugh' in just nine days. Unsure whether the story would be passed by the censor, Andreev suggested that 'Red Laugh' should be published with fifteen to twenty pictures from Francisco de Goya's (1746–1828) *The Disasters of War*, as this would enhance one of the thematic lines in the story – 'the line of madness.'[8]

Teleshov remembers that Andreev reached such a nervous state while writing this story that it was frightening to be in the room with his friend. Only Andreev's wife, Aleksandra, remained in his office as he wrote for nights on end without sleep.[9] Afterwards, physically and mentally exhausted, Andreev felt as though he was near a breakdown. He wrote to Veresaev: 'For eight months [after writing 'Red Laugh'] my head was shattered. I was not able to work and I thought that I would never recover. There were days when frankly [I thought that] by-and-by I would go crazy. I healed myself alone – gave up work, read Dumas and Jules Verne, the boat, the bicycle, the baths, for the summer I went ga-ga, like a minister – and in the fall I was able to proceed freely with work.'[10] Rimma also remembers that while the entire family had rented cottages in Finland that summer to relax, Andreev was still feeling the effects of

'Red Laugh.' He seemed to be overly excited, possibly manic, and constantly on guard. Aleksandra was quite worried about his mental health and would not leave her husband alone. Rimma's patience was tested as she, Pavel and Aleksandra, spent two weeks trying to talk Andreev through this psychologically difficult state.[11]

Viewed in the context of illness narrative theory, 'Red Laugh' takes on new relevance. As already noted, Andreev was concerned with his public image and realized that his fame was connected to his celebrity as much as to his literary works. At the time, mental illness, unlike the Romantic notion of the tortured artist, was something to hide and deny since it was becoming more closely related to the psychopath and social deviant. In the United States, neurasthenia and its resulting treatment were different for men and women. Women were obliged to rest, while men required vigorous activities. Tom Lutz writes that many men took cures that involved militaristic discipline, moral accountability and incessant exercise such as horseback riding and alpine hiking.[12] Morris makes an interesting argument that mental illness of the time was regularly associated with 'female pain.' Male pain was much more open and tended to be exhibited in public spaces: street fights and combat.[13] Therefore, it is not surprising that Andreev would be ashamed of his neurasthenic condition and might try to contextualize it in the 'male' arena of war. By transferring his illness experience into a military context, he associates his experience with neurasthenia with valor and duty as opposed to hysteria and weak-mindedness. The sufferer is heroic in his struggle with mental illness, not frail and unable to cope with the demands of life.

Andreev's exploration of mental illness is thus conveyed through narrative fragmentation in which time and space are confused, underscored by the depiction of sleeplessness, resulting in disorientation, exhaustion and anxiety. Andreev uses the metaphor of war to communicate the struggle that occurs within the individual when there is no clear enemy or alien force. A battle may be fought, but eventually the *self* is traumatized and mutilated – both physically and mentally. For Andreev, there is no cure or hope for treatment; therefore the discourse is of inevitable insanity. Doctors offer no medical remedy and seem mad themselves.

For sufferers of mental illness, writing a personalized text often becomes a means of gathering a fragmented self into a narrative whole. The individual must confront the problem that this 'natural self' is rooted in disease, in the abnormal, and that the lack of control over himself, his own mind, constitutes a confused sense of personal identity.[14] 'Red Laugh' is Andreev's attempt to bring narrative coherence to his own struggle with neurasthenia. This is a quite plausible alternative to the standard *anti-war* reading that 'Red Laugh' usually receives, and better situates this story into the larger context of Andreev's life and literary works.

The critical response to 'Red Laugh'

In 1904–1905 several highly patriotic works were published in support of Russian troops fighting in the Far East. Tolstoi wrote 'Come to your senses!' (Odumaites'!) in opposition to the war. This led to other anti-war texts, and Andreev's 'Red Laugh' was read in the same context.[15] Most of the authors opposing war wrote in a realistic, historically accurate style. Andreev's story was different in that it used what has been called an 'expressionistic' style and concentrated on the destruction of the human psyche. Although others wished to read the story as pertaining directly to the Russo-Japanese War, Andreev called it a fantasy on the theme of a future war between future peoples.

When the story was published, most critics from the various ideological camps (including later Soviet scholars) praised the story without giving it in-depth analysis. Negative criticism concentrated on structural problems such as confusion over the narrative voice(s); abuse of artistic license in the depiction of war; dissatisfaction with the grotesque imagery of psychosis. Very few of the author's contemporaries or later critics paid attention to Andreev's 'psychological analysis' of war or his stated goal of wanting to depict 'madness and horror.' Those who did pay attention to this theme ignored Andreev's description of individual torment, instead reading it as a collective psychological experience.

Shortly after reading a draft of 'Red Laugh' in 1904, Gor'kii wrote to Andreev that critics would concentrate on the soldier's 'psychiatric abnormalities' and that he could even envision an article entitled: 'A Madman's Portrayal of War.'[16] Six years later, Dr Aleksandr Mumortsev (1879–?), a clinical psychiatrist who published several articles on the psychopathological nature of Andreev's literary characters, wrote that 'Red Laugh' was one of the more exact descriptions of mental confusion and the progressive loss of mental capabilities that had been offered. He proposed that Andreev chose the subject 'war' because it enabled him to describe the 'sensations' associated with such a loss.[17] Mumortsev stopped short of suggesting that Andreev might have experienced these anxieties himself.

Laughter as a marker of madness

'Leonid Andreev never laughed with an expansive, loud laugh, the way unblighted people laugh, only a passing, pale smile curled his lips,' describes Sergei Elpat'evskii (1854–1933). 'He never roared with laughter.'[18] Nikolai Evreinov (1879–1953) wrote that Andreev associated the sad and terrible elements of life not with tears or even disgust, but with laughter.[19] To understand madness in Andreev's literary works, it is important to identify the major themes as well as the signifiers that he employs. One of the most consistent signifiers of madness is laughter, which Andreev utilizes as an outward sign of mental illness. This device is used because insanity is difficult to identify and describe. There are no distinct physical markers and the afflicted is not quite sure whether or not he is insane. Bezzubov argues that laughter is connected to the psychological condition of Andreev's characters,[20] thereby providing a shorthand marker for the mental condition of the individual, even if the character is not aware of it.

In one of Andreev's early works from 1901, 'Laughter,' republished in 1904 as 'Three Questions' (Tri voprosa), we find an initial experiment with the signifier. In this story Elena Nikolaevna has left the main character waiting in the cold for two and a half hours, having gone instead to a Christmas party. He and some friends decide to rent costumes and crash the party. The main character's costume of a 'Chinaman,' causes great laughter among his friends due to the facial expression of the mask. After some time at the party the main character speaks to Elena Nikolaevna, who also finds him quite funny in his costume. He says to her: 'It is shameful to laugh. Do you mean that behind my funny mask you do not feel the real suffering face – after all I wore [the mask] only so that I could see you? Why didn't you come [to our date]?'[21] She answers this question with 'cruel laughter' and he looks at himself in the mirror and also begins to laugh angrily and despairingly at how ridiculous he appears. He shouts at her: 'You should not laugh!' He proceeds to tell her about his love for her, his jealousy and the despair that she causes him. Just as he thinks that he has touched her heart, she again begins to laugh at him. On the way home, the main character's friend tells him that he and his costume were the hit of the party, but he is in such despair that he tears the costume apart. According to Fatov, this story is based on a real event that occurred between Evgeniia Khludeneva and Andreev.[22] In this story Andreev begins to associate laughter with despair, pain and rejection. We find no joy or happiness in Andreev's laughter.

Two months after writing 'Laughter,' Andreev published 'The Lie' in the 20 February 1901 number of *Courier*. He edited the final draft of the story while under the treatment of Professor Cherinov for acute neurasthenia.[23] It is in this story that laughter is first associated with madness. The hero is consumed by rage caused by the infidelity and deception of his beloved. He is quite literally driven mad by jealousy and eventually kills her. In this early work, we find the confusion associated with mental illness and witness the signifier of madness in the character's laughter:

> I killed her. I killed her and while a lifeless and flat mass, she lay at this window, beyond which the dead field turned white. I stood with my feet on her corpse and laughed. This was not laughter of the insane, oh no! I laughed because my chest breathed evenly and easily, and the inside of it was happy, calm, and empty, and from my heart fell the worm, having oppressed it. And, bending over, I stared into her dead eyes. Large, hungry for the light, they remained open and were similar to the eyes of a wax doll – so round and dim, exactly like they were covered with mica. I was able to touch them with my fingers, close and open, and it was not frightening, because in the black, impenetrable pupil already this demon of lies and doubt did not live, which for so long, so greedily drank my blood.
>
> When they grabbed me I was laughing and to these clutching people it seemed horrible and wild. A few, with disgust, turned away from me and went to the side; others directly and menacingly, with a reproach on their lips, approached me but when their eyes fell on my bright and happy look, their face turned white and the earth riveted their legs to the spot.
>
> 'Insane,' they said and it seemed to me these words comforted them because it helped them understand the riddle: how, being in love, I was able to kill my loved one – and laugh. And only one, fat, red cheeked and happy called me by other words, and it hit me and eclipsed the light in my eyes.
>
> 'Poor thing!' he said with compassion and without spite, because he was fat and happy. 'Poor thing!'
>
> 'Don't!' I shouted. 'Don't call me that!'
>
> I do not know why I rushed at him. Of course, I did not want to kill him, not even touch [him] but all of these frightened people, having seen in me the craziness and villainous [actions], were frightened even more and began to shout such that it again became funny.
>
> When they led me from the room, where lay the corpse, I loudly and persistently repeated, looking at the happy, fat man:
>
>> 'I am happy! I am happy!'
>> And this was true.[24]

Although the character denies being insane, and instead suggests that his laughter is a sign of the relief of being liberated from jealousy, the reader is quite aware that the character is ill. All of the witnesses understand him to be insane and it is only when one of them takes pity on the main character that he becomes upset.

Following this work, laughter becomes a semi-regular indicator of madness in Andreev's repertoire. Bezzubov argues that laughter represents more than just the psychological state of the lone character, and is an expression of madness itself.[25] Vasilii Fiveiskii chuckles at his own madness at the end of the story 'The Life of Vasilii Fiveiskii' (1904).[26] In 'Phantoms,' Andreev writes:

> He wore spectacles with very thick lenses, and when he laughed he bared his gums, so that it looked as if the whole of him was laughing, both outside and inside, and that even his hair was laughing too. He laughed very often. His voice was low – a gurgling bass that sounded as though someone was sitting on him and bouncing up and down; but when he laughed very much it changed to a high tenor.[27]

In *Black Maskers* (1908), Andreev's directions to the actors suggest that there should be a note of insanity in Duke Lorenzo's laughter, and later in the play laughter is further connected to his madness.[28] In Andreev's novel *Sashka Zhegulev* (1911), Foma Nevernyi appears in the camp of Sashka Zhegulev and plays the role of the holy fool.[29] In the story 'He' (1913), laughter is one of the signs that the narrator is insane although he is not sure of this himself:

> I remember ever since that convulsive, absurd, idiotic laugh, which pulled my mouth apart like the bridled mouth of a horse. I remember that agonizing feeling of fear and some kind of wild submission, when, left alone, completely alone in my own room or on the shore of the ocean, I suddenly began to experience a strange pressure on the muscles of my face, an insane and insolent demand for laughter, even though for me it was not only humorless but even joyless.[30]

In a collection of anecdotes, which are anything but funny, Andreev tells us that prisoners are often driven to madness. In one case a prisoner is deprived of sleep and falls into states of uncontrollable laughter, which usually then turn into a yawn.[31] Here Andreev plays with the notion of laughter on two levels: on the surface 'My Anecdotes' (Moi anekdoty; 1915) is a collection of tragic stories which might elicit only a 'humorless and joyless' laughter, and in a deeper sense it is an indication of the sleep deprivation and madness of the prisoner.

Bezzubov views Andreev's use of laughter as grotesque and carnivalesque, connecting it to both European and Russian traditions. He pays particular attention to the Satanic and demonic laughter that represents 'cosmic provocation' and the 'terrible world' (control over man's fate and psyche). This is an important connection in that phantoms, devils and Satan are linked to madness in many of Andreev's works. Bezzubov argues that Andreev's use of laughter allows his characters to fight against fate, while laying bare the mechanism of the psyche and providing an element of catharsis.[32] As Bezzubov notes, Andreev's use of laughter is complex and contains multiple meanings. However, it must also be argued that laughter is more often an indicator of the psychological state of the main character, representing terror rather than joy.

'Red Laugh'

'Red Laugh' is also subtitled 'Fragments of a Manuscript' and is just that – textual fragments loosely arranged in chronological order, which often have no definite beginning or end. The first nine fragments constitute the story of a soldier. The first fragment begins with the line: 'madness and horror.'[33] The reader is immediately plunged into a world gone mad as the soldier's unit marches under a burning sun and then comes under attack. In this world, there is no sleep. For three days the unit fights the enemy at a distance, enduring a barrage of shells. Constant reference is made to hours and days on end without slumber. The lack of rest promotes a distorted understanding of reality for the characters in the story – 'ten hours without a break, without slowing down, without picking up those who collapsed but leaving them to the enemy.'[34] In the second fragment: 'We had not slept or eaten for twenty hours. Hellish thunder and screeching had shrouded us in madness for three whole days, cutting us off from the earth, the sky, our own men – those of us still alive, stumbling around like lunatics.'[35] This disorientation creates confusion between reality and dream. For a moment the hero thinks that he is home and then realizes that he has finally fallen asleep, if only for a second. The third fragment brings him back to the lunacy of the present moment.

> madness and horror.
>   They say that a lot of men suffering from mental illness have appeared in our army and in the enemy's as well. Four psychiatric wards have been set up on our side. When I was at headquarters, one of the adjutants showed me around.[36]

After the battle, the soldier visits some of his comrades in the field hospital, where he learns that his unit is to go on the offensive the following day. Five days he has been without sleep and each time he begins to doze off, a doctor prods him. The doctor asks for his help because he needs to move patients onto the train, but everyone is asleep – everyone except the soldier and the doctor. The doctor is mad (or perceived to be so by the soldier). As they collect bodies, the soldier watches as one orderly, driven mad, shoots himself. Another orderly bangs his head against the train and threatens to do the same.

The next day, the soldier takes part in the offensive and both of his legs are blown off. He is sent home and, once there, it is apparent that the soldier is going insane. His family is clearly concerned by his state and only his brother is able to relate to him. The soldier's illness finally gives way to a type of dementia where there is no concept of temporal markers and general cognition is lost: 'I had become absentminded and often could not identify familiar faces. Even in a simple conversation, words would escape me, or else I could not, for the life of me, remember the meaning of a word. I had a clear picture of my days: they were strange, short, chopped off like my legs, with mysterious empty spaces, long hours when I was unconscious or insensible, of which I remembered nothing.'[37]

In Part II of 'Red Laugh,' there is a narrative shift to the soldier's brother, as the soldier has died after a period of 'creative ecstasy.' The brother tells the reader that the soldier wrote steadily for two months without leaving his wheelchair, refusing to eat. He did not sleep until he was twice medicated and forced to sleep for a couple of hours: 'but, after that, even drugs were powerless to overcome his creative fever.'[38] He smoked cigarette after cigarette and was highly agitated: 'at the slightest touch he would have a fit of weeping or of laughter. Once in a great while he would relax, blissfully, and would chat with me [i.e. the brother] in a benevolent way.'[39] The death of the soldier leads the brother to contemplate his own mental health. The brother claims that he feels 'like a fly between the panes of a double window. I rush around striking transparent, impenetrable barriers.'[40] He understands his illness as a debilitating disease that affects the brain.[41] He spends three days without sleep, which brings on feelings of remoteness and alienation.[42] The brother begins then on a downward spiral into madness which results in hallucinations and disorientation, similar to those experienced by the soldier. The brother is aware that he is going mad. He follows the war in newspapers, rails against it and associates the battles with his own struggle against psychosis. The red laugh comes to symbolize both the madness of war on the battlefield and the brother's deteriorating mental condition. The red laugh eventually invades the brother's reality and he runs for cover amid explosions during a street battle with an undefined enemy. It seems that the brother is caught in the middle of a war, but it is more likely that he is employing a metaphor to express his mental state, which he perceives as a struggle against the red laugh. The brother's mind finally collapses and the war begins to close in around him in the form of mounting corpses which he fears will crush him – leading ultimately to his death.

The myth of battle

Dr Mumortsev's task was to show how Andreev successfully described an individual's loss of cognition in 'Red Laugh.' He was not attempting literary criticism, but using popular literature to explain medical theory. Almost a century later, illness narrative theory has applications in medicine, sociology and, recently, in literary theory.[43] Mumortsev indicated that 'Red Laugh' was an illness narrative, but he did not say that the story might be informed by Andreev's own illness experience. However, we can now make this assertion to provide a more dynamic critical understanding of Andreev and his literary work.

One can argue that in 'Red Laugh' Andreev mirrors the soldier; the soldier's experience is that of the author.[44] Once home, the young man finds comfort in his bike, his son and a love of photography. One may remember that Andreev, in his diary, believed that a bike would relieve his melancholy, while Azov tells of how Andreev turned to bicycling after his discharge from the clinic in 1901. Andreev was also an avid photographer and his obsessive tendencies often fueled his pursuit of this hobby.[45] It seems that when Andreev writes of the soldier, 'the photographic equipment neatly arranged on the shelves. [He] would take up photography again, take pictures of peaceful landscapes, of [his] son walking, laughing, playing,'[46] there is an association between the relative experience of author and character. By 1905 Andreev's son Vadim was two years old. Further evidence of a shared biography occurs with the mention of an unresponsive hand. The former soldier, like Andreev, is a writer and he is distraught that due to nerves, his hand now shakes so badly that he cannot write. His response to the problem is that he will dictate his ideas. Andreev also suffered from a hand injury and could not hold a pen for prolonged periods, so he either dictated or typed his stories and letters.[47]

Andreev can be seen, therefore, as associating himself with the soldier, giving the reader a clue to the identity of the unnamed protagonist. This can lead to the conclusion that the soldier's battle with madness reflects Andreev's own illness experience. The task of an illness narrative is to not only describe the sensation of being ill, but also to create a meaning that can bind that experience with the self.[48] Frank suggests that illness narratives can overlap with various other modes of narrative, including stories of inflicted trauma such as war.[49] In this way

Andreev contextualizes his mania in the loose framework of 'the madness of war' in order to give meaning to his own sense of reality.

War offers interesting insights when conceptualized as a metaphor for madness. Anne Hunsaker Hawkins addresses the 'Myth of Battle and Journey' in illness narrative in which the disease is depicted as an enemy to be vanquished. Disease is most commonly perceived as something alien, lacking an organic relation to the ill person; therefore, certain illnesses result in treatments which *attack* the disease, casting the patient in the role of battleground where the war is fought as well as warrior against the alien forces of disease.[50] Hawkins does not address mental illness in her discussion of the battle myth, instead concentrating on cancer, AIDS and other diseases that can be *attacked*, *bombarded* and *forced into submission*. Andreev was unsuccessful in attacking or forcing his neurasthenia into submission, so it is the symptoms of this war – disorientation, anxiety, weariness, confusion and much more – which the author explores in 'Red Laugh.'

Although this story was read at the time of its writing as a depiction of the Russo-Japanese War, neither side is ever referred to by nationality in the narrative. The soldier sees the enemy advancing and for a moment he is confused when his opponent seems to be wearing the same uniform as his own. The enemy approaches calmly with 'happy anticipation of an unexpected encounter.' There is a moment of relief when it seems that there will be no battle:

> When they began firing on us, for a time we could not understand what was happening, and went on smiling under a great hail of shrapnel and bullets that cut down hundreds of men. Someone yelled that there had been a mistake, and – I remember very clearly – we realized at last that it really was the enemy before us, wearing their own uniforms, not ours, and we immediately returned their fire.

The soldier loses both of his legs in the battle and awakens in a hospital. When he asks about the battle, he receives evasive answers. Finally he learns the disturbing news that 'it appears that they were from our side, that it was one of our own shells, fired from one of our cannons by one of our own soldiers that had torn off my legs.' No one wants to explain to the young man that 'two regiments of the same army, a half mile from each other, had spent a full hour almost destroying each other, fully convinced that they were fighting the enemy.' Few speak of the battle, but later 'certain people' suggest that the enemy had slipped away during the fighting. For a while, the soldier almost believes this excuse, but later he reads that the enemy had also engaged in a battle in which two divisions of the same army had fought hand-to-hand combat against each other.[51]

Unlike those metaphorical battles where the knights of the healthy host fight the alien forces of cancer, Andreev seems to depict a confused state in which one wages war with oneself. This evidently represents the nature of mental illness: the initial anticipation of a manic episode, leading to confusion and disorientation and, when one returns to a state of normalcy, evasion and pity from friends and family. The battle myth that Andreev describes is not like the war on cancer; the combatants are not so easily identified as *self* and *other*. With mental illness the *other* is the *self*, leading to an undifferentiated relationship between friend and foe. In Andreev's version of the battle myth, there is no treatment that destroys the alien invader. There is no chemotherapy, AZT cocktail or even lithium. For Andreev, it seems there can be no valiant victor in the war with mental illness. Instead, corpses surround the soldier's brother and foretell his ultimate demise.

Only the first seven fragments of 'Red Laugh' are located on an actual battlefield. The next twelve fragments take place in the hometown of the soldier. The war continues for the soldier and his brother, but it is now a war that is waged within. The battlefield, as Hawkins suggests, is the body, or in this case the mind, but the enemy is not clearly identifiable and there is no medical treatment which will bring ultimate victory.

Andreev uses war as a tangible expression of the realities of mental illness. The brother states: 'My mind refuses to conceive what is fundamentally insane. A million men assembled in a certain place to kill one another systematically, and they all suffer, and they all are miserable. What is that if not madness?'[52] The connection between war and madness becomes even more apparent as the soldier's brother slowly goes insane. He is far removed from the battlefield and yet the war continues to agitate his condition. Andreev's war is a series of battles waged against the self; a period of disorientation when an unspecified enemy turns out not to exist in any tangible sense. This does not make the battle any less real, but simply suggests the helplessness of those suffering from mental illness.

Indications that this story is as much about mental illness as it is about war are also provided by the depiction of medical treatment. The patients are referred to as lunatics and madmen: 'There are more madmen than wounded.'[53] They wander about disoriented, bang their heads against objects and display other behavior suggestive of severe mental illness. This is not surprising considering that Andreev had spent time in a sanatorium, but had never been in a combat hospital. Another interesting point, however, is that the doctors are also clearly mad, or at least the soldier perceives them as such. Therefore, there seems to be no hope for recovery, no course of action or plan for treatment.

The illness experience

If the red laugh represents encroaching insanity, then what is Andreev telling us about his life with neurasthenia? Andreev depicts serious disorientation and loss of spatial and temporal cognition in his use of a fragmented narrative structure. Most fragments begin with an ellipsis, as if starting in the middle of a particular event, and the reader must discern how far forward in time the story has progressed, where the events are now taking place, what has occurred in the ellipsis, and how the fragment relates to previous fragments. Within a fragment, one paragraph sometimes ends with an ellipsis and the next one begins with an ellipsis, once again forcing the reader to search for the orientation of the story. Linear timelines and plotlines are not used in this structure, causing confusion for the reader, which mirrors that of the characters.

Shlomith Rimmon-Kenan rhetorically asks: 'Wouldn't narrative fragmentation be the most suitable form for the experience of disrupted narrative identity?' in order to suggest that sometimes illness narrative is not a 'triumph over disillusion' (as suggested by Frank and others) but 'an entrapment in the chaos they tell.'[54] The supposition is that fragmentation conveys chaos and defies the notion that the illness can be conquered. Read within this context, Andreev's use of fragmentation may express his understanding of insanity as ultimately unavoidable.

The disorienting nature of the narrative structure is combined with the character's illness experience. The concept of time is compromised for those suffering from a manic episode as the brain is flooded with unusually rapid mental activity, resulting in a decreased need for sleep and eventually developing into a fractured sense of reality and mental fatigue.[55] In 'Red Laugh,' reference is made to ten hours, twenty hours, and two weeks without slumber. The lack of sleep results in a distorted understanding of reality for the soldier. The confusion of battle and the horrors of war also convey Andreev's fractured sense of self, time and space:

> These simultaneous sensations, thoughts, this suffering and horror sweep the ground from under my feet, and I feel like a chip of wood tossed on the waves, a speck of dust in a whirlwind. I am torn violently from everyday existence, and every morning there is a terrible moment when I am suspended over the black abyss of madness. And I will fall into it; I must fall into it.[56]

Further confusion is created by the character shift from the soldier to his brother. Weaknesses on the level of plot structure and narrative coherence actually form the basis for what one might suggest is the nature of this specific literary illness narrative. In the brother's narrative, we are provided with a description of how one rationalizes illness rather than with the symptoms of mania given to us by the soldier. The illness narrative of the two brothers allows Andreev to describe both the experience of mental illness at the moment of mania, as well as the fears and rationalizations of an individual at the onset of psychosis. In this way, the narrative is structurally problematic; yet as an illness narrative it is multifaceted and complex in the best sense of these words. Rather than choosing to give only one side of illness (symptom or meaning), Andreev explicates different facets of the same experience. The reader learns about the reality of mania for the soldier: hyperactivity, sleeplessness, spatial and temporal fragmentation, impaired cognitive abilities and more. In the experience of the brother, one confronts the meaning of mental illness: the realization of the onset of madness, the panic and the great effort to maintain a semblance of sanity. In both instances, we see the alienation, loneliness and hopelessness of the sufferer.

For the soldier, the experience is immediate and the reader is meant to witness the psychosis:

> My eyes would not stay open. Their pupils, shrunken to the size of poppy seeds, searched in vain for shade beneath the cover of lowered eyelids. It felt better if I shut my eyes. [...] When someone fell, he fell silently. I myself stumbled and fell several times, and then, involuntarily, I would open my eyes. What I saw was fantastic, the leaden ravings of a world gone mad. The burning air quivered, and the stones, too, quivered in silence. They seemed to be on the point of melting.[57]

The lack of sleep impairs the soldier's sense of reality. His experience is of disorientation:

> Our movements were sure and swift, our orders precise; they were carried out accurately, but had any one of us been asked who he was, he would not have been likely to find an answer in his darkening mind. As in a dream, faces seemed to be those of old friends; everything that was happening seemed familiar, natural, a repetition of previous events. Yet when I looked closely at one or another of the faces around me or at a gun or listened to the roaring, it all struck me as being novel and infinitely mysterious.[58]

The soldier realizes that he is going mad: 'He himself felt very strange, though he had not touched anything all day: his head was spinning, and for minutes on end, his fear became wild ecstasy – the euphoria of fear.'[59] Elation eventually gives way to confusion and alienation. The soldier then begins to feel the 'presence of the irrational.'[60] Later, the soldier describes the approach of madness: 'It was still hanging over the earth – thin, hopeless, like a child crying or like the whimpering of a thousand abandoned, freezing puppies. It entered my brain like a sharp, icy needle and moved back and forth.'[61] When he finally goes home, his hair is white, his face haggard, his body shakes uncontrollably and his legs have been amputated; he is maimed both physically and psychologically. Here the fragmentation of the narrative structure is also realized in the physical reality of the body. This ties the loss of spatial and temporal referencing of the mind together with the trauma of the body, so that the soldier is no longer perceived as *whole*. The amputation of his legs due to war can be a metaphor for his crippled mental state caused by mania; his experience is mental as well as physical.

The brother's experience is psychological but not physical. He struggles with the knowledge that he is going mad and the reader shares the meaning of his madness. The brother states:

> To tell you the truth, I am very afraid of going mad. I do not understand what is happening. I do not understand, and that appalls me. [...] I am beginning to lose track of what is permitted and what is forbidden, what is rational and what is sane. [...] While you were still there, there were nights when I could not sleep. I had strange thoughts: I wanted to take an ax and kill them all – our mother and sister, the maid, the dog. [...] Feel how hot my head is. It is burning. Sometimes it grows cold and everything in it freezes, becomes numb, turns into terrible, deathly ice. I must go mad – do not laugh brother – I must go mad.[62]

Mumortsev argues that the brother plays the role of the psychoanalyst, taking down the words and actions of the soldier, as well as engages in self-reflection about his own mental health. He believes that formal psychosis for the brother does not occur until the last lines of the story.[63] The idea of self-reflection and dealing rationally with mental illness is important in this argument. Clearly, this is something that Andreev constantly struggled to do in order to function with the conditions of his illness, and he is able to explore this experience through the brother:

> I do not understand war and I am bound to go mad, like my brother, like thousands of others who have been brought back from it. This does not frighten me. The death of my reason will be as honorable as the death of a sentry at his post. But waiting for it – this slow, inexorable approach of madness, this impression of something enormous falling into an abyss – this is what my mind cannot bear.[64]

The twelfth fragment begins with the line 'is beginning.'[65] This would seem to indicate that the brother is starting to go mad, as does the ensuing narrative:

> A bloody mist is settling over the earth, clouding our vision, and I am beginning to think that a universal catastrophe is at hand. Madness is

coming from out there, from those fields red with blood. I am a strong, healthy man; I do not suffer from debilitating diseases that might affect my brain. Yet, I can see the infection spreading to me. [...] During the day I can still fight it off, but at night, like everyone else, I become the slave of my dreams, and my dreams are full of horror and madness...[66]

The brother has reached a point at which he is frightened to enter his empty house and refuses to unlock the soldier's study. He limits himself to the use of the living room. He hallucinates and sees the soldier for a second time and the soldier explains to him, 'That is the red laugh. When the world goes mad it laughs like that. You do know, do you not, that the world has gone mad?'[67] The brother knows that the soldier is right and that the rest of the world is also beginning to realize that universal violence against reason is affecting their weak minds. For the brother, unlike the soldier, the narrative is about the inevitable approach of madness and how he relates to this inevitability. Once the brother accepts insanity, he is able to enter his house without fear and he unlocks the soldier's study.

> This morning I read that the battle is still raging, and again, I am seized by anxiety and a sense of something falling inside my brain. It is coming, it is near, it is already at the threshold of these bright, empty rooms. Remember, remember me, my dear girl. I am going mad.[68]

The brother finally decides to wait for the arrival of madness. He goes into the living room and opens the window. He feels there are people in the room with him, but he states, 'I knew that I was imagining they were there because I was ill, running a fever, but I could not overcome the fear that was making my whole body shiver as if I had a chill.'[69] Even as the brother goes mad, he is aware of this process of psychosis and it is finally realized when corpses surround him and he looks out the window to see the red laugh.

Woodward sees in 'Red Laugh' not a tale of war between two nations but the conflict that was raging within the mind of twentieth-century man. He views Andreev's depiction of war as an exploration of man's basic instincts which are transformed in one of two ways: 'either his instincts, so long repressed, assume absolute control of him, in which case he is transformed into a savage, like Nemovetsky, or his hyper-sensitive reason collapses before the spectacle of unparalleled horror. The words "madness and horror" epitomize these two metamorphoses.'[70]

Given the theme of madness and Andreev's own medical history, what insight is gained by reading 'Red Laugh' as an illness narrative? It has been argued that we construct master narratives in order to make sense of the events that constitute a life. Illness upsets the coherence and continuity of this narrative.[71] The disruption of Andreev's narrative led to a story in which illness *is* the narrative continuity. Rather than trying to counteract the disruption, the narrative in 'Red Laugh' embraces it. Andreev describes an illness experience through both the brother and the soldier. The latter conveys the physical experience of exhaustion, disorientation, and alienation. Andreev employs the ellipsis with great frequency and makes little effort to create continuity between the fragments concerning the soldier. In the brother's experience, there is a much more rational narrative approach. No longer is the reader made to feel disoriented; the ellipses become less frequent and the fragments seem to follow in a more coherent progression. The brother calmly accepts the slow approach of insanity. How does one react when confronted with the fact that he is going insane? Andreev captures the fear and dread of the individual at the beginning of the process and then seems to suggest that one must give oneself over to the inevitable.

In 1905, Aleksandra informed her husband that a literary circle had met to discuss a paper by the psychiatrist V.V. Chekhov on the psychological elements of 'Red Laugh.' The literary circle concluded that: '1) L[eonid] A[ndreev] based his story on his own psychology, in the same way that Tolstoi and Garshin have; 2) the horrors, depicted in the story, conform to reality in both a psychological and a physical sense; 3) the significance of such stories for the Russian public is enormous.'[72]

Frustrated by the negative criticism of 'Red Laugh,' Andreev wrote to his friend Aleksandr Serafimovich (1875–1958), 'What so ever, I will not write anymore about the insane, and you know the reason: the reservoir has run dry! Not one more insane person! Plain as day. Dozens of stories are [to be] composed, but not about the insane, not even one.'[73] Of course, this would not be the case. Andreev's literary success had been built on sensational psychopaths – murderers, rapists and the criminally insane. These were degenerates, who represented the demise of Russian society. It is true that Andreev would attempt to address religious themes, to write symbolic plays, but he could not completely abandon his insane characters or the theme of madness.

Dionysus: madness, death and regeneration

At the beginning of the twentieth century, it was readily accepted that interpretive philosophies had a degenerative effect on individuals, especially youths.[74] The philosophies of Schopenhauer and Nietzsche were believed to be especially infectious and could result in insanity. A pessimistic worldview that valued destruction and the unlimited importance of the individual was deemed extremely dangerous as it promoted ruthless, egocentric attitudes leading often to deviant behavior. The threat was clearly to the church and state, charged with maintaining moral and social order, respectively. The Nietzschean undertones in Andreev's works challenged these institutions.

Andreev first became acquainted with Nietzsche in the 1890s when a friend, who was a university student, asked if he wanted to read *Thus Spake Zarathustra*. Their combined knowledge of German was limited so the level of comprehension is debatable, but their reading formed the basis of Andreev's 'The Story of Sergei Petrovich'. Vasilii Brusianin (1867–1919) writes that the philosophical influence of Nietzsche, and even more so of Schopenhauer and Hartmann, was an important part of the cultural fabric of Andreev's youth and is readily evident in his literary works.[75] One of Andreev's productive symbols of madness for a short period of time was Dionysus (or Bacchus). In Russian literature and culture, this mythological figure was invested with added meaning due to the influence of Nietzsche's *The Birth of Tragedy* (1872) and the cultural ethos of the symbolist and neo-realist movements' development of Nietzschean thought.[76]

Dionysus was the Greek god of wine and vegetation. There are many versions of his birth, but all of them involve Zeus' seduction of a mortal woman. When Hera, Zeus' wife, learns that Zeus has impregnated Semele, she tries to destroy the unborn child. In all versions, Zeus saves some part of Dionysus and he is reborn, which is why he is typically known as 'twice-born.'[77] In the most common version, Zeus seduces Semele and then Hera tricks Semele into demanding that Zeus come to her in his full glory. When Zeus comes to Semele as a lightning bolt she dies of fright, but Zeus takes the unborn child from Semele's womb and sews it into his own thigh. Eventually, Dionysus is raised by Semele's sister Ino. When Hera discovers this she punishes Ino with madness and eventually inflicts the same upon Dionysus himself.

Dionysus runs away from his nurses and wanders through Egypt. In Phrygia, Cybele cures him of his madness. At this time, Dionysus adopts an oriental costume and institutes many of his own rites, and soon becomes a full-fledged god. His followers are rewarded with many blessings, particularly the cultivation of the grape and the pleasures of wine. Male and female votaries achieve communion with their god in nocturnal, orgiastic rites on mountains, and often have visions of him as a bull or a goat at the peak of their religious frenzy (aided by ample amounts of wine). These ceremonies are associated with overt sexuality and the ritual killing and ingesting of animals. Dionysus often drives his enemies mad, but is generous to his loyal worshipers. When he firmly establishes a following from the eastern Mediterranean to as far east as India, he leaves the earth and takes his place in Mount Olympus with the other gods.

Dionysus is recognized as a fertility god. Grapes and other crops are planted and then harvested. The harvest celebration is associated with a drunken orgy which ultimately leads to Dionysus' destruction and dismemberment, thereby fertilizing the ground and preparing it for rebirth and regeneration in the spring.

At the beginning of the twentieth century, Dionysus regained cultural currency based on the lasting influence of Nietzsche's *The Birth of Tragedy*. In this early work, Nietzsche explores the function of the aesthetic and argues for a binary opposition of forces – Dionysian and Apollonian. For Nietzsche, Dionysus is the god of chaos, fruitfulness and ecstasy, representing the fundamental human disposition – instinctive and intuitive. Apollo is the god of order and of dream (a higher truth). He represents measured restraint and the silent recasting of life. In Andreev's works, we see a similar dichotomy between the mathematician and the artist, the rational and the intuitive, control and performance. For Nietzsche, there is a fundamental interplay between these two forces, between life and knowledge, which creates tragedy (or in a larger context, aesthetic harmony). Repression or denial of one of these two forces results in either too much chaos or too much order.

Bernice Glatzer Rosenthal notes that the primary Nietzschean text for the symbolists was *The Birth of Tragedy* and the 'aesthetic justification of the world and human existence, [Nietzsche's] celebration of the Dionysian, and his belief that myth is essential to the health of the culture.'[78] The symbolists were opposed to positivism, rationalism and materialism while searching for a higher reality that could only be comprehended intuitively. The neo-realists, generally speaking, were more interested in recasting Nietzsche's superman into a social revolutionary who would transcend Russian bourgeois society.[79] The myth of Dionysus, therefore, is perceived differently by the two groups based on political and philosophical agendas. However for both, broadly stated, Dionysus becomes a Christ-figure or proletarian superman who represents the rebirth and resurrection of higher ideals (political and social fertility) after a period of revolutionary madness, chaos and destruction.

Edith Clowes pays specific attention to Andreev's 'The Story of Sergei Petrovich' in which the character tries to read *Thus Spake Zarathustra* in German but is unable to gain anything meaningful from it. He then attempts to transform himself into a superman, but finds that he is destined to be a nameless bureaucrat. Unable to accept this, Sergei Petrovich decides to kill himself. Clowes sees in this story a contamination of Nietzschean thought with elements of Dostoevskii's moral rebellion.[80] This connection is quite obviously stated, but similar themes of madness and persecution are evident in other of Andreev's works. Like 'The Story of Sergei Petrovich,' these texts display the contamination of Nietzschean and Dostoevskian philosophy, but are more interested in the subtle theme of Dionysian madness and destruction than in the emergence of a moral superman.

Traces of the Dionysian theme, as part of the larger Dostoevskian-Nietzschean influence, appeared in 'The Life of Vasilii Fiveiskii,' Andreev's story about a village priest's rebellion against God. Published in 1904, the story was influenced by the death of Vasilii Mikhailovich Fiveiskii (1873–1903), the senior sanitary inspector of Nizhnii Novgorod, who had died of a disease of the brain at the age of thirty. The story of his death made an impression on Andreev, whose visit to Nizhnii Novgorod coincided with the man's funeral in February 1903.[81]

Andreev's story recounts the trials and tribulations which eventually drive Father Fiveiskii insane. After their son drowns in a river, Father Fiveskii's wife turns to alcohol and, in an attempt to bear another son, gives birth to an idiot. She eventually dies in a house fire, and Father Fiveiskii sends his daughter away and raises the idiot alone. After so much tragedy in his own life, Father Fiveskii begins to internalize the sorrows of others, and when a worker dies in a landslide he believes that he has been prepared by God to create a miracle. However, when Father Fiveskii cannot raise this worker from the dead, he goes insane and dies.

At this time, under the influence of modern scientific discourse, Russian Orthodox priests were encouraged to work with secular zemstvo doctors to heal moral sickness.[82] The church seized on psychiatric issues surrounding heredity, moral bankruptcy and insanity to stigmatize dissenters and schematics. Beer writes: 'By the late 1880s, terms and concepts explicitly drawn from the epidemiological models of society presented by crowd psychologists at home and abroad came to inform the writings of the ecclesiastical authorities.'[83] Religious dissent, consequently, was recast in the scientific language of psychopathology. By the early twentieth century, religious and social opposition in Russia was recognized as a symptom of moral illness, confusing religious theory with medical and social science.[84]

Kaun sees a Nietzschean subtext in the story, that faith is the enemy of reason: 'Faith keeps the unfortunates in obedience and submission, by justifying the unjustifiable, by lulling discontent to sleep with the aid of such narcotic illusions as sin and penalty, virtue and reward, God and future life.'[85] Woodward views 'The Life of Vasilii Fiveiskii' in parallel with 'The Thought' – the latter is about a struggle with reason, while the first involves a struggle with faith. However, both Kerzhentsev and Father Fiveiskii suffer from the same mortal sin – pride.[86]

In 'The Life of Vasilii Fiveiskii' there is a tension between the Orthodox and the Pagan worlds. Father Fiveiskii as the village priest is stranded between the two, but in both worlds pride is often punishable by madness and death. One of the first references to the Dionysian is when Father Fiveiskii's wife convinces him that they will defy the will of God and again bear a son to replace the one that was taken from them. It is autumn, his wife is described as a bacchante, and 'madness stood guard at the door' when she conceived.[87] The word *resurrect* is used several times to describe their attempt to bear a child and undoubtedly plays into the Dionysian-Christ trope that from destruction and chaos comes rebirth. The priest's wife grows healthy with her pregnancy but, as Andreev almost gleefully notes, what is conceived in madness comes into the world mad.[88] Their child is physically and mentally deformed. Woodward argues that the half-man, half-beast child is a symbol of Father Fiveiskii's deformed subconscious.[89] More specifically, one could suggest that it is punishment for the priest's first act of pride.

Turning away from God, Father Fiveiskii begins to see his parishioners' experiences as an extension and reflection of his own. Unlike Job, the priest cannot bear the relentless test of faith. When a mentally ill cripple confesses to raping and killing a girl, Father Fiveiskii admits to killing his own wife and child, foreshadowing what is to come. He endures a terrible night of visions and in the morning says that he is leaving the priesthood.

A farmer, Father Fiveiskii seems happy and renewed with a return to the earth. However, his prideful rejection of God results in disaster, just like his wife's pregnancy. His house catches on fire and his wife is burned alive. This event causes Father Fiveiskii to send his daughter away (the only positive element in his life), rebuild the house, recommit to the care of his deformed son, and return to the priesthood. Reinvested, Father Fiveiskii now bears the misfortune of his life with joy.

The priest's religious mania, however, leads him to his third act of pride – when he determines that he is prepared to raise a man from the dead. Instead of the corpse rising from the coffin, the priest sees his own deformed child clutching at its side, causing his entire psyche to collapse. Here, as in 'The Thought,' the reasoning of a madman betrays itself as irrational and warped at the crucial moment of perceived victory. Pride again has brought an individual low and the punishment is madness and death.

The cultural context for Andreev's presentation is complex, but the line of discourse unquestionably uses Dionysus, Christ, Dostoevskii and

Nietzsche among its signposts of degeneration. Afonin reads this story as one example of many among fellow neo-realist writers in which a priest becomes a politically active figure rebelling against the dominant power structures.[90] Clearly too, Andreev was still under the influence of Gor'kii, a proponent of Nietzschean ideas, so it is not unlikely that Gor'kii had a strong hand in formulating the philosophical underpinnings of 'The Life of Vasilii Fiveiskii.'

These connections are further developed in Andreev's play *To the Stars*, published in the tenth *Znanie* anthology in 1906. Andreev had read *Astronomical Evenings* by the German astronomer and meteorologist Hermann Klein (1844–1914) in 1900 and wanted to write, with Gor'kii, a play about astronomy and revolution. The two never did collaborate, but both wrote plays on the original theme. Gor'kii completed *Children of the Sun* (Deti solntsa) during his imprisonment in the Peter and Paul Fortress in 1905. Andreev began work on *To the Stars* in 1904 and it was first staged in Vienna in October 1906, and in Imperial Russia, in Terijoki, Finland, only in May 1907 due to problems with the censor.

The play is concerned with the astronomer Sergei Nikolaevich Ternovskii who is inspired by the majesty of the universe and disconnected from the trivialities of everyday life. He lives halfway up a mountain isolated from the rest of the world. However, he is drawn into a revolution by his children who are taking part at the base of the mountain. Ternovksii learns that his son Nikolai has been arrested when wounded victims of the revolution appear at the doorstep of his mountain retreat. In the final act, Nikolai's wife brings news that her husband has gone insane in prison. The conflict centers on the scientist's indifference to life on earth. Ternovskii concentrates on a higher set of ideals, on a larger life system, thereby displaying a disregard for basic humanity and his fellow individuals, even his own children.

This play was written under the influence of the social and political strife of the time, but we will pay attention to Nikolai's imprisonment and resulting madness, described in Act IV. This is an early example of the role that prisons/punishment and asylums/madness play in Andreev's work. Although there are only subtle references to the Dionysian-Dostoevskian theme of madness and resurrection, illuminating this theme gives some insight into Andreev's philosophical position and his intellectualization of madness around 1905.

Marusia tells how her husband was thrown into prison. She recounts how the prisoners raised a mutiny and were trampled and beaten by the guards. Nikolai is injured much like Dionysus is torn apart by his frenzied disciples: 'They beat them with their fists, they trampled upon them with their feet. [...] They beat them terribly and for a long time –

these stupid, cold-blooded beasts. They had torn his mouth – the beautiful lips that had never uttered a falsehood, had nearly gouged his eyes out – the eyes that saw only the beautiful.'[91]

Following this beating a 'deadly melancholy' overtakes Nikolai. His depression grows more severe, his memory fails him and finally he is completely silent. Madness was a form of punishment first inflicted upon Dionysus by Hera and later used by Dionysus himself to punish his enemies. For Andreev too, madness is a form of punishment. Marusia says: 'When I went to see him today he had already been taken to the hospital. When they took him for a walk yesterday he wanted to throw himself out through the window, but he was caught in time. Then – madness, the strait-jacket and that's all.'[92]

Marusia refers to Nikolai's 'beautiful face' and 'beautiful form' that have been shattered. Ternovskii refers to his son as a prophet and asks what the doctors say of his condition. Marusia says that Nikolai is an idiot. *Idiot* is repeated three times and certainly Andreev is evoking Dostoevskii's Prince Myshkin, a Christly figure who goes insane at the end of the novel *The Idiot* (Idiot) and suggests that 'Beauty will save the world.' Like Christ, Marusia claims that Nikolai said to her as mental illness began to overtake him: 'I carry within my soul the sorrow of the whole world.'[93] Ternovskii says of his son: '[Nikolai] – an idiot! How difficult it is to imagine that. This beautiful man, this harmonious, luminous spirit plunged into darkness, into wearisome, miserable, barely movable chaos.'[94]

At this point Marusia and Ternovskii split ideologically. In discussing what to do with Nikolai, Marusia says that she will build a city for the displaced – the insane, blind and diseased. Ternovksii shows no remorse for his son, claiming that he has no children as all human beings are alike to him. He sees the whole of life and therefore cannot mourn the loss of only one person. He then seems to return to the theme of resurrection by claiming that life is everywhere and that Nikolai could be reborn, but later rejects this notion. Marusia asks if Nikolai is to be reborn 'to go mad, to perish.'[95] Ternovskii insists that Nikolai exists in everything. Marusia, calling again upon the symbols of Dionysus asks: 'But death, madness and the wild [jubilance] of slaves?'[96] Nietzschean time moves cyclically, coming back eternally to the same forms of consciousness and experience. Dionysian temporality is emblematic of this cycle of life, madness, chaos, death and return. Ternovskii again claims that Nikolai is in everything and that through death we all find immortality. Marusia states that she will keep Nikolai's memory sacred: 'Let them again and again kill him within me, but high above my head I shall carry his pure, uncorrupted soul.'[97]

Although Marusia and Ternovskii differ in their value of the individual, both see Nikolai as a Christlike / Dionysian symbol of regeneration. The conflation of these various ideas were the talk of literary and intellectual circles around 1905 and fascinated Andreev's contemporaries Merezhkovskii, Viacheslav Ivanov (1866–1949) and Chulkov. Clowes writes: 'Dostoevsky as a religious thinker is treated implicitly as the Russian parallel to Nietzsche. Merezhkovsky views Nietzsche's moral inquiry and his "solutions" as forms of "sickness" that signal regeneration.'[98] She states that Ivanov 'formalizes the parallel between Dionysian orgy and Christian crucifixion. Both rites ultimately celebrate human existence because they embrace its deepest paradoxes.'[99] Chulkov viewed Christ as a revolutionary and revolution as a creative act.[100] Therefore, it is not unreasonable that Andreev invested threads of Dionysus, Christ, Nietzsche and Dostoevskii in his descriptions of Nikolai and Father Fiveiskii.

Dionysus, however, loses its symbolic value and after 1905 Andreev only rarely uses it as a shorthand signifier of madness. A possible explanation is that as his friendship with Gor'kii deteriorated, Andreev moved further away from these philosophical positions. But the way in which madness and punishment are once again united thematically is important to this discussion. Like Dostoevskii's moral rebels, both Nikolai and Father Fiveiskii attempt to fight against the prevailing power structures. For Dostoevskii's characters, punishment often comes in the form of prison sentences (Raskolnikov and Ivan Karamazov) or suicide (Svidrigailov and Stavrogin), although both Rogozhin and Prince Myshkin go insane. The Nietzschean-Dinonysian influence, more specifically, calls for madness and death in a process of pagan destruction that ultimately leads to rebirth and regeneration. Andreev never embraced Nietzschean philosophy as enthusiastically as some of his contemporaries, but still we find evidence of this philosophical discourse in his depiction of madness around 1904–6.

Prison and death

On 9 February 1905, Andreev allowed a meeting of the Social Democratic Labor Party to be held in his apartment. He was sick in bed with the flu, but when the police raided the apartment Andreev was sent to the Taganka jail along with the participants of the political meeting. At first, Andreev was in good spirits, but in prison his health began to rapidly deteriorate. By 21 February, he was complaining of heart palpitations, for which he sought treatment from the prison doctor.[101] Aleksandra, in the meantime, obtained medical certificates attesting to

Andreev's fragile mental state – from her brother-in-law, Dr Filipp Dobrov (1869–1941), and from Dr Georgii Pribytkov, junior member of the clinic for nervous disorders and a student of the psychiatrist Kozhevnikov.

After he graduated from the medical faculty of Moscow University, Dobrov became a resident physician at the First Gradskii Hospital. He was married to Aleksandra's older sister, Elizaveta Mikhailovna Veligorskaia (1871–1943), and became very close friends with Andreev. They shared an interest in literature and Andreev greatly appreciated Dobrov's literary opinions. Dobrov was especially knowledgeable about music and the theater and often hosted members of the Moscow arts community at his home. It was natural then, that Aleksandra would turn to Dobrov when she needed a medical certificate to present to the commandant of the Moscow penitentiary system to gain the release of her husband after his arrest.

Dobrov's certificate of 11 February 1905 states that Andreev had sought medical treatment from various doctors (Tokarevskii, Mitakov, Cherinov and Pribytkov) for a nervous disorder.[102] These doctors had employed hypnosis, water treatments and other medical remedies to treat Andreev. Over the past two years as the author's family physician, Dobrov had addressed Andreev's complaints about a variety of physical and mental ailments including a predominance of morose and melancholy feelings, a fear of death and an aversion to life, bouts of hypochondria, severe migraines, neuralgic pains and anginal seizures.

In Dobrov's opinion, these medical issues in conjunction with certain hereditary facts suggested that Andreev suffered from a severe form of schizophrenia rooted in degenerative defects of the nervous system. Based on this diagnosis, Dobrov believed that Andreev's condition was incurable and would lead to further deterioration. Therefore he warns that the author's imprisonment might result in the most lamentable and inveterate consequences.

The second certificate by Pribytkov was sought when it was deemed that Dobrov's was not florid enough to gain Andreev's release.[103] Pribytkov's certificate identifies all of the symptoms that we have confronted in Andreev's diaries and literary works – headaches, bouts of depression, a fear of going insane and heart problems, which resulted in pathological drunkenness, insomnia and intense feelings of loneliness. Pribytkov writes:

> On 16 September 1902 [Aleksandra Mikhailovna's] husband, Leonid Nikolaevich Andreev, came to me for medical advice, complaining of headaches, in the form of migraines, the onset of melancholy, anxiety, a fear of going insane, palpitations, an anginal phenomenon (of a type

termed angina pectoris). [...] Taking into account everything noted above and other less important nervous and psychological abnormalities, I conclude that Leonid Andreev suffers from severe neurasthenia due to a degenerative predisposition – that, in fact, his illness ought to be considered incurable and any nervous or psychological disturbance for him is certainly not only detrimental, but dangerous.[104]

Some critics have interpreted these medical certificates as fabricated documents to ensure Andreev's release from prison.[105] Certainly, they were used to this end, but this does not mean that the symptoms and diagnoses themselves were falsified. The laws at this time were quite strict regarding the falsification of medical documents and both Dobrov and Pribytkov would have severely jeopardized their medical careers by providing phony medical certificates. Further, Andreev wrote from jail, 'It is embarrassing, that I am so ill, that I have to bother, to grovel, as every conversation with these gentlemen is a humiliation. If only I were healthy!'[106] Afonin also attests that many of Andreev's closest friends and family feared for his health while he was in prison.[107] Andreev spent two weeks in jail and was only released on 25 February after Savva Morozov (1862–1905), a wealthy industrialist, paid ten thousand roubles in bail money.

In the autumn of that same year, on 20 September, Andreev's youngest sister, Zinaida died of a possible brain hemorrhage at the Imperial university clinic for nervous disorders in Moscow, where Andreev had also been a patient. Rimma remembers that at the end of 1904, Zinaida and her family were living below Andreev and his family in the same house. One day she started bleeding from the nose to such a degree that they called for a doctor. All through the winter, Zinaida continued to have regular nosebleeds, which quite worried the family. Doctors treated her with arsenic, but this only seemed to make her condition worse. There was a feeling among the Andreevs that Zina's husband was not taking her condition seriously, and it was decided that she would start having her meals upstairs at her brother's. Andreev also wrote to a well-respected Professor Usov, who responded that Zina should be taken immediately to the clinic for treatment. Three days after she was admitted to the clinic, Zinaida passed away.[108] Pavel writes:

This death, the first in our family since our father's death, struck Leonid so forcibly that for a long time we feared for his sanity. Previously there had been thoughts of death; now they had received a concrete, real form – moreover, in the image of his younger sister whom he loved so much and who, incidentally, was so like him. I remember this night in [Leonid's] apartment. A long wide corridor, many rooms, in one of these, mother is in a state of psychological paralysis pacing from corner to corner and mumbling something to herself ... [...] On the morning of the second day Leonid himself comes to me and says that we must save mother... [...] It was a long time before the oppressive and painful mood caused by her death eased and was replaced by a feeling of sadness induced by the irretrievable loss and the instability of everything on earth.[109]

Prior to gaining access to Rimma's memoirs, I had argued in earlier publications that Zina's death was related to a brain disorder, knowing the place of her treatment and based on some references to her death in memoirs about her brother.[110] Alekseevskii, however, remembers that 'she died due to the presence of hemophilic symptoms caused by a brain hemorrhage' at the tender age of twenty-one.[111] Rimma also refers to hemophilia as the cause of her sister's death.[112]

Although hemophilia was not a brain disorder, it was associated with degeneration as a blood taint like that suffered by the Romanov Dynasty. This, coupled with other illnesses in the family, certainly did little to ease Andreev's fears about hereditary illness. It is clear that Andreev's father, his brother, Pavel, as well as the author himself, displayed pathological behavior. Alekseevskii says that Pavel 'died from symptoms of a painful neuralgia due to the degeneration of [his] nerve endings.'[113] Zinaida's death of a possible brain hemorrhage drastically influenced Andreev's psyche, and negatively influenced his understanding of medical treatment, blood taints and the overall health of his family.

Aleksandra Mikhailovna

The Romans had been some of the first to believe that the robust growth of a civilization must be followed by stagnation, decay and death. The decadence and decline of Roman society was thus a natural evolution from its earlier vigor. In a similar sense many in the 1880s–1890s, influenced by scientific theories that further anthropomorphized societies, believed that they were caught in a state of organic decomposition and that cultural decadence was only one of the manifestations of this degeneration of civilization. As a result, it made sense that the decadent individual was sickly and very possibly depraved. As such Nietzsche could argue that Wagner's decadent genius was 'characterized by pathological manifestations such as hysteria, nervous excitability, histrionics, mendacity, visual restlessness, sensationalism, aesthetic fragmentation, effeminacy and more.' As Bernheimer notes, it was the psycho-medical rhetoric of degeneration that Nietzsche used to brand his former friend a decadent.[114]

By February 1906, Andreev's literary success was international in scope, but so too was his rumored history of mental illness. Like so many

European decadents, Andreev too was depicted in the foreign press as a degenerate. In *The Independent Review*, Simeon Linden wrote:

> Another peculiarity of Andreieff's writings is his partiality for describing the workings of the mind of the mentally unbalanced. In all probability the following fact may not be altogether without its influence in this relation. The young Russian is of a very emotional temperament and liable to attacks of nervous depression and melancholy, which, on more than one occasion, necessitated his placing himself under special treatment for the cure of acute nervous trouble. There can be no doubt that his personal experiences played a part in those of his stories which give us a present-ment of the psychology of certain of his mentally unbalanced characters[115]

Closer to home, Andreev's release from prison and then the tragic nature of his sister's unexpected death were further compounded by a perceived threat from the Black Hundreds, loyalist gangs supporting the autocracy, because of his revolutionary works. As a result, Andreev, Aleksandra and their son, Vadim, left the country and went to Finland, Germany, Italy and Switzerland, again back to Finland and finally settled in Berlin, Germany.

Still trying to cope with the death of Zinaida, Andreev wrote the story 'Lazarus', in which the focus is not on resurrection and life, but the ultimate victory of death over the living. Afonin claims that Andreev wished to confirm the decadent position that the truth of death is greater than the truth of life.[116] Andreev's story begins just after Lazarus has been raised from the dead. He lives alone due to the danger that he poses to the people around him – his gaze saps the life from the living. Once tales of his resurrection spread, Lazarus is visited by a Roman sculptor, who is forever damaged by this meeting, as well as by the Roman Emperor Augustus, who is able to overcome Lazarus' gaze because of a sense of responsibility for the Empire. Following their meeting, Augustus has Lazarus' eyes burned out with hot irons, and Lazarus spends the rest of his days shuffling in the wilderness, with his hands outstretched, in search of the heat of the sun. One day he simply disappears and this is the end of Lazarus' second life.

On 21 October 1906, Andreev's play, *To the Stars*, debuted in Vienna and was an unexpected success. The director, Richard Vallentin (1874–1908), also played the lead role of Treich. This was the first production of the Freie Volksbühne organization, which aligned itself politically with the social-democrats of the newspaper *Die Arbeiter Zeitung*. The positive reviews in both the local newspapers and those back home in Russia made Andreev ecstatic. His first attempt at drama was a hit.[117]

This theatrical triumph was soon followed by the birth of Andreev's second son, Daniil, on 2 November. Yet, joy soon turned to despair as Aleksandra suffered from a postnatal infection for some three weeks before passing away. Extremely distraught, Andreev sent the newborn to Moscow with Aleksandra's mother and went to the island of Capri to seek refuge and solace with his friend Gor'kii, who was also in self-imposed political exile from Russia. Aleksandra was buried, as was Andreev's sister Zinaida, in the cemetery within Moscow's Novodevichii monastery.

In the span of a year and a half, Andreev had tragically lost both his sister and wife. The death of Aleksandra would prove to be an especially crucial turning point in the author's life. Gone was his balance, the stabilizing force. Turning to Gor'kii, Andreev thought that their friendship might help him to deal with his grief. Gor'kii writes of this period on Capri:

All his thoughts and words centered on recollections of the senselessness of [his wife's] death.

'You understand,' he said with strangely dilated pupils, 'she was still alive as she lay in bed, but already her breath smelt of a corpse. It was a very ironic smell.'

Dressed in some kind of a black velvet jacket, he even seemed outwardly crushed, down-trodden. His thoughts and words were eerily concentrated on the question of death. It so happened that he settled down in the Villa Caraciollo, [...]

One evening when I arrived I found him in a chair in front of the fireplace. Dressed in black and bathed in the crimson glow of the smoldering coal, he held on his knees his little son Vadim and in low tones, with sobs, was telling him something. I quietly entered and it seemed to me that the child was falling asleep. I sat down in a chair by the door, and listened – Leonid was telling his son how Death stalks over the earth and strangles little children. [...]

When his grandmother took him away, I remarked that it was hardly necessary to frighten the boy with stories like that, stories about death, the invincible giant.

'And if I cannot speak of anything else?' he said sharply. 'I've finally grasped how indifferent 'beautiful Nature' is, and I only want one thing – to tear my portrait out of this trite pretty frame.'

It was difficult, almost impossible, to speak to him. He was nervous, irritable, and it seemed as though he deliberately rubbed salt on his own wounds.

'The idea of suicide haunts me; it seems to me that my shadow crawls after me, whispering, "leave, die!"'[118]

Unfortunately, this time on Capri was disastrous for the authors' friendship and did little to relieve Andreev's grief. Instead of providing emotional support, Gor'kii encouraged Andreev to channel his emotions into literary activities. While on Capri, Andreev reportedly wrote or outlined such works as: 'Judas Iscariot and Others,' 'Darkness,' *Sashka Zhegulev*, 'My Notes,' *Black Maskers*, *The Ocean* and a caustic satire 'Love of One's Neighbor.'[119] Although Andreev was able to process some of his grief into creative energy, it was a very dangerous time for him. To Andreev's relief, his friend Veresaev came to Capri for a month. To Veresaev's dismay, however, he found that Andreev had returned to his destructive behavior – drinking binges, depression, talk of death and suicide.

In the spring of 1907 Andreev returned to Russia from Capri, still expecting to be arrested for his political (real and imagined) activities. Almost immediately upon arriving in Moscow he visited Daniil, intending to take his youngest son to live with him. Andreev faced a vigorous protest, however, from Aleksandra's family and it was decided that Daniil would be looked after by the Veligorskii-Dobrovs. While in Moscow, Andreev and his family stayed in the Loskutnaia Hotel where the author's life was 'disorderly and noisy.'[120] Zaitsev remembers:

> Often he stayed in the Loskutnaia Hotel near the Iverskaia Gate and the Historical Museum. The *European* Petr Dmitrievich Boborykin who also stayed there, told me, slightly horrified, 'Imagine, I get up at six in the morning; by nine I've already done some work, and that's the time *he* comes back.' Petr Dmitrich who has never gone to bed after midnight, who drank mineral water, and wore snow-white collars, and our Leonid Andreev had adjacent rooms at the Loskutnaia Hotel! Oh, Rus', Rus'![121]

As before, Andreev sought female comfort in an attempt to ward off his depression, finding many willing companions. Even so, he was unable to escape the memories of Aleksandra and their life together in Moscow. So, Andreev took his family to St Petersburg. Chulkov writes of this period:

> Once I visited Andreev, when he lived in St Petersburg, in a large house on the St Petersburg side. His mother met me and said with a whisper that Leonid was 'ill.' This meant that he was drunk. I wanted to leave but Andreev heard my voice, came out and drew me into his office. Before him stood a bottle of cognac, and he continued to drink. It was obvious that he had already been drinking for about three days. He said that life in general was 'one hell of a thing,' and that his life was ruined: 'she is gone, the one who was a star for me. Deceased!' he said in a whisper, mysteriously and grimly. Then he put his head on the table and began to cry. And again

there was that mysterious whisper and ravings. Suddenly he became silent and began to listen, having turned to the glass door, which, it seems, led out onto the balcony. 'Do you hear?' he said. 'She is there.' And he resumed his ravings, and it was impossible to understand whether he was indeed hallucinating or whether he needed all of this to express the enigmatic feelings – which he himself could not understand – that weighed upon his soul at that time.[122]

Besides escaping from memories associated with Moscow, Andreev also moved to St Petersburg to be near the capital's literary and theatrical circles. He was still writing short stories, but became increasingly interested in developing plays for the stage. In February 1907, at Vera Komissarzhevskaia's theater in St Petersburg, Vsevolod Meyerkhold's (1874–1940) production of *Life of Man*, completed just before Aleksandra's death, was warmly received. In five acts the play traces the course of a man's life from the moment of birth through poverty, love, success and disaster to death. The allegorical figures are called 'Man,' 'Wife,' 'Neighbors,' etc. A prologue is spoken by 'Someone in Grey,' who remains on stage though invisible to the protagonists, commenting occasionally on the action, and holding a burning candle to symbolize the gradual ebb of Man's life and his ultimate return to oblivion.

Not since 'The Abyss' and 'In the Fog' had a work by Andreev received so much attention from all quarters. The play won several prestigious dramatic prizes, but it also insighted riots by the Black Hundreds in several cities. Gor'kii and those around him disliked it, while some of the modernists, such as Blok and Belyi, found it absolutely innovative.[123] Blok would later write of the experience:

It seems that *The Life of Man* in this sense was his most autobiographical play. I had occasion to see it from the stage, for which I am indebted to the directorial tricks of Meyerhold. I will never forget what a stunning impression the first act made. It was presented 'on burlap.'[124] In the very back of the stage there was a little couch with old women and a screen, and in the front there was a round table with chairs all around. The stage was lit only with a lamp on the table and with a narrow circular spot from an upper light. And so, standing in the dark, almost right next to the actors, I looked at the theater, at the flashes of ruby opera-glasses here and there. *The Life of Man* unfolded right next to me – next to me a mother in childbirth cried out piercingly, next to me a doctor in a white apron and with a cigarette nervously paced the space diagonally, and most importantly, next to me was the square back of 'Someone in Grey', who cast his lines into the theater from a dull column of light.

Those lines were – and still are – considered by many to be banal. I remember that the actor Kazimir Vinkent'evich Bravich,[125] grew bored to death of them (Bravich, too, is also now deceased). But there is something in them that troubles me to this day . . .

Andrei Belyi called the mood that permeates this play 'sobbing despair.' This is true; sobbing despair burst from the breast of Leonid Andreev more than once, and for this several of us were eternally grateful.[126]

On 12 December, *Life of Man* debuted at the Art Theater, directed by Konstantin Stanislavskii (1863–1938), and was the smash hit of the Moscow theatrical season. The night of the debut, Andreev was called out onto the stage for prolonged ovations after the second, fourth and fifth acts. Stanislavskii's stage design uniquely captured the mood of the production. The entire stage was covered in black velvet and Stanislavskii used colored ropes to reduce all objects to mere outlines, heightening the symbolic quality of the play. Ropes marked the contours of chairs, tables, windows and doors. Some of the actors also wore black velvet and seemed to appear and disappear from the stage. Audiences were utterly captivated and a good portion of the play's popularity was due to Stanislavskii's staging.

After the success of *Life of Man*, Andreev attempted several more symbolic dramas including *Tsar Hunger* (1908) and *Anathema* (Anatema, 1909). In parallel with these, he wrote realistic works for the stage, such as *Days of our Life* (1908) and *Gaudeamus* (1910), raising questions among his colleagues and critics as to his artistic allegiances.

Despite the success of his latest play, Andreev was drawing ever sharper reviews from literary critics. He was aware of what was being written about him and raised this issue in an interview with Izmailov in November 1907. Andreev stated: 'Every day I receive a pile of press clippings and articles about me from the Press Bureau. These almost entirely consist of profanity and fabrication. Already long ago I adopted a rule not to appear with rebuttals and I have never betrayed myself except for one exception, when someone wrote that I am insane, and then someone began to read a lecture about me, examining me under this lens.'[127] As we have noted, Andreev was much talked about in the press and in such an atmosphere in which *Andreev the individual* was as equally interesting as *Andreev the writer*, he had to actively manage this public reputation. The modernist reading of life and art as one in the same is typical of the time, although in this case it is complicated by Andreev's desire to avoid the stigma of mental illness. This media attention only became more focused once he moved to the capital.

While in St Petersburg, Andreev lived on Kamennoostrovskii prospect in a large apartment with big bay windows that provided a wonderful view of the island and Finland in the distance. Here Andreev tried to recreate the *Sreda* literary circle by inviting some of its old Moscow members, along with new literary colleagues such as Blok and Sologub. Andreev was looking to recapture the camaraderie and friendship that he had enjoyed in Moscow, but this St Petersburg version proved a failure. At the end of September 1907, Andreev held his first *Sreda* meeting at his apartment. Andreev had a sore throat and asked that Blok read his story 'Darkness.' This story was a distortion of the revolutionary Pinkhus Rutenberg's activities in a bordello, while hiding from the police. 'Darkness,' once published, angered Gor'kii and further estranged the two writers. A second *Sreda* meeting was held on 9 October, at which Andreev read a draft of his play *Tsar Hunger*. The play was a continuation of his dramatic experimentation with symbolism in which Andreev criticizes all layers of Russian society (church, government, intelligentsia, art, science, etc.) as being subservient to the moneyed classes.

As noted, these literary meetings were unsuccessful and did little to recreate the collaborative energy of the earlier Moscow version. The excitement of youth and newfound literary success could not be regained among, mainly, established authors. In this attempt, we might find another instance in which Andreev was looking to surround himself with the positive personal relationships that had for a time dispelled his anxiety of the meaninglessness of life.

Once in the northern capital, Andreev lived what Chulkov called 'a double life' – on the outside he was actively pursuing his literary career with critics, actors and publishers, but on the inside he was experiencing 'excruciating anxiety,' tormented by his solitude.[128] On 9 October, following the failed *Sreda* meeting, Andreev made an addendum to one of his last adolescent diaries. It speaks to his loneliness and his constant search for a companion:

On 10 February 1902 I was married to Shurochka [the nickname of Aleksandra Mikhailovna]. 25 December 1902 a son, Vadim, was born in Moscow. 19 February 1903 I quit drinking. 20 October 1906 a son, Daniil, was born in Berlin. 1 November, on the twelfth day after giving birth Shurochka grew sick with a postnatal-infection and on the 28th she died. All of those years with her were overwhelmingly happy. After her death I began to drink. Very unhappy.

In the beginning of March 1907 [having just returned] from Capri, Nadezhda Aleksandrovna Fokht [neè Antonova] visited. She gave herself to me. We thought about getting married, but it turned out that I did not love her, that I love only Shurochka. Now she lives with her second husband in Moscow and often writes to me. And she loves me deeply and is miserable.

As an author I am still on the rise. And I am already half European. In Russia they consider me, it seems, first (of course after Tolstoi). And I am very unhappy. I live in Petersburg. In Finland I bought land and am building a large dacha. I am spending from 12 to 18 thousand a year.

I am searching for a wife, whom I might be able to love and whom I might be able to marry. So far I am unsuccessful. In the summer I found someone who was somewhat agreeable, and she gave herself to me, but she was pregnant and went back to her husband. I loved again a woman, but she was also pregnant, and as soon as I caught wind I grew very cold [to the idea]. There are two women, with whom I could compel myself to fall in love, but so far I have been unsuccessful. I dream about a chambermaid with whom I could fornicate.

I think that I have reached the limit of suffering. Further is either death or a reversal towards happiness. And my heart singly and terribly is possessed by the death of Shurochka.

So am I on 9 October 1907. It is five o'clock in the morning, after reading at the Wednesday literary circle my *Tsar Hunger*, which was called genius. I drank a lot, but I am not drunk.[129]

Again, Andreev felt that he needed a female companion to balance his life, to drive away the black dog of depression, to participate in his periods of mania. More importantly, a companion was Andreev's defense against feelings of loneliness. Arguably, Andreev's main illness experience was an aversion to solitude and the perceived meaninglessness of life. This theme occupies considerable space in his diaries and literary works and is reflected in his life choices. Secondarily, Andreev experienced attacks of anxiety, which also found a place in his fiction. The two seem often to interact with each other. The futility of life mingled with isolation leads to anxiety and fear of a heart attack; and the issue of treatment in Andreev's literary works underscores the hopelessness of the situation in the author's mind.

Solitude

Andreev's adolescent diaries indicate various degrees of perceived isolation. In some cases it is mild: 'Boring: nothing to do and no reason to live.'[130] In others, his feelings are tied to his romantic pursuits: 'At the present time [my] life is composed of three elements: work – intense and persistent; vodka and illness; feelings of loneliness for Aleksandra Mikhailovna, which the loneliness underscores.'[131] Yet, it was his existential feelings of solitude that fueled Andreev's anxiety; the idea that even among others he was alone:

In fear and disgust I think about the onslaught of every new day. They are all so empty, all so meaninglessly-melancholy wanderings in space, boring experiences of boring moments of a humdrum life, solitude, depression, a yearning to hang onto the soul of the world, a dissatisfied and painful yearning. Alone with my own head, in which there is gloom and depression. I could not feel more lonely if I were on the wildest and most secluded island in the Great Ocean, than right now 'in the circle of family,' among people.[132]

An argument can be made that this angst concerning the meaninglessness of life provides a unifying thematic thread for Andreev's realistic, symbolic and allegorical works. Not just a reflection of the larger social panic over the alienation of the individual in an increasingly complicated industrialized society, however, Andreev's brand of isolation is more complex in its various manifestations: trauma – 'Silence,' guilt – 'In the Fog,' banal existence – 'Grand Slam' or hopelessness – 'In the Basement.' The source is psychological anguish, rather than social angst, resulting in separate, individualistic expressions of futility.

Vera Katonina remembers that everything was 'difficult' for the author – difficult to live, difficult to think, difficult to gain a sense of himself. 'Almost constantly, into each of his moods, crept and could be felt such pessimism, such a deep sense of loneliness, that by the moment, in conversations with him, it became intolerably dreary, [and you felt] sad for someone, seemingly for him.' She remembered that Andreev often contemplated this disparagement, with his face set in a gloomy expression, while on long walks.[133] Andreev once said to his neighbor: 'No, there is nothing more hopeless, more interminable and more horrifying than to experience the feeling of everlasting loneliness.'[134] Another neighbor in Finland, Beklemisheva, writes: 'We often took walks in groups or just the two of us. During these walks Leonid Nikolaevich spoke about despair, loneliness, the fear of death and about the fact that solitude caused in him physical anxiety.'[135]

One of his earliest works from 1899 explores the anxiety of solitude in the story of an owner and his dog.[136] In 'The Friend' (Drug) Vladimir Mikhailovich is a writer whose friends think that he should take on a more lucrative occupation and refrain from drinking vodka, which is ruining his health. He is sickly and suffers from fits of depression. When drunk he insults his friends and beats his dog. Even so, when sober, he considers his dog, Vasiuk, his only real friend. When Vladimir Mikhailovich becomes famous, his loneliness vanishes, he stops drinking and he is kind to his friends. He also falls in love with a woman and begins to pay less attention to his dog. When Vasiuk becomes ill, Vladimir Mikhailovich is too concerned with his new romance and delays calling the veterinarian. He finally buys the dog some medicine, but it is too late and Vasiuk dies while Vladimir Mikhailovich is with his girlfriend. Shortly after the dog's death, the writer's incredible fame turns into angry disappointment from his critics and he begins to feel like he is trapped in a coffin. The young woman leaves him and once again he is alone. It is then that Vladimir Mikhailovich feels the full weight of his solitude and the death of his only true friend.

Isolation occurs for both the dog and the man and, maybe unintentionally, Andreev sheds light on the selfishness of those suffering from clinical depression, who, in their attempt to address their own problems, become so self-possessed that they further alienate themselves from others. This story is highly autobiographical, with Andreev in the part of Vladimir Mikhailovich and Moisei Moseevich in the role of the dog Vasiuk. Alekseevskii attests to the fact that 'The Friend' was written about Moisei Moseevich, the Andreev family pet. He argues that Andreev's faithful companion knew all of his different moods and would act accordingly. If, for example, Andreev came home drunk, Moisei Moseevich knew to hide under the bed, but if Andreev came home sober, he would jump about and lick his master's hand. While Andreev studied for his final exams, Moisei Moseevich was his constant companion, seemingly reading each page along with his master.[137] Pavel also remembers that his brother often turned to his dog when he was sick or when he locked himself in his room for several days due to depression. Moisei Moseevich soothed Andreev's 'yearning for love, incomprehensible melancholy, and the extreme, notwithstanding [his] acquaintances, solitude.'[138]

As mentioned previously, 'In the Spring' is an autobiographical story about a young man, Pavel, who contemplates suicide but finds meaning in life once he must support his mother and siblings following his father's death. The puzzling question is why did Pavel want to kill himself in the first place? Andreev writes: '[Pavel] was not in love with anyone, he was not experiencing any sorrow, and he wanted to live, but everything in the world seemed to him unnecessary, meaningless and therefore repugnant to the point of aversion, to the point of ill-tempered spasms on his face.'[139] The question is answered in Pavel's transformation after examining his father's coffin. As he leaves the barn, the 'deep remorse of an exhausted heart' and 'unsolved pathological melancholy' is replaced with a new appreciation for life and, eventually, a new goal in life – to save his family. Typical of Andreev, it is the ailing heart and the pervasive sadness that represent the physical and psychological symptoms of illness which lead to thoughts of suicide. Possibly even more important is that family and human contact saved the character as well as the author himself.

Woodward argues that the problems of estrangement and miscommunication influence an entire cycle of Andreev's early stories and are closely tied to his own sense of reality and self-criticism.[140] Isolation and loneliness thematically underpin the previously discussed stories involving prisons, insane asylums and hospitals. Viacheslav Grechnev, for example, claims that 'Phantoms' is essentially about alienation and solitude as the patients, doctor and nurse in the asylum are unable to communicate with each other.[141] This is also a consistent element of Andreev's failed personal and literary romances, as well as in works like 'In the Basement,' 'At the Window,' 'The City' (Gorod) and 'Ipatov' where the ill are marginalized; at best voyeurs and at worst disenfranchised.

The issue of finding meaning in his life was clearly exacerbated by the death of Aleksandra and his ensuing search for companionship. Much like during his years at school and university, Andreev was once again in need of the balance that would help him negotiate his self-perceived high wire act above madness and death. Nadezhda Antonova (now Fokht) briefly re-entered his life when she accompanied him from Berlin to Capri, but due to his grief and heavy drinking she soon left, although Andreev believed that they would eventually marry.[142] Veresaev writes of Andreev, while on Capri: 'The impression from him was such: [his] soul thrashed about and grieved, frozen in dismal solitude and it seemed to him that if he could find a loving female soul that everything in him would right itself and everything would be fine.' Veresaev suggests, however, that it was not easy for Andreev to find such a person, especially when he offered his hand in marriage to every passing woman.[143] As mentioned in his diary entry above, Andreev again met with Nadezhda in 1907, after she had divorced her husband, but they were unable to establish a permanent relationship.

One of the more telling memoirs of this period comes from the actress, Alisa Georgievna Koonen (1889–1974), who caught Andreev's fancy during rehearsals for his play *Life of Man*, just after his return from Capri. According to Koonen, the author was attracted to her because she reminded him of his recently deceased wife. This awkward comparison was made even more memorable when Andreev proclaimed: 'Our generation is a generation of insane people, searching for truth, rebelling and suffering. Such people are always drawn to the young, serene. Here I am and I would like to be more often near you.'[144]

Andreev began to write long letters to Koonen from St Petersburg. When in Moscow, he would appear unexpectedly and was often in a good mood – buoyant and happy. After her performances, Andreev would take Alisa on long evening sleigh rides in various parks. However, this outward buoyancy and success masked a more troubled internal life – 'in front of me was a lonely person, deeply unhappy, and I began to relate to him with a funny feeling of tenderness and pity, rejoicing when I was successful in driving away the gloominess, despair, which so often tortured him.'[145] Andreev tried to hide this morose side by being especially attentive and constantly joking.

On one of his visits, Andreev brought the plans for his large house which was to be constructed in Vammelsuu, near the Gulf of Finland. He told Koonen he would like her to live in this house with him and she, feeling uncomfortable, tried to turn the conversation in a more humorous direction. The next time Andreev came to Moscow, he brought his mother to meet Alisa. The meeting did not go well as Anastasiia Nikolaevna told of her son's illness – of hallucinations when he thought he saw his dead wife or, better yet, when he awaited her arrival. After this, there was a break in their relationship. Koonen intentionally avoided meeting Andreev and he also stopped going to the theater.

One evening, after everyone had gone to bed, Andreev rang at Alisa's door. When her father opened it, he found the author in a terrible state asking to speak to Koonen. Her father convinced Andreev to leave, reasoning that it was not appropriate to speak to a young lady in such a condition, at such an hour of the evening. Koonen later spoke to Andreev and explained that she could not marry him or be a part of his life. The two did not see each other until a year later, when Alisa happened to be performing in St Petersburg. 'Pale, thin, terribly excited, he came up to me in the dressing room and unexpectedly pulled a revolver from his pocket.'[146] Koonen grabbed him and made him sit on the couch. His excited desperation turned to depression and the two sat in the theater talking until the evening performance. They only saw each other once more in the Passazh shopping center in St Petersburg after Andreev had married again, and the exchange was complicated when Andreev took offense at what he perceived as Alisa's attempt to ignore him.

This fascinating glimpse into Andreev's failed courtship of Koonen replicates the pattern of behavior that is central to Andreev's personality before and after these events. His fear of solitude repeatedly drives Andreev to find a companion who will alleviate the melancholy and anxiety that haunt him. These difficult psychological periods result in abuse of alcohol and the contemplation of suicide. Ironically, this behavior isolates him further from the people with whom he most wants to connect because they cannot meet his emotional demands. As Kleinman correctly argues 'bizarre actions of florid mental illness stigmatize because they break cultural conventions about what is acceptable appearance and behavior, while invoking cultural categories of what is ugly, feared, alien, or inhuman.'[147] Andreev wished to avoid the stigmatization of mental illness, and yet his volatile emotional behavior is remembered as a major part of his posthumous legacy.

In 1908, Andreev rewrote the final act of his play *Life of Man* to better express the loneliness and solitude of his main character.[148] He also published 'Curse of the Beast' (Prokliatie zveria), the story of a schizophrenic who is caught between his love for nature and his fascination with city life. In his tormented mind, the main character is disturbed by the cramped city-dwellers' prison-like existence. He eventually feels oppressed by his own solitude and is disillusioned with the city, which is embodied by a caged seal in the zoo. Soon many more of Andreev's characters would associate the prison cell with the isolation of mental illness, a physical representation of a psychological reality.

'Curse of the Beast' was written with Aleksandra Mikhailovna's death in Berlin in mind and was dedicated to her memory. Therefore, it is reasonable to read it in the context of Andreev's own mourning process. Yet, once we plumb a little deeper, we find many of the same ideas that have informed Andreev's own descriptions of mental illness prior to his loss. For example, the introduction speaks of 'many doors – without an exit' recalling 'Phantoms' or 'a corridor between two deaf stone walls' that might evoke a similarly impenetrable obstacle in 'The Wall.'[149] The story is constructed in fragments, much like 'Red Laugh,' creating disorientation for the reader, while the main character's madness creates several doubles, one of whom is a 'semi-insane erotomaniac' – a similar claim that Tolstoi's wife made about Andreev.[150]

Of possibly more importance is the character's actual illness experience, described as a loss of individuality by which he becomes a part of the collective body of the city until he 'takes on all of the typical characteristics of a degenerate.'[151] The idea that the city saps the energy out of the individual is nothing new, therefore Andreev's character hopes that by escaping to a park, that he might be able to regain his sanity. Yet, as he staggers his way through the city, he realizes that he is alone, as everyone else has also lost their individuality (and possibly humanity) becoming mere phantoms or animals. Once in the park, where there is a zoo, the main character finds that the cages for the animals are just as restrictive as the city is for the individual. While there he believes that he is cursed by a caged seal. Like Father Fiveiskii, the curse is, in fact, the realization of his own madness. Eventually, the main character decides to return to the city now that he is most certainly cursed / insane.

In his own personal life, Andreev eventually did find a companion who could assuage his feelings of solitude. Her name was Anna (Matil'da) Il'inichna Denisevich. One version suggests that Andreev originally hired her as his literary secretary, upon the recommendation of Chukovskii, and within a month they were married. Liudmila Ken and Leonid Rogov, however, have found evidence that Andreev actually knew Anna as early as November 1907 and engaged in correspondence (as well as declarations of love) well *before* Anna became his secretary.[152] At the beginning of April, the couple stopped in Orel on their way to the Crimea to be married. There, Andreev celebrated the tenth anniversary of the beginning of his literary career by reading from his new work 'The Story of the Seven Who Were Hanged' to a crowd of about twenty-five people.[153] Afterwards, the couple continued south and was married on 21 April 1908 in Yalta. Finally, Andreev had found a companion to fill the perceived void in his soul. The house that he had hoped to share with the actress Koonen, in May of that same year, became home to Leonid Niko-laevich, Anna Il'inichna and their combined families.[154] There, they had another three children together: Savva (1909–1970), Vera (1910–1986) and Valentin (1912–1988).

With his marriage to Anna, Andreev believed that he had finally escaped his solitude. He had found a woman with whom he could rebuild his life – a new life of literary success and financial comfort. After several years of loneliness and depression, Andreev could now settle down in the Finnish countryside and enjoy the comforts that his literary and dramatic triumphs had won him. Yet, even with the newfound stability of family life, Vadim writes that his father 'was beset with insu-perable loneliness.'[155]

Shipovnik

Andreev's isolation from his former Moscow life was evident not only in his attempt to recreate the *Sreda* literary circle, but also actualized in his movement to the *Shipovnik* publishing house in St Petersburg. Shortly after declining the editorship of the *Znanie* almanac because Gor'kii did not support the inclusion of Blok and Sologub as mentioned previously, Andreev began to publish in the *Shipovnik* literary almanacs. His play *Life of Man* appeared in their first number and 'Darkness' in the third. By the fourth number, Andreev had become one of the literary editors. 'The Story of the Seven Who Were Hanged' was in the fifth number and *Tsar Hunger* was published by *Shipovnik* as a separate book with illustrations by Evgenii Lansere (1875–1946). Working closely with Zinovii Grzhebin (1877–1929), Andreev had a significant say in what appeared in the almanacs. Within these pages were found some of the old *Znanie* writers, such as Kuprin, Bunin and Zaitsev, symbolist artists like Leon Bakst (1866–1924), Aleksandr Benois (1870–1960) and Mstislav Dobuzhinskii (1875–1957) and many of the symbolist writers and poets, including Blok and Sologub. The almanacs in a sense broke many of the former literary allegiances, mixing authors from rival literary camps as well as those from the same camps who had significant disagreements over their movements' development. In many ways, *Shipovnik* reflected Andreev himself – a realist, as considered by the decadents and a suspicious symbolist according to his former realist colleagues.

During the period 1904–8, Andreev lost both his youngest sister and his wife, destabilizing the *balance* that he had momentarily found in his personal life. His literary works became more rebellious, while both reflecting the political uncertainty of the times and a growing fascination with symbolism. Although madness became a less dominant theme of his works during this period, we might view this as a stage of creative gestation as Andreev would soon intertwine the various themes of mental illness, criminality, political rebellion and incarceration into coherent statements about the devolution of Russian society.

Notes

1 'The Governor' was first published in the third number of the journal *Truth* in 1906. Andreev, 'Gubernator,' vol. 2, *Sobranie sochinenii v 6 tomakh*, 128–9. In English, I use the translation of Andreieff, Leonid. *His Excellency the Governor*. Translated by Maurice Magnus (London: C.W. Daniel, Ltd., 1924) 60–1.

2 Greenslade, William. 'Fitness and the *fin de siècle*.' In *Fin de Siècle/Fin du Globe*. Edited by John Stokes (London: Macmillan, 1992) 38–9.

3 Beer, *Renovating Russia*, 76.

4 Anisimov, *Literaturnoe nasledstvo*, 218. Elpat'evskii claims that the two Turks were working for Andreev's neighbor. See Elpat'evskii, S. 'Leonid Nikolaevich Andreev: Iz vospominaniia.' *Byloe*, 27–8 (1925): 280.

5 Ken and Rogov, *Zhizn' Leonida Andreeva*, 130.

6 Andreev, 'Prizraki,' 90–1 / 174–5.

7 Anisimov, *Literaturnoe nasledstvo*, 228.

8 Chuvakov, V., ed. 'Iz pisem L. Andreeva – K.P. Piatnitskomu.' *Voprosy literatury*, 8 (1971): 166.

9 Teleshov, *Zapiski pisatelia*, 118 / 92.

10 Veresaev, 'Leonid Andreev,' 410.

11 OGLMT, f. 12, op. 1, no. 165 (KP 5693 of), 61–61b.

12 Lutz, Tom. *American Nervousness, 1903: An Anecdotal History* (Ithaca: Cornell University Press, 1991) 32–4.

13 Morris, *The Culture of Pain*, 104.

14 Hogan, Joseph and Rebecca Hogan. 'When the Subject Is Not the Self: Multiple Personality and Manic-Depression.' *a/b: Auto/Biography Studies*, 16, 1 (Summer 2001): 40–1; 44.

15 This section is a synopsis of Iezuitova's chapter on the history of the

reception and resulting scholarship dedicated to 'Red Laugh.' See Iezuitova, L. "Krasnyi smekh' ego literaturnoe okruzhenie, kritika, analiz.' In *Tvorchestvo Leonida Andreeva (1892–1906)*, 151–86.

16 Anisimov, *Literaturnoe nasledstvo*, 243.

17 Mumortsev, *Psikhopaticheskiia cherty v geroiakh Leonida Andreeva*, 15–16.

18 Elpat'evskii, 'Leonid Nikolaevich Andreev,' 277.

19 Evreinov, N. 'O «Krivom Zerkale». Kak Leonid Andreev smeialsia v borodu.' *Novyi zhurnal*, 35 (1953): 207.

20 Bezzubov, V. 'Smekh Leonida Andreeva.' In *Tvrochestvo Leonida Andreeva: Issledovaniia i materially*. Edited by G. Kurliandskaia (Kursk: Kurskii gos. ped. institut, 1983) 15–16.

21 Andreev, 'Smekh,' vol. 1, *Sobranie sochinenii v 6 tomakh*, 267.

22 Fatov, *Molodye gody Leonida Andreeva*, 70.

23 OGLMT, f. 12, op. 1, no. 78 (KP 1957). Letter of Isaak Novik dated February 1901.

24 Andreev, 'Lozh', vol. 1, *Sobranie sochinenii v 6 tomakh*, 274.

25 Bezzubov, 'Smekh Leonida Andreeva,' 16. Bezzubov does not directly say madness. He states that laughter comes from the 'terrible world' that Andreev wants to depict. This is a shorthand reference to Feodor Tiutchev's poetic cycle, which was concerned with the chaos that inhabits and unites the natural elements with the human soul. This cycle is also referenced in Aleksandr Blok's memoir of Andreev in which he tells of Andreev's internal 'chaos.' For a discussion of how one might understand Bezzubov's use of the phrase 'terrible world' see White, *Memoirs and Madness*, 243–55.

26 Andreev, 'Zhizn' Vasiliia Fiveiskogo,' vol. 1, *Sobranie sochinenii v 6 tomakh*, 552–4. In English, see Andreyev, Leonid. 'The Life of Father Vassily.' In *When the King Loses His Head and Other Stories*. Translated by Archibald J. Wolfe (New York: International Book Publishing Company, 1920) 270–1.

27 Andreev, 'Prizraki,' 76 / 149–50.

28 Andreev, *Chernye maski*, vol. 3, *Sobranie sochinenii v 6 tomakh*, 367; 369; 387; 388. In English, see Andreyeff, Leonid. *The Black Maskers*. In *Plays by Leonid Andreyeff*. Translated by Clarence L. Meader and Fred Newton Scott (New York: Charles Scribner's Sons, 1918) 24; 29; 52–3; 54.

29 Andreev, *Sashka Zhegulev*, vol. 4, *Sobranie sochinenii v 6 tomakh*, 192–6. In English, see Andreyev, *Sashka Jigouleff*, 194–9.

30 Andreev, 'On,' vol. 4, *Sobranie sochinenii v 6 tomakh*, 265–66; also see 284; 287; 288.

31 Andreev, 'Moi anekdoty,' vol. 5, *Sobranie sochinenii v 6 tomakh*, 33–4.

32 Bezzubov, 'Smekh Leonida Andreeva,' 24.

33 Andreev, 'Krasnyi smekh,' vol. 2, *Sobranie sochinenii v 6 tomakh*, 22. In English, see 'Red Laugh' in Andreyev, *Visions: Stories and Photographs by Leonid Andreyev*, 81.

34 Ibid.

35 Ibid., 25 / 84.

36 Ibid., 28 / 87.

37 Ibid., 51 / 114.

38 Ibid., 51 / 116.

39 Ibid., 52 / 116.

40 Ibid., 53 / 118.

41 Ibid., 56 / 120–1.

42 Ibid., 62–5 / 128–33.

43 Couser, G. Thomas. 'Critical Conditions: Teaching Illness Narrative.' In *Teaching Literature and Medicine*. Edited by Anne Hunsaker Hawkins and Marilyn Chandler McEntyre (New York: Modern Language Association, 2000) 282–8.

44 Woodward avoids making a one to one comparison, but suggests in relation to 'Red Laugh' that Andreev has 'the ability to experience, as though they were his own, the emotions of his characters.' See Woodward, *Leonid Andreyev: A Study*, 102.

45 Chukovskii, *Kniga o Leonide Andreeve*, 79 / 61.

46 Andreev, 'Krasnyi smekh,' 49 / 112.

47 There are various stories about what happened to Andreev's hand. Pavel Andreev claims that the injury to his brother's hand occurred when he was cut with a blade while ice-skating. See Pavel Andreev, 'Vospominaniia o Leonide Andreeve,' 152–3. Sof'i Panova claims that Andreev ran a shard of glass through his hand. See Fatov, *Molodye gody Leonida Andreeva*, 201. Brusianin claims that while ice-skating, Andreev fell on some broken glass. See Brusianin, *Leonid Andreev. Zhizn' i tvorchestvo*, 27.

48 Hawkins, Anne Hunsaker. *Reconstructing Illness: Studies in Pathography* (West Layfayette, Indiana: Purdue University Press, 1993) 2.

49 Frank, Arthur. *The Wounded Storyteller: Body, Illness, and Ethics* (Chicago: University of Chicago Press, 1995) 69.

50 Hawkins, *Reconstructing Illness*, 61–90.

51 Andreev, 'Krasnyi smekh,' 39–40 / 100–2.

52 Ibid., 47–8 / 110.

53 Ibid., 35 / 95.

54 Rimmon-Kenan, Shlomith. 'The Story of "I": Illness and Narrative Identity.' *Narrative*, 10, 1 (January 2002): 19–24.

55 Jamison, Kay Redfield. 'Manic-Depressive Illness and Creativity.' *Scientific American* (February 1995): 66–7; Jamison, Kay Redfield. *Touched with Fire: Manic-Depressive Illness and the Artistic Temperament* (New York: Free Press, 1993) 32.

56 Andreev, 'Krasnyi smekh,' 49 / 112.

57 Ibid., 22–3 / 81.

58 Ibid., 25 / 84.

59 Ibid., 29 / 88.

60 Ibid., 32 / 92.

61 Ibid., 39 / 100.

62 Ibid., 47–9 / 110–12.

63 Mumortsev, *Psikhopaticheskiia cherty v geroiakh Leonida Andreeva*, 13.

64 Andreev, 'Krasnyi smekh,' 53 / 118.

65 Ibid., 55 / 120.

66 Ibid., 56 / 122.

67 Ibid., 61 / 128.

68 Ibid., 65 / 132.

69 Ibid., 71 / 140.

70 Woodward, *Leonid Andreyev: A Study,* 104.

71 Rimmon-Kenan, 'The Story of "I": Illness and Narrative Identity,' 11–12.

72 Andreev, Leonid. 'Pis'ma iz Taganskoi tiur'my.' Edited and commentary by L. Afonin. *Zvedza,* 8 (1971): 172.

73 Fatov, N., ed. 'Pis'ma Leonida Adreeva k A.S. Serafimovichu.' In *Moskovskii al'manakh,* book 1 (Moskovskii rabochii: Moscow, 1926) 289.

74 Gilman, *Difference and Pathology,* 59–75.

75 Brusianin, *Leonid Andreev. Zhizn' i tvorchestvo,* 47–9; 53; 108–11.

76 For the role and influence of Nietzschean philosophy at the beginning of the twentieth century in Russia see Clowes, Edith W. *The Revolution of Moral Consciousness: Nietzsche in Russian Literature, 1890–1914* (DeKalb, Illinois: Northern Illinois University Press, 1988); Rosenthal, Bernice Glatzer, ed. *Nietzsche in Russia* (Princeton, NJ: Princeton University Press, 1986); Rosenthal, Bernice Glatzer. *New Myth, New World: From Nietzsche to Stalinism* (University Park, Pennsylvania: Pennsylvania State University Press, 2002).

77 The information about the Greek god Dionysus is from Tripp, Edward. *The Meridian Handbook of Classical Mythology (Formerly Titled: Crowell's Handbook of Classical Mythology)* (New York: New American Library, 1970) 203–11.

78 Rosenthal, *New Myth, New World,* 33.

79 Clowes, *The Revolution of Moral Consciousness,* 84–113; 175–200.

80 Ibid., 84–96.

81 Woodward, *Leonid Andreyev: A Study,* 87, footnote 6.

82 Beer, 'The Medicalization of Religious Deviance,' 461.

83 Ibid., 469.

84 Ibid., 482.

85 Kaun, *Leonid Andreyev: A Critical Study,* 206.

86 Woodward, *Leonid Andreyev: A Study,* 89–90.

87 Andreev, 'Zhizn' Vasiliia Fiveiskogo,' 495–6 / 173–6.

88 Ibid., 498 / 179.

89 Woodward, *Leonid Andreyev: A Study,* 93–4.

90 Afonin, *Leonid Andreev,* 112–20.

91 Andreev, *K zvezdam,* vol. 2, *Sobranie sochinenii v 6 tomakh,* 367. In English, see Andreieff, Leonid. *To The Stars.* Translated by Dr. A. Goudiss. *Poet Lore,* 18, 4 (Winter 1907): 462.

92 Ibid., 367 / 463.

93 Ibid., 367 / 462.

94 Ibid., 368 / 463.

95 Ibid., 369 / 465.

96 Ibid., 370 / 466. The translation is incorrect in that *torzhestvo* should not be translated as *orgy.*

97 Ibid., 371 / 467.

98 Clowes, *The Revolution of Moral Consciousness,* 129.

99 Ibid., 137.

100 Ibid., 141.

101 Andreev, 'Pis'ma iz Taganskoi tiur'my,' 180–1. It probably did not help that Andreev had decided to quit smoking as well.

102 LRA, MS. 606 \ G.1.ii.b*.

103 Andreev, Valentin. 'Chto pomniu ob ottse.' In *Andreevskii sbornik: Issledovaniia i materialy.* Edited by L. Afonin (Kursk: Kurskii gos. ped. institut, 1975) 259.

104 White, Frederick H. '«Tainaia zhizn'» Leonida Andreeva: Istoriia bolezni.' *Voprosy literatury*, 1 (2005): 323–4. Also see White, Frederick H. 'Leonid Andreev's Release from Prison and the Codification of Mental Illness.' *New Zealand Slavonic Journal*, 41 (2007): 19–42.

105 Aingori et al., 'Zabluzhdenie ili obman: o tak nazyvaemom sumasshestvii Leonida Andreeva,' 105.

106 Andreev, 'Pis'ma iz Taganskoi tiur'my,' 182.

107 Ibid., 183, footnote 2.

108 OGLMT, f. 12, op. 1, no. 165 (KP 5693 of), 59–60.

109 Pavel Andreev, 'Vospominaniia o Leonide Andreeve,' 203–4.

110 See White, '«Tainaia zhizn'» Leonida Andreeva: Istoriia bolezni,' 325; White, Frederick H. 'Leonid Andreev: Litsedestvo i obman.' *Novoe literaturnoe obozrenie*, 69 (2004): 143; White, *Memoirs and Madness*, 230. Russian critics have taken exception to this argument. See Aingori et al., 'Zabluzhdenie ili obman: o tak nazyvaemom sumasshestvii Leonida Andreeva.'

111 OGLMT, f. 12, op. 1, no. 144 (KP 5692), 86.

112 OGLMT, f. 12, op. 1, no. 165 (KP 5693 of), 28.

113 OGLMT, f. 12, op. 1, no. 144 (KP 5692), 85.

114 Bernheimer, *Decadent Subjects*, 12–13.

115 Linden, Simeon. 'Leonidas Andreieff.' *The Independent Review*, (February 1906): 216–17.

116 Afonin, *Leonid Andreev*, 181.

117 Ken and Rogov, *Zhizn' Leonida Andreeva*, 174–5.

118 Gor'kii, *Kniga o Leonide Andreeve*, 58–60 / 43–4.

119 Ibid., 61–2 / 45–6.

120 Vadim Andreev, *Detstvo*, 24–6 / 18–19.

121 Zaitsev, *Kniga o Leonide Andreeve*, 136–7 / 99.

122 Chulkov, *Kniga o Leonide Andreeve*, 121–2. In English, see White, *Memoirs and Madness*, 87–8.

123 Woodward, *Leonid Andreyev: A Study*, 157–9.

124 Meyerhold left the entire stage bare and simply hung gray linen (Blok describes it as burlap) to create a smoky monotone gray space, which curled about the figures on stage. Meyerhold wished to create for each scene a source of light which would illuminate a certain area and the actors were to appear as sculptures. Andreev was unhappy with this presentation as he felt that it was too mystical and gloomy.

125 Kazimir Vinkent'evich Bravich (Baranovich) (1861–1912), actor.

126 Blok, *Kniga o Leonide Andreeve*, 100–1. In English, see White, *Memoirs and Madness*, 74.

127 Aiaks [A. Izmailov].'U Leonida Andreeva.' *Berzhevye vedomosti* (Vech. vyp.), 10225 (28 November 1907): 1.

128 Chulkov, *Kniga o Leonide Andreeve*, 109 / 87.

129 LRA, MS. 606 \ E. 8; Entry for 9 October 1907.

130 LRA, MS. 606 \ E.1 *12 March–30 June 1890; 21 September 1898*; Entry for 23

March 1890. See also LRA, MS. 606 \ E.2 3 *July 1890–18 February 1891*; Entry for 30 July 1890.

131 LRA, MS. 606 \ E. 8 *27 March 1897–23 April 1901; 1 January 1903; 9 October 1907; 28 April*; Entry for 6 April 1900.

132 Ibid., Entry for 27 November 1898.

133 Katonina, V. 'Moi vospominaniia o Leonide Andreeve.' *Krasnii student*, 7–8 (1923): 17.

134 Ibid., 21.

135 Daniil Andreev and Beklemisheva, *Rekviem*, 205.

136 Andreev, 'Drug,' vol. 1, *Sobranie sochinenii v 6 tomakh*, 134–9. In English, the story can be read as 'The Friend' in Andreyev, *The Little Angel and Other Stories*. Translated by W. H. Lowe (New York: Alfred A. Knopf, 1916) 135–46.

137 OGLMT, f. 12, op. 1, no. 144 (KP 5692), 24. Rimma says the same thing about the relationship between Andreev and Moisei Moseevich. See OGLMT, f. 12, op. 1, no. 165 (KP 5693 of), 25–6.

138 Pavel Andreev, 'Vospominaniia o Leonide Andreeve,' 194.

139 Andreev, 'Vesnoi,' vol. 1, *Sobranie sochinenii v 6 tomakh*, 369.

140 Woodward, *Leonid Andreyev: A Study*, 59–60.

141 Grechnev, 'Rasskaz L. Andreeva «Prizraki»,' 75.

142 Ivanova, L. and and L. Ken, eds. 'Leonid Andreev. Pis'ma k Pavlu Nikolae-vichu i Anne Ivanovne Andreevym.' *Russkaia literatura*, no. 1 (2003): 171–2.

143 Veresaev, 'Leonid Andreev,' 416.

144 Koonen, Alisa. *Stranitsy zhizni* (Moscow: Kukushka, 2003) 72.

145 Ibid.

146 Ibid., 74.

147 Kleinman, *The Illness Narratives*, 159.

148 Andreev, *Zhizn' cheloveka*, vol. 2, *Sobranie sochinenii v 6 tomakh*, 491–92. In English, Andreev's explanation for the changes to Act V of *The Life of Man* is in Andreyeff, *Plays by Leonid Andreyeff*, 141–2.

149 Andreev, 'Prokliatie zveria', vol. 3, *Sobranie sochinenii v 6 tomakh*, 17.

150 Ibid., 41.

151 Ibid., 22.

152 Ken and Rogov, *Zhizn' Leonida Andreeva*, 203–4.

153 Ibid., 206.

154 Anna Il'inichna had a daughter from her first marriage – Nina Konstanti-novna Karnitskaia (1906–1987).

155 Vadim Andreev, *Detstvo*, 40 / 28.

6

Feigned and performed

But the most amazing – fall 1908, when I suffered through that terrible situation with A[nna]. Undoubtedly, in relation to personal suffering, for those months I was in a state of psychosis, severe semi-madness; and all my thoughts were given to Anna, to new unexpected facts and revelations, to [this] morbid investigation. A desire to know the whole truth was my idée fixe; exclusively, logic was [my] instrument – in other words, the most intensive work of [my] mind [was focused] in this one direction. And at this same time with unexpected ease and quickness (my hand was still hurting and I dictated) was written: 'My Notes', moreover several times work was interrupted by revelations-surprises of the truth, akin to suicide or madness; and then *Days of our Life, Black Maskers, Earthborn Son* and *Anathema*. And all of them were complete improvisation.

Leonid Andreev, from his Finnish diary.[1]

As Andreev began to rebuild his life around his new family in Vammelsuu, various ideas from his earlier works started to coalesce in coherent and consistent ways. In dramatic and literary works of this period the performance is a way of interacting with madness in an attempt to hide its effects from the public, because there exists the threat of incarceration for those deemed abnormal or dangerous (including the insane), therefore verisimilitude (giving a *truth* that the public wants to see) is necessary to avoid the stigma of madness.

Institutional spaces: prisons

Andreev bought a plot of land near the Finnish fishing village of Vammelsuu in the summer of 1907. He then bought many of the adjacent fields, eventually owning nearly fifteen hectares, or thirty-seven acres, of land. Here Andreev built an enormous house in 1908, which he would later jokingly call his 'Villa Advance' as it had been bought with

6.1 A photograph of Andreev taken in the 1910s.

money advanced to him for future literary works by the publishing house *Niva*. Many of the capital's intellectuals rented cheap summer cottages in the area, while literary critic Kornei Chukovskii, professor of psychiatry Vladimir Bekhterev, and painter Il'ia Repin (1844–1930), also established permanent residences in villages around Vammelsuu. This new residence was perceived by some as an ostentatious display of wealth and success.

Although still under construction, by May 1908 the scaffolding had been removed and the Andreevs could move into a house still pungent with the scent of resin and fresh paint. It was built in the Nordic style with heavy wood beams, high ceilings, large windows and big porcelain fireplaces. There were twenty stoves to heat fifteen rooms, a tower fifteen meters high and a multi-layered sloping roof made of red tiles that gave the impression of either royal grandeur or a massive factory depending on the visitor's disposition towards the author. Outside, among the piles of beams, bricks and tiles there was also an entire complex of structures: woodshed, coach house, stables, ice house and barn. At the bottom of a steep slope, next to the Black rivulet, there was a bathhouse, a pump house and two landing stages for Andreev's boats. The landscape around the house was quite barren and though Andreev had trees planted, few took to the Finnish clay soil.[2]

Although Andreev still took part in literary society in St Petersburg and Moscow, he confined himself mainly to his villa where he engaged in various hobbies, including photography and boating. Literary society and his family, therefore, came to him and, occasionally, one could count as many as fifty visitors at once. In this case, Andreev housed guests in his neighbors' empty winter chalets after a long evening of socializing. Even with such generosity, Vadim suggests that many of these guests did not actually like his father. When entertaining guests Andreev was like an actor who has taken the stage, but remains completely disconnected from his audience. Vadim believed that it was a result of this need to play certain roles that his father was beset by an insuperable loneliness his entire life.[3]

Even as Andreev sought refuge in Vammelsuu from the outside world, the political turmoil of the times continued to weigh upon him. Possibly as a result, we can trace the theme of institutional spaces in his works, from hospitals to asylums and finally to prisons. Andreev expressed his association of prisons with insane asylums to the journalist and translator Herman Bernstein (1876–1935): 'Russia today is a lunatic asylum. The people who are hanged are not the people who should be hanged. Everywhere else honest people are at large and only criminals are in prison. In Russia the honest people are in prison and the criminals are at large.'[4]

In 1908 Andreev wrote 'The Story of the Seven Who Were Hanged' about how seven prisoners meet their day of execution. In this story, the prison is associated with an insane asylum: '[I]t appeared to the warden, who passed all his life in the prison, and who looked upon its laws as the laws of nature, that the prison and all the life within it was something like an insane asylum, in which he, the warden, was the chief lunatic.'[5] Following this statement, each character deals in his or her own way with the fear and anxiety of execution.

The story begins with a plot to assassinate a government official. The plot is foiled and several terrorists are arrested, tried and condemned. In prison, along with the five terrorists, there are also two murderers: Ianson and a freedom-loving gypsy. Andreev psychologically explores each character's relationship with life and death. Woodward gives special significance to how the characters are paired as they walk to their execution, understanding Ianson and the gypsy as the least advanced, with the women Musia and Tania fusing with Werner to show 'the progression of increasing enlightenment' towards a 'spiritual and philosophical conquest of death.'[6] In a similar way, Kaun sees it as a story in which the revolutionaries 'prove victorious over death in the last moments of their life, and at their very executions.' He argues that in spite of the death sentence, the story 'is most exhilarating and stimulating, in that it justifies life, struggle, striving, self-sacrifice, through the exalted feeling of immortality.'[7]

Yet, death is tinged with the shadow of madness for several characters in this prison. Musia gives herself over to the music of life, although very briefly she is afraid that these are hallucinations of a sickly mind.[8] Sergei Golovin follows a strict training regime, but then begins to doubt the necessity of physical fitness. His fear grows and overtakes him and 'every thought seemed to him but madness, every motion – madness.'[9] However, once he masters his fear he returns to his training routine, accepting his death as a final exercise – hanging from the neck. Werner's relationship with life and death is negotiated through logic and the game of chess. Prior to his arrest, Werner felt 'deadly fatigue. By nature rather a mathematician than a poet, he had not known until now any inspiration, any ecstasy and at times he felt like a madman, looking for the squaring of a circle in pools of human blood.'[10] Werner overcomes his fear, continues playing chess, and embraces death as something joyous. It is only then that 'the [dull] fatigue that had tormented Werner during the last two years [...] disappeared.'[11] Werner thinks that he will overcome death and yet, on the way to the gallows he realizes that 'reality was intoxicated with madness and Death, united with Life [...].'[12] Even so, Werner is sure that he will transcend death.

The characters overcome their fear of death, and madness is only a passing concern. However, their comrade Vasilii Kashirin loses all control and is plagued by phantoms and automatic puppets.

> Madness came crawling painfully. His consciousness was dying out like an extinguished bonfire, growing icy like the corpse of a man who had just died, whose heart is still warm but whose hands and feet had already become stiffened with cold. His dying reason flared up as red as blood again and said that he, Vasily Kashirin, might perhaps become insane here, suffer pains for which there is no name, reach a degree of anguish and suffering that had never been experienced by a single living being; that he might beat his head against the wall, pick his eyes out with his fingers, speak and shout whatever he pleased, that he might plead with tears that he could endure it no longer – and nothing would happen. Nothing could happen. And nothing happened.[13]

Even in his madness, which is described as a great physical torture, Kashirin accepts his death and finds some level of peace from the phantoms and puppets. When he is led out to execution with the other prisoners they are shocked at his disheveled appearance and vacant gaze. Andreev links death and madness in the character of Kashirin, as Musia says of Kashirin: 'He is dead already'[14] and a few moments later refers to him as a corpse.

The next story that Andreev published in 1908 was 'My Notes.' Woodward believes that Andreev wrote this story so soon after 'The Story of the Seven Who Were Hanged' in order to contrast Werner's ability to physically and psychologically transcend the prison with the doctor of mathematics' incorporation of the prison into his philosophical sense of individuality.[15] It would be just as productive to concentrate on the antagonistic relationship between logic and intuition, intellectual activity and the artistic temperament.[16] This binary opposition is very useful in understanding Andreev's narrative of illness, especially in reading 'My Notes.' Here Andreev contrasts the mathematician with the artist and how the rules and regulations of the prison influence their psyches. The mathematician-type in Andreev's works represents the rational in opposition to the emotional (artistic-type). Whether it is Kerzhentsev or Werner, the scientific, logical (Apollonian), mathematical mind attempts to understand, tame and control the irrational. Talent, creativity and uncontrolled (Dionysian) emotions are represented by the artist, an individual who courts the irrational. For Andreev, as for many at this time, these represent the two extremes of the struggle for life. They may also represent Andreev's own perception of his illness experience in which he was forced to balance his perceived *talent* with his need for stability and *meaning* in life.

In 'My Notes,' there are two main characters – the doctor of mathematics and the artist K. The doctor is in prison for killing several of his family members in order to gain a large inheritance, but he maintains his innocence. The mathematician suggests that people prefer the appearance of truth, rather than truth itself, and this is how he justifies being condemned to prison although, he claims, he did not commit the crime. His theory is that he *appeared* guilty and, therefore, was guilty in the eyes of the jury. He accepts his sentence and writes his notes to explain how, after being condemned to death, he discovered the great purpose of the universe, expressing disgust that those living free continue to slander life.[17]

The mathematician refers to his diary, to which the reader is not privy, and claims that it bears evidence that he is mentally ill.[18] In his youth he experienced 'a certain dreaminess [...]; a self-respect which was easily offended and which revolted at the slightest insignificant provocation; a passionate impetuosity in solving world problems; fits of melancholy alternated by equally wild fits of merriment,' which gave him 'a character of extreme unsteadiness, of sad and harsh discord.'[19] The artist K also appears to be mentally unstable. The difference between the two is their approach to life – the mathematician is logical and rational, while the artist is intuitive and creative.

When first imprisoned, the mathematician vigorously protested his confinement, and the difficulty of these first few years was compounded by the loss of his fiancé to another man, his mother's death, and failed friendships with those on the outside, which left him completely alone. After he accepted the fact that he would never be released, he was able to find peace. He embraced the idea that 'the infinite may be conceived by the human mind only when it is brought within certain boundaries,' thereby accepting his prison cell as a positive unifying limit and rejecting his desire to escape as useless and absurd.[20] However, Andreev was not advocating the mathematician's theories; rather, the acceptance of the prison by the character is rebuffed by Andreev, as we have seen in other stories.If there is any doubt about this, Andreev gives a description of the prison via the mathematician which reminds us of the hospitals and asylum we have already visited:

> Our prison is a huge five-storey building. Situated in the outskirts of the city, at the edge of a deserted field, overgrown with high grass, it attracts the attention of the wayfarer by its rigid outlines, promising him peace and rest after his endless wanderings. Not being plastered, the building has retained its natural dark red colour of old brick, and at a close view, I am told, it produces a gloomy, even threatening, impression, especially on nervous people, to whom the red bricks recall blood and bloody lumps of

human flesh. The small, dark, flat windows with iron bars naturally complete the impression and lend to the whole a character of gloomy harmony, or stern beauty. Even during good weather, when the sun shines upon our prison, it does not lose any of its dark and grim importance, and is constantly reminding the people that there are laws in existence and that punishment awaits those who break them.[21]

The mathematician takes great pleasure in his isolation from the outside world. He proudly describes the corridors with heavy locked and grated doors and the stone walls which encircle the prison. He even helps to design a more efficient prison – because, after all, it is the structure of the prison which enables him to maintain his *sanity*.[22] As a free man he had been nervous and weak, susceptible to illness, but the regularity of the prison has made him considerably stronger.[23]

The mathematician's rules and regulations are in direct opposition to the creative energy of the artist K. The warden asked the mathematician to pacify the young artist after he became enraged that he was provided with only a chalkboard for his drawings. The artist is driven to near madness each time he must destroy his art in order to create something new. Against prison policy, the artist draws on the walls of his cell with his own blood. To maintain order, the mathematician asks him to wash the walls but promises to get the artist paper and a pencil.

The warden suggests that the artist create a series of portraits, beginning with the mathematician. The mathematician describes his own portrait:

> My portrait would remind you, my indulgent reader, of that mysterious peculiarity of artists, according to which they very often transmit their own feelings, even their external features, to the subject upon which they are working. Thus, reproducing with remarkable likeness, the lower part of my face, where kindness and calm dignity are so harmoniously blended, K undoubtedly introduced into my eyes his own suffering and even his horror. Their fixed, immobile gaze; madness glimmering somewhere in their depth; the painful eloquence of a deep and infinitely lonely soul – all that was not mine.[24]

It seems that the mathematician is denying his own insanity, the madness to which he admitted earlier in the story. By disowning such a 'terrible face, full of wild contradictions,'[25] the mathematician holds to his original view that people prefer verisimilitude rather than veracity. The mathematician chooses to believe that his face transmits kindness and dignity rather than madness and suffering.

Failing to accept the restrictions of the prison, the artist K commits suicide by throwing himself from a table onto the stone floor. The artist could no longer paint portraits, and prior to his death the mathematician had seen 'the madness which shortly led him to his untimely grave.'[26] The difference in the two is that the mathematician is able to lie to himself in order to maintain some level or appearance of control. The artist could not delude himself and saw life for all of its realities. The mathematician laments, 'I cannot help feeling sorry for those unfortunate people who, like K, because of a peculiar construction of their brains, always turn their eyes toward the dark side, whereas there is so much joy and light in our prison!'[27] For a moment the mathematician also contemplates suicide as an escape from the prison, but the lack of structure causes him to reject this idea – not knowing what death entails would take him out of his controlled environment. Again, we think of Gor'kii and Andreev, Pomerantsev and the endlessly knocking patient; there are those individuals who can lie to themselves to create the appearance of harmony in life and there are those who cannot, who become victims of life.[28]

The mathematician's beliefs, however, are put to the test. Invited to the warden's house, he recounts details of his family's murder that seem to point to his own participation but, just as he is about to lose control, he performs for the warden's family as would be expected of an innocent man – he demands justice and the punishment of the *real* murderer – restoring the appearance of innocence. Afterwards, the mathematician sees the ghost of his dead father in his cell, but is able to ward off this phantom. He questions himself: 'I understand that the human ear and eye can be deceived – but how can the great and lucid human mind fall into such coarse and ridiculous deception?'[29] And then, in an act of self-deception, he rejects the possibility of his own guilt, reconfirming his belief in verisimilitude and maintaining his sanity by means of his intellect (something that Kerzhentsev could not do).

This successful performance leads the warden to fight for the mathematician's release and two months later he is liberated from prison. However, in freedom he finds 'self-deception and falsehood.'[30] He is visited by his former fiancé who tries to tell him that she still loves him, but she retreats in horror when he begins to laugh at her (Andreev's signature for madness). The mathematician realizes that he is losing his mind. In reaction to this he decides to recreate for himself the rules and regulations of the prison. In a small house on the outskirts of town he builds a cell and hires a jailer to maintain the prison's rigid regime. In this way he is able to reclaim his *sanity* although the rest of the town believes that he is completely insane.[31]

In the mathematician's argument, Natal'ia Generalova finds elements of the scientific theories of Auguste Comte (1798–1857), Henry Thomas

Buckle (1821–1862) and John Stuart Mill (1806–1883) on society and humanity.[32] She argues that the issues of confinement and rebellion, in several of Andreev's stories, are connected to both madness and political subjugation.[33] The characters who try to avoid madness are, in fact, attempting to avoid personal repression. The important point is that Andreev is now connecting madness with incarceration rather than treatment.

Foucault argues that a period of confinement began when the insane were contained and housed apart from the general population.[34] Previously, the mentally ill had been allowed to live on the outskirts of towns, but once identified as *dangerous*, governments created institutional spaces that confined the sick. The original intention was not to treat the ill, but cull the *abnormal* from society. Even after William Tuke (1732–1822) and Philippe Pinel (1745–1826) supposedly ushered in more humane methods of treatment, according to Foucault, fear was essential for the management of the mentally ill. Tuke 'substituted for the free terror of madness the stifling anguish of responsibility.' Guards using tactics of surveillance and judgment, initiated at Tuke's York Retreat, became standard for nineteenth-century mental asylums, and a dynamic was established by which the insane were given minority status and treated like children.[35] The state was the father figure and exercised sovereignty over the minor patient.[36]

Pinel believed that creating a domain of virtue, labor and social responsibility, without the fantastical aspects of religion, would be beneficial in reaching a basic morality that remained untouched by madness. However, '[i]n one and the same movement, the asylum becomes, in Pinel's hands, an instrument of moral uniformity and social denunciation.'[37] According to Foucault, madness had originally been combined with vice, laziness and indigence. After Pinel, insanity became a form of social failure, and fifty years later it was associated with social degeneracy.[38] Both the York Retreat and Pinel's asylum stood in judgment of patients, without possibility of appeal, and doled out punishment otherwise reserved for criminals.[39]

The theories of Tuke and Pinel led to the creation of a new authority in eighteenth century society – the medical professional. Rather than bringing scientific knowledge to the asylum, medical experts exercised moral and social authority over the madman's minority status. Physicians relied on age-old techniques of authority, judgment, punishment and love to create a semblance of medical practice, just when the treatment of mental illness was seeking acceptance as objective science.[40]

According to Julie V. Brown, the basis of the asylum system in Russia was institutional control and the incarceration of dangerous elements of society. The expansion of the asylum system was rationalized on similar grounds.[41] Madhouses, schools and hospitals had been under regional self-government jurisdiction since 1864. But the change to a singular controlling body for the mentally ill led to the incarceration of the insane in prisons and workhouses, while convicted criminals were often housed in asylums to evaluate their mental competence.[42] At the beginning of the twentieth century, many psychiatrists agreed with Pavel Iakobii's assessment that they were involved in *police* psychiatry, but attempted to place the blame on the tsarist government. Whereas psychiatrists had once embraced the role of protecting society from the dangerously ill, they now began to emphasize their limited responsibility in asylum admittance and blamed the government for gross violations of civil rights, especially with the incarceration of 'political' dissidents who were often shackled under the watchful eye of military guards; a common feature of the mental asylum after 1905.[43]

The role of institutional control over the mentally ill is an important thematic strand in Andreev's works. In 'Grand Slam' Prokopii Vasil'evich spends two months in a mental hospital after the death of his wife.[44] Kerzhentsev is incarcerated after he murders Savelov. It is noted that the mental asylum in 'Phantoms' houses fourteen *nonviolent* patients. In the play *Gaudeamus* the old student tells of spending a year in a mental hospital after both his wife and daughter died of diphtheria.[45] In *Sashka Zhegulev*, Timokhin commits suicide and his funeral is interrupted by a lunatic in the asylum where it is being held.[46] In *Diary of Satan*, Magnus tells Wondergood the story of a political exile who escapes and begins living with a group of religious fanatics. At a ceremony the exile ritually kills a small child believing it will save the innocent fools from committing a sin. The exiled man then goes mad and dies in an insane asylum.[47]

Clinically insane characters who have not been afforded treatment are also ubiquitous in Andreev's works. In 'Day of Anger',[48] *Tsar Hunger*,[49] 'He'[50] and *King, Law and Freedom* (Korol', zakon i svoboda),[51] characters are identified as insane. Vasilii Fiveiskii goes insane when he cannot raise a man from the dead.[52] Duke Lorenzo in the play *Black Maskers* recognizes that he is mad when he confronts his double.[53] Ipatov, a rich merchant, goes insane and removes himself from society, relying on his wife for comfort.[54] Insane Dan is a character in *The Ocean*.[55] Elena Dmitrievna kills herself in 'Sacrifice.'[56] Each one of these characters and many, many others would seemingly have benefited from some kind of psychiatric, if not institutional, care.

Andreev's representation of institutional control in the form of hospitals, asylums and prisons reflects the cultural anxiety of the Russian nation about irrational behavior. Illness, madness and criminality all were met with the same response – incarceration. In 1906, Andreev wrote lightheartedly to his friend Goloushev, 'Oh, what kind of straight forward plays I will write. Not one theater will produce them. And if produced, the theatrical manager and the entire troupe will be placed in an insane asylum or a prison. Or possibly it will be like this: first to the madhouse and only then to the prison.'[57] Andreev was of a generation that viewed the irrational within the context of Lombroso's atavistic characteristics and degenerate criminal *typology*. Given this understanding of mental illness, Andreev undoubtedly wanted to avoid such identification and actively promoted a healthy public image of himself. In 1908, he again published an open letter refuting various stories which suggested that he was ill.[58] Clearly, Andreev saw these reports as an effort to stigmatize him as a degenerate and not as an attempt to frame his illness in the romantic ideal of the tormented artist, which had to some degree benefited some writers only two decades earlier.[59]

I have already suggested that the performance of sanity was Andreev's defense against being identified and stigmatized as mentally ill. As a result, institutional spaces often become the backdrop for the author's fictional dramas. Institutional intervention took the form of hospitals, asylums, and prisons in which illness was controlled by separating individuals from the outside world. Once isolated, patients and prisoners were treated virtually in the same manner. Rehabilitation is a late twentieth-century phenomenon, so it is not surprising that Andreev would conflate these institutional spaces and thematically combine the mentally ill with the falsely accused; prisoners with the clinically insane.

Verisimilitude: the appearance of truth

'The Thought' and 'My Notes' are not the only works in which Andreev explores the relationships between performance and deception. In several other pieces, Andreev suggests that people want the appearance of truth more than they want truth itself. In Andreev's play, *Black Maskers*, which he began writing at the same time as 'My Notes,' we find yet another expression of the concepts of deception, performance and verisimilitude. The setting for the play is the castle of Lorenzo, Duke of Spadaro and Knight of the Holy Spirit. The castle is really Lorenzo's psyche turned into external space, and he invites guests to represent various aspects of himself. Lorenzo is not aware of this, however, and is confused by the ugliness of his visitors. Empirical reality becomes chaotic as the guests multiply and change masks, as various versions of his wife appear and Lorenzo duels with and kills his double. Lorenzo then loses his mind, becoming paranoid and confused. Woodward writes: 'The joust is resolved in the triumph of the true personality. The false Lorenzo is killed and is now subjected to the penance of being made to lie in the coffin and listen to the record of his sins from those whom he has wronged. The illusions have been swept away and the masks stripped off; only truth remains.'

The important aspect in Woodward's explanation is that by stripping away the masks, truth is revealed. Brusianin, Andreev's literary secretary, interprets the play less optimistically, calling Lorenzo 'demented' and 'insane' following the duel, noting that he perishes in 'darkness.'[60] Beklemisheva is also less confident and suggests that an underlying message of the play is: 'if you are going insane, then do this alone in your own room, in a hospital, but do not drag your madness out onto the stage.'[61] The play ends with Lorenzo setting the castle (his psyche) on fire. However, it is important to recognize that issues of mental health are again couched in theatrical terms. For example, once Lorenzo has gone insane, his wife asks those in the castle to keep an appearance of normalcy:

> I beg of you, ladies and gentlemen, to do me a favour. You are no doubt aware that the Duke, my husband, is somewhat indisposed. He is expecting guests, though none are invited, and since he will probably assume, my dear friends, that you are his guests, I beg of you not to express surprise or alarm. The Duke's memory is somewhat impaired, so that he forgets even persons who are dear to him. Divert him, gently and cautiously, from his illusions.[62]

Performance and deception are perpetrated to simulate the facade of regularity. Of course, this leads to greater confusion for Lorenzo, who states: 'These charming masks beget so many ridiculous misunderstandings. Some jester, assuming my voice and features, has long been deceiving you with a base falsehood.'[63] This comment calls into doubt the success of the performance.

Another example of the theme of performance is Andreev's play *He Who Gets Slapped*, which premiered at the Moscow Art Theater on 27 October 1915 and at the Aleksandrinskii Theater in in Petrograd a month later, which takes place in a circus in a French city. The character He is running from a failed marriage after his wife has left him for their mutual friend. He finds solace in the world of the circus and there is a definite contrast between the real world and the circus world.

In the real world He is an intellectual, but in the circus he is a clown who is slapped in the face as part of his act. In the circus world Count Mancini is trying to marry his adopted daughter Consuelo to the Baron for his own gain. Everyone, including He, is in love with her. He tries to dissuade her, to save her from the outside world, but Consuelo understands that she must marry the Baron. In the end, He poisons Consuelo and himself, and the Baron shoots himself in a race to meet Consuelo on the other side.

In the play there are various references to He's identity prior to entering the circus and what he has or wants to become in this new world. He has clearly suffered from his loss in the outside world and now claims to be mad: 'Never in your life did you use such a precise expression. I am mad!'[64] However, we are not quite sure if this is the case or if this is another aspect of his performance. This confusion partially stems from the fact that He is just a role that the intellectual from the outside world is now playing. He admits:

> Don't be angry, Jim. It's a play, don't you understand? I become happy when I enter the ring and hear the music. I wear a mask and I feel humorous. There is a mask on my face, and I play. I may say anything as a drunkard. Do you understand? Yesterday when I, with this stupid face, was playing the great man, the philosopher [*he assumes a proud monumental pose, and repeats the gesture of the play – general laughter*] I was walking this way, and was telling how great, how wise, how incomparable I was – how God lived in me, how high I stood above my head [*his voice changes and he is speaking faster*] then you, Jim, you hit me for the first time. And I asked you, 'What is it, they're applauding me?' Then, at the tenth slap, I said: 'It seems to me that they sent me from the Academy?' [*Looks around him with an air of unconquerable pride and splendour. Laughter. Jim gives him a real slap.*][65]

As in 'The Thought,' performance is employed to hide the main character's true emotions and psychological state. Even as he suffers on the inside, He plays the part of a clown and entertains the audience, demonstrating that people prefer the appearance of normalcy to the truth.

Andreev employs the themes of performance and deception for the last time in a story written in 1916 entitled 'Sacrifice.' In this story Iakov Sergeevich Vorob'ev dies, leaving his wife and daughter in a difficult financial situation. Salvation seems to come in the form of Mikhail Mikhailovich Verevkin. He is attracted to both mother and daughter, which causes a conflict between the two women. After a confrontation with her daughter over Verevkin, the mother comes unhinged.[66] As a result, the mother decides to buy life insurance and kill herself, but must figure out how to do it so that it does not look like a suicide. In the end, the mother dies under the wheels of a train and the daughter marries Verevkin and receives the money from her mother's insurance policy.

Even after her death, Verevkin is still in love with the mother and grows very happy when, after the birth of their second child, the daughter begins to look like her mother.

The mother, Elena Dmitrievna, realizes that in order for her daughter to collect the insurance money, she will have to hide her madness and make her death look accidental. She conceptualizes her suicide, therefore, as a theatrical performance.[67] After her death, the reader understands that she has been successful in her performance, as no one seems to suspect that her death was intentional. In town, Elena Dmitrievna had bought apples and other goods, something a suicidal person would not do, and then as she was boarding the train she momentarily turned her head and inadvertently fell between the rails. In a final line that foreshadows Vladimir Nabokov's (1899–1977) wry literary smile, Andreev writes: 'these types of situations often occur, and not without reason was she afraid of railroads and not without reason was she insured!'[68] The performance is a great success. The police believe that it was an accidental death. The appearance of normalcy is maintained to disguise madness and the desire to commit suicide.

In each of these works, mental illness is associated with performance for the benefit of an audience. The performer attempts to convey to his or her audience the appearance of *normalcy*. It is the appearance that is important as the audience, according to Andreev, does not desire so much the truth as the appearance of truth (i.e. *normalcy*). Society does not want to confront the uncomfortable reality of mental illness. This is the reason for the incarceration of the ill. To avoid incarceration, therefore, the ill must *act* normal. The desire for an appearance of truth, of familiarity, in his literary works is not unlike Andreev's own behavior in maintaining and defending his mental health for his literary audience, while possibly also betraying his own illness experience.

Critics and psychiatrists

Not surprisingly, critics and psychiatrists paid special attention to Andreev's public incidents of reported illness, especially when they were closely followed by literary works that could be characterized as *psychopathological*. In 1908, Izmailov gave a positive review of Andreev's story 'My Notes,' indicating its connections with 'The Thought.' He addressed the tension between highbrow and lowbrow literature as well as the general opinion that Andreev's works qualified as the latter – 'a literature of ecstasy and illness, mental fatigue and perversion.' Izmailov, however, was not prepared to subscribe to such markers as high (represented by Dostoevskii) and low (represented by Andreev) literary representations of mental illness.[69] Either way, the critic was clearly reflecting the opinion held by some elements of society that Andreev was a purveyor of social ills and deviant discourse.

Two months later, Izmailov reviewed Andreev's play *Black Maskers*, which had debuted on 2 December 1908 at the theater of Vera Komissarzhevskaia (1864–1910), and understood the play's theme of split personalities within the Russian literary context of Nikolai Gogol''s (1809–1852) 'Nose' (Nos), Dostoevskii's *The Double* and Chekhov's 'The Black Monk' (Chernyi monakh). All three works deal with mental illness and the creation of an imaginary double. However, Izmailov felt that Andreev was unsuccessful in adding anything to this line of inquiry in his attempt 'to peer into the psychological, or more specifically, psychopathological abyss.'[70]

At the same time, in Lunacharskii's literary criticism we find Andreev clearing corpses from the streets of a decaying and putrid society:

> While some of us, scenting the breath of the Plague, carry on a loathsome orgy of perverted instincts, and endeavor to warm up their benumbed sensuality by means of sodomy, Sadism, and all sorts of abomination; while others burn candles and send up smoke to heaven and into the eyes of their neighbors, lisping variegated psalms and sermons – Leonid Andreev, in a leather mask, black and terrible, with a long hook in his hands, goes up and down the city streets, rummages in heaps of corpses and semi-corpses, hurls the rotten flesh into a large pit, pours lye on it, burns it. Should he at this performance perchance deal with this plague-hook a final blow to one who still rattles – what matter? Burn the corpses. Purify life.[71]

One cannot ignore the allusion to a plague, the destruction of society by an uncontrolled epidemic of degraded morals and false religions.

Medical experts were equally interested in Andreev and his works. Feodor Rybakov (1868–1920), a former student of Korsakov and head of the Department of Psychiatry at Moscow University from 1911 to 1917, was involved in experimental psychiatric research on alcoholism and affective psychosis. In 1908 he published *Contemporary Writers and Sick Nerves* in which he argued that, under the philosophical influence of Nietzsche and the literary influences of Verlaine and Baudelaire, contemporary writers had begun to explore a type of extreme individualism, leading them to delve into the recesses of their psyches. Sick writers thereby gained special advantage in a literary milieu devoid of social decorum.[72] According to Rybakov, Andreev's characters are nothing more than melancholic automatons – referencing mainly *Life of Man*, *Tsar Hunger* and 'The Curse of the Beast.'[73] Rybakov assumes that the writers themselves are degenerates and that society must resist this sickly cultural discourse. Anguish over a deteriorating social order as reflected in literature is a natural argument from a psychiatrist of this time and, once again, Andreev is representative of this moral and psychological decline.

The following year Ol'ga Kube published *Nightmares of Life: A Critical-psychological Study about L. Andreev, Pshebyshevskii and Other Contemporary Writers*, in which she called Andreev a *sick talent*. 'If he is not mentally ill, then by all means he possesses a sick psyche/soul.'[74] Kube, however, is light on psychological theory in discussing Andreev's play *Life of Man*. Striking a more religious than scientific tone she states that Andreev's continual question 'Why do I live?' should be reframed as 'How should I live?' Kube's interpretation of the Russian word *dukhovnii*, which has both the meaning *spiritual* and *mental*; as well as *dusha* – *soul* and *psyche* is problematic. Although she claims that her study is psychological, Kube is more concerned with Andreev's dogma, faith and beliefs.

Even with a focus on a degenerate erosion of morals, Kube's vague argument that 'a clear mind and love should defeat evil and suffering' misses the psychiatric mark.[75] However, her significant contribution was in not separating Andreev from his literary works. Kube believed Andreev, the man, was ill – psychologically and, possibly, spiritually.

Also in 1909, Dr M. O. Shaikevich, who studied in St Petersburg under Bekhterev and specialized in the intersections between literature and psychopathology, published 'The Psychological Side in the Works of Leonid Andreev.' Shaikevich argues that his research method attempts to identify the sickly elements of both the author and his literary works. However, he examines only the psychopathological elements of Andreev's oeuvre.

Beginning with the classifications of Andreev's texts by other critics, Shaikevich refutes the notion that the author's stories can be categorized as either *good-hearted* or *psychological*. Below the surface of even the altruistic stories, the doctor finds a psychological experience that informs the narrative, suggesting that all of the stories should be re-categorized along psychological lines: healthy and sick characters affected by loneliness;[76] stories involving fear and terror;[77] stories in which philosophical ideals impede real lives;[78] characters who rely on morals to buttress their psychological well-being (including moral degenerates).[79] After a lengthy discussion of several of Andreev's individual works, Shaikevich concludes that only 'The Thought' and parts of 'The Abyss' and 'The Life of Vasilii Fiveiskii' utilize psychopathological material. He holds that the line between madness and normalcy is not sharply defined, but is determined mostly by physical rather than moral factors.

Shaikevich believes that the psychopathological elements in Andreev's works play a secondary role and act as an unpleasant solution for primarily religious and moral-philosophical problems.[80]

In 1910, Dr Mumortsev published a collection of essays titled *Psychopathic characteristics in the characters of Leonid Andreev*, in which he gave critical attention to 'Red Laugh,' 'The Abyss,' 'In the Fog,' 'The Life of Vasilii Fiveiskii' and 'My Notes.' He argues that 'in the works of Andreev such sufficient evidence of the sickly psyche is depicted and yet many critics turn what is unclear to them into philosophical or poetic questions.'[81] It is difficult to say if this was a specific reaction to Shaikevich's article, but Mumortsev definitely saw accurate depictions of clinical pathology in Andreev's works.

Mumortsev argues that progressive psychological paralysis and paramnesia are depicted accurately in 'Red Laugh.'[82] Referring to the works of Krafft-Ebing and Kovalevskii, Mumortsev reads 'The Abyss' and 'In the Fog' in the context of sexual deviance. Nemovetskii (The Abyss) is a degenerate with sexual perversions and Pavel (In the Fog) is a neurasthenic with sexual hyperesthesia.[83] In Father Fiveiskii, Mumortsev argues for basic insanity with elements of paranoia. He references psychiatric theory on paranoia by Magnan, Josef Berze (1866–1958), Gustav Störring (1860–1946) and Wilhelm Wundt (1832–1920). Relying partially on Lombroso, Mumortsev believes that the mathematician in 'My Notes' suffers from delusions of grandeur. This in turn results in an atrophied sense of morality, reduced psychological and intellectual capacity, hallucinations, and grandiose ideas that limit his capacity for logical reasoning.[84]

Mumortsev concludes that 'L. Andreev essentially recreates the psychology of ill people. In this area he is a complete master and one should marvel at how accurately he describes the types of mental illness. It seems that this is not an artist-belletrist, but an artist-psychiatrist writing, one who is familiar with all of the fine points of the science of mental disorders.'[85] The doctor concludes that Andreev is a product of his time, tuned in to the degeneration of his own society, and thereby illustrates it with precision.

The literary critic Nikolai Smolenskii attempts to interrupt the critical discourse on Andreev by disproving the notion that the author is a theomochist, sociologist or psychologist. Smolenskii argues that Andreev is really just reflecting the decadent, capitalistic strains of ongoing cultural discourse.[86] He finds that there is no larger objective idea in Andreev's works, but only a personalized subjective interest.[87] An author of psychological subject matter, Smolenskii feels that there is no artistry in Andreev's descriptions. The outward psychological expressions may seem authentic, but the internal logic or evolution of thought is not well crafted.[88]

There is a disconnect, however, between the artistic and scientific representations of human frailty in Smolenskii's criticisms. He finds fault in Andreev's lack of artistry and uses Dostoevskii and Gogol' as stellar examples of how it should be done. Smolenskii is even willing, grudgingly, to recognize decadent writers like Wilde, Maupassant and Sologub.[89] What Smolenskii dislikes in Andreev's works is the movement away from a romanticized depiction of the inner workings of man towards a more medicalized (here we could substitute the word *decadent*) line of discourse. Smolenskii is correct that Andreev is reflecting the cultural and social conversations of his time, but the critic misses that fact that the cultural dialogue is now non-romantic and scientific.

Elena Menchikova, also in 1910, argued that although Dostoevskii and Andreev both wrote about sick, abnormal characters, the authors were distinct because their own ailments were different. Dostoevskii suffered from epilepsy while Andreev is a degenerate, Menchikova gingerly asserts.[90] She claims that Dostoevskii's illness experience, exacerbated by his prison sentence and religious doubts, led to constant self-analysis. Having provided nearly twenty pages about Dostoevskii, and how his physical and mental condition influenced his literary works, when Menchikova discusses the abnormal behavior of Andreev's characters it is quite apparent that she is associating these abnormalities with the author's psychological state. This is further underscored in using Garshin as a segue – an author who committed suicide after well-known bouts with mental illness – before giving critical attention to Andreev's works.

Menchikova states that Dostoevskii's disturbed characters receive relief and comfort from other characters, while Andreev's are alone and further alienate themselves from others.[91] Both authors populate their works with fallen women, but Andreev does not delve as deeply as Dostoevskii into their psyches. Andreev is more interested in the outward expressions of his characters' psychological problems and less in their underlying causes.[92] Menchikova argues that Andreev is not a psychologist, but an artist whose works are filled with a hopeless pessimism and a pathological fear of life, love and death.[93] Dostoevskii, on the other hand, is introspective and searches for meaning in his characters' (and his own) suffering. By association, Menchikova is suggesting that Andreev, the degenerate, is a lonely pessimist who suffers from bouts of anxiety, which is different from Dostoevskii the epileptic, who explores the philosophical underpinnings of madness. For this reason we find different illness experiences reflected in their literary works.

The literary and scientific discourse linking Andreev's life and works with mental illness was further substantiated in 1910 when three articles appeared in the press claiming that Andreev had gone mad and was suffering from an acute nervous disorder.[94] Andreev answered these articles in an open letter entitled, *The Madness of L. Andreev*. He wrote sarcastically that he was tired of the ongoing questions about his health and that he would admit to being insane if everyone would leave him in peace to work.[95]

Possibly due to this continual attention by the media, Brusianin began *Leonid Andreev: Life and Works* (Leonid Andreev. Zhizn' i tvorchestvo), published in 1912, with a description of a hot day in July when Andreev's guests were treated to a newspaper story claiming that he was gravely ill. Andreev told everyone to verify from the papers that he was raving mad, had howled like a dog and chased everyone around after lunch. Brusianin argued that such sensationalist stories of madness could not be further from the truth, that Andreev was happy and full of vigor.[96] The fact that Brusianin was Andreev's literary secretary suggests that either Andreev was quite healthy and considered these claims of mental illness a constant nuisance, or that Brusianin was only too happy to oblige Andreev's desire to deflect attention away from his medical problems. In either case, it is quite telling that Brusianin begins his book in this way.

In fact, Brusianin's critical study is in its entirety a defense of Andreev's mental health and literary legacy. Brusianin states that Andreev had been called a pornographer ('The Abyss'), an anarchist (*Savva*), and an apologist for the petty bourgeois (*Life of Man*). The isolation felt by so many of Andreev's characters logically led critics to suggest that Andreev himself had psychological problems. Brusianin refers to critics by name and argues that these same individuals had not been as judgmental of Andreev's literary contemporaries.[97] In one instance, Brusianin names and chastises a critic who made connections between the works of Dostoevskii and Andreev, stating: 'Who really knows among critics and readers what worries the author when, during a sleepless night of work, he alone stands over the abyss of human existence?' Brusianin then remarkably asserts that Andreev's sleepless nights are sometimes caused by migraines which doctors have been unable to diagnose.[98] These rebuttals are often supported by comments from Andreev as though Brusianin had conducted several interviews. It might be suggested that this was Andreev's attempt at self-defense via his literary secretary, and certainly indicates that Andreev was actively engaged in the cultural and critical discourse about his literary legacy and was specifically concerned about the stigma of mental illness.

After Brusianin's defense, medical discourse pursued even greater concentration on Andreev as the main representative of degenerate society. In 1913, Dr T. Tkachev argued that Andreev's literary works were harmful for readers, especially children and the mentally ill.[99] Like other psychiatrists and critics, Tkachev asserts that fear of life is the leading pathological symptom of a majority of Andreev's characters. 'If it is a story – not the history of an illness, copied from the sorrowful certificate of a psychiatric hospital, but an artistic work, wherein does there exist his idea and his artistic material?'[100] Tkachev notes that a disproportionate number of Andreev's characters are mentally ill, leading a reader to think that the entire world is turning into a madhouse.

In response to such criticism, in an open letter to the editor of the *Stock Exchange News* in 1913, Andreev writes, 'Concerning gossip about my insanity, arising occasionally, I should say in advance that this is not true.'[101] Yet in reality, Andreev suffered from and sought treatment on several occasions for some kind of mental fatigue, while in the public sphere, for his reading audience, he played the role of the healthy and sane writer – *Leonid Andreev*. In order to avoid the stigma of madness, Andreev was forced to perform – to act sane. He once wrote a cautionary note to a friend: 'Here is a bit of friendly advice that I give to you so as not to become lost in the filthy labyrinth of life: read not what these liars fabricate about a writer, read what he himself writes.'[102] Even with so much attention given to his perceived illness, Andreev continued to explore these complex issues in his literary works.

Anxiety

In 1910, the literary critic Ivanov-Razumnik wrote that the unifying theme of Andreev's literary works was death. They lacked an overarching philosophical idea, but reflected the author's subjective experiences, which included the meaninglessness of life, fear of living, and a feeling of solitude in which death was the last absurdity.[103] We have already discussed in the previous chapter the theme of isolation in Andreev's literary works, and I have also made the assertion that his existential feelings of solitude fueled Andreev's anxiety. 'He was frightened,' remembers literary critic Elpat'evskii. 'A dark fright, a fear of life lived in his psyche and life was wrapped by him in a gloomy shroud.'[104]

Anxiety can have rational and irrational triggers. Free-floating anxiety occurs when emotional and physical responses to fear are elicited without obvious association with a particular event, object or situation. It becomes pathological when the anxiety is excessive, chronic and interferes with an individual's ability to function in normal daily

activities. Anxiety attacks can be influenced by a large array of factors –
stress, lack of sleep and environmental circumstances. In several of
Andreev's diary entries and in memoirs about the author we find
instances of and references to anxiety attacks. Certainly, Andreev felt a
great deal of stress due to financially supporting his entire family while
attending university. His bouts of insomnia and irregular sleeping
patterns were also well-known and thought to contribute to his
pessimistic literary works. Andreev's failed romantic endeavors, various
health problems, and heavy drinking could also have played a role in
these anxiety attacks. This cycle seems to have informed Andreev's
literary descriptions of mental illness in which *fear* (strakh) plays an
important role as an indicator of psychosis.

Andreev's family was aware of his anxiety attacks. His brother Pavel
remembers: 'To [his bouts of melancholy] should be added the feeling of
some kind of incomprehensible fear, fear of sleep, fear of himself, fear of
everything.'[105] This is also evidenced in his diary entries:

An indescribable fear haunts me, for example, in my dreams and in
waking. I am afraid – but of what I do not know. Today, for example, in the
afternoon I was walking along the street, completely empty in reality, was
not presenting, of course, the least danger – but I was afraid. I was afraid of
the factory pipes – especially of one, which periodically produced a flame.
I was afraid of the blackest tall wall with an embedded screen in the
window. I was afraid of every passerby, but I did not know why I was
afraid. Subsequently, what disturbs me even more than this fright is the
sensation of a certain kind of confusion in my head. It feels as if each
thought has jumped the tracks and now snarls, flounders, jostles with each
other – only the devil knows what to do with them. And all of their jostling
is cloaked by some kind of hazy fog, from which slips along the surface the
sliver of an idea, now it again disappears and is replaced by the wisp of
another idea that shows itself at once as the vague outlines of many more
ideas. A desire arises to beat your head against a wall, or to do anything of
the sort, so that this agonizing Sabbath somehow comes to an end.[106]

From where does the fear come? I know only one thing: that this fear is a
sickness and abnormal, like my inclination for vodka is abnormal, like my
passions are abnormal. In my mind I cannot find a justification for this
fear – and solely [my] body, [my] vile body produces it. I know the
reasons: a heart ailment. Day after day, hour after hour while forcing me to
peer at death, [my heart] forces me to amass a fear of death, has increased
it to an unnatural size, so that the last exit for me has been closed.[107]

The fear of losing one's mind is a leitmotif in several of Andreev's
literary works. 'Red Laugh,' 'The Life of Vasilii Fiveiskii,' 'Phantoms,' 'The
Thought,' 'The Story of the Seven Who Were Hanged,' 'My Notes' and

others employ fear as a signifier for the approach of insanity or as an indication of actual psychosis. I will focus on another three stories where anxiety is employed in a similar way.

Published in 1899, 'At the Window' is the story of Andrei Nikolae-vich, one of Andreev's many marginalized and lonely characters. He sits by the window each day plagued by anxiety and melancholy. In his mind's eye, life is strange and terrible with a variety of pitfalls. Bad things happen to his neighbors, confirming his fears. When he is given a chance to marry the pretty girl from across the street he rejects the offer in favor of his seemingly safe detached existence. Andrei Nikolae-vich's alienation from society is not greatly different from a long line of Russian literary fugitives – the little men (Gogol'), underground men (Dostoevskii) and gooseberry types (Chekhov). Therefore we might argue that his level of anxiety is no more or less than that of many similar characters.

Feodor Iurasov is a different type of character – a thief, three times convicted – yet he too, according to Iezuitova, is 'fatally lonesome.'[108] Andreev published 'The Thief' in 1905 about Iurasov's trip by train to see his former mistress who lives just outside Moscow. As the story begins he picks the pocket of a man out of habit, although he does not need the money. The victim suspects something is amiss, but remains on the platform somewhat perplexed as Iurasov departs on the train. Iurasov is dressed in English cloth and hopes to be taken as a respectable German clerk from a commercial house, but quickly realizes that he is more ridiculous than convincing. He feels better once he leaves the train car and looks out into the fields rushing by.

This sense of peace does not last long as his psychological condition begins to shift: 'The indifference of the fields, their aloofness, filled him with utter loneliness. The feeling of being discarded from life like a dead man terrified him. Had he been asleep for a thousand years and awakened in a new world among new people, he could not have felt lonelier than now.'[109] A gypsy song from another compartment enrages him and he decides that he will beat his lover when he arrives, simply as an act of revenge for his wretched life.

His mood changes for the better at a scheduled stop, but as he gets back on the train, Iurasov overhears two conductors joking that the gendarme is looking for someone on the train. It is unclear about whom they are speaking, but Iurasov is obsessed with the idea that the gendarme is after him. He begins to panic and although there is no evidence that he is being sought, he rushes through the compartments in an attempt to get to the front of the train. Everyone and everything represents danger and he is gripped by an 'animal fear.'[110] This terror overcomes him and he leaps from the train into the path of an oncoming postal train, still convinced that he was being pursued by the gendarme.

Shaikevich, a professor of psychiatry at Moscow University and a contemporary of Andreev's, suggests that Iurasov is forced to confront his loneliness at the scheduled stop when he is not allowed into a private dance; this, rather than some ambiguous pursuit by the gendarme, triggers his psychosis. He argues that a criminal thrice sentenced should not panic at the possibility of being caught for a petty crime and that the real reason for his sickly terror is psychological.[111] Significantly, it *is* the threat of solitude and a life lacking meaning which seems to prompt Iurasov's anxiety attack. His fear is irrational as there is no evidence that the gendarme are even interested in or searching for a pickpocket. The anxiety is self-generated and results in a rather grotesque act of suicide.

Menchikova argued in 1910 that 'almost all of the works of L. Andreev are infiltrated by one domineering mood – a pathological feeling of fear, which assumes diverse shades.'[112] 'The Thief' has been aligned with other stories in which there is a sharp distinction between the city and the country. Woodward suggests that for Andreev the city denoted people and a relief from solitude, despite opposite indications in his stories 'The City' and 'The Curse of the Beast.'[113]

In 1913 Andreev wrote 'He' about a poor student who finds work as a tutor with a rich family. Reminiscent of the works of Poe, Andreev's student finds himself in an odd house populated by a sick and reclusive woman and her husband, Norden, who is having an affair with the English governess. The married couple have a son, Volodia, and had a daughter, Elena, who drowned some years before. The oddities of the house compound the student's fragile mental state, causing him to imagine a strange visitor and to believe that Elena is still alive. He is eventually driven out of the house in a fit of madness and nearly freezes to death. When the student recovers consciousness, he is in a hospital being treated for frostbite and an unspecified illness – probably madness.

As with most stories in which the narrator is mentally disturbed, the reader cannot trust the perceived reality of the narrative. In 'He,' it is not clear that the student is ill until the end, which bothered some critics when the story was first published. Izmailov disliked the fact that the inconclusive nature of the character's psychological state necessitated a reread of the story to ascertain if the student really was insane.[114] Upon close examination, mental illness is indeed united thematically with fear and solitude, compounded by depression.

The first indication of illness is outwardly represented by laughter, and an 'agonizing feeling of fear and some kind of wild submission, when, left alone, completely alone in my own room or on the shore of the ocean.'[115] Fear is also manifest in the appearance of both the strange visitor and the dead daughter. The themes are united when the student begins to realize that he is losing his mind: 'Fear before the stranger completely disappeared; it is true, I never attempted myself to touch him or start a conversation, but this was not from fear, but from some sort of feeling of the irrelevance of all words; and in appearance it was all done so calmly and simply, as if *he* was not the greatest evil and my death, but a simple, orderly, silent doctor, daily visiting just such an orderly and silent patient. But the depression was horrible.'[116]

Depression, a perceived meaninglessness of life, feelings of solitude, and the resulting anxiety are a large part of Andreev's illness experience. It is probably impossible to say where the feelings of isolation stop and the anxiety begins; they are intertwined in a fluid association causing an increase or decrease of psychological intensity at various times. The importance of this interaction for understanding Andreev's self-perception is readily found in his diaries and literary works. Unquestionably, it is the one thematic thread that can be followed through Andreev's oeuvre. In addition, the awareness that there was no treatment or cure available certainly generated still more angst for Andreev.

The third act

Having reached the height of his material success and settled in Vammelsuu, Andreev indulged in his various passions – photography, painting, boating, gardening and a new gramophone. He trained his manic energy on these activities as a type of release. For example, he spent entire days in his darkroom, which was playfully called 'Ward No. 6,' a reference to Chekhov's story about an insane asylum.[117] Chukovskii writes of Andreev's passion for photography:

> It was as if he himself was an entire factory, working ceaselessly in shifts, preparing all those masses of large and small photographs which were stacked up in his study, contained in special boxes and chests, overflowing on every table, mounted on the window panes. There was no corner in his dacha, which he had not photographed several times over. Some photographs were extremely successful, for instance spring landscapes. It was hard to believe that they were photographs at all, so suffused were they with elegiac musicality, reminding one of Levitan.[118]
>
> In the course of a month he made thousands of photographs, as if fulfilling some colossal order, and when you visited him he made you look through all those thousands, sincerely convinced that for you, too, they

were a source of bliss. He could not imagine that there might be people who could find his plates uninteresting. It was touching to hear him trying to persuade everyone to buy a color photograph.[119]

Andreev could just as easily spend several days in front of the easel or digging in his garden. His nights would then be consumed with books about painters, sailing boats, or whatever had captured his latest fancy.

In the summers, Andreev was particularly drawn to the sea. He would cruise for weeks at a time on his yacht *Distant One*, built by his own design. The entire family was expected to join in many of these expeditions and Vadim remembers spending the entire summer of 1912 on the island of Bjerke, inhabited only by birch trees. Andreev spent each summer on the sea until war broke out in 1914.[120]

Kaun writes that with his second marriage and life in Finland, Andreev struggled once again with his own solitude. This void was filled to some degree by Anna, upon whom he relied for his literary endeavors, both as his stenographer and as a critic. Kaun notes:

> He needed her sympathetic ears, her fine response, her delicate sensitiveness, her unflagging alertness, and her constant watchful presence, in order to overcome the depression of his black solitude, and to be in a position to create. With the selfishness of a genius or a child (he possessed the elements of both) he monopolized all her time, all her attention and interest, all her strength and energy. During his creative periods he would dictate his productions to her all night long, striding up and down his huge study, smoking incessantly, consuming quantities of strong tea from the always active samovar, and utterly oblivious of the fatigue and exhaustion of [his wife].[121]

Although his literary and critical success was in a slow decline, Andreev was still a popular cultural figure during the first two decades of the twentieth century, with a public eager to read his new works and attend the premiers of his plays. Andreev's friend and literary colleague Zaitsev viewed this period of Andreev's life as broken and isolated. Failing health and seclusion from former friends seemed to Zaitsev a terrible end to a once vibrant literary life.[122] In contrast, Andreev's neighbor Beklemisheva noted that this period was full of family activities and personal hobbies. Croquet and sailing, as well as a house full of visitors, allowed Andreev to escape the aggravations of the literary and theatrical circles of the capital.[123] The reality of life along the Black rivulet, however, was most certainly more complex and nuanced than either of these two interpretations of the author's final years.

Even as Andreev created a life in Vammelsuu, he continued to write for the theaters in Moscow and St Petersburg. Andreev scored a success with audiences in November 1908 with *Days of Our Life* at the New Theater under the direction of Evtikhii Karpov (1857–1926). For the first month, the play about Andreev's own student experiences ran every day. *Black Maskers* did not fare as well the following month at the theater of Vera Komissarzhevskaia in St Petersburg (2 December) or at the theater of Konstantin Nezlobin (1857–1930) in Moscow (7 December). Many, even the actors in the two theaters, were unsure of the play's meaning. Yet, the disappointment of *Black Maskers'* reception was alleviated to some degree by the birth of Leonid and Anna's first child together, Savva, on 25 March 1909.

After a summer trip to Europe with Chirikov, Andreev readied his new play, *Anfisa*, for the 1909–10 season at the New Dramatic Theater in St Petersburg (the former theater of Vera Komissarzhevskaia). The play, about three sisters, adultery and murder, premiered on 10 October under the direction of Aleksandr Sanin (1869–1956) and was an abject failure with audiences and critics. *Anfisa* was in rehearsals at the Malyi Theater in Moscow with a new emphasis, but in December the production was canceled. At the same time, Andreev was working with the Art Theater in Moscow on another one of his symbolic dramas, *Anathema*, about the cruelty and injustice of life. The Jew David Leizer is told by Anathema, in the guise of a lawyer, that he has inherited a great amount of money, but Leizer will accept it only if he can do some good with it. The need is so great from so many people, however, that Leizer and his money prove to be insufficient to address all of the suffering in the world. Eventually, an angry mob stones Leizer to death, proving Anathema correct about the brutality of life. The play, which premiered on 2 October, was an immense success, with special praise reserved for the main actor Vasilii Kachalov (1875–1948). A production of *Anathema* at the New Dramatic Theater in St Petersburg, once again directed by Sanin, did not fare as well after its debut on 27 November. Even so, *Anathema* was the theatrical hit of the season throughout the entire Russian empire.

Until World War I, the Andreevs did live comfortably in this cottage community, not far from St Petersburg. On 12 May 1910 a daughter, Vera, and on 24 December 1912 a son, Valentin, were born to the couple. At this time, Andreev was almost constantly surrounded by family and friends who often visited his house in the Finnish countryside. Many representatives of the literary scene (critics, reporters and other hangers-on) also made the trek to Vammelsuu for scintillating tidbits about Andreev's life that could be used later for their articles and weekly columns. Once back in St Petersburg or Kiev or Moscow, they wrote of his unorthodox daily routine and *disorderly* life. Andreev was bothered by this vindictive distortion of the truth. Yet, many of his contemporaries attested to the fact that Andreev had a strange compulsion to read all of the press clippings about him collected and sent by the Press Bureau, which often then poisoned his mood for the rest of the day.[124]

Vadim compares the years 1908–1914 to the third act of *Life of Man*, in which a ball is held in the house of Man. The house is full of people, visible wealth and perceived joy, but underneath the façade there is a tangible tediousness and vacuity. The praise for Man, his wife and their house is fawning and hypocritical. Similarly, Andreev was surrounded by a lot of noise, fame and material affluence but this was a 'strange, very nervous and, along with this, unreal life.' People came and went and slowly the accolades began to diminish.[125] His daughter's memories of the period are associated with her father's failing health and headaches. 'It occurred by degrees that everyone began to relate to papa as to an invalid.'[126]

Ekaterina Ivanovna and Salomé

At the end of the 1910 summer Anna, alone, went on a trip abroad for several months and Andreev again started drinking heavily. He was depressed and had little time for his children, other than Savva. When Anna returned at the end of October, his mood improved. The couple then decided to go on a trip together the following month to Germany, France and Italy. Why Anna went abroad without her husband is not exactly clear, although it was reported in the popular press that Andreev had suffered a mental breakdown. What is clear is that the marriage had not brought Andreev the new *balance* that he so desired.[127]

Shortly after their marriage, Andreev had been shattered when he learned that Anna had lied to him about her love-life prior to their marriage. An indication of the emotional toll caused by this revelation is found in the epigraph that began this chapter. Anna had led Andreev to believe that other than her ex-husband, she had had no other lovers. All through the courtship, Andreev doubted this claim, but Anna had confirmed it time and again. After their marriage and while Anna was in St Petersburg, Andreev had come across a letter from a former lover who was upset that Anna was leaving him for Andreev. In the letter it was revealed that Anna had had yet another lover previous to the author of the letter. For Andreev, this was a great betrayal of faith and long after he struggled with the issues of infidelity, deception, dishonesty and disloyalty. These struggles are displayed in his plays *Anfisa*, *Professor Storitsyn*, *Ekaterina Ivanovna*, *Waltz of the Dogs* (Sobachii val's) and *Samson in Chains* (Samson v okovakh). Similarly, some of these themes appear in his final novel *Diary of Satan* (Dnevnik Satana).[128]

Andreev's play, *Ekaterina Ivanovna*, literally starts with a bang. In the first scene, Ekaterina's husband, Stibelev, fires three shots at his wife because of an unsubstantiated suspicion that she has committed adultery with Mentikov, an unscrupulous social parasite. The bullets miss Ekaterina in a physical sense but they shatter her psychologically. Act II takes place six months later at the estate of Ekaterina's mother. The audience learns that Ekaterina fled there with her children the night of the shooting and that Mentikov followed her. While at the estate she committed adultery with Mentikov, became pregnant and had an abortion. In so doing, Ekaterina makes real the false charge that was leveled against her by her husband. Stibelev arrives at the estate and begs Ekaterina to return to him. For a moment she believes that reconciliation is possible, but when it becomes clear that her husband is driven only by desire, thoughts of salvation are lost. In Acts III and IV, two years later, Ekaterina has given her body to an assortment of male suitors. In Act IV, Ekaterina's original association with dance and the bacchantes turns into a more grotesque reference to Salomé's dance of the seven veils in the artist Koromyslov's studio. At this point Ekaterina is lost both spiritually and psychologically.

Woodward argues that the philosophical basis for this conflict is reflected in Andreev's other works (such as *Anfisa*) in which feminine principles of instinct and intuitive knowledge are contrasted with masculine principles of self-assertion and self-gratification.[129] He believes that there is a moral scale to the play with Mentikov, the parasite, at one end and Ekaterina, the victim, at the other. In the end Ekaterina's higher feminine truth is rejected by rational male logic.[130]

In terms of its literary perspective, *Ekaterina Ivanovna* was written under the influence of Andreev's theories on a new type of theater which would relinquish external action for use in the cinema, while maintaining the internal, psychological and intellectual developments of a character for the stage. In 'A Letter on the Theater' (Pis'mo o teatre) Andreev argued that life had moved inward and that the theater of spectacle must be supplanted by a theater of the mind.[131] Although this was certainly a criticism of realist theater and a nod to the future of cinema, it marks also the growing importance Andreev gave to the psyche. In *Ekaterina Ivanovna*, Andreev probes the notion of moral insanity, deviant sexuality, and the degeneration of civilized Russian society. The play begins with an external action, the gunshot, but then focuses on the moral and psychological devolution of the main character.

The play, which premiered at the Art Theater in Moscow on 17 December 1912, generated a great critical response, with few supporting

Andreev's creative vision.[132] One of the more fascinating reactions was written by Dr K. Platonov in what he called a 'judicial-psychopathological essay.'[133] He describes a pseudo-court proceeding, conducted to decide whether Ekaterina Ivanovna was a 'type of contemporary Russian woman – wife and mother, or, possibly a monstrous and ill person.'[134] Platonov bases his essay on mock court proceedings held in Kharkov on 14 February 1913, which imitated a similar event that occurred in Moscow three weeks earlier.[135]

The Kharkov court heard testimony from psychiatric experts that Ekaterina Ivanovna was pathological, showing signs of acute hysteria. However, some in the jury doubted this diagnosis. In what is probably the most intriguing part of his essay, Platonov explains how mental illness is differentially understood by disparate sectors of society. For the average person madness exists only when the disorder is obvious and visible, while psychiatrists and neuropathologists recognize that mental illness can exist with only minor perceivable symptoms, or in their absence. Therefore, a psychiatrist must interpret immoral behavior as an early indication of illness.[136]

This assertion was clearly an attempt by psychiatry to claim authority over the irrational. We might recall Foucault's claim that medical professionals had exercised moral and social authority over the madman's minority status since the eighteenth century, relying on age-old techniques of authority, judgment, punishment and love to create a semblance of medical practice, just as the treatment of mental illness was seeking acceptance as objective science. Platonov's essay positions his profession as the only one competent to diagnose and treat moral insanity.

Platonov continues that everyone is capable of less than ideal behavior, but this does not mean that everyone is mentally ill. Unfortunately, Andreev did not provide enough information to ascertain Ekaterina Ivanovna's medical history – hereditary issues, upbringing or prior living conditions – which doctors rely on to make a diagnosis. However, the reader is led to infer that Ekaterina Ivanovna was a good mother and wife until the attempted shooting. This event caused the change in her behavior. Platonov argues that a mental illness can remain dormant until a singular event causes it to rise to the conscious level. He asserts that the 'psychological trauma' of the gunshot caused Ekaterina to become an automaton: 'Ekaterina Ivanovna, in the last two acts, displays all of the symptoms of a hysteric-psychopathological condition, the type of condition which doctors, psychiatrists and neuropathologists are often asked to observe.'[137]

An intriguing element of this essay is that Platonov, as well as the others involved in the mock trial, unblinkingly provided a diagnosis for a fictional character. This may speak to the fact that psychiatry was still in its infancy and not completely established as science, rather than art. Absent is any sort of query as to how Andreev might be able to so accurately depict mental illness – especially given that Platonov had just argued that the general public viewed psychosis differently than trained medical professionals. Platonov and the others also seem to separate Andreev from Ekaterina Ivanovna – it is the character, not the author, whom they put on trial.

Andreev uses different literary clues to lead his audience to the same conclusions reached by psychiatrists and neuropathologists. He relies on the images of the bacchante[138] and Salomé to signify Ekaterina Ivanovna's descent into madness. What might seem like two completely different lines of discourse – scientific and biblical – are, in fact, complementary. The image of the femme fatale of the *fin de siècle* was connected to degeneration theory and social deviance, uniting these two lines of discourse in a larger cultural context.

The biblical story from which the cultural Salomé arises is in Mark 6:21–9.[139] Salomé is the stepdaughter of Herod Antipas and dances before him and her mother, Herodias, on Herod's birthday. Herod promises Salomé whatever she would like after her performance and, on Herodias' recommendation, she asks for the head of the prophet, John the Baptist, who had called the marriage of Herodias to Herod adulterous.

In the late nineteenth century, European authority was under assault on political, social and metaphysical fronts, as represented in, among others, the figure of the femme fatale.[140] A patriarchal culture associated a rise in female self-awareness as a sign of cultural anarchism and social decay. Salomé became a particularly productive symbol representing the perversity of women, while degeneration theory suggested that immoral behavior was an indication of the decline of modern society as a whole. Therefore, Salomé was grouped with the dandy, the homosexual, the prostitute, the syphilitic, and other representatives of sexual deviance.[141]

In Act IV Ekaterina Ivanovna is directly associated with Salomé as she has reached the depth of her depravity and sexual licentiousness. Everyone has gathered at Koromyslov's studio and in the corner is the artist's latest project, 'Salomé with the head of the prophet.' Andreev begins the act by providing the immediate association: 'Katerina is Salomé. Half-naked she stands on the platform, with lowered head and eyes. In her outstretched hands she holds a thin decorative vessel in which is supposed to be the head of John the Baptist.'[142] This image is then confirmed by the characters as well. Teplovskii says, 'What sort of a lady are you? You are the maiden Salomé, and in the hands of this Herod [referring to Koromyslov] into the bargain.'[143] Two other artists debate Ekaterina Ivanovna's fidelity to the part, although Teplovskii and Mentikov both exclaim 'Bravo, Salomé!' in defense.[144]

As Act IV continues, Ekaterina Ivanovna returns to her pose as Salomé until the men decide that she should perform the dance of the seven veils. Andreev then provides the following stage directions:

> Katerina, looking questioningly and coquettishly as before, comes to the centre, and pauses irresolutely. Dances. At one moment it seems as if she would start to cry. Koromilsov [sic] exclaims, 'Bravo, Bravo!' He holds a glass of wine and watches her. Katerina exclaims strangely, helplessly and wildly waving her hands, and then assumes the pose of shameless defiance. Her lips are somewhat curled into an angry smile, her eyes look arrogantly and with contempt.[145]

Ekaterina Ivanovna's husband enters and the audience is given to understand that this is not the first time that he has witnessed this dance (or behavior). And so, the play begins with her husband's irrational jealousy and ends with his broken acceptance of her sexual depravity. Ekaterina Ivanovna asks if she can take a ride with Teplovskii and her husband agrees. She then states, 'For two hours, I have been holding an empty dish. What for? That's stupid, I don't want it. Give me the head of the prophet, I want the head of the prophet!' She continues, though Koromyslov tries to calm her down, 'You wanted me to be Salomé, but there is no prophet here – that's impudence! They are all such insignificant people, [toads].'[146] Andreev leaves his play open-ended, although it is clear that Ekaterina Ivanovna is insane and morally depraved. It is a psychological drama about deviant psychopathology in civilized Russian society.

Toni Bentley associates the revitalization of the Salomé motif with the passion for the Orient in late nineteenth-century Europe. Orientalism was at the very height of fashion since, in Western minds, the East was ruled by exotic non-Christian forces. The veiled women, Salomé and others emerged as a personification of a mysterious world of rapturous sex.[147]

In 1876 Gustave Moreau (1826–1898) painted *Salomé*, inaugurating 'the late nineteenth-century's feverish exploration of every visual detail expressive of this young lady's hunger for St John the Baptist's head.'[148] At the same time that Moreau's painting was exhibited in a Paris salon, Flaubert was writing a story entitled 'Herodias' in which Salomé's mother is depicted as an ambitious woman who controls the effeminate Herod and uses the virginal Salomé as her tool. 'Thus, Flaubert makes that daughter into a virgin whore, instinctively mimicking in dance the details of passion her body had not yet experienced in fact.'[149]

The two versions of Salomé provided by Flaubert and Moreau were united in the public's mind in 1884 by Huysman's *Against the Grain*. His character Des Esseintes views Moreau's painting of Salomé as the symbolic incarnation of old-world vice and establishes a tinge of masochistic euphoria in the understanding of Salomé. In turn, French symbolist poet Jules Laforgue (1860–1887) 'developed an aspect of the virgin whore's bloodlust' in his *Six Moral Tales*, influenced by the poetry of Heinrich Heine (1797–1856). However, Laforgue does not allow Salomé to revel in her aggression against the prophet, and she is dashed against the rocks after trying to throw the head of John the Baptist into the ocean. Bram Dijkstra credits these four innovators in the Salomé myth as inspiration for Wilde's famous play of 1891.[150]

Best known to Andreev, Wilde's account makes Salomé the central figure, reassigning Herodias' actions in the biblical story to her. Wilde's version concentrates on four main events – John's delayed entrance, Salomé's dance, her kissing of John's severed head, and her death at the hands of Herod's soldiers. Wilde's depiction of Salomé exhibits the female destructiveness, dark obsession and apocalyptic bestiality of earlier accounts, but he humanizes these characteristics by providing an interiority for her that had been lacking previously.[151] The original version of the play was written in French under the influence of the avant-garde and symbolist theater of Paris. Written for Sarah Bernhardt (1844–1923), Wilde envisioned his play in yellow tones with Salomé either in green, with associations to a poisonous lizard, or naked, wearing only ropes of exotic jewels. However, the play was banned by the Lord Chamberlain's office because it depicted a biblical subject.[152] It was not performed in Paris until 1896.

An English version of the play was published in England in 1893 with the Japanese-inspired sinuous illustrations of Aubrey Beardsley (1872–1898). Elliot L. Gilbert sees this edition as a representation by Wilde and Beardsley of perverse sexuality that acts as 'an attack on the conventions of patriarchal culture even as they express their horror at the threatening female energy which is the instrument of that attack.'[153]

In Germany, Max Reinhardt's (1873–1943) productions of *Salomé* in 1903 inspired Richard Strauss (1864–1949) to compose an opera of the same name. Strauss envisioned Salomé as a Wagnerian heroine in the body of a ballerina. His vision was realized in 1905 when the soprano singing the part in German refused, as a 'decent woman,' to perform the nine-minute *Dance of the Seven Veils*, ceding this part to a ballerina from the opera house.[154]

In Strauss' opera, the *Dance of the Seven Veils* is accompanied by a soundtrack and Salomé performs a striptease, solidifying the associations of dangerous seduction and unabashed sexuality. Less about a biblical subject, Strauss' work was understood by his contemporaries as an opera about sexual perversion. Salomé was characterized as morally repugnant, a sexual hysteric, and critics attacked the opera as decadent.[155]

In 1904, Wilde's play was translated into Russian by the symbolist poet Bal'mont. In 1907 an attempt by the Moscow Art Theater to produce Wilde's play was blocked by the Russian Orthodox Church. Andreev, however, attended the dress rehearsal of *Salomé* at the theater of Vera Komissarzhevskaia on 27 October 1908. To avoid the outrage of the church, the biblical names for this production were changed, and Salomé did not address the severed head of John the Baptist but spoke into a cistern, at the bottom of which supposedly lay the saint's corpse. The changes, however, did not pacify the church and the play was banned prior to the first public performance, causing a furor in the Russian press.[156]

Ida Rubenstein (1885–1960) finally introduced Russian audiences to *Salomé* on 20 December 1908. Relying on influential friends, Rubenstein agreed to stage her version in mime, although she distributed the text in advance of the debut. Just prior to the first performance in the St Petersburg Conservatory, the prefect of the police confiscated the papier-mâché head of John the Baptist. Even without a head or the text, Rubenstein's performance of *Salomé* and the *Dance of the Seven Veils*, which left her nearly naked, was met with ecstatic applause.[157]

Sergei Diaghilev (1872–1929) saw Rubenstein's performance, and then cast her in similar roles for his Ballets Russes. She played Cleopatra and danced with twelve veils instead of seven. The following year, Rubenstein played Zobeida, the sultan's wife, who releases the sultan's slaves and, along with her concubines, engages in an orgy. When the sultan witnesses this, everyone is slaughtered and Zobeida stabs herself in the heart. Bentley writes, '*Schéhérazade* introduced yet another variation in the genesis of the nineteenth-century femme fatale. Here, in a symbolic gesture, she dies from a self-inflicted wound as atonement for her unleashed sexuality.'[158]

The association of mental illness with immoral behavior became common in Russia at the beginning of the twentieth century. Laura Engelstein argues that the events of 1905 were believed to be the work of young people in revolt against familial authority and respectable society. This revolt not only included 'hooliganism' but vicious forms of sexual transgression, which pointed to the general social malaise of the time. Lax censorship following the failed revolution seemed to allow sex to take center stage in literature and the press, wherein homosexuality, sodomy, lesbianism, bestiality and pornographic images were pushing what was considered *normal* sexual relations to the side.[159]

As social boundaries began to rapidly deteriorate, vice was no longer limited to the lower classes (peasant girl prostitutes) and in this was realized the fears of degeneration theory – that Russian society as a whole was devolving into deviance. Not surprisingly, this perverse desire to engage in acts of insubordination, usually with sexual connotations, was often diagnosed as a psychological problem in women. Engelstein states: 'Once reluctant to identify popular deviance as pathological in an organic or clinical sense, physicians were now more willing to apply such distinctions.'[160]

Early in his literary career, Andreev reflected society's growing apprehension about deviant sexuality in 'The Abyss' and 'In the Fog.' A decade later Andreev returned to the debate with a more nuanced approach in which *guilt* could not be so easily assigned. Stibelev's jealousy and sexual obsession led to the destruction of his wife and family. After escaping his attempt on her life, Ekaterina Ivanovna is psychologically shattered, which is expressed outwardly by her sexual promiscuity. Relying on Salomé and degeneration, Andreev creates a Russian *femme fatale* who is less the villainous seducer of men and more the victim of male desire and the general social malaise. At the end of the play, Ekaterina Ivanovna is unfulfilled and insane, still looking for her prophet.

In the European post-Enlightenment, sexuality and its hidden forces of seduction were understood as a corruption of the rational. Physical excess, particularly unbridled sexual activity, was often punished by madness and associated with the feminine.[161] By the end of the nineteenth century, medicine equated female sexuality with hysteria and mental illness. Andreev's accurate presentation of the cultural and scientific discourse of the day allowed for, if not promoted, social debates about and mock trials of his play. Platonov and others were responding to these lines of discourse when they provided a psychiatric diagnosis for Ekaterina Ivanovna. This is why Platanov was able to argue that Ekaterina was 'one of the women of our epoch' representing a layer of abnormal society that is unable to channel sexual impulses into a 'superior psychic energy,' but instead allows them to 'serve perverse gratification.' Ekaterina Ivanovna was surrounded by this social rebellion and it slowly seeped into her subconscious. When she endured the psychological trauma inflicted by her husband, rage born of sexual jealousy, her subconscious responded in kind with its own brand of sexual aggression. This, among other reasons, is why Platonov is confident in diagnosing Ekaterina Ivanovna with a condition he calls sexual-pathological, linking her immoral behavior with mental illness.[162]

The Thought: the play

Andreev wrote The Thought, a theatrical version of his story of the same name, which premiered at the Moscow Art Theater on March 1914. Nearly twelve years had passed and Andreev's conception of the basic theme had changed. In the 1902 story, Kerzhentsev thought that he could control his madness, but by 1914 the question was whether the psychiatrists could make an accurate diagnosis. Andreev intended the play to be independent of the story and, in a letter, suggested to the lead actor that he misinterpreted the role due to an 'unnecessary reading of the story.' Andreev explained that Kerzhentsev does not know if he is insane. The key to the performance, according to Andreev, was the *not knowing*.[163]

The play begins in Kerzhentsev's study where there is a large cage containing an orangutan, dying of despair and melancholy. According to Kerzhentsev this despair results from the orangutan's realization that he could have been a king, but was prevented from this and reverted into an animal that stands on all fours. Degeneration theory remains at the core of the play as madness is associated with regression, the bestial and incarceration. Kerzhentsev too will aspire to greatness and be prevented by the frailty of his own mind. For him, the murder of Savelov is an experiment conducted to test the power of his intellect, an attempt to rise up and stand on two legs.

In the second act, we learn that Savelov is a writer who is greatly dissatisfied with his own literary works. He is tired of writing only about what he knows: 'There is an entire enormous world living somewhere behind my back and I feel how pleasant it is, but am unable to turn my head.'[164] Savelov is a man of limited intellect while Kerzhentsev sees himself as a man of great intelligence. There is further tension between the two men because of Kerzhentsev's love for Tat'iana Nikolaevna, Savelov's wife.

Kerzhentsev kills Savelov in the third act and when Kerzhentsev encounters his housekeeper, he finally realizes that he has gone insane. At the mental hospital the doctors discuss Kerzhentsev's condition: 'The one who thinks that he is insane is still healthy, but the one who stops thinking will go mad.'[165] Kerzhentsev speaks with the nurse, trying to understand where his theory went wrong. By the doctors' definition then, Kerzhentsev is not insane. In a final meeting with Tat'iana Niko-laevna, Kerzhentsev argues that he was not insane when he killed Savelov, that he wanted to climb to the heights of free will and free thought but that his intellect, which he had worshiped like a god, had become his worst enemy, and he had lost the border between in/sanity. By the end of the play, the audience learns that, like the orangutan, Kerzhentsev is caged and terribly alone. Kerzhentsev's strength at the beginning of the play: 'I don't have friends and I don't want them,'[166] is his torment at the end: 'I am terribly alone, like no one in the world.'[167] Therefore, philosophical ideas of becoming a king or a beast give way to practical fears of loneliness and despair.

Elements of performance[168] and deception[169] carry over from the short story to the play. However, in the latter Kerzhentsev is less certain of his ability to straddle the boundary between in/sanity, to control the *dangerous fire* of madness. Andreev wrote to Vladimir Nemirovich-Danchenko (1858–1943) that *The Thought* would examine the regal power of the unconscious, suggesting that the focus would shift from insanity to the suffering of the madman.[170] In the span of twelve years, Andreev seems to have become more pessimistic about the effects of madness. The theme now is less about masking and controlling the symptoms and more about *not knowing* if one is insane.

Moscow psychiatrist Dmitrii Amenitskii (1875–?) wrote *An Analysis of the Hero of L. Andreev's* The Thought in 1915. Amenitskii was responding to the production of Andreev's play at the Moscow Art Theater, believing that the author had probed one of the most important problems of contemporary psychiatry – the difficulty of psychiatrists in establishing a psychological diagnosis of congenital and hereditary defects of the psyche in a legal context.[171] Amenitskii explains the various types of degenerative illness. The fourth type, a paranoid consti-tution, plagued Kerzhentsev. However, when presented with the three choices offered by the court in determining Kerzhentsev's guilt, Amenit-skii finds it nearly impossible to make a decision. The court essentially wants to know if he is sane – then he goes to prison, or insane – then he remains in the hospital. Amenitskii argues that the basis for a degenerat-ing constitution can remain unrealized in an individual from birth but, if triggered, can produce varying degrees of mental illness (psychosis or madness). In most cases it is not clear when the trigger occurs – before, during or after the crime. These issues are further compounded when an entire society is in a state of degeneration, since what once might have been considered a clinical form of psychosis is now the social norm.[172] Amenitskii states that Russian psychiatrists are not expected to heal the sick but to protect society from dangerous elements. In this capacity they are being cast into the role of jailers by the courts.[173]

On all fours

Ernest Haeckel's (1834–1919) theory of recapitulation, prevalent in the 1870s, attempted to explain the similarities between humans and animals. Haeckel argued that the individual organism repeats the entire history of the species in its own physical evolution. The development of an embryo passes through fish, reptile, and other phases on its way to becoming a fully formed human fetus. The German biologist understood insanity as an example of arrested brain development in which the individual did not completely transition from a lower evolutionary state. This theory offered an explanation for defective biological structures and led to further ideas on arrested development.

Galton's theories on the inheritance of abilities, along with Haeckel's recapitulation theory, influenced Ellis' explorations in the field of eugenics. Ellis positioned human beings on the axis between horizontal quadrupeds and vertical bipeds. The ape was classified as an imperfect biped with quadrupedal attitudes, while civilized man walked completely erect. Greenslade writes of Ellis' theory, 'Apes, infants, savage races, country people, plebeians and women would be seen fumbling in some evolutionary egg-and-spoon race, yards from the finishing tape.'[174]

These theories and others played into fears of biological reversion in which the beastly remained somewhere only slightly below the surface of the civilized visage. 'The unmasking of vice beneath the hitherto civilized surface, or the moments glimpse, glance or gaze, by a witness to it, drew on a poetics with a long history, but it is now invigorated with the spectacle of the devolutionary and degenerating self,' argues Greenslade.[175] In turn this influenced the evolution of the romantic doppelgänger into a far more monstrous double – Marlow and Kurtz in Conrad's *Heart of Darkness* and Stevenson's Jekyll and Hyde.

At this same time, Lombroso discovered cranial anomalies in the skulls of criminals which he used as empirical evidence of atavism, arguing that the ferocious instincts of the criminal were similar to those of inferior animals. Criminals, savages and apes displayed similar bone structure as well as a related inclination for mutilation and murder. The born criminal was a reversion to a distant primitive ancestor. Through the scientific theories of recapitulation, atavism and regression, the deviant criminal was drawn closer in lineage to the untamed beast.

In turning his story 'The Thought' into a play, Andreev most certainly searched for distinctive visual and thematic clues which an audience might recognize as indicators of criminal insanity. He unites Kerzhentsev's intellectual overconfidence with the primitive elements of criminality, as argued by Lombroso and others. In the Bible, Andreev found a figure whose overwhelming pride resulted in punishment in the form of bestial madness – Nebuchadnezzar.

Nebuchadnezzar II (or Nebuchadnezzar the Great) was the ruler of Babylon in the Chaldean Dynasty from 605 BC to 562 BC, marking the high point of the second Babylonian Empire. He is known today for his conquests of Judah and Jerusalem, his monumental architectural feats in the capital of Babylon and construction of the Hanging Gardens. When the Pharaoh Necho was marching his troops towards Assyria, Nebuchadnezzar, prior to his ascension to the throne, was put in command of an army to force the pharaoh to retreat. Nebuchadnezzar was victorious in engagement after engagement and gained all of the territory once held by the Egyptians – even chasing the pharaoh into Egypt itself. When news of his father's death reached Nebuchadnezzar, he was forced to return to Babylon to secure his right to the throne. After his ascension, Nebuchadnezzar fought several more military campaigns to increase Babylonian influence and to quell rebellions within the conquered lands. He captured Jerusalem in 597, again in 588, and finally the city and temple were destroyed with most of the prominent citizens deported to Babylon in 587.[176]

After the various military victories, Nebuchadnezzar turned his attention to construction with the aim of making Babylon one of the world's great wonders. With this in mind, old temples were restored and new monuments to Babylonian gods were erected. He finished the palace begun by his father and united both parts of Babylon, divided by the Euphrates, by an underground passage and a stone bridge. He also built a triple-lined wall of defense around the city. His construction projects were not limited to the capital city and most of the Babylonian Empire benefited from his industriousness.

In the Book of Daniel, however, Nebuchadnezzar is punished for boasting of his numerous achievements. He is driven mad by God and for seven years lives like a wild animal. Daniel writes:

> 30 The king spake, and said, Is not this great Babylon, that I have built for the house of the kingdom by the might of my power, and for the honour of my majesty? 31 While the word *was* in the king's mouth, there fell a voice from heaven, *saying*, O king Nebuchadnezzar to thee it is spoken; The kingdom is departed from thee. 32 And they shall drive thee from men, and thy dwelling *shall be* with the beasts of the field: they shall make

thee to eat grass as oxen, and seven times shall pass over thee, until thou know that the most High ruleth in the kingdom of men, and giveth it to whomsoever he will. 33 The same hour was the thing fulfilled upon Nebuchadnezzar: and he was driven from men, and did eat grass as oxen, and his body was wet with the dew of heaven, till his hairs were grown like eagles' *feathers*, and his nails were like birds' *claws*.[177]

After seven years, Nebuchadnezzar regained his sanity and returned to the throne, but little more is written about his reign. The biblical interpretation is that Nebuchadnezzar suffered for his pride and therefore was forced to carry the burden of madness and to walk on all fours, which the Greeks called lycanthropy (made famous in the character of the Werewolf), or today might be diagnosed as boanthropy (victims believe that they are an ox). This puts into some perspective Kerzhentsev's overconfidence in his intellect and his concentration on reducing himself to the bestial as proof of his madness.

Kerzhentsev looks upon the nurse Masha with contempt because she is a religious woman. In the play he becomes adamant that religion is a lie and compares it to the theater.[178] This rejection of God, and of Masha as its representative, furthers the story's connection to the book of Daniel:

I, Dr Kerzhentsev, wanted to howl. Not to shout but to howl, like that other inmate. I wanted to tear my clothes and claw myself with my nails. I wanted to grab my shirt at the collar, pull at it a little at first and then rip it apart. I, Dr Kerzhentsev, wanted to get down on all fours and crawl. It was quiet all around, and the snow beat at the window, and somewhere nearby Masha was silently praying.

Kerzhentsev thinks that he might draw attention to himself if he were to howl or to tear his shirt so he decides to crawl. He then asks himself, 'But why crawl? Am I really insane?' Although he is seized with terror by his desire to howl and claw, he eventually succumbs:

And so, rolling up my sleeves I got on the floor and started to crawl. I had not yet crossed half the room when I became so amused by the absurdity of it that I sat there and laughed and laughed. [...] Evidently the urge to crawl and the rest of it were the result of autosuggestion. The persistent thought that I was insane had given birth to insane desires, and as soon as I began to gratify them, it turned out that they did not exist and that I therefore was not insane.

Kerzhentsev, however, is not ultimately convinced that he is sane.[179] Such a description not only echoes the biblical story of Nebuchadnezzar, but may draw on William Blake's (1757–1827) 1795 image of the fallen ruler who is on all fours, caught in the transition from man to beast. It is possible that when Kerzhentsev speaks of autosuggestion, he is referencing the madness of Nebuchadnezzar.

There are further references to this biblical story in 'The Thought.' For example, after crawling about on all fours in his cell, Kerzhentsev later tells how he loved only himself and looked down upon religious people, like 'a medieval baron in his eagle's nest in an impregnable castle, proudly and imperiously surveying the valleys below, so as I, unconquered and proud, in my castle.'[180] The eagle's nest is a fascinating reference since Nebuchadnezzar grows hair like eagle feathers and, like the king of Babylon, Kerzhentsev is dragged from his impregnable castle.

For much of 1904 Andreev had worked on a story, 'From the Depths of Ages' (Iz glubinyi vekov), with the alternative titles 'The Tsar' (Tsar') and 'Nebuchadnezzar' (Navukhodonosor), a psychological study of an autocrat and his megalomania. Due to Gor'kii's criticism of the story, Andreev did not finish this version, but did rework it over the summer and eventually published it in October 1905 as 'So It Was.' This suggests that the biblical figure of Nebuchadnezzar was a part of Andreev's creative vocabulary early in his literary career.[181]

In the play *The Thought*, Kerzhentsev no longer crawls on the ground. However, an orangutan is added as a symbol of Kerzhentsev's loneliness and isolation. At the beginning of the play the dying orangutan is discussed with a friend Kraft, a possible reference to Krafft-Ebing, and at the end Kerzhentsev realizes that he, like the orangutan, will also die alone in a cage. The howling is left to another patient, Kronilov, who keeps Kerzhentsev up at night. Certainly, the orangutan as a symbolic double for Kerzhentsev was not chosen arbitrarily. Darwin's ape, Lombroso's criminal atavist, Thomas Carlyle's (1795–1881) criminal ape faces, and a whole host of simian references employed at this time represented both the source of evolution and the dangerous degradation of contemporary man. Kerzhentsev begins the play as a scientist conducting research on an orangutan, only to identify with the animal at the end, thereby charting his complete devolution from a healthy, sane medical theorist to a lonely, insane criminal beast.

We can only speculate on how Andreev's understanding of madness changed over time. It would have been very effective to have Kerzhentsev crawling on all fours in the dramatic version of *The Thought*. As argued previously, however, Andreev increasingly identified madness with criminal behavior and incarceration. Therefore, we might interpret this change as a move away from a biblical reference towards a more visually striking image of a caged animal. At the time this would have been considered a more *scientifically accurate* symbolic representation of criminal atavism. Further, Andreev wished to leave the question of

Kerzhentsev's sanity to the psychiatrists, and therefore reduced the obvious allusions to insanity. The orangutan represents Kerzhentsev's two extremes: medical theorist and primitive throwback, leaving the audience (and science) to decide whether or not the doctor is insane.

Although Andreev's literary reputation began to wane during this period (1908–14), his works continued to be cited by medical personalities (doctors and psychiatrists) as accurate depictions of mental illness.[182] Andreev's notion of feigned and performed madness also remained an intriguing artistic theme.[183] Throughout Andreev's literary career, the actor and the performance in the context of mental illness was a productive theme. Variable mood swings, oscillating between manic highs, depressive lows and periods of normalcy, can be constructed as various roles, corresponding to each period. The roles bring meaning to life, the excess energy of mania is directed into the role, and the performance suggests that the actor is healthy, normal and creative.

Chukovskii describes this process as characteristic of Andreev: how he fixated on certain activities and created a persona for each one of them. 'Andreev's costumes suited him like those of an operatic tenor – the costume of an artist, a sportsman, a sailor. He wore them as actors wear their costumes on stage.'[184] Similarly, Andreev created a character who was fixated on the murder of a friend, who took on the role of the madman or the doctor of mathematics who proves that the appearance of truth, or sanity, is much more important than reality.

The performance is not to entertain, but is a way to engage the illness. Andreev played the role of the painter, sailor or photographer to focus his manic energy, to be constructive rather than destructive. Although his family and friends were aware of this performance, it was not really for their benefit, but for his own. It was a way to bring some coherence to his illness experience. Andreev's characters channel their mental illness in similar ways. Kerzhentsev comes to the conclusion that his role as madman may not have been for the audience, but actually to mask his own illness. The clown He, from *He Who Gets Slapped*, realizes that his pain and despair does not disappear with a slap in the face. Like Duke Lorenzo (*Black Maskers*), Kerzhentsev is willing to kill his double (Savelov) in an attempt to find the truth. In Andreev's life and literary works there is an element of the performance, utilized in order to avoid being stigmatized as mentally ill. The performance, in turn, becomes a type of deception, replicating *normal* behavior to give meaning to the illness experience. As a result, I argue that by maintaining the appearance of normalcy, Andreev wished to avoid the criticism à la Nordau that the author was as morally corrupt as his decadent works of art.

Notes

1 Andreev, *SOS*, 22–3.
2 Vadim Andreev, *Detstvo*, 33–38 / 24–6.
3 Ibid., 39–40 / 27–8.
4 Bernstein, Herman. *Celebrities of Our Time: Interviews* (New York: Books for Libraries Press, 1968) 49. According to Woodward, the story was written after the government suppressed revolutionary activities in Kherson and Warsaw in 1908. See Woodward, *Leonid Andreyev: A Study*, 190–1.
5 Andreev, 'Rasskaz o semi poveshennikh,' vol. 3, *Sobranie sochinenii v 6 tomakh*, 62. In English, see Andreyev, Leonid. *The Seven Who Were Hanged: A Story by Leonid Andreyev*. Translated by Herman Bernstein (New York: Illustrated Editions Company, 1941) 56.
6 Woodward, *Leonid Andreyev: A Study*, 193–6.
7 Kaun, *Leonid Andreyev: A Critical Study*, 243.
8 Andreev, 'Rasskaz o semi poveshennikh,' 83 / 113.
9 Ibid., 88 / 126.
10 Ibid., 94 / 143.
11 Ibid., 96 / 148. The English translation is inaccurate. Andreev describes it as a 'mutnaia' or 'dull' fatigue.
12 Ibid., 102 / 164.
13 Ibid., 93 / 140.
14 Ibid., 104 / 168.
15 Woodward, *Leonid Andreyev: A Study*, 198.
16 Ibid., 80. Woodward makes this point in his reading of 'The Thought.' However, it has relevance for 'My Notes,' which Woodward understands as a continuation of 'The Thought.'
17 Andreev, 'Moi zapiski,' vol. 3, *Sobranie sochinenii v 6 tomakh*, 115. In English, I use the translation of 'The Man Who Found the Truth' and page references for: Andreyev, Leonid. *The Crushed Flower and Other Stories*. Translated by Herman Bernstein (New York: Harper and Brothers, 1916) 272.
18 Ibid., 115–16 / 273.
19 Ibid., 116 / 275.
20 Ibid., 124–5 / 284.
21 Ibid., 126 / 286.
22 Ibid., 127–9 / 288–90.
23 Ibid., 129 / 290.
24 Ibid., 141 / 307.
25 Ibid.
26 Ibid., 152 / 323.
27 Ibid., 153 / 324.
28 I have already addressed this point in *Memoirs and Madness*. For Gor'kii's seeming need to create a sanitized version of life for himself see Chapter 8 (257–81). For Andreev's need to constantly question the status quo, refer to Aleksandr Blok's literary portrait (73–4).
29 Andreev, 'Moi zapiski,' 160 / 334.
30 Ibid., 162 / 339.
31 Ibid., 177 / 354.

32 Generalova, N. '«Moi zapiski» Leonida Andreeva. (K voprosu ob ideinoi problematiki povesti).' *Russkaia literatura*, 4 (1986): 178–9.
33 Ibid., 176.
34 Foucault, *Madness and Civilization*, 44–5.
35 Ibid., 232; 234; 238–9.
36 Ibid., 241.
37 Ibid., 244–6.
38 Ibid., 246.
39 Ibid., 252–3.
40 Ibid., 257–9.
41 Brown, 'Peasant Survival Strategies in Late Imperial Russia,' 324.
42 Brown, 'Psychiatrists and the State in Tsarist Russia,' 270.
43 Ibid., 280–1.
44 Andreev, 'Bol'shoi shlem,' vol. 1, *Sobranie sochinenii v 6 tomakh*, 149.
45 Andreev, *Gaudeamus*, vol. 3, *Sobranie sochinenii v 6 tomakh*, 556; 562.
46 Andreev, *Sashka Zhegulev*, vol. 4, *Sobranie sochinenii v 6 tomakh*, 137.
47 Andreev, *Dnevnik Satana*, vol. 6, *Sobranie sochinenii v 6 tomakh*, 193.
48 Andreev, 'Den' gneva,' vol. 3, *Sobranie sochinenii v 6 tomakh*, 219–21.
49 Andreev, *Tsar' Golod*, vol. 3, *Sobranie sochinenii v 6 tomakh*, 283–5; 291–2.
50 Andreev, 'On,' vol. 4, *Sobranie sochinenii v 6 tomakh*, 283–90.
51 Andreev, *Korol', zakon i svoboda*, vol. 5, *Sobranie sochinenii v 6 tomakh*, 149–50; 175.
52 Andreev, 'Zhizn' Vasiliia Fiveiskogo,' vol. 1, *Sobranie sochinenii v 6 tomakh*, 550.
53 Andreev, *Chernye maski*, vol. 3, *Sobranie sochinenii v 6 tomakh*, 381.
54 Andreev, 'Ipatov,' vol. 4, *Sobranie sochinenii v 6 tomakh*, 37–8.
55 Andreev, *Okean*, vol. 4, *Sobranie sochinenii v 6 tomakh*, 408.
56 Andreev, 'Zhertva,' vol. 6, *Sobranie sochinenii v 6 tomakh*, 112–13.
57 RGALI, f. 734, op. 1, ed. khr. 6 l. 1–4.
58 *Rech'*, 300 (7 December 1908): 4; *Obozrenie teatrov*, 602 (10 December 1908): 8.
59 For an interesting discussion of how Vsevolod Garshin benefited from associations with mental illness see Wessling, Robert D. 'Vsevolod Garshin, the Russian Intelligentsia, and Fan Hysteria.' In *Madness and the Mad in Russian Culture*. Edited by Angela Brintlinger and Ilya Vinitsky, 75–89. For Andreev, nearly two decades later, mental illness was associated with deviance and degeneration.
60 Brusyanin, V. 'The Symbolic Dramas of Andreyeff.' In *Plays by Leonid Andreyeff*, xxi.
61 Daniil Andreev and Beklemisheva, *Rekviem*, 245.
62 Andreev, *Chernye maski*, vol. 3, *Sobranie sochinenii v 6 tomakh*, 388. In English, I use the translation of *The Black Maskers* and page references for: Andreyeff, *Plays by Leonid Andreyeff*, 54.
63 Ibid., 393 / 61–2.
64 Andreev, *Tot, kto poluchaet poshchechiny*, vol. 5, *Sobranie sochinenii v 6 tomakh*, 347. In English, see Andreyev, Leonid. *He Who Gets Slapped: A Play in Four Acts*. Translated by Gregory Zilboorg (Westport: Greenwood Press, 1975) 112.

65 Ibid., 329 / 60.
66 Andreev, 'Zhertva,' vol. 6, *Sobranie sochinenii v 6 tomakh*, 107; 111.
67 Ibid., 110; 111.
68 Ibid., 113.
69 Izmailov, A. 'Novaia povest' Leonida Andreeva.' *Berzhevye vedomosti*, 10741 (5 October 1908): 6.
70 Izmailov, A. "Chernye maski' v teatre Komissarzhevskoi.' *Russkoe slovo*, 282 (5 December 1908): 2.
71 Lunacharskii, 'T'ma.' As quoted in Kaun, *Leonid Andreev: A Critical Study*, 17.
72 Rybakov, Feodor. *Sovremennye pisateli i bol'nye nervy: Psikhiatricheskii etiud* (Moscow: V. Rikhter, 1908) 4–5.
73 Ibid., 7; 29; 45.
74 Kube, Ol'ga. *Koshmary zhizni: Kriticheski-psikhologicheskii ocherk o L. Andreeve, Pshebyshevskom, i dr. sovremennykh pisateliakh* (St Petersburg, 1909) 26.
75 Ibid., 76.
76 Shaikevich, M. 'Psikhologicheskaia storona v proizvedeniiakh Leonida Andreeva.' *Vestnik psikhologii, kriminal'noi atropologii i gipnotizma*, 6, 1, St Petersburg (1909): 32–3. The stories involving healthy characters include: 'Grand Slam,' 'The Foreigner' (Inostranets), 'Silence,' 'In the Dark Distance,' 'Once There Was,' 'An Original Person' (Original'nyi chelovek), 'At the Station' and 'No Forgiveness' (Net proshcheniia). The stories involving sick characters include: 'The City,' 'Phantoms' and 'The Thief.' This group also includes characters who are extremely egocentric or anti-social: Petrov ('Phantoms'), Kerzhentsev ('The Thought'), Vasilii Fiveiskii ('The Life of Vasilii Fiveiskii') and Sergei Petrovich ('The Story of Sergei Petrovich').
77 Ibid., 33. The stories listed by Shaikevich are 'The Abyss,' 'In the Fog,' 'Darkness,' 'The Life of Vasilii Fiveiskii,' 'The Alarm-Bell,' 'The Wall' and 'Red Laugh.' He secondarily lists stories that are specifically concerned with a fear of life ('At the Window') and a fear of death ('Grand Slam,' 'Once There Was,' 'Lazarus' and *Life of Man*).
78 Ibid., 34. The stories listed here are *Savva*, 'Darkness,' *To the Stars* and *Tsar Hunger*. Stories with a specifically pessimistic philosophical underpinning include 'The Governor,' 'The Story of Sergei Petrovich' and 'The Life of Vasilii Fiveiskii.'
79 Ibid., 37–8. This group includes 'The Thought,' 'The Abyss,' 'The Life of Vasilii Fiveiskii,' 'Ben-Tovit' and 'Judas Iscariot and Others.'
80 Ibid., 54–5.
81 Mumortsev, *Psikhopaticheskie cherty v geroiakh Leonida Andreeva*, 2.
82 Ibid., 3; 7. Progressive paralysis was mainly associated with untreated syphilis, but also psychological stress and/or trauma, and severe alcoholism. Reduplicative paramnesia, associated with brain injury and later with neurological disorders, was a delusional belief that a place or location had been duplicated.
83 Ibid., 16.
84 Ibid., 9.
85 Ibid., 11.

86 Smolenskii, Nikolai. *Zashchitnikam Leonida Andreeva!* Second Edition (Moscow: V.I. Logachev, 1910) 14–16.

87 Ibid., 30.

88 Ibid., 62–3.

89 Ibid., 70–2.

90 Menchikova, Elena. 'Psikhopatologiia v proizvedeniiakh Dostoevskogo i L. Andreeva.' *Vestnik vospitaniia*, 4, 1 (1910): 189. For more on Dostoevskii's epilepsy see Rice, James L. *Dostoevsky and the Healing Art: An Essay in Literary and Medical History.* Ann Arbor: Ardis, 1985.

91 Ibid., 195.

92 Ibid., 196.

93 Ibid., 206–8; 211.

94 *Obozrenie teatrov*, no. 1159 (30 August 1910): 17; *Penzenskie vedomosti*, 188 (2 September 1910): 3; *Penzenskie vedomosti*, 191 (5 September 1910): 4.

95 *Utro Rossii*, 242 (5 September 1910): 3.

96 Brusianin, *Leonid Andreev. Zhizn' i tvorchestvo*, 5–6.

97 Ibid., 6–9.

98 Ibid., 70–1.

99 Tkachev, *Patologicheskoe tvorchestvo*, 19.

100 Ibid., 22.

101 *Birzhevye vedomosti*, 13810, evening edition (18 October 1913): 4.

102 Iezuitova, L. 'Deviat' pisem Leonida Nikolaevicha Andreeva k Lidii Semenovne Ramenskoi.' *Russkaia literatura*, 3 (1992): 151.

103 Ivanov-Razumnik [Razumnik Vasilievich Ivanov]. *O smysle zhizni. F. Sologub, L. Andreev, L. Shestov.* Introduction by P.D. Rayfield (Letchworth: Bradda Books, 1971) 86–7; 107–10; 115; 139–40; 146.

104 Elpat'evskii, 'Leonid Nikolaevich Andreev,' 275.

105 Pavel Andreev, 'Vospominaniia o Leonide Andreeve,' 194.

106 Generalova, 'Leonid Andreev, Dnevnik 1891–1892,' 98.

107 LRA, MS. 606 \ E. 8 *27 March 1897–23 April 1901; 1 January 1903; 9 October 1907; 28 April*; ii. Entries for 8, 11, 12 August 1898 are torn from the original manuscript.

108 Iezuitova, *Tvorchestvo Leonida Andreeva (1892–1906)*, 78.

109 Andreev, 'Vor,' vol. 2, *Sobranie sochinenii v 6 tomakh*, 14. In English, I use the translation of 'The Thief' and page reference for Andreyev, *Visions: Stories and Photographs by Leonid Andreyev*, 160.

110 Ibid., 20 / 167.

111 Shaikevich, 'Psikhologicheskaia storona v proizvedeniiakh Leonida Andreeva,' 32–3.

112 Menchikova, 'Psikhopatologiia v proizvedeniiakh Dostoevskogo i L. Andreeva,' 207.

113 Woodward, *Leonid Andreyev: A Study*, 186–7.

114 Izmailov, A. 'Poeziia bol'nogo uma i proza zdorovogo cheloveka: («On» Leonida Andreeva).' *Novoe slovo*, 6 (1913): 127–8.

115 Andreev, 'On,' vol. 4, *Sobranie sochinenii v 6 tomakh*, 265.

116 Ibid., 288.

117 Vadim Andreev, *Detstvo*, 60–1 / 42.

118 Isaak Il'ich Levitan (1861–1900), painter.

119 Chukovskii, *Kniga o Leonide Andreeve*, 79 / 61.
120 Vadim Andreev, *Detstvo*, 62–4 / 43–4.
121 Kaun, *Leonid Andreyev: A Critical Study*, 86.
122 Zaitsev, *Kniga o Leonide Andreeve*, 125–46 / 93–105.
123 Daniil Andreev and Beklemisheva, *Rekviem*, 195–276.
124 Woodward, 205–7.
125 Vadim Andreev, *Detstvo*, 60 / 42. I translated this passage into English as I feel that Roper's version is flawed.
126 Andreeva, *Dom na chernoi rechke*, 19–20; quote is on 46–7; 64.
127 Ken and Rogov, *Zhizn' Leonida Andreeva*, 238–43.
128 Ibid., 213–14.
129 Woodward, *Leonid Andreyev: A Study*, 232–3.
130 Ibid., 233–4.
131 Andreev first published 'A Letter on the Theater' in the March 1912 issue of the journal *Masks* (Maski). This letter was republished with a second letter in 1914 as 'Letters on the Theater' (Pis'ma o teatre) in volume 22 of the *Shipovnik* almanac.
132 Woodward, *Leonid Andreyev: A Study*, 235–6.
133 Platonov, K. *'Ekaterina Ivanovna' L. Andreeva. (Sudebno psikhopatologicheskii etiud)* (Kharkov: 'Utro' Zhmudskogo, 1913).
134 Ibid., 3.
135 At the end of January 1913, a mock trial was held in the studio of Feodor Komissarzhevskii (1882–1954) in Moscow, organized by the journal *Masks*. Various artistic personalities took part in the proceedings, including Andreev's friends and colleagues Veresaev, Gloushev and Nemirovich-Danchenko. It seems that these *court proceedings* were probably friendlier than the Kharkov version held on 14 February. See *Rannee utro*, 18 (22 January 1913): 5; *Teatr*, 1219 (22 January 1913): 5; *Odesskoe obozrennie*, 240 (31 January 1913): 9.
136 Platonov, *'Ekaterina Ivanovna' L. Andreeva*, 4.
137 Ibid., 6.
138 Andreev, *Ekaterina Ivanovna*, vol. 4, *Sobranie sochinenii v 6 tomakh*, 453; 456. In English, see Andreyev, Leonid. *Katerina (Yekaterina Ivanovna): A Drama in 4 Acts*. Translated by Herman Bernstein (New York: Brentano's, 1923) 123; 125; 133.
139 There is a Salomé in Mark and Matthew who is the mother of the sons of Zebedee. Salomé is the name given to the daughter of Herodias, which is not given in the biblical passage.
140 Bentley writes of the cultural shift: 'Fears about the sexual woman were especially prevalent in both Europe and America during the late 1800s as a "medical" preoccupation with the virus of female insatiability gathered momentum. [...] The psychological climate in France during the late nineteenth century was rife with insecurity, fertile ground for Salomé's insurrection. The devastating defeat in the Franco-Prussian war in 1870 and the divisive turmoil of the Dreyfus affair filled political life with confusion, shame and loss. The rise of industrialization challenged the individual's place in the world, while both rampant venereal disease and the legalization of divorce in 1884 left women vulnerable as scapegoats. As

issues of women's rights edged forward, so did the anxiety.' Bentley, Toni. *Sisters of Salome* (New Haven: Yale University Press, 2002) 22–3.

141 Meier, Franz. 'Oscar Wilde and the Myth of the *Femme Fatale* in *Fin-de-Siècle* Culture.' In *The Importance of Reinventing Oscar: Versions of Wilde during the Last 100 years.* Edited by Uwe Böker, Richard Corballis and Julie A. Hibbard (Amsterdam: Rodopi, 2002) 119.

142 Andreev, *Ekaterina Ivanovna*, 460–1 / 144.

143 Ibid., 461 / 146.

144 Ibid., 462–3 / 149–50.

145 Ibid., 466 / 160.

146 Ibid., 470 / 170–1. The English translation uses 'crabs,' but the Russian word is 'toads,' which seems more appropriate.

147 Bentley, *Sisters of Salomé*, 23.

148 Dijkstra, Bram. *Idols of Perversity: Fantasies of Feminine Evil in* Fin-de-Siècle *Culture* (Oxford: Oxford University Press, 1986) 380.

149 Ibid., 381.

150 Ibid., 382; 395–6. Huysman's quote is taken from a passage presented by Dijkstra.

151 Gilbert, Elliot L. '"Tumult of Images": Wilde, Beardsley, and *Salome*.' *Victorian Studies*, 26 (Winter 1983): 142–4.

152 Showalter, Elaine. *Sexual Anarchy: Gender and Culture at the* Fin de Siècle (New York: Viking, 1990) 149–50.

153 Gilbert, "Tumult of Images", 133–4.

154 Bentley, *Sisters of Salomé*, 35.

155 Gilman, *Disease and Representation*, 166–8.

156 Matich, Olga. 'Gender Trouble in the Amazonian Kingdom: Turn-of-the-Century Representations of Women in Russia.' In *Amazons of the Avant-garde. Alexandra Exter, Natalia Goncharova, Liubov Popova, Olga Razanova, Varvara Stepanova, and Nadezhda Udaltsova.* Edited by John E. Bowlt and Matthew Drutt (New York: Guggenheim Museum, 2000) 83; Strutinskaia, E. 'Legenda o Salome.' *Russkoe isskustvo*, 1 (2004): 140–3.

157 Bentley, *Sisters of Salomé*, 137–40. It might be under this influence that Andreev's Ekaterina Ivanovna holds a platter without a head in Act IV of his play.

158 Ibid., 142–3.

159 Engelstein, *Keys to Happiness*, 264–8.

160 Ibid., 290.

161 Gilman, *Disease and Representation*, 64–7.

162 Platonov, 'Ekaterina Ivanovna' L. Andreeva, 6–8.

163 Daniil Andreev and Beklemisheva, *Rekviem*, 79–82. Letter from Leonid Andreev to Leonid Leonidov, 13 February 1914.

164 Andreev, *Mysl'*, vol. 5, *Sobranie sochinenii v 6 tomakh*, 95.

165 Ibid., 122.

166 Ibid., 91.

167 Ibid., 133.

168 Ibid., 92; 105; 112; 116.

169 Ibid., 96; 103; 118.

170 Balatova, N. and V. Bezzubov, eds. 'Pis'ma L.N. Andreeva k Vl.I.

Nemirovich-Danchenko i K.S. Stanislavskomu (1913–1917).' *Uchenye Zapiski Tartuskogo Gosudarstvennogo Universiteta*, 266 (1979): 238. Letters of 31 October and 6 November 1913.

171 Amenitskii, *Analiz geroia «Mysl'»*, 3.

172 Ibid., 24–7.

173 Ibid., 28.

174 Greenslade, *Degeneration, Culture and the Novel*, 70.

175 Ibid., 72–3.

176 Information about Nebuchadnezzar was compiled from Henze, Matthais. *The Madness of King Nebuchadnezzar: The Ancient Near Eastern Origins and Early History of Interpretation of Daniel 4* (Leiden: Brill 1999); Sack, Ronald. *Images of Nebuchadnezzar: The Emergence of a Legend* (London: Associated University Presses, 1991).

177 Daniel 4: 30–3.

178 Andreev, *Mysl'*, 125.

179 Andreev, 'Mysl'', 414–15 / 70–1.

180 Ibid., 418 / 74.

181 Woodward, *Leonid* Andreyev: *A Study*, 129.

182 A frequently referenced example is offered by Dr Jerome M. Schneck, who published a paper in 1970 on pseudo-malingering, using Andreev's 'The Thought' as the primary text. Schneck, a psychiatrist with the St Vincent Hospital and Medical Center of New York, defined the condition as one suffered by people who misrepresent their illness in order to repress the very symptoms that constitute their condition. Simply put, an individual convinces himself that he is 'faking it,' in order to avoid having to admit that he is, in fact, actually suffering from an affective illness. Schneck argues that although Andreev's story is an extreme case, it does accurately describe this condition. See Schneck, Jerome M. 'Pseudo-malingering and Leonid Andreyev's "The Dilemma".' *Psychiatric Quarterly*, 44, 1 (December 1970): 49–54.

183 Czech author Pavel Kohout (b. 1928) wrote the play *Poor Murderer*, which opened on Broadway in 1976, based on 'The Thought.' In this version, Kerzhentsev is a former actor now confined to an insane asylum. Kohout employs the play-within-a-play device to tell the story of how Kerzhentsev, in the role of Hamlet, killed Savelov, in the role of Polonius. Tired of his charade as a madman, Kerzhentsev asks for the opportunity to show how he cunningly murdered his friend by reenacting his Hamlet performance. Following the reenactment he becomes increasingly anxious about his performance; whether he convinced the audience of his sanity and efficacy as an actor. The professor who is to determine Kerzhentsev's sanity remains unconvinced and asks that the scene be reenacted again, but with a different actor as Hamlet. This actor, playing Kerzhentsev playing Hamlet, does not kill Polonius but drops to his knees and barks like a dog at the anticipated moment of the murder. It turns out that the actors brought to the insane asylum for the performance are in fact Savelov and Tatiana, who have come to try to bring Kerzhentsev out of his madness. However, Kerzhentsev is even more distraught once he realizes that he is mentally ill. Tantiana, moved by his madness, leaves her husband in order to nurse Kerzhentsev

back to health. In Kohout's version, Kerzhentsev kills Savelov symbolically, without a rapier (or a paperweight). Kohout compellingly reemploys the important elements of Andreev's story (madness and the performance) using a mirroring effect. Susan Harris Smith correctly suggests that 'Kerzhentsev's madness in-authenticates everything; the entire play must be reevaluated in terms of his genuine madness.' See Kohout, Pavel. *Poor Murderer*. Translated by Herbert Berghof and Laurence Luckinbill (New York: Viking Press, 1977); Smith, Susan Harris. 'Ironic Distance and the Theatre of Feigned Madness.' *Theatre Journal* (Theatrical Perception: Decay of the Aura) 39, 1 (March 1987): 63.

184 Chukovskii *Kniga o Leonide Andreeve*, 83 / 64.

7

Diaries and death

The attitude which the Allied Governments have assumed with
regard to tormented Russia is either *betrayal* or *madness*.

Leonid Andreev, *SOS* (1919)[1]

For most of 1912–13, Andreev suffered from constant migraines,
insomnia and a pain in his arm. Finally in 1914, he decided to go to
Rome with Anna and Savva to convalesce.[2] The final act of Andreev's life
was one of failing health and diminished artistic abilities. These
problems were complicated further by war and revolution, which
monopolized a great amount of Andreev's attention. This chapter
concentrates on the author's Finnish diary, where the illness experience
is once again at the fore, as well as Andreev's own pursuit of treatment.
As noted at the beginning of this study, if we examine Andreev's
narrative of illness from adolescent diary, through his literary works, to
his final Finnish entries, we gain perspective on how neurasthenia influenced the author's life and works.

Panpsyche theater

Andreev first published 'A letter on the Theater' in the March 1912 issue
of the journal *Masks* (Maski). This letter was republished with a second
letter in 1914 as 'Letters on the Theater' (Pis'ma o teatre) in volume 22 of
the *Shipovnik* almanac. In these letters, Andreev argued for a new type of
theater that would maintain the internal, psychological and intellectual
development of a character for the stage. The theater of spectacle must
be supplanted by a theater of the mind, a theater of the 'panpsyche,' like
the productions offered by the Art Theater in Moscow. *Drama* must
occur internally, whereby the characters' external actions are driven by
the internal psychological struggles within the character, the joys and
suffering of the human experience.

To appreciate Andreev's theory of the panpsyche, it is necessary to

7.1 Leonid Andreev in 1914, while under the treatment of
Dr Iosif Gerzoni in Petrograd.

remember his understanding of *verisimilitude*, which meant providing a
truth that people wanted to see, rather than the often painful truth that
might lead to disappointment or a sense of betrayal. Andreev's theory of
the panpsyche theater seemingly grew out of this concept in which there
is an outward acceptable truth, a thin veneer, which often hides a less
attractive, psychologically complex truth about the individual. At certain
moments, this unattractive truth shows through the veneer and creates
dramatic, often psychological, tension.

Andreev's most popular play of this period, *He Who Gets Slapped*, is
populated by individuals who have a circus persona and a real life
history that is only revealed for brief moments during the play. The
Count is not really royalty. The circus performer Consuelo is not really
Count Mancini's daughter. The dashing horse trainer Bezano is actually

quite shy and reserved in person. The unattractive truth about the clown, He, is that he is running from a failed marriage, betrayed by a good friend and his own wife. He is hiding from this psychological pain within a circus, where he can be a clown whose humiliation is viewed by those around him as part of a humorous act. These circus colleagues have their own secrets to keep and do not want to know why the clown suffers so greatly. They are more than willing to accept this veneer, a clown who is repeatedly slapped and humiliated, as the real man. Tension, therefore, is created by the psychological dissonance found in the veneer of a circus clown, covering the tragic loss and betrayal of an intellectual who has turned his back on his former life.

Once this is understood by the theater audience, the secondary story of He's love for Consuelo reveals added meaning as the clown tries to save the young girl from a similar type of betrayal and humiliation that he has himself just experienced. The clown's love is further intensified because his rival for Consuelo's affection is the Baron, the same kind of scoundrel as the former friend who betrayed He's trust and stole his wife. For each external story-line, there is an even more dynamic internal story-line that is developed in parallel. In these parallel story-lines, we find the psychological tension that Andreev wished to maintain and develop for the Russian stage. In order to hide their true emotional and psychological states, Andreev's characters perform, maintaining an appearance of normalcy for the other characters in the play, as well as for the theater audience. This false normalcy interacts with the unattractive truth that is slowly revealed throughout the course of the play to provide the psychological motivation for the characters' actions, which then unites the two parallel story-lines into what Andreev called a panpsyche drama.

In Andreev's theater of the panpsyche we find many of the ideas and themes of his previous literary and dramatic works. Psychological disharmony is interconnected with the performance and a desire for verisimilitude, which allows for the depiction of two *truths* – one that exists for public consumption and a second that festers within the individual. Andreev suggests that the tension that exists between this external persona and the internal, *real* self is what creates *drama*. When viewed within the context of Andreev's life and works, his theories on panpsyche drama interrelate profoundly with his own reported illness experience. As noted in the previous chapter, the performance replicates *normal* behavior while providing meaning for the illness experience – an individual's internal truth.

Chronic illness

At the end of January 1914, Andreev and part of his family took a vacation to Italy. There, Andreev continued to suffer from ill health. At one point, he suffered a minor heart attack that was accompanied by deep despair.[3] At the beginning of March, Anna wrote to Aleksandr Kipen (1870–1938) that her husband was full of 'blackness,' identifying his state of depression with the dark bile of Hippocratic medicine, which represented melancholy.[4] 'He does not want to go to the doctor. And I do not know what is with his heart: nerves or some sort of a physical defect that is appearing. Probably a little bit of both. How wonderful it would be if he were healthy. That would be a treat, what a rare treat.'[5] Andreev too wrote to Kipen at the end of the summer that he had been sick for three weeks with acute neuralgia in his right arm and shoulder, an uninterrupted pain that negatively impacted every aspect of his life.[6]

In August 1914, Andreev wrote to his youngest brother Andrei: 'Since about the 25th of July I have been unwell: at first there were bad signs of an appendicitis; it seems that this was not the correct diagnosis, as upon our return to Vammelsuu (27th) I had severe neuralgia in my right arm, [and] a relentless pain seemingly in my tooth, that did not allow me to sleep.'[7] Possibly as a result of these symptoms, Andreev sought treatment from Dr Iosif Gerzoni in Petrograd from 27 September through to 20 November 1914.[8] His medical care consisted of a strict diet of semolina and no more than four glasses of weak tea a day. This was the typical treatment for neurasthenia. Andreev claimed that the diet did not have a noticeable effect and that he felt like he was trapped in a cage.[9] Andreev writes to his brother from the hospital: 'The first couple days I began to feel better, but suddenly something unexpectedly snatched my head and heart and I began to feel bad.'[10]

Vadim, who visited in November, remembered the uneaten breakfast, his father's 'sullen and haggard' look and the complaint that his arm never stopped aching. Andreev's mother went to the hospital every day, convinced that her son would not recover without her help.[11] At the end of December, Andreev wrote to his brother: 'For the last while the pain in my head rages with particular strength, damn it, I live like a semi-invalid, surprising even myself with how this is turning out. I have started treatment with a new good doctor, perhaps it will work.'[12] Vadim writes that his father returned home even though he was still suffering from pain in his arm and nervous blindness (black spots which clouded his vision). His spirits lifted, however, while writing the play *Samson in Chains*, although he became 'morose and irritable' after its completion.[13]

For April and May 1915, February through April 1916, and March

1917 Andreev was under the care of Dr L.S. Abramov, who prescribed semolina and electric shock therapy for fatigue.[14] Again, this indicates that Abramov was treating him for neurasthenia. Andreev wrote to Veresaev of his treatment in a typically whimsical fashion:

> We counted on spending the spring in Moscow, but instead of this I have already been in the clinic (Tverskaia 10) for five weeks, where with limited success I treat my numerous illnesses. How many of them there are! And the liver, and the digestion, and the uretic diathesis, and a complete abnormality of the nervous, vasculomotor and other systems. And there is the constant, almost incessant headache![15]

Beklemisheva remembers that Andreev did not like being left alone and that on at least one occasion he called his mother in the middle of the night to return to the clinic so as to alleviate his anxiety.[16] Once again, he needed the calming influence of a female companion. Even so, he masked his fear in humor. Andreev used to joke with his mother that she did not know the difference between the physician Ivan Merezheevskii and the symbolist poet Dmitrii Merezhkovskii. He supposedly jested: 'Mamasha is undergoing treatment with Merezhkovskii.'[17]

In July 1915, Andreev wrote to Andrei after returning from a visit to the doctor: 'He did not find any organic defects but one, neurasthenia.'[18] In September, Andreev admits in a note to a friend that it is not the war that has left him in a state of depression and unable to write, but the various illnesses and the melancholy. He concentrates his illness in two areas, his head and heart, and views his entire life in a constant state of exhaustion.[19] 'I am still far from recuperation, I'm turning sour, my head aches, as are the other elements of my personality,' complained Andreev to Andrei on 7 March 1916. 'Yes it is so boring undergoing treatment. Complete attention is paid to [my] health, my head is empty, I don't have any kind of life, with a withering discipline of baths, electrification, injections and medicine.'[20] In May, after returning to Vammelsuu, Andreev wrote to Goloushev, 'I am a melancholic, a hypochondriac, a nervous case, a psychasthenic.'[21]

Beklemishva claims that from around 1913 until the end of his life, Andreev suffered from constant headaches and pain in his arm. She writes that he was first under the care of Merezheevskii, a leading degeneration theorist and a professor of psychiatry at the Military-Medical Academy in St Petersburg, and then from 1913 to 1917 was treated by a Dr Niurenberg, although these claims cannot be corroborated.[22]

Treatment

Andreev's experience with hospitals and asylums was probably better than the norm given that he was treated in Moscow and Petrograd and not in provincial madhouses where conditions were at their worst. Also it is likely that Andreev received the latest treatments for neurasthenia as a literary personality. This involved dietary limitations, rest and electric shock therapy.[23] However, the treatments did not cure Andreev and must have seemed to him like only temporary solutions to his ongoing struggle. The types of treatment his literary characters receive allow suppositions about Andreev's faith, or lack thereof, in modern medicine.

At the beginning of the story 'The Thought,' the reader is told that Kerzhentsev was committed to the Elizavetinskaia Psychiatric Hospital for examination by several experienced psychiatrists. Possibly Andreev had in mind the Ekaterinskaia Hospital in Moscow as his model for the fictional Elizavetinskaia. The Ekaterinskaia was established in 1775 and by 1795 had evolved into a correctional home for criminals and others who had brought 'shame and dishonor' on society. It was also believed that the Ekaterinskaia provided space to the Secret Chancellery for people punished for social and/or political crimes. In 1808 the Preobrazhenskaia Hospital in Moscow was opened specifically for the treatment of the mad. The hospital was originally designed for the humane care of patients but, as the hospital quickly became over-crowded, guards were added and restraining devices were used frequently as the police began to incarcerate madmen whom they felt were violent and incurable. By the 1820s the director complained that the hospital was being used as a detention facility for political prisoners with faulty diagnoses of mental illness. In the 1850s, a section of the Ekaterinskaia was used for the preliminary observation of patients. In 1862 the Ekaterinskaia was closed and all the patients were moved to the Preobrazhenskaia.[24] Although Andreev probably never had to endure direct contact with criminals and political prisoners during his hospital stays, the idea that this could eventually happen if his condition rapidly deteriorated, must have been unnerving.

At the end of the nineteenth century, the psychiatric profession suggested that it was the only authority equipped to diagnose and treat the insane. Julie V. Brown writes '[Psychiatrists] became active propagandists for the institutionalization of the insane. [...] Their journals were rife with accounts of dangerous acts committed by madmen, and they advocated the removal of all of the insane from society for the protection of the latter.'[25] In 1899, the government confirmed psychiatrists' concerns about the danger of madmen, but left admission to mental institutions in the hands of the courts and police. This ruling eroded psychiatrists' control over entrance to overpopulated asylums and minimized their role in court proceedings.[26] Psychiatrists eventually rejected their role in *police* psychiatry and began to blame the government for the erroneous conflation of the criminally deviant and the clinically insane.

In *The Thought* Kerzhentsev is watched by the nurse, Masha, whom Kerzhentsev believes is insane herself. In a small note he mentions that the intern Petrov has refused him the necessary dose of chloralamide so that he can sleep and that this will drive him mad.[27] As in the play, Andreev develops the idea that sanity is all about power. Those in power are designated sane and those incarcerated are insane:

> Help me, you learned men! Let your authoritative words tip the scales in this or that direction and so resolve this wild, dreadful dilemma. [...]You have one enormous advantage, which grants to you alone the knowledge of truth: you have not committed a crime, you are not under indictment, and you have been invited to explore my psychic condition for a substantial fee. This is why I am insane. On the other hand, if it were you who were confined here, Professor Derzhembitsky, and I who had been invited to observe you, then you would be the madman and I the king of the roost – the expert, the liar, who differs from other liars only in that he lies under oath.[28]

The issue is less about diagnosis and treatment in Kerzhentsev's mind than about the doctors playing the roles of judge and jury in deciding his guilt. Unfortunately for Kerzhentsev, when it comes to the trial, the doctors are divided equally in their opinions, denying him a definitive statement about his sanity. The role of the doctors is to decide Kerzhentsev's suitability to stand trial and there is no pretense of treatment or rehabilitation.

The only doctors found in 'Red Laugh' are at the battle front, and they are all insane according to the soldier narrator:

> 'The doctor's mad, too. Take a look at him.'
> The doctor was not listening. He was squatting on his haunches, swaying, his lips and fingertips moving noiselessly. In his eyes I saw that same fixed, dumbfounded, stunned look.[29]

> Still looking at me in the same stern way, [the orderly] shook his finger again, then took out his revolver and shot himself through the temple. I was neither surprised nor frightened. Shifting my cigarette to my left hand, I felt his wound with my finger. [...] Still yelling at me [the doctor] turned his back to me, and I went up to the man who had said he would shoot himself next. He, too, was an orderly, a student. His forehead pressed to the side of a car, he was sobbing, his shoulders heaving.[30]

Our doctor, the one who had amputated my legs, a gaunt old man who stank of iodoform, tobacco smoke, and carbolic acid and was always smiling with this spare yellow-gray mustache ... [...] And in his old eyes so close to mine, I saw that same vacant, stunned look. And something horrible, unbearable, like the collapse of a thousand buildings at once, flashed through my brain, and turning cold with fear I whispered, 'The red laugh.' [...] 'You're out of your mind doctor!'[31]

Once home, the soldier seems to be cared for exclusively by his family and as his mental condition deteriorates, there is no treatment mentioned other than twice he is heavily sedated to induce sleep.[32]

In 'Phantoms' Dr Shevyrev does not admit any violent cases into the asylum and seems simply to house the mentally ill. The patients have little confidence in the doctor. Pomerantsev says that Dr Shevyrev 'is here to tell us untruths.'[33] Petrov thinks that the doctor is 'a drunkard and a very selfish and immoral man, who runs a nursing-home with the sole object of fleecing fools.'[34] Maria Astaf'evna, the nurse, believes that there are deficiencies in the way the asylum is operated.[35] The only treatment available to the patients are daily walks, as the doctor seems unable or unwilling to provide any other remedy: 'Every day Dr Shevyrev sat now by the side of one patient, now by another, listening very attentively, so that it seemed that he talked a great deal, but in reality he was always silent.'[36]

It is not surprising that Andreev's characters avoided asylums given their lack of effectiveness. Such a decision is depicted in the story 'Ipatov,' published in *Russian Word* (Russkoe slovo) in 1911. Nikolai Pavlovich Ipatov was a wealthy merchant with financial troubles which caused him great stress and possibly brought on a condition which left him in silence and tears. Ipatov tried to hide his condition by continually smiling or talking nonsense and would leave the room if he felt he must cry. His wife went to the priest to ask for help, but to no avail. She also sought advice from monks and doctors but they had no answers. Each time he was examined, Ipatov seemed to experience an anxiety attack which rendered him unable to explain his condition. He suffered in this way for a year. The constant weeping had an effect on his eyes and throat. 'Someone else suffering from such [an illness] would have laid hands on himself long ago, but either Ipatov lost his ability to reason, or the suffering had moved him to such a place where a person no longer has the power to even raise his hand against himself.'[37]

For the next twelve years Ipatov lived in a dark storeroom under the stairs and continued to weep and groan because of an unspecified, terrible sorrow. His wife was his sole provider during this time. Any other wife 'would have given the old man to a poorhouse or an insane asylum.'[38] The story is disturbing for the present-day reader because Ipatov is offered no relief from his suffering. Andreev's point is that people do not suffer from catastrophic illnesses because they are morally corrupt or sinful, but because they are unlucky.[39] This seems to refute the science of the day that argued that mental illness was a sign of moral deficiencies. As we have seen in Andreev's work, the insane asylum is no more therapeutic than a dark storeroom, and the medical profession offers no help to those suffering from affective illnesses. Ipatov is fortunate that he has a wife who is willing to care for him and yet, he is left to groan and weep from despair until his dying day.

Two years later, Andreev wrote the story 'He,' about the student who imagined visitations from a strange man and the family's deceased daughter. As with Ipatov, there is no attempt to treat or cure the student's condition and he is released to the care of his friend. In a telling confession the student says: 'As a matter of fact, I am dying of something. They all interrogate me, what is wrong with me and why am I silent and from what am I dying – and these questions are the most difficult for me and painful. I know that they ask out of love and want to help me, but I am terribly frightened of these questions. Do people really always know from what they are dying?'[40]

In the play *The Thought*, Kerzhentsev is treated by the doctors Ivan Petrovich and Sergei Sergeevich Primoi, as well as the professor of psychiatry Evgenii Ivanovich Semenov. It seems that even the professionals are undecided as to whether their patient is mentally ill. There were witnesses to his attacks, although Semenov claims that this does not prove that the patient is mad. Kerzhentsev has always been a bit strange, but Semenov points out that 'strange' does not mean 'insane' and offers the opinion that Kerzhentsev should be sentenced to fifteen years of penal service. The young Dr Primoi, however, notes that psychiatry is quite complex and wonders if he himself would be considered sane were he examined. Semenov argues that those who question themselves are sane, but Primoi says 'All the same I am bothered, Evgenii Ivanych. [The head] is a complex mechanism.'[41]

Moments later Semenov seems to agree with Primoi when asked about Kerzhentsev's written confession. Semenov argues that when Kerzhentsev confesses that he is insane, he is actually perfectly healthy, and when he argues that he is sane, he is completely mad. A bit like Dr Shevyrev at the *Babylon*, Professor Semenov is seemingly less concerned with his patients during his time on stage, and more interested in the nurse Masha, thereby calling into doubt his commitment to curing the clinically ill.

In the next episode, Kerzhentsev speaks to Masha and asks her for more medication to treat his insomnia. Masha says that the doctors are aware that he has not slept. Kerzhentsev then says: 'Ignoramuses! Louts! Jailers! They place a person in such conditions, so that a completely healthy person could go insane, and they call this a test, a scientific trial.'[42] Kerzhentsev is bothered by another patient who wails continually, even after he has been put in a straightjacket, and believes that the doctors themselves are nearly insane. He asks Masha if he is insane (she thinks not) and then tells her that he has been betrayed by his intellect.

When Ivan Petrovich enters the cell, he tells Kerzhentsev that he looks 'fresh.' When Kerzhentsev disagrees, Ivan Petrovich tells him that he deserves penal servitude rather than medication. Certainly there is no treatment or rehabilitation meant for the patient as now two of his physicians have expressed the opinion that Kerzhentsev should be sent to hard labor. Again, we see Andreev's conflation of prison and asylum, crime and madness, doctor and jailer. No attempt is made to diagnose his condition and Kerzhentsev is left to figure out for himself whether he is a madman who committed murder, or a murderer who went mad after committing a crime.

Andreev himself sought treatment on numerous occasions with little success, and it is not unreasonable to think that this contributed to the fact that his characters suffer a similar fate. His progression of thought on the issue seems to be that the ill are first treated without success ('Once There Was,' 'The Present,' and 'Phantoms'), then they are incarcerated as criminals ('The Thought,' 'My Notes' and *The Thought*), and finally left to die outside of institutional control ('Ipatov,' 'He' and 'Sacrifice'). This evolution of thought possibly reflects Andreev's experience with the psychiatric profession and his resignation that, like Ipatov, he would have to depend on his wife for his care and wellbeing.

The Finnish diary

The years following the start of World War I were difficult for most Russians, given that Russia was also plagued by the revolutions of 1917 and civil war during this period. Andreev's health was declining and his financial situation became very tenuous. He continued to create literary and journalistic works, and took a job in Petrograd as an editor for the newspaper the *Russian Will* (Russkaia volia) in order to stabilize his family's financial situation. In December of 1917, Finland declared independence from Russia and the Andreevs were suddenly in emigration, caught in the middle of the Finnish civil war. Although the First World War had stirred Andreev's patriotism, the failure of the February

Revolution to consolidate the military campaign against the Central Powers left him deeply disappointed.

In August 1914, Andreev began again to keep a regular diary until his death in 1919, thereby completing the narrative arc: from adolescent diary, through literary fame, to adult diary. In some sense, if we read his literary works from a semi-autobiographical perspective, Andreev's narrative of illness covers twenty-nine of his forty-eight years of life.[43] In these final years Andreev was plagued by ill health, financial problems and the threat of war. This would be difficult for anyone, but it must have seemed to Andreev that his life had come full circle.

In October 1915, Andreev reflected on his literary career stating, 'Curiously, I wrote almost all of my best things in moments of the most personal dislocations, during periods of the most difficult mental experiences.' He explains how, consumed by grief, 'Judas Iscariot and Others' was written shortly after Aleksandra's death. 'Sick, crazy with drunkenness, not thinking, I wrote "The Seven Hanged".' In 1908, after finding out that Anna had not been completely honest about her sexual history, Andreev was 'in a state of psychosis, and severe semi-madness.' During this time he wrote 'My Notes,' *Days of Our Life*, *Black Maskers*, *Earthborn Son* and *Anathema*. 'Aside from this, there were many other cases, when ill health, which interfered with my thinking, or household woes and suffering, the children's illnesses, conflict with people – heightened the quality of my work.' In contrast, Andreev was sure that his literary works suffered during times of relative tranquility. He believed that he was a better writer when he followed his intuition, rather than his intellect. 'I write well when my personal life is so agonizing that it is frightening for me to think about myself and frightening to think in general.' The illness narrative of degeneration is evident in this entry, as Andreev contemplates how much of his success has been based on 'genius' as opposed to talent. Genius, associated with psychologically traumatic moments, is negated by the rational and clear-thinking elements of his talent. We have seen this in depictions of the artist and the mathematician. Andreev believed that drunkenness enlivened his genius: 'If I could drink without losing consciousness and turning for the most part into a beast, and if the alcohol did not act so meanly and destructively on my body, on my heart, I ought of course to drink for work.'

Andreev wrote that his artistic production had suffered in the last seven or eight years (c. 1908–15) due to the harshness of critics, which had negatively impacted his genius and talent. 'Who, of the critics, knows me? It seems no one. Loves me? Also no one. But several of the readers love me – even if they do not know it. Who are they? Either the sick, or the suicidal, or those close to death, or the mad. People in whom have intermingled the genius and the untalented, life and death, health and sickness – such a mix like me.'[44]

Alekseevskii offers a similar retrospective diagnosis in 1926, equating Andreev's genius with his diagnosis of 'hysteric-neurasthenia' as though both were necessary for his creativity. He calls this the author's 'black spot' because Andreev had complained of suffering from black spots just before some catastrophic events in his life. Alekseevskii even suggests that Andreev's play *Black Maskers* was named after these spots. As with Chukovskii and many others, Alekseevskii sees in Andreev's deep emotions and excessive passions the basis for his creativity, be it photography, drawing or literature.[45]

In May 1915, having just arrived home, Andreev was forced to return to the clinic due to a pain in his arm that quickly intensified, causing great agony. The undiagnosed pain lasted for five days and only subsided once he received salt water treatments, which he was required to continue for several weeks along with an austere dietary regime.[46] Andreev complained that he had to spend his entire spring in the hospital,[47] but continued his diet, gymnastics and medicines throughout the summer.[48]

Following the short lived success of Andreev's anti-war play *King, Law, Freedom*, his financial situation became challenging as his literary fame perceptibly started to wane. The Moscow Art Theater had recently declined to produce his play *Samson in Chains* and the critics' attacks on his works had intensified and grown ever cruder. Andreev had for months tried to convince Nemirovich-Danchenko of *Samson's* worth, but to no avail. Similarly, he had offered his play *Waltz of the Dogs* to the Moscow Art Theater, but it too was rejected. Andreev's last great success was the premiere of his play *He Who Gets Slapped*, at which he had responded to fourteen curtain calls.

On 9 December 1915, Andreev's brother, Vsevelod, died of tabes dorsalis, probably the result of an untreated syphilitic infection. According to Vera, a few days before his death, her uncle went completely insane and kept repeating the nonsense phrase 'Pavel is on the terrace! Pavel is on the terrace!'[49] Syphilis was considered an illness of degeneration that resulted in moral and physical insanity. Once thought to be a hereditary disease, by the beginning of the twentieth century it was associated with the socially aberrant prostitute and the sexually deviant male customer.[50] Vsevolod's death must have deeply affected Andreev and confirmed many of his worst fears about his own struggle with neurasthenia.

As a possible result of his brother's death, Andreev returned to the autobiographical themes of 'In the Spring' more than a decade later. The play *Youth*, published in 1916, explores further the issues of suicide, failed love and a father's death. The main character Vsevolod contemplates suicide, like Pavel from 'In the Spring,' because he finds no meaning in life. 'For everyone it is spring, but for me in spring there is such intolerable, acute, agonizing melancholy – why is this, when I die, I will croak like the last dog, I will die, like soon my father will die!'[51] The fact that Zoia, Vsevolod's love-interest in the play, has left him has only added to his despair.

Later in the play, Vsevolod contemplates suicide. He blames it on 'intolerable, unthinkable, growing day by day, melancholy.'[52] He underlines the fact that he is young and healthy, but no longer wants to live. When his friend Nechaev tries to persuade him that he could become a famous lawyer, Vsevolod argues that a beautiful life is a fraud, more like a squirrel running on a wheel, borrowing a phrase used to describe his own mental condition from Andreev's adolescent diary. Looking back on his adolescence at the age of forty-four, Andreev drives away the despair of his youth by placing in the mouth of Nechaev and then Vsevolod the slogan: 'One needs to live fearlessly and intensely.'[53] The seemingly upbeat conclusion to the play is possibly a nostalgic glance at the tumultuous adolescence that Andreev endured.

Kaun suggests as much by disregarding *Youth* as a 'popular trifle.'[54] He draws our attention instead to Andreev's *Waltz of the Dogs*, bearing the subtitle *A poem of solitude*, 'permeated as it is with black sadness.'[55] In the play, published posthumously in 1922, Henry Tile is prepared to marry Elizabeth but learns that she has married another. This destroys Henry and, although he continues to work at the bank, he begins drinking heavily, stifled by the futility of his life, which is exemplified by the simple piano piece that he bangs out from time to time. His brother Karl develops a plan to kill Henry in order to collect a large life insurance policy. At the same time Henry develops a plan to steal money from the bank and go to America. In the meantime, Elizabeth returns and becomes Karl's lover. Unexpectedly, Henry kills himself; destroying everyone's plans of deceit.

At the end of his literary career, Andreev reinforced the narrative themes of lost love, solitude and suicide over the more courageous demand to live life fearlessly and intensely. Plumbed by Andreev in his adolescent diaries, solitude remained a hallmark of a majority of his literary works. In Andreev's own life there are numerous examples of these patterns of behavior – heartbreak, alcohol, suicide, depression and a reckless search for love. Andreev's personal illness narrative is about perceived and real loneliness – the depths to which it took him and his frenetic need to avoid it at all costs. This is seen in his relationship with friends and family, and is especially realized in his interaction with lovers, wives and mistresses. Andreev's solitude was all-consuming and selfish.

In February 1916, Andreev returned to the clinic for nervous disorders in Petrograd under the care of Dr Abramov. Having already completed one course of treatments, Andreev still suffered from continuous headaches which did not allow him to sleep, leaving him in a semi-catatonic state. During his stay, he reread his adolescent diaries and did not like the life he had depicted; deeming his adolescent persona boring and self-absorbed.[56]

Even after Andreev returned to Vammelsuu, he was depressed and viewed both his past and present as 'so sad, so bleak, so melancholy.' He was lethargic, laying in bed day and night, ruminating and feeling alone in 'the dark solitude.' The cost of maintaining his house and the war added to his problems, and in the second half of March he returned to the clinic. He suffered from an agitated anxiety that was close to 'fear, tears and an enormous sadness.'[57] In May, Anna wrote to Andreev's good friend Gouloshev:

> [Andreev] fell into such despair that from general advice, he is smoking again. Last night he spoke very gloomily. He spoke about how a person loses his willpower and is ready to grab a gun and shoot himself, for example. His headaches. [...] It is truly unlucky that we never happened to meet an intelligent, real doctor.[58]

In early September 1916, Andreev joined the editorial staff of the *Russian Will* as head of the fiction, stage and criticism sections, and moved with his family into an apartment in Petrograd. The building was ornate, constructed from 1823–27 for a rich merchant by the architect Domenico Adamini (1792–1860), near The Field of Mars, the Griboedov Canal and The Church of the Savior on Spilt Blood.[59] The apartment was decorated with the same heavy, large furniture that was in his house in Vammelsuu. There were dark brown curtains on the windows, dark oak furniture and a blue carpet. Andreev also hung some of his drawings on the walls – three musicians from his play *Life of Man*; a strange figure vanishing through an archway; Judas and Christ crucified together on the same cross. As in Finland, the apartment was constantly populated with guests. Aleksandr Amfiteatrov (1862–1938), Shaliapin and Sologub were regular visitors.[60]

During the summer, Andreev tried to convince his literary friends in Moscow to contribute pieces to the newspaper and was greatly disappointed when many declined his invitation. By the fall, *Russian Will* was struggling with its own internal strife and rumors that it was an organ of the Ministry of the Interior. It was believed that this seemingly progressive newspaper was actually financed by the government in collusion with industry, backed by German capital, and was created to diffuse the revolutionary movement among workers. At first Andreev seemed to believe that the progressive aims of the paper were genuine and thought that the steady income would allow him to write plays without financial worries, but neither was the case.

On 17 December 1916, Andreev premiered his one-act play *Requiem* (Rekviem) at a small theater studio in Moscow, but the production was closed after eleven performances. Yet by January, Andreev was in better spirits with hope that the coming year would bring revolution and an end to war. This desire for political change was realized in February, and Andreev was enlisted as a propaganda writer for the Provisional Government, although he quickly grew disenchanted. Vadim describes his father during a return home to Vammelsuu: 'Not a trace of his former cheerful humor, so noticeable in the early days of the revolution, now remained. He was jaded, pinched, while the lines above his eyebrows cut even deeper into his high forehead. His movements were slow, measured and severe. More and more frequently he complained about his heart and constant headaches. I thought his silence most startling: instead of his former monologues, his lively, convincing speeches, he filled the rooms of our house with silence.'[61]

The *Russian Will* was sold on the eve of the October Revolution and Andreev found himself out of work. On 26 October 1917, Andreev took his family back to Vammelsuu. Not surprisingly, Andreev's extravagant villa had not fared well in the absence of upkeep and repairs. Vadim writes that damp patches had formed on the dining room walls and that it was so cold in the house during the winter, accidentally spilled soup froze within minutes. First the dining and front rooms became uninhabitable, but quickly so did most other rooms in the house as mold covered the rafters and the leaky windows allowed heaps of snow to gather on the floor.[62] By the spring of 1918, Andreev wrote in his diary, 'I do not like sick people or sick houses.'[63] As his home showed evidence of disrepair, Andreev's health was also deteriorating. Seeing a parallel between leaky ceilings and headaches, warped floors and a bad heart, the fear of war, revolution, and a lack of money compounded his suffering. 'Every bit of my head aches. Yesterday evening it also ached. [...] Every day, almost every hour, is an uninterrupted negotiation with pain.'[64]

On 20 April 1918, Andreev was disappointed that no one had remembered the twentieth anniversary of his literary debut. Surely, this strengthened his feelings of loneliness and isolation. Five days later,

Andreev pondered his poor health and provided a rather synoptic illness narrative:

As long as I can remember, I almost always suffered from some kind of illness, even though over the course of my life I have never spent *one entire day* in bed. Serious illnesses, as such, I have not had, but there has been a frequent, and in recent years, almost uninterrupted sensation of pain. Every single one of the smallest defects in [my] mechanism [...] I feel as an intense and occasionally violent pain. After my attempted suicide in [18]94, I suffered for 8–10 years from a most cruel 'nervous heart,' one of the most agonizing tortures on this earth: an hourly expectation of death and a fear of it, lingering and uninterrupted, standing behind your will and consciousness. [...] Then there are the headaches. Three-day migraines, from which I have suffered since my youth and which duly continued until the death of Shura; after her death suddenly there was a strange interruption for five months and my head did not ache at all. And in general nothing then ached, a very curious thing. The headaches then came once again, without the former regularity, although more frequently; and each year they were all the more frequent. It was already common that I might have a headache for a *month* – that is literally for a month, every day and every night. Now it is even *difficult* for me to remember a day when my head did not ache at all, or even a little bit.

The heart and the head – these are my leitmotifs. Around these themes are facile minor motifs and endless variations: the liver, the stomach, neuralgia of the arm, (two months I underwent treatment in the hospital), uninterrupted pain of the neck muscles – like before a 'backache,' lighten-ing-like, breath-taking flashes of pain in my head before a cough or even laughter, the small of my back, my spine, a hemorrhoid.

Until the war I saved myself by means of [my yacht] *Distant One* and the skerries. In the summer, there were days of complete physical bliss: burnt by the sun, fanned by the wind, a large part of the day spent naked – bronze skin at the glorious end of summer – no reading, no thinking, genuinely and deeply experiencing 'the sea dog,' I stopped feeling the pain. Then again, not always, as there is one [symptom] I preserved unfailingly and wherever – insomnia, and from it, of course, came nothing good. On the sea insomnia appeared out of the utmost interest in the surroundings: all of my crew sleeps like the dead after a difficult day, but I peer outside, what is out there, I hasten to sleep, I hasten the entire night and indeed leap at it, not giving anyone the chance to sleep in earnest. And, in every case, towards the fall my health started to improve and I was able to work a lot. The war suspended my entire existence on the sea, and for the last four years without the slightest success I have been in the hospital four times for a month at a time and for two, received treatment for my arm, my liver, and so on and so on.

Then I became severely fatigued from [my work on] the *Russian Will*; it is from this that I really grew tired and lost something from my gold reserve. But I was still able to live and work and then there was the Bolshevik's October [Revolution]. It was with this, one could say, that my health immediately and completely abandoned me, basta. All that remained were the uninterrupted pains. Probably there is already something organic that is genuine, from which finally [these pains] will die. I know one thing: it all originates in the psyche. As it is poisoned so is everything else, so that every morning you get up in confusion: am I to get up?[65]

In this entry, we find a perception of life as a negotiated relationship with illness originating in the psyche. Scholars who have read Andreev's works through the single critical lens of pessimistic philosophy or social disadvantage, are asked to consider that this illness narrative suggests that Andreev's life is viewed more appropriately through a lens attentive to the constant pain of mental and physical illness.

Following this entry, Andreev continued to suffer from headaches and to reflect on his past.[66] At the end of April, he again read through some of his adolescent diaries and wondered at his own bold predictions of literary success – at the age of twenty.[67] The rest of Andreev's last years were spent in contemplation of war and revolution. Vadim claims that by 1918 his father had lost interest in photography and painting, that even writing in his diary became an arduous task. For so much of his life, Andreev had literally been consumed by his various passions, but now he could barely muster energy for daily living. Vadim writes:

[Father] no longer had any physical or mental strength left to keep up the struggle. He dropped his eyes, by now faded and lusterless. All of their restless brilliance, which at one time struck everyone, who came into contact with father, had vanished. The grey streaks in his long hair swept straight back, showed through more visibly. Senile bags appeared under his eyes emphasizing his general and profound weariness. He lost weight, perhaps from malnutrition, or even from the incipient starvation, while his velvet jacket sat loosely on his shoulders, investing his entire figure with a premature flabbiness. At times, he seemed like a sixty-year-old, though in reality he was only forty-six.[68]

As his house became less and less inhabitable, Andreev felt more and more isolated. Many of his friends and literary colleagues had settled in Neuvola, about sixty-five kilometers from Petrograd, while Andreev chose the more distant Vammelsuu because it was close to the ocean. 'Evidently, fate willed me here to prolong my honorable isolation. Previously I did not regret it – the drunkenness, squabbles, all those trifles – it was better to be alone, but (now) it would be better to be even in this company.'[69]

Added to his personal loneliness, Andreev became ever more disappointed by political events. In March 1918, Vladimir Lenin (1870–1924) signed the Treaty of Brest-Litovsk which gave enormous concessions to the Germans, but also brought some relief to the Bolsheviks who were fighting a civil war. Disenchanted with the political actions of the Bolsheviks, Andreev began to conceptualize Russia as a large mental asylum run by the insane. Lenin, Lev Trotskii (1879–1940), and others did not receive as much rebuke from Andreev for their counterproductive political actions as they did for their immorality, stupidity and barbarism. Andreev perceived the Bolshevik takeover and resulting collusion with the Germans as the final destruction of civilized Russian society leading to moral corruption and eventual imbecility.[70] These political set-backs seemed to contribute further to his poor health.

As Andreev's physical health continued to deteriorate, he once again experienced an *attack* on 16 May 1918. The following day he felt 'poisoned' and suffered from a severe headache and pain in his left arm. Two days later, he joked that it had been a 'coalition of pain: liver, stomach, heart and the rest.'[71] His ill health left him almost twenty pounds lighter than the previous year; and roughly forty pounds thinner than he had been in 1910. This gave him a flat stomach, which he liked, but still left his grey hair, which he did not appreciate.

Complaints about headaches and various pains are a regular part of most diary entries of this period.[72] Vadim writes, 'Father's walks became increasingly rare, as he found it difficult to go far. With every passing day, his headaches became more tortuous and tedious, as he struggled with his approaching death from a brain hemorrhage.'[73] After experiencing recurring dreams, Andreev believed that his extended illness even affected his subconscious, and this caused him further anxiety.[74] His poor physical condition was aggravated by an inadequate diet; as concessions were made so that the children received the majority of the food.[75] By mid-July 1918, however, the situation seemed to improve and Andreev enjoyed being out in the abandoned countryside, isolated from the machinations of the capital. Although he was still suffering from multiple ailments, he tried to sunbathe and give himself cold water treatments, which he claimed soothed his nerves.[76]

Andreev had always been conscious of his health and a need for exercise. The bicycle, as an example, was a recurring motif in his attempt to regulate his mental health with physical activity. He had a 'gymnasium' with a trapeze, rings, chinning bar, bench and other fitness equipment on the second floor of his house. Vera remembers that her father spent a lot of time in this room, especially during the winter months when he could no longer exercise outside.[77]

By the end of summer 1918, Andreev's mood became more

pessimistic. In his adolescence, he had turned to the philosophy of Schopenhauer and Hartmann in search of meaning for his bouts of depression, when his life seemed pointless and full of pain. He now employed a different set of intellectual touchstones to make sense of the war, revolution and his deteriorating health. He felt that the ideas of Darwin and Karl Marx (1818–1883) were to blame for the 'genuine horror' that had resulted in 'blood and murder everywhere.'[78]

After reading a book on the French Revolution, Andreev rhetorically asked how, after achieving something so wonderful, had it so quickly devolved into 'filth, blood and madness?' His answer: the very essence of man is animalistic wickedness and a predisposition to madness. 'The genius begins, but the idiot and the brute continue and finish.'[79] Andreev no longer views the world in terms of overcoming the Will, but in the context of a devolution of morals and mental capabilities that degrades the wonderful ideas of the genius into something deformed and sick. With overwhelming scientific evidence that humanity could regress, this was a legitimate explanation for the horrors of war and revolution. Andreev entertained similar ideas in early stories, such as 'The Abyss' and 'In the Fog,' but now devolution was occurring not just individually, but at the level of entire nations.

Early in the twentieth century, European nations had been threatened by the growing military and economic power of Germany. This had played on their fears of national weakness, possibly resulting from theories about physical deterioration caused by degeneration.[80] Defeat at the hands of the Japanese had caused similar national self-doubt among Russians, but the chaos of war with Germany combined with civil unrest had seemed to provide overwhelming evidence that degeneration had run its full course. For Andreev and others, there was plentiful evidence of Russia's complete devolution.

European thinkers such as William Ralph Inge (1860–1954) also recognized the Bolshevik Revolution as a threat to European civilization. Long seen as a primitive nation, the revolution nudged Russia, poisoned and sickly after war, into complete regression. By the mid-1920s Inge and other intellectuals medicalized political discourse to render the Bolsheviks and their European communist sympathizers a disease with symptoms of degeneration.[81]

Even with such a grim outlook, on 22 August 1918, Andreev cele-brated his forty-seventh birthday. He began the entry with: '[My birthday] is an exceptional situation by its own ugliness. Insomnia all night, a hemorrhoid, a headache, [my] heart – I barely got up.' Rumors of an impending German invasion compounded Andreev's feelings of despair and helplessness. 'Melancholy, when one wants to howl, cut your stomach open with a knife, drink poison, shoot yourself or someone else in the head, throw yourself from a tower – and howl until you have lost your voice and your wits.' Andreev wrote that he had only one worse birthday, in 1915, when he suffered the entire summer from headaches and a bad heart and yet, a month later he experienced great success with his play *He Who Gets Slapped*. This gave him some glimmer of hope for the days to follow his forty-seventh birthday.[82]

A week later, the author and his family moved out of their home to a dacha in nearby Tyrisevä after being able to secure a mortgage on the villa. The move was good for them because they now had reliable electricity and Andreev was close to the ocean. Water had always promoted a sense of tranquility in the author's physical and emotional states. 'My head ached, physically I was wretched, but it seemed tolerable if there was that smell and the lively sound [of the ocean].'[83] Most days, Andreev walked to the beach and, even though he suffered from constant headaches, he was able to make significant progress on his novel *The Diary of Satan*.

On 27 September, Andreev wrote: 'Agonizing health, an agonizing mental condition. Painful. Again I think about suicide. I think [about it] or does it think about me? But the ocean is splendid.'[84] Andreev took solace from the ocean as well as the proximity and companionship of friends and fellow refugees. However, he continued to complain constantly of headaches, chest pains and insomnia: 'At times all of my illnesses, having united, exhibit something like an extended attack. It is already the third or fourth day that my head and heart ache, and I am entirely filled with the peculiar feeling of a painful poison. My head is also poisoned. All the same I attempt to maintain a solid frame of mind, I laugh and loudly rejoice and this is very similar to a happy little house with windows onto a cemetery.'[85] In October, Andreev wrote to his brother Pavel, 'I am very ill. Insomnia, head and heart aches, neurasthenia and the like – for some time it has become difficult to live possessing such rotten health.'[86]

That year Tyrisevä, which had been a small summer cottage community for residents of St Petersburg, suddenly became the center of a colony of white émigrés. New houses were built and summer homes were made habitable for all seasons as bankers, stockbrokers and the capital's *nouveau riches* waited for the Bolshevik government to fall. Vadim writes that this influx of people made his father feel even more alone as they were the very same Philistines against whom he had fought his entire life.[87]

December 1918 was especially difficult for the Andreevs. Leonid's infatuations with other women had caused conflicts with Anna. One such woman was the wife of a St Petersburg business man, thirty years her senior. Vadim remembers that the woman had a light, incorporeal air and that his father became a frequent guest of hers that December until she left to join her husband abroad.[88] The rift between the Andreevs was only resolved once Andreev gave his wife his diary to read and proclaimed that Anna was his best friend and the only love of his life.[89]

A further problem was that their residence was unable to withstand the winter conditions, so the family was forced to move to another location in Tyrisevä on 10 December. On 15 December, Andreev experienced a prolonged heart attack, which he believed to be the worst he had ever experienced. Vadim argues that his father never completely recovered from this episode and remained until his death a semi-invalid who quickly grew tired at the least physical exertion.[90] Five days later, he broke one of his front teeth which caused him great pain and forced him to make three separate trips to Vyborg.[91] By the end of January 1919, however, Andreev felt much better, no longer bothered by his heart condition, and was quite warm and cozy in his new apartment.[92]

During this time, Andreev became an ardent anti-Bolshevik. He turned his attention to a political tract entitled '*SOS*,' which was directed at the West. He believed that once it was published in Paris and London, the civilized world would come to the aid of Russian society.[93] Andreev advocated intervention by Entente forces even if it meant national humiliation. Having offered his services to the Whites, but receiving a rebuff, Andreev set his sights on a lecture tour of the United States. He believed that he could awaken sympathy in the Americans for the Russian people.

Andreev's enthusiasm buoyed his health until April 1919, when he again fell quite ill. During Passion Week he wrote, 'My condition is no worse than that of Christ at this time. But he rose again! ... It is dark, like in a casket. The last few days and evenings the attacks have been asphyxiating, from which the melancholia and weakness and complete aversion to life are evolving into a wretched sensation.'[94]

On 10 May, the Andreevs returned to their villa in Vammelsuu. This exacerbated Leonid's depression, as the house had begun to rot and fall apart, and looters had stolen and defaced some of their property. At the same time, Andreev learned from his doctor that his heart had 'weakened,' leading him to believe that he was 'already up to his waist in a grave.'[95] As in his adolescence, money and illness became constant concerns. 'Apart from thoughts about my health, thoughts about money oppress me when I am not sleeping.'[96]

In September, prior to Andreev's planned departure for the United

States, he and his family moved to Mustamäki to stay at the house of Feodor Fal'kovskii (1874–1942). Fal'kovskii was a writer and director whose theater had premiered Andreev's *Days of Our Life* in 1908. The two had worked together at the *Russian Will* and had become exceptionally close after 1917. Andreev wrote on 8 September: 'I am unhealthy, congested. My mental state is agonizing.'[97] Four days later he died of a possible brain hemorrhage.

On that final day, Andreev woke up with a headache and spent most of the morning in his bedroom. He took lunch apart from his family and wrapped himself in a dark green velvet jacket and a brown silk scarf to avoid getting a chill.[98] Mariia Iordanskaia (1879–1965) recalls that Andreev went for a nap after lunch, but after some time called out to Anna. Seated on the bed, but breathing with difficulty, he said 'Anna, I am not well.' As his wife went for his medicine, Andreev fell onto his back. She gave him a few drops of medicine, he vomited, and after a time his breathing returned to normal, but for the last two hours of his life, he did not regain consciousness.[99] Andreev's death certificate states that he died of a brain hemorrhage, although most believed and then propagated that he had died of a heart attack. Andreev's own protestations about a bad heart probably contributed to this supposition, yet his father had also died of a brain hemorrhage. It would be, therefore, pure supposition to speculate on which of Andreev's numerous illnesses directly or indirectly contributed to his death.

Life of Man

Andreev's life came full circle, much as it was foretold in his play *Life of Man*. A youth of poverty and loneliness evolved into an adulthood of amazing success and incredible material wealth. Pavel believed, however, that despite his brother's outward success with his family life in Finland and his literary career, 'internally [Andreev] remained the same, suffering and alone, as he had been almost his entire life.'[100] Vadim argues that underneath his father's fame was a vacuity that eventually contributed to the precipitous decline of Andreev's literary and financial capital. Sick and insolvent at a difficult time in Russian history, Andreev died as an exile, all but forgotten by the people who once fawned over him.

Consistent throughout all of these periods of his life was the belief that he was ill. Whether it was a weak heart or a broken heart, migraines, alcoholic binges, acute neurasthenia or depression, Andreev's self-perception was closely linked to his personal illness narrative. This narrative was influenced by the scientific, medical and popular discourse of the time that combined a multitude of symptoms into a single pathology – degeneration. Since 1902, Andreev had been officially diagnosed as an acute neurasthenic. In turn, this diagnosis was reflected in his literary works, offering further insight into his personal illness experience.

Ivanov-Razumnik wrote that Andreev's works lacked an overarching philosophical idea, but reflected his own subjective experiences, which included the meaninglessness of life, fear of living, and a feeling of solitude in which death was the last absurdity.[101] Through the course of Andreev's life and literary works, one can easily find the themes of isolation and anxiety. As a result of his own experiences, Andreev had little faith in the treatment that the medical profession could provide or in hopes for a cure. As such, he viewed incarceration as the reality of the Russian medical system for dealing with *dangerous* elements of society. Degeneration theory was clearly the guiding principle of the day and many believed that Andreev effectively captured the finer points of this epidemic of degeneration in his plays and stories, as well as exhibited its symptoms in his own life.

Consequently, we can argue that Andreev's personal and artistic relationships with sickness reflected *fin de siècle* medical theories on mental illness. In turn, Andreev's literary fare was cited and discussed in popular publications by psychiatrists and critics alike as reliable evidence of the decline of Russian society, not to mention the deviance of the author himself. It is difficult, therefore, to dismiss this interaction as anything other than vital to the author's literary and autobiographical self-perception. As a result, we can reinterpret Andreev's life and works as symbolic of Russian decadence in much the same way that other authors have become emblematic of their own national decadent movements. Arguably, only by embracing Andreev's life and works as a narrative whole do we gain a complete picture of the author and the man.

Notes

1 Andreev, *SOS*, 337.
2 Ken and Rogov, *Zhizn' Leonida Andreeva*, 267–77.
3 Ibid., 270.
4 Porter, *Madness: A Brief History*, 38.
5 Chuvakov, V., ed. 'Leonid Andreev. Pis'ma A.A. Kipenu.' *De Visu*, 3/4 (1994): 11.
6 Ibid., 12.
7 Liubatovich, N., ed. 'Pis'ma k bratu. Andreiu Nikolaevichu Andreevu, unter-ofitseru vol'noopradelaiushchemusia deistvuiushchei armii.' *Zalp*, 1 (1933): 68.

8 Chuvakov, V. 'Perepiska L. Andreeva i E. Chirikova.' In *Leonid Andreev: Materialy i issledovaniia*. Edited by V. Keldysh and M. Koz'menko (Moscow: Nasledie, 2000) 83, footnote for letter 26; Andreev *SOS*, 430, footnote 4 (25 April 1918).

9 Liubatovich, 'Pis'ma k bratu,' 69.

10 IRLI, f. 9, op. 2, n. 4 l. 20. Letter of 07 October 1914 from Andreev to Andrei Andreev.

11 Vadim Andreev, *Detstvo*, 107–9 / 74.

12 IRLI, f. 9, op. 2, n. 4 l. 30. Letter of 31 December 1914 from Andreev to Andrei Andreev.

13 Vadim Andreev, *Detstvo*, 118–19 / 81–2.

14 Chuvakov, V., ed. 'L.N. Andreev: Pis'ma k A.P. Alekseevskomu.' In *Ezhegodnik rukopisnogo otdela Pushkinskogo Doma na 1977 god*. Edited by A. Khramtsova (Leningrad: Nauka, 1979) 192, footnote 1; Andreev *SOS*, 430, footnote 4 (25 April 1918). In a letter to S. Goloushev of May 1915, Andreev talks about electric shock therapy. See LRA, MS 606/F. 24. i.(22). Also see Daniil Andreev and Beklemisheva, *Rekviem*, 115.

15 RGALI, F. 1041, Op. 4, Ed. kh.r. 182.

16 Daniil Andreev and Beklemisheva, *Rekviem*, 214.

17 Ibid., 212.

18 Liubatovich, 'Pis'ma k bratu,' 70.

19 Iezuitova, 'Deviat' pisem Leonida Nikolaevicha Andreeva k Lidii Semenovne Ramenskoi,' 154.

20 Liubatovich, 'Pis'ma k bratu,' 71.

21 LRA, MS 606/F. 24.i. Letter of 5 May 1916 from Andreev to S. Goloushev.

22 Daniil Andreev and Beklemisheva, *Rekviem*, 233.

23 White, *Memoirs and Madness*, 230–2.

24 Dix, Kenneth Steven. 'Madness in Russia, 1775–1864: Official Attitudes and Institutions for Its Care.' Ph.D. dissertation (Los Angeles: University of California, 1977) 87–8; 90–3; 97; 99.

25 Brown, 'Psychiatrists and the State in Tsarist Russia,' 273.

26 Ibid., 275–7.

27 Andreev, 'Mysl',' 402 / 56.

28 Ibid., 415–16 / 72.

29 Andreev, 'Krasnyi smekh,' 35 / 95.

30 Ibid., 38–9 / 99.

31 Ibid., 41 / 102–3.

32 Ibid., 51 / 116.

33 Andreev, 'Prizraki,' 78 / 152.

34 Ibid., 83 / 162.

35 Ibid., 85 / 166.

36 Ibid., 79 / 155.

37 Andreev, 'Ipatov,' vol. 4, *Sobranie sochinenii v 6 tomakh*, 39.

38 Ibid., 40.

39 Ibid., 42.

40 Andreev, 'On,' vol. 4, *Sobranie sochinenii v 6 tomakh*, 293.

41 Andreev, *Mysl'*, 122.

42 Ibid., 124. In the play, 'jailers' is added in one of the epitaphs referring to the

doctors, possibly indicating the transformation of Andreev's thought about asylums and prisons. In the story, a similar outburst is used for Kerzhentsev's friends who try to subdue him. Clearly then, the reference to jailers is added specifically for the doctors.

43 Paul de Mann and others have argued that every fictional text has an element of autobiography and every supposed autobiography has an element of fiction. See de Man, Paul. 'Autobiography as De-Facement.' *MLN*, 94, 5 (December 1979): 919–30; Elbaz, Robert. 'Autobiography, Ideology and Genre Theory.' *Orbis Litterarum: International Review of Literary Studies*, 38, 3 (1983): 187–204. Mikhail Koz'menko reads Andreev's adolescent diaries in parallel with his literary works, seeing little difference in the two, and even going so far as to call them a diary-novel. Koz'menko, Mikhail. 'Psikhokhronika Leonida Andreeva: rannie dnevniki kak protoformy poetiki pisatelia.' In *Russkaia literatura kontsa XIX – nachala XX veka v zerkale sovremennoi nauki*. Edited by V. Polonskii (Moscow: IMLI RAN, 2008) 204–18.
44 Andreev, *SOS*, 22–5.
45 OGLMT, f. 12, op. 1, no. 144 (KP 5692), 91–6.
46 LRA, MS 606/F. 24.i. Letter of 19 May 1915 from Andreev to S. Goloushev.
47 LRA, MS 606/F. 24. i. (22). Also see Daniil Andreev and Beklemisheva, *Rekviem*, 115.
48 LRA, MS 606/F. 24.i. Letter of 1 July 1915 from Andreev to S. Goloushev.
49 Andreeva, Vera. *Dom na Chernoi rechke: Povest'* (Moscow: Sovetskii pisatel', 1974; 1980) 53. Alekseevskii suggests that Vsevolod died of progressive paralysis in a mental hospital. See, OGLMT, f. 12, op. 1, no. 165 (KP 5693 of), 85. In a conversation with the director of the Andreev museum in Orel, Olga Vologina claimed that Vsevolod died of meningitis.
50 Engelstein, *Keys to Happiness*, 165–211; Greenslade, *Degeneration, Culture and the Novel*, 163–5; Gilman, *Disease and Representation*, 252–6.
51 Andreev, 'Mladost', vol. 5, *Sobranie sochinenii v 6 tomakh*, 264.
52 Ibid., 272.
53 Ibid., 303.
54 Kaun, *Leonid Andreyev: A Critical Study*, 314.
55 Ibid., 317.
56 Andreev, *SOS*, 26.
57 Ibid., 27–29.
58 RGALI, f. 734, op. 1, ed. kh. 7, l. 6–8. Letter from A.I. Andreeva to S. Goloushev of May 1916.
59 More in Russian on the Adamini House can be found at: www.encspb.ru/article.php?kod=2804002919 accessed on 14 August 2007.
60 Vadim Andreev, *Detstvo*, 163–5 / 113–14.
61 Ibid., 182–3 / 128.
62 Ibid., 198–9 / 139.
63 Andreev, *SOS*, 37.
64 Ibid., 48.
65 Ibid., 50–1.
66 For references to headaches and other illnesses see Andreev, *SOS*, 57; 65; 67; 77; 81; 83; 89.

67 Ibid., 62–3.
68 Vadim Andreev, *Detstvo*, 202–3 / 142.
69 Andreev, *SOS*, 74.
70 Ibid., 78–84.
71 Ibid., 90.
72 Ibid., 90; 95; 99; 101; 103; 104; 107; 108–9; 110; 114; 123; 131.
73 Vadim Andreev, *Detstvo*, 221 / 155.
74 Andreev, *SOS*, 100.
75 Ibid., 101; 103; 104; 105.
76 Ibid., 107–8.
77 Andreeva, *Dom na chernoi rechke*, 78–9.
78 Andreev, *SOS*, 120.
79 Ibid., 132.
80 Greenslade, *Degeneration, Culture and the Novel*, 185–90.
81 Ibid., 243–5.
82 Andreev, *SOS*, 137–8.
83 Ibid., 142.
84 Ibid., 149.
85 Ibid., 155.
86 Ivanova and Ken, 'Leonid Andreev. Pis'ma k Pavlu Nikolaevichu i Anne Ivanovne Andreevym,' 183.
87 Vadim Andreev, *Detstvo*, 244–6 / 172–3.
88 Ibid., 246–9 / 173–5.
89 Andreev, *SOS*, 164–5.
90 Vadim Andreev, *Detstvo*, 241 / 169.
91 Andreev, *SOS*, 165.
92 Ibid., 168.
93 Kaun, *Leonid Andreyev: A Critical Study*, 165.
94 Andreev, *SOS*, 173.
95 Ibid., 177.
96 Ibid., 180.
97 Ibid., 187.
98 Vadim Andreev, *Detstvo*, 263 / 185.
99 Andreev, *SOS*, 385–7.
100 Pavel Andreev, 'Vospominaniia o Leonide Andreeve,' 205.
101 Ivanov-Razumnik, *O smysle zhizni*, 86–7; 107–10; 115; 139–40; 146.

8

Conclusions

We have scarcely begun to reflect on the physiology of the criminal, and yet we are already confronted with the indisputable realization that there is no essential difference between criminals and the insane – presupposing one believes that the customary way of moral thinking is the way of thinking of spiritual health. No faith, however, is still as firmly believed as this, and so we should not shrink from drawing its consequences by treating the criminal as an insane person: above all, not with haughty mercy but with the physician's good sense and good will.

Friedrich Nietzsche, 'The Dawn'[1]

By reopening the fourth line of critical discourse, I have attempted to reexamine Andreev's literary output in light of his personal and medical history. In doing this, the primary goal was to confront, and possibly refute, the Soviet biography of the author that has dominated discussions of Andreev since the 1960s. Specifically, in addressing why it might be that Andreev was so interested in the theme of madness and how this influenced his literary career, I have touched upon many of the issues that have remained *unanswered* by scholars. Although there will always be differing opinions, Andreev's experience with neurasthenia (specifically depression and anxiety) offers keys to understanding his personal life (drinking binges, mood swings, romantic endeavors) and literary themes (performance, institutional spaces, illness narrative). In so doing, I have attempted to show how this might then alter our understanding of Andreev's literary allegiances (realist or symbolist), how his literary works interacted with the popular science of the day (degeneration theory) and why this interaction may be the key to Andreev's immense success during his lifetime. Granted, each one of these issues could warrant its own study, but the purpose of this book was to reopen the line of discourse for further discussion of Andreev and his time. In this concluding chapter, the intention is to outline new ways of interpreting Andreev's life and works in order to encourage future scholarly

8.1 Leonid Andreev from February 1901, while a patient at the Imperial clinic for nervous disorders.

investigations that go beyond the author presented by Soviet scholars to satisfy the demands of the Soviet and post-Soviet literary markets and to be candid about the role that neurasthenia played in his life and works.

Madness in the *fin de siècle*

There is a long thematic tradition of madness and the mentally ill in Russian literature; in the works of Pushkin, Vladimir Odoevskii (1803–1869), Gogol', Dostoevskii and many more. Andreev was a product of the evolution in cultural perceptions of madness during the Russian *fin de siècle*. As a representative sample, I will compare three stories, each written a decade apart. Garshin, who suffered from mental illness and eventually committed suicide, published 'The Red Flower' in 1883. Chekhov, a medical doctor, published 'Ward No. 6' in 1892. Andreev published 'The Thought' in 1902. In each of these works, mentally ill characters are confined in an institution, but the tone of their incarceration is significantly different.

In Garshin's story, a mentally ill patient believes that all of the world's evil is concentrated in three poppies in the asylum's garden. He thwarts the vigilance of the hospital staff and finally plucks all of the flowers, but dies of nervous exhaustion. Robert D. Wessling argues that Garshin's story played a role in stylizing mental illness for the Russian intelligentsia in the 1880s. Garshin's cult of mental illness was informed in large part by the romantic ideal of madness as 'a glamorous enhancement of both the artistic temperament and exterior body.'[2]

The patient in Garshin's story performs a heroic and noble deed – he rids the world of evil. We find no hint of deviant or criminal behavior in his act of defiance. Rather, the patient's madness is a result of benevolent inspiration. Although it is overcrowded and employs primitive methods of treatment, the hospital is diligent in trying to shield the patient from over-exhaustion. The doctors are sensitive to the patient's loss of weight, pacing and sleepless nights. Therefore, the patient's death is viewed as a tragedy.

As previously noted, the assassination of Alexander II caused a tidal shift in the cultural discourse of Russian society. Following the regicide, articles in the press frequently referred to crime and sedition as a plague infecting Russian society. At the same time, Vladimir Mikhnevich (1841–1899) chronicled life in the capital as *Plagues of Petersburg* (Iazvy Peterburga), a series of tales about the moral and social diseases of contemporary Russia. The romantic notion of illness and progress was replaced by social pathology and infection, and these became prominent cultural themes in the popular press of the late Imperial period.[3]

Fitting of this shift toward a more scientific discourse, Chekhov's 'Ward No. 6' depicts the abuse of psychiatry in which Dr Ragin becomes a patient in his own hospital after befriending one of the patients who suffers from persecution mania. As Margarita Odesskaya argues, the story describes the poor conditions of psychiatry in the Russian provinces of the 1890s. She reasons that Chekhov disagrees with those who had high hopes for zemstvo social medicine, engages Nordau's theories on degeneration, and demonstrates the 'helplessness of medicine and society in the face of mental illness.'[4] Chekhov's story is representative of the movement away from the previous decade's romantic vision of mental illness toward a more *scientifically* informed approach – although clearly with misapprehensions.[5]

In 'Ward No. 6' there is a growing trepidation that abnormal behavior can be classified and identified, eliciting a general distrust of psychiatry's *objective science*. Chekhov's character states: 'Once prisons and asylums exist, someone must inhabit them. If it is not you it will be I, if not I then someone else.'[6] In this story the struggle between art and science finds its way into popular culture. Chekhov, himself a physician, suggests that if Dr Ragin can be incarcerated, then anyone can be deemed abnormal and, therefore, clinically insane. Mental illness is no longer heroic or romantic, but a medical condition that results in physical confinement.

In 1902 the focus of 'The Thought' is criminal homicide, reflecting the de-romanticized influence of degeneration theory. There is no doubt that Kerzhentsev is guilty of murder. The question is whether psychiatry is advanced enough to diagnose him as criminally insane. In Andreev's work we find evidence of the final victory of science and medicine over the romantic notions of artistic inspiration. By 1914, Andreev had rewritten *The Thought,* less as a depiction of madness and more as a judgment on psychiatry, and his contemporaries certainly read it in the context of degeneration theory and medical discourse.[7]

The insane in many of Andreev's stories are dangerous murderers, thieves, and terrorists. They are not saving the world from evil. They are not innocent victims of an overly aggressive psychiatric diagnosis. The mathematician in 'My Notes' states: 'Even during good weather, when the sun shines upon our prison, it does not lose any of its dark and grim importance, and is constantly reminding the people that there are laws in existence and that punishment awaits those who break them.'[8] Andreev's characters reflect the scientific theory of biological devolution and criminal *typology*. Because they are insane, they are morally corrupt and can commit crimes without remorse or even a genuine understanding of their transgressions.

Garshin was one of Andreev's main literary influences, and it is likely that mental illness played some part in their affinity. Iezuitova argues that Andreev developed many of Garshin's literary themes on the intelligentsia (opposition to Populism), social isolation (involving suicide and imprisonment), and war (psychology of battle).[9] Andreev's views were further shaped by the influential texts that were published following Garshin's popularity: Lombroso's *Genius and Madness* (1864; Russian translation 1892), Krafft-Ebing's *Psychopathia Sexualis* (1886; Russian translation 1887), Nordau's *Degeneration* (1892; Russian translation 1893) and many others. Therefore, we must take into account the fact that Andreev read Garshin's literary works in the context of the developing scientific language of degeneration. This difference was then realized by Andreev's contemporaries such as the critic Gekker, who argued that whereas Garshin depicted in part the process of madness in order to show readers the heights to which the psyche could ascend, Andreev's Kerezhentsev forced readers to the edge of madness itself.[10]

Even as the perception of mental illness evolved in the popular imagination, Andreev could not escape comparisons to Garshin. The actor Nikolai Khodotov (1878–1932) once tried to drive away Andreev's melancholic mood by joking that he did not need to become suicidal like Garshin. Andreev responded seriously that his doctors had already predicted madness for him and that for both of them the color red represented insanity.[11] In this context, Andreev understood mental illness as a fatal disease – in both Garshin's 'The Red Flower' and Andreev's 'Red Laugh' the main character dies of nervous exhaustion, basically neurasthenia, following prolonged bouts of psychosis.

This is a cursory look at a much larger literary topic, but it is representative of the way in which the depiction of madness and mental illness evolved in Russia over the course of three decades, influenced by the prevailing medical science. For Garshin's audience in the 1880s, mental illness was still a romantic enhancement of artistic creativity. In the 1890s Chekhov viewed the issues in scientific terms and saw little hope for a cure. Andreev in the 1900s reflected the belief that mental illness was synonymous with deviant behavior and, at times, led to criminal acts of violence. By depicting madness in this way, Andreev was giving cultural currency to degeneration theory and the psychiatrists who were claiming the authority to describe and *treat* the irrational, thereby protecting society.

The critical response

This study is a narrow look at a complex subject, not a comprehensive statement about the theme of madness in the Russian *fin de siècle* or the ways in which literary critics engaged the boundary between art and science. Instead, it aims to underscore the evolution of thought on madness at the turn of the century and asks scholars to consider the growing importance of medical discourse in Russian culture at the time. It also seeks to dispel the notion that most writers of the period were pretending to be ill as part of a decadent literary masquerade. Certainly, there were some who ascribed to this romantic pose. There were others who believed the popular theories on national decline and put their faith in the healthy proletariat. Finally, those diagnosed with ailments based on this negative discourse of degeneration reflected the anxiety of the mentally ill in their artistic works. Scientific conjecture was readily accepted and incorporated into the cultural production of the *fin de siècle*, and these cultural products were in turn cited by medical authorities as confirmation of their own theories, creating a circular argument. In effect, artists like Andreev and the critics who reviewed their works helped to prove scientific theory *correct*, ultimately ceding control over the irrational to medical authorities.

More specifically, many literary critics viewed Andreev's works within a degenerate and scientific context. In 1901, M. Chunosov [I. Iasinskii] (1850–1931) wrote that Andreev 'works with the help of a scalpel and microscope' in creating his psychological stories.[12] In 1903 Vladimir Botsianovskii (1869–1943) said that Andreev captured the animalistic quality of his characters with particular clarity, and that it was this bestial excess that was at the root of a majority of his works. The critic makes specific reference to Krafft-Ebing in his discussion of Andreev's 'The Abyss' and 'In the Fog.'[13] A year later, Aleksandr Skabichevskii (1838–1910) discussed Andreev's 'The Life of Vasilii Fiveiskii' in an article entitled 'Degenerates in Our Contemporary Fiction.'[14] Amfiteatrov called Andreev a gladiator, alluding to the artistic brutality of Roman decadence, comfortable in 'publicly ripping out the stomach of one of his own heroines and then continuing on to commit still worse to another.'[15] Allusions to Rome represented the decadent decline and fall of nations. In 1906, Dmitrii Ovsianiko-Kulikovskii (1853–1920) criticized Andreev's play *Savva* for its psychology of anarchy, claiming that the main character was a psychopath. Andreev wrote to Gor'kii of this review: 'Ovsianiko-Kulikovskii simply declares him insane, with clearly expressed delusions of grandeur, rudiments of religious derangement, degeneracy.'[16]

In 1908, T. Ganzhulevich (1880–1936) wrote that Andreev was the first to speak about decadence and degeneration; he alone described the inner world of an individual and its outward expression.[17] Nikolai Efros (1867–1923) wrote a positive article in June of that same year, celebrating ten years of Andreev's literary activities. In it, he claimed that Andreev had addressed all of the burning issues of the day. However, Efros warned that these literary works should not be read as journalism or even as historical documents. 'They are only psychological documents, from the history of his soul, from the history of the pain of his soul, of the sick incomprehension of the meaning of life, and a thirst to understand it.'[18]

In a December 1908 review of Andreev's play *Black Maskers*, Leonid Galich [Leonid Gabrilovich] (1878–1953) united the content and structure of the play with the author's medical history. 'Andreev was always subjective, was always excessively inclined towards lyricism. He always *rushed* his own creative works. This is a weakness of neurasthenics (ask any doctor): for them it is enough of a destructive irritation, as to immediately use up their nerves.' Galich argued that neurasthenia causes immediate outbursts that then result in decline and weakness. In these symptoms, Galich offered an explanation for Andreev's *rushed* literary works but also his 'Great talent. Distinctive psyche. And a clear hypertrophy of sensitivity.'[19] Here, we still find remnants of the belief that madness and genius are intertwined.

In 1909, Vladimir Friche (1870–1929) argued that Andreev's characters were neurasthenics with an unpredictable inclination towards madness, while his brand of individualism represented the final echoes of an expiring petty bourgeois society.[20] In 1910, Konstantin Arabazhin (1866–1929) suggested that Andreev gained rapid success because he was able to tap into the psychology of contemporary society as it 'is living through a difficult moment of spiritual decline, standing at the crossroad [...].'[21] L'vov-Rogachevskii reasoned that all of Andreev's characters were abnormal and that the diagnosis given to Kerzhentsev applied to all of them – degenerate. 'The degeneration of Pavel, the school pupil, of Kerzhentsev and of Nemovetskii express particularly clearly an entire array of deeds of sexual perversion and sometimes complete amoralism.'[22]

In December 1912, the Russian Futurist manifesto, *A Slap in the Face of Public Taste* (Poshchechina obshchestvennomu vkusu), dedicated an entire line to Andreev and writers like him, suggesting that readers needed to wash their hands after touching such filthy slime. Plainly, by this time Andreev was considered the leading representative of a type of decadent boulevard literature that depicted the filthy underbelly of Russian society.

A decadent conclusion

Chirikov argued that Andreev did not like to burden his friends with his psychological problems and bouts of deep despair.[23] These periods of severe depression, however, have become a leitmotif in Andreev's posthumous legacy.[24] Combine this with his recurring anxiety over solitude and the meaninglessness of life, his abuse of alcohol, and his reckless search for a love that would save him from madness and death, and an unfortunate picture of Andreev's illness experience begins to materialize. At the beginning of the twentieth century, Andreev was diagnosed as an acute neurasthenic and suffered from insomnia, persistent migraines, neuralgia of the arm, a weakening heart, and anxiety attacks. The medical science of that day asserted that neurasthenia was a hereditary degenerative illness that would eventually lead to idiocy and possible death. For Andreev, medical treatment seemed to have no lasting positive effects, and the psychiatric profession could offer no hope for a cure. Even more to the point, Andreev's doctors had predicted that the author would eventually reside in a madhouse – or so Andreev had described his condition to Khodotov.

Andreev wanted, however, to avoid being stigmatized as a psychopath, a madman or a deviant. He realized that his popular success was as reliant on his public image as it was on his literary works. Therefore, we find contradictory statements from the author about his health, depending on the audience. After all, Nordau's book *Degeneration* had transferred Morel's scientific theory from the insane asylum to the literary avant-garde. Employing psychiatric models, Nordau argued that the cultural avant-garde was not modern and progressive, but rather atavistic and regressive. Nordau's goal was to stigmatize cultural figures as perverted and sick. The key assertion was that not only the art, but also the artist, was degenerate. The literary critic Lev Kleinbort (1875–1950) remembers a discussion with Andreev about the characteristics of illness and wellness. Andreev complained, 'they always write this about me: sick thoughts ... a sickly acuteness of feeling ... All of my characters are degenerates, eaten by worms, because I myself have been physically eaten, [and] I am a degenerate. As far as I am concerned, this is sheer nonsense. My physical health can only be envied. Both my father and mother were healthy people, very robust.'[25] However, friend and fellow author Skitalets remembers that Andreev suffered from a constant fear of sudden death and an unexplained illness. 'Besides this, he had these attacks, almost monthly, of these unbearable headaches, lasting for several days, also, it seemed, groundless. Maybe it really was a hereditary illness, owing to hereditary alcoholism, which he himself suspected: it was as if there rested on his brain some black taint.'[26] These recollections encapsulate Andreev's dilemma. Nordau and the theorists of degeneracy were claiming that both the author and his literary works were demented and sick. Andreev's ill health seemed to support these notions and was reported in the press as evidence of such. To quell this stigma, Andreev made public pronouncements refuting these assertions and defending his mental health, literary works and public image.

Yet, he could not escape either the literary critics or the medical personages (doctors and psychiatrists) who used his works as examples of psychopathology. Lev Voitolovskii (1875/7–1941) graduated from the medical faculty of Kharkov University in 1900, and four years later he was sent to the front to treat patients of the Russo-Japanese War.[27] In 1905 he wrote an article for the journal *Truth*, entitled 'Social-psychological types in the stories of Leonid Andreev,'[28] arguing that social conditions influenced the psychology of Andreev's characters. He organized one group of stories ('The Thought,' 'Laughter,' 'The Lie,' 'Silence,' and 'In the Fog') around the idea of 'moral blindness' in the characters' psyches, which was exacerbated by loneliness and anxiety. Relying on the theory of degeneration, Voitolovskii argued that this condition leads to impotency and death.[29] Voitolovskii eventually became both a respected social psychologist and literary critic, and wrote about Andreev's literary works *more than ten times*.[30]

Such scholarly works again show the uneasy relationship of literary criticism presented as medical theory. This attention might be seen as positive in that it legitimated Andreev's literary talents, and negative as it drew further attention to the psychopathological elements of his works. Keeping in mind that Nordau's argument that decadent authors infected society via their degenerate artistic works, the medical discourse around such stories as well as the media attention surrounding Andreev's perceived ill health placed him in an awkward position, in which his life and works became further entwined within the imagination of his reading public.

More specifically, the codification of illness in *fin de siècle* Russia was based on the social construction of disease and the individual's internalization of these constructs.[31] Critics have tried to make connections between Andreev's literary themes and those of Dostoevskii.[32] Madness, criminality and alienation, however, are themes which cannot be ascribed to a single author or literary influence; these are a reflection of larger social anxieties. As a result, this study has asked scholars to look more broadly at the scientific discourse on degeneration found in Russian culture at the turn of the century; to reexamine the definitions of Russian decadence. A vast number of intellectuals in all fields of cultural, political and social production were influenced by this medical discourse, as well as the social construction of its pathology. Stigmatized as an acute neurasthenic, Andreev was possibly more attuned to the latest medical theories on mental illness than many of his contemporaries. In turn, his literary works, inhabited by all sorts of degenerates, should be read within the context of decadence and understood as important signposts of anxiety over the decline of civilized Russian society. Doing such allows a reinterpretation of Andreev's life and works. Asking literary scholars to reconsider Andreev's works in light of European and Russian decadence, also liberates the author to some degree from the 'not a realist, not a symbolist' discourse that has practically eliminated him from most contemporary scholarship on the period.

By reexamining Andreev's life and literary works through the cultural discourse of pathology, we can see the influence of literary decadence and the development of Russian psychiatry, especially in the context of degeneration theory. This also provides perspective on Andreev's struggle with mental illness and why some critics have argued that he was one of the most spiritually and psychologically unsettled Russian writers of his time.[33] Andreev's illness experience as an acute neurasthenic was informed by numerous factors that were ultimately infused into his literary works; reflecting his very private battle with ill health, a public battle to maintain his personal reputation, and the struggle waged between art and science for the authority to define the irrational at the turn of the twentieth century.

One might suggest that, similar to Wilde, Andreev's struggle with acute neurasthenia became a public sign of his deviance – personal and literary. Although he was never tried in a court of law like Wilde, his works were given mock trials and his life was discussed in the court of public opinion. Andreev's understanding of his condition was informed by the medical science of the day. These concepts were realized in his literary works, which were in turn used by psychiatrists and medical professionals to support the legitimacy of their science. As Wilde's life and works are emblematic of British decadence today, we might view Andreev's life and works within a similar framework, in which one cannot disentangle the discourse about the author's life from the discussion of his literary works. The two are intertwined because of the way they were read and discussed by his contemporaries.

In conclusion, this study offers avenues for further discussion of Andreev's role in Russian decadence and his relationship with the psychiatry of Russian culture. It attempts to reopen for argument aspects of Andreev's personal and literary life that were either ignored or purposely hidden by Soviet scholars. In so doing, I offer initial ways in which to contextualize troubling aspects of his personality that most certainly found expression in his creative works.

It may seem that this study is doing exactly what the author's critics did during his lifetime: Call him crazy and show how his madness is reflected in his creative works. Rather than such a simple equation, I am attempting to show that the culmination of many factors surrounding Andreev's life with neurasthenia influenced this relationship. It is not my argument that Andreev was mad and as a result he created mad characters. My argument is that Andreev was diagnosed as a neurasthenic and suffered from real problems (depression, insomnia, anxiety and others); he was told by doctors that this was a disease that resulted in moral and mental depravity, probably leading to the madhouse; he was stigmatized by some critics as a degenerate and madman. In an attempt to address the effects of his neurasthenia he self-medicated with alcohol, black tea and cigarettes; he looked for a woman to cure him of his affliction; he struggled to find meaning in a world seemingly devoid of it. All of these factors influenced his creative process. In his literary works, he explored in a personal way facets of madness, treatment, incarceration, asylums, performance, verisimilitude and much more. After all, authors often write about what they know best.

By claiming that this was part of Andreev's illness experience is not to say that his characters' experiences were his experiences. Andreev used his own familiarity with illness to create a fictional experience. In this fiction are found remnants of Andreev's own experience, but also elements of the cultural context which informed this knowledge of illness. By examining his complete works, I am suggesting, we find themes that allow us to gain insights into Andreev's relationship with neurasthenia and to better understand the theme of madness in his creative works.

If we extrapolate this further, we can make a supposition that Andreev's own relationship with neurasthenia mirrored the Russian public's anxiety about the devolution of Russian society, which explains why Andreev was such a popular literary figure. Yet another step further, we can suggest that Andreev's own relationship with neurasthenia, as found in his literary works, also united him with the larger decadent discourse of the time and is one reason why scholars still seem to struggle with literary classifications for his works.

The argument is that there were many factors in Andreev's relationship with neurasthenia that influenced his life and works and that by accepting this we might look with renewed interest at Andreev in the *fin de siècle* cultural context. After all, he was not immensely popular during his lifetime because he was a friend of Gor'kii or because his 'understanding of the "folk" [was] quite vast, universal' as some Soviet scholars have suggested.[34] He was immensely popular because he wrote about the moral decline of Russian society, interacting with the other decadent strains of modernist culture, and articulated for many the relevant issues of the day, most of which revolved around the scientific discourse of degeneration. Consequently, it is extremely relevant to consider the role that neurasthenia played in the life and works of Leonid Andreev. In questioning past classificatory practices, we might then accept Andreev as a representative of Russian decadence, and include him in scholarly discussions, once again, as a transformative figure of the Russian *fin de siècle*.

Notes

1 Nietzsche, Friedrich. *The Portable Nietzsche*. Edited and translated by Walter Kaufmann (New York: Penguin Books, 1976) 85–6.

2 Wessling, 'Vsevolod Garshin, the Russian Intelligentsia, and Fan Hysteria,' 77.

3 Beer, 'Microbes of the Mind,' 539–40.

4 Odesskaya, Margarita. "Let Them Go Crazy': Madness in the Works of Chekhov.' In *Madness and the Mad in Russian Culture*. Edited by Angela Brintlinger and Ilya Vinitsky, 194; 197; 202–5.

5 For a discussion of Chekhov's knowledge of contemporary scientific theory on psychopathology see: Gatrall, Jefferson J.A. 'The Paradox of Melancholy Insight: Reading the Medical Subtext in Chekhov's "A Boring Story".' *Slavic Review*, 62, 2 (2003): 258–77; Meve, E. *Meditsina v tvorchstve i zhini A.P. Chekhova* (Kiev: Gosmedizdat, 1961); Swift, Mark Stanley. 'Chekhov's "Ariadna": A portrait of Psychopathy and Sin.' *Slavonic and East European Review*, 68, 1 (January 2008): 26–57.

6 Chekhov, Anton. 'Palata No. 6.' In Chekhov, Anton. *Sobranie sochinenii*, vol. 7. Edited by K. Muratova (Moscow: Khudozhestvennaia literatura, 1956) 146. In English, I have quoted from 'Ward No. 6' in Tchekhoff, Anton. *The Black Monk and Other Stories*. Translated by R.E.C. Long (New York: Books for Library Press, 1970) 253.

7 Afonin, *Leonid Andreev*, 121–2.

8 Andreev, 'Moi zapiski', 126/287.

9 Iezuitova, L. 'Leonid Andreev i Vs. Garshin.' *Vestnik Leningradskogo universiteta*, 8 (1964): 97–109.

10 Gekker, *Leonid Andreev i ego proizvedenie*, 36.

11 Khodotov, Nikolai. *Blizkoe-dalekoe* (Leningrad: Iskusstvo, 1962) 231.

12 Chunosov, M. [I. Iasinskii]. 'Hevyskazannoe. (L. Andreev. Rasskazy. SPb. 1901).' *Ezhemesiachnye sochineniia*, 12 (1901): 384.

13 Botsianovskii, 'Leonid Andreev,' 32; 46–7.

14 Skabichevskii, Aleksandr. 'Degeneraty v nashei sovremennoi bellestristike.' *Russkaia mysl'*, 9 (1904): 90–101.

15 Amfiteatrov, A. *Literaturnyi al'bom* (St Petersburg: Obschestvennaia pol'za, 1904) 69–70.

16 Anisimov, *Literaturnoe nasledstvo*, 274.

17 Ganzhulevich, T. *Russkaia zhizn' i ee techeniia v tvorchestve L. Andreeva*. Second edition (St Petersburg: M.O. Vol'f, 1908) 6; 13; 48–51.

18 Efros, 'Leonid Andreev'. Possibly in *Literaturnaia nedelia*, June 1908. A clipping, without a full citation, at OGLMT n. 12, op. 1, 11980 of.

19 Galich, Leonid. 'O chernykh maskakh.' *Teatr i iskusstvo*, no. 51(21 December 1908): 913.

20 Friche, V. *Leonid Andreev. Opyt kharakteristiki* (Moscow, 1909) 72–3; 76.

21 Arabazhin, K. *Leonid Andreev. Itogi tvorchestva* (St Petersburg: Obshchestvennaia Pol'za, 1910) 4–5.

22 L'vov-Rogachevskii, *Dve pravdy. Kniga o Leonide Andreeve*, 55.

23 Chirikov, E. 'Leonid Andreev.' In *Russkie sborniki*, book 2. Edited by E. Grimm and K. Sokolov (Sofia: Rossiisko-bolgarskoe izdatel'stvo, 1921) 61–2.

24 For example, the following paragraph is found in a literary biography from 1939: 'Already in early childhood his parents were astounded by the abruptness of his character heightened by [his] irritability: the young boy was now gratuitously, loudly happy, then he fell into sadness, a brooding mood uncommon for a child. This psychological dissonance subsequently, with advancing age, intensified everything in Andreev.' See N/A. 'Literaturnyi kalendar': L.N. Andreev.' *Literaturnaia ucheba*, no. 11 (1939): 87.

25 Kleinbort, L. 'Vstrechi. L. Andreev.' *Byloe*, 24 (1924): 181.

26 Skitalets [S.G. Petrov]. 'Vstrechi. L. Andreev.' *Krasnaia nov'*, 10 (1934): 164.

27 For more on the Voitolovskii, see: www.hronos.km.ru/biograf/bio_we/voitolovsky.html; http://ru.wikipedia.org/wiki/%D0%92%D0%BE%D0%B9%D1%82%D0%BE%D0%BB%D0%BE%D0%B2%D1%81%D0%BA%D0%B8%D0%B9,_%D0%9B%D0%B5%D0%B2_%D0%9D%D0%B0%D1%83%D0%BC%D0%BE%D0%B2%D0%B8%D1%87; www.sakharov-center.ru/asfcd/auth/author.xtmpl?id=172. These websites were accessed on 14 August 2007.

28 Voitolovskii, Lev. 'Sotsial'no-psikhologicheskie tipy v rasskazakh Leonida Andreeva.' *Pravda*, 8 (August 1905): 123–40.

29 Ibid., 136–7.

30 Chuvakov, V. *Leonid Nikolaevich Andreev: Bibliografiia, vypusk 2; Literatura 1900–1919*. Edited by M. Koz'menko (Moscow: Nasledie, 1998) 584.

31 Gilman, *Disease and Representation*, 3–4.

32 Babicheva, Iu. 'Tri «Mysli» Leonida Andreeva.' *Nauchnye doklady vysshei shkoli «Filologicheskie nauki»*, 5 (1969): 30–41; Generalova '«Moi zapiski» Leonida Andreeva,' 175–6; Iasenskii, S. 'Iskusstvo psikhologicheskogo analiza v tvorchestve F.M. Dostoevskogo i L.N Andreeva.' In *Dostoevskii. Materialy i issledovaniia*, vol. 11. Edited by G. Fridlender (St Petersburg: Nauka, 1994) 156–87.

33 Grechnev, 'Rasskaz L. Andreeva «Prizraki»,' 71.

34 Iezuitova, *Tvorchestvo Leonida Andreeva*, 238.

Bibliography

Afonin, L. *Leonid Andreev*. Orel: Knizhnoe iz-vo, 1959.

——, ed. *Andreevskii sbornik: Issledovaniia i materialy*. Kursk: Kurskii gos. ped. institut, 1975.

Aiaks [A. Izmailov].'U Leonida Andreeva.' *Berzhevye vedomosti* (Vech. vyp.), 10225 (28 November 1907): 1.

Aingori, L.E., O.V. Vologina, V.Ia. Grechnev, L.A. Iezuitova, L.N. Ken and L.I. Shishkina. 'Zabluzhdenie ili obman: o tak nazyvaemom sumasshestvii Leonida Andreeva.' *Russkaia literatura*, 4 (2005): 103–14.

Alexander, Franz G. and Sheldon T. Selesnick. *The History of Psychiatry: An Evaluation of Psychiatric Thought and Practice from Prehistoric Times to the Present*. New York: Harper & Row, 1966.

Alsop, Stewart. *Stay of Execution: A Sort of Memoir*. Philadelphia: Lippincott, 1973.

Amenitskii, D. *Analiz geroia «Mysli»: K voprosu o paranoidnoi psikhopatii*. Moscow: MVO, 1915.

Amfiteatrov, A. *Literaturnyi al'bom*. St Petersburg: Obschestvennaia pol'za, 1904.

Andreev, Daniil and V. Beklemisheva, eds. *Rekviem: Sbornik pamiati Leonida Andreeva*. Moscow: Federatsiia, 1930.

Andreev, Leonid. 'V kholode i zolote.' *Zvezda*, 16 (19 April 1892): 418–22.

—— 'On, ona i vodka.' *Orlovskii vestnik*, 240 (9 September 1895): 1.

—— 'Zagadka.' *Orlovskii vestnik*, 312 (21 November); 314 (24 November); 316 (26 November 1895): 1.

—— *Bezdna. S stat'ei L'va Tolstogo i polemicheskoi literaturoi*. Berlin: Ioanna Rede, 1903.

—— 'Influentiki, neirasteniki, i alkogoliki.' In *Leonid Andreev: Sobranie sochinenii*, vol. 1, 88–92.

—— *Leonid Andreev: Sobranie sochinenii s portretom avtora i vstupitel'noi stat'ei professora M.A. Reisnera*. 13 vols. St Petersburg: Prosveshchenie, 1911.

—— 'Pis'ma k N.K. Mikhailovskomu.' In *Literaturnyi arkhiv*. Edited by K. Muratova, 51–62.

—— 'Pis'ma V.S. Miroliubovu.' In *Literaturnyi arkhiv*. Edited by K. Muratova, 65–117.

—— 'Pis'ma iz Taganskoi tiur'my.' Edited and commentary by L. Afonin. *Zvedza*, 8 (1971): 163–83.

—— *SOS: Dnevnik (1914–1919), Pis'ma (1917–1919), Stat'i i interv'iu (1919),*

Vospominaniia sovremennikov (1918–1919). Edited by Richard Davies and Ben Hellman. Moscow, St Petersburg: Atheneum/Feniks, 1994.

—— *Sobranie sochinenii v 6 tomakh*. 6 vols. Moscow: Khudozhestvennaia literatura, 1990–6.

Andreev, Pavel. 'Vospominaniia o Leonide Andreeve.' *Literaturnaia mysl'*: *Al'manakh* 3, Leningrad: Mysl' (1925): 140–207.

Andreev, Vadim. *Detstvo: Povest'*. Moscow: Sovetskii pisatel', 1963.

Andreev, Valentin. 'Chto pomniu ob ottse.' In *Andreevskii sbornik: Issledovaniia i materialy*. Edited by L. Afonin, 233–42.

Andreeva, Rimma. 'Trudnye gody.' *Orlovskaia pravda*, no. 275 (21 November 1971): 3.

Andreeva, Vera. *Dom na chernoi rechke: Povest'*. Moscow: Sovetskii pisatel', 1974; 1980.

Andreieff, Leonid. *To The Stars*. Translated by Dr. A. Goudiss. *Poet Lore*, 18, 4 (Winter 1907): 417–67.

—— *His Excellency the Governor*. Translated by Maurice Magnus. London: C.W. Daniel, Ltd., 1924.

Andreyeff, Leonid. *The Black Maskers*. In *Plays by Leonid Andreyeff*, 1–64.

—— *The Life of Man*. In *Plays by Leonid Andreyeff*, 67– 155.

—— *Plays by Leonid Andreyeff*. Translated by Clarence L. Meader and Fred Newton Scott. New York: Charles Scribner's Sons, 1918.

Andreyev, Leonid. 'The Man Who Found the Truth.' In *The Crushed Flower and Other Stories*, 269–361.

—— *The Crushed Flower and Other Stories*. Translated by Herman Bernstein. New York: Harper and Brothers, 1916.

—— 'The Friend.' In *The Little Angel and Other Stories*,135–46.

—— *The Little Angel and Other Stories*. Translated by W. H. Lowe. New York: Alfred A. Knopf, 1916.

—— 'The Life of Father Vassily.' In *When the King Loses His Head and Other Stories*, 161–272.

—— *When the King Loses His Head and Other Stories*. Translated by Archibald J. Wolfe. New York: International Book Publishing Company, 1920.

—— *Katerina (Yekaterina Ivanovna): A Drama in 4 Acts*. Translated by Herman Bernstein. New York: Brentano's, 1923.

—— *Sashka Jigouleff*. Translated by Luba Hicks. Edited and introduced by Maxim Gorky. New York: Robert McBride & Company, 1925.

—— *The Seven Who Were Hanged: A Story by Leonid Andreyev*. Translated by Herman Bernstein. New York: Illustrated Editions Company, 1941.

—— 'The Phantoms.' In *Judas Iscariot and Other Stories*, 144–89.

—— *Judas Iscariot and Other Stories*. Translated by Walter Morison and E.M. Walton. London: John Westhouse, 1947.

—— *He Who Gets Slapped: A Play in Four Acts*. Translated by Gregory Zilboorg. [1922] Reprint. Westport, Connecticut: Greenwood Press, 1975.

—— 'The Thought.' In *Visions: Stories and Photographs by Leonid Andreyev*, 31–78.

—— 'The Red Laugh.' In *Visions: Stories and Photographs by Leonid Andreyev*, 79–142.

—— 'The Thief.' In *Visions: Stories and Photographs by Leonid Andreyev*, 152–68.

—— *Visions: Stories and Photographs by Leonid Andreyev*. Edited and introduced by Olga Andreyev Carlisle. San Diego: Harcourt, Brace, Jovanovich, 1987.

Andreyev, Vadim. *Childhood.* Translated and adapted by Neil Roper. London: Cromwell Publishers, 2003.

Anisimov, I., ed. *Literaturnoe nasledstvo. Gor'kii i Leonid Andreev: Neizdannaia perepiska*, vol. 72. Moscow: Nauka, 1965.

Arabazhin, K. *Leonid Andreev. Itogi tvorchestva.* St Petersburg: Obshchestvennaia Pol'za, 1910.

Augustein, Hannah Franziska. 'J C Prichard's Concept of Moral Insanity: A Medical Theory of the Corruption of Human Nature.' *Medical History,* 40 (1996): 311–43.

Azov, V. [V.A. Ashkinazi]. 'Otryvki ob Andreeve.' *Vestnik literatury,* 9 (1920): 5.

Babicheva, Iu. 'Tri «Mysli» Leonida Andreeva.' *Nauchnye doklady vysshei shkoli «Filologicheskie nauki»,* 5 (1969): 30–41.

Baer, Joachim T. 'Anregungen Schopenhauers in eineigen Werken von Tolstoj.' In *Die Welt Der Slaven. Halbjahresschriften für Slavistik.* Edited by Peter Rehder, 225–47.

Balatova, N. and V. Bezzubov, eds. 'Pis'ma L.N. Andreeva k Vl.I. Nemirovich-Danchenko i K.S. Stanislavskomu (1913–17).' *Uchenye Zapiski Tartuskogo Gosudarstvennogo Universiteta,* 266 (1979): 231–312.

Beard, George M. *American Nervousness: Its Causes and Consequences*: New York: G.P. Putnam, 1881.

Becker, George. *The Mad Genius Controversy: A Study in the Sociology of Deviance.* Beverly Hills: Sage Publications, 1978.

Beer, Daniel. 'The Medicalization of Religious Deviance in the Russian Orthodox Church(1880–1905).' *Kritika: Explorations in Russian and Eurasian History,* 5, 3 (Summer 2004): 451–82.

—— '"Microbes of the Mind": Moral Contagion in Late Imperial Russia.' *Journal of Modern History,* 79, 3 (September 2007): 531–71.

—— 'Blueprints for Change: The Human Sciences and the Coercive Transformation of Deviants in Russia, 1890–1930.' *Osiris,* 22 (2008): 26–47.

—— *Renovating Russia: The Human Sciences and the Fate of Liberal Modernity 1880–1930.* Ithaca: Cornell University Press, 2008.

Belousov, Ivan. *Ushedshaia Moskva: Vospominaniia.* Moscow: Russkaia kniga, 2002.

Belyi, Andrei. 'Vospominaniia ob Aleksandre Aleksandroviche Bloke.' In *Aleksandr Blok v vospominaniiakh sovremennikov v dvukh tomakh.* Edited by V. Orlov, 204–322.

Bentley, Toni. *Sisters of Salome.* New Haven: Yale University Press, 2002.

Bernheimer, Charles. *Decadent Subjects: The Idea of Decadence in Art, Literature, Philosophy, and Culture of the Fin de Siècle in Europe.* Edited by T. Jefferson Kline and Naomi Schor. Baltimore: Johns Hopkins University Press, 2002.

Bernstein, Herman. *Celebrities of Our Time: Interviews.* [1924] Reprint. New York: Books for Libraries Press, 1968.

Bezzubov, V. 'Smekh Leonida Andreeva.' In *Tvrochestvo Leonida Andreeva: Issledovaniia i materially.* Edited by G. Kurliandskaia, 13–24.

—— *Leonid Andreev i traditsii russkogo realizma.* Tallin: Esti Raamat, 1984.

Bogdanov, Konstantin. *Vrachi, patsienty, chitateli: Patograficheskie teksty russkoi kul'tury XVIII–XIX vekov.* Moscow: O.G.I., 2005.

Böker, Uwe, Richard Corballis and Julie A. Hibbard, eds. *The Importance of Reinventing Oscar: Versions of Wilde during the Last 100 years.* Amsterdam: Rodopi, 2002.

Botsianovskii, V. *Leonid Andreev.* St Petersburg: Gerol'd', 1903.

Bowlt, John E. and Matthew Drutt, eds. *Amazons of the Avant-garde: Alexandra Exter, Natalia Goncharova, Liubov Popova, Olga Razanova, Varvara Stepanova, and Nadezhda Udaltsova.* New York: Guggenheim Museum, 2000.

Brintlinger, Angela and Ilya Vinitsky, eds. *Madness and the Mad in Russian Culture.* Toronto: University of Toronto Press, 2007.

Brown, Avram. 'Leonid Nikolaevich Andreev.' In *Dictionary of Literary Biography, Volume 295: Russian Writers of the Silver Age, 1890–1925.* Edited by Judith E. Kalb and J. Alexander Ogden, 21–33.

Brown, Julie V. 'Psychiatrists and the State in Tsarist Russia.' In *Social Control and the State.* Edited by Stanley Cohen and Andrew Scull, 267–87.

—— 'Peasant Survival Strategies in Late Imperial Russia: The Social Uses of the Mental Hospital.' *Social Problems,* 34, 4 (October 1987): 311–29.

—— 'Heroes and Non-Heroes: Recurring Themes in the Historiography of Russian-Soviet Psychiatry.' In *Discovering the History of Psychiatry.* Edited by Mark S. Micale and Roy Porter, 297–307.

Brusianin, V. *Leonid Andreev. Zhizn' i tvorchestvo.* Moscow: K.F. Nekrasov, 1912.

Brusyanin, V. 'The Symbolic Dramas of Andreyeff.' In *Plays by Leonid Andreyeff,* xi–xxvi.

Burenin, V. 'Kriticheskie ocherki.' *Novoe vremia,* 9666 (31 January 1903): 2.

Carlisle, Olga Andreyev. *Far from Russia: A Memoir.* New York: St Martin's Press, 2000.

Carlson, Eric T. 'Degeneration and Medicine: Theory and Praxis.' In *Degeneration: The Dark Side of Progress.* Edited by J. Edward Chamberlin and Sander L. Gilman, 121–44.

Chamberlin, J.E. 'An Anatomy of Cultural Melancholy.' *Journal of the History of Ideas,* 42, 4 (October–December 1981): 691–705.

Chamberlin, J. Edward and Sander L. Gilman, eds. *Degeneration. The Dark Side of Progress.* New York: Columbia University Press, 1985.

Chekhov, Anton. *Sobranie sochinenii,* vol. 7. Edited by K. Muratova. Moscow: Khudozhestvennaia literatura, 1956.

—— 'Ward no. 6.' In Anton Tchekhoff. *The Black Monk and Other Stories,* 213–302.

—— 'Palata no. 6.' In Anton Chekhov. *Sobranie sochinenii,* vol. 7, 121–76.

Chirikov, E. 'Leonid Andreev.' In *Russkie sborniki,* book 2. Edited by E. Grimm and K. Sokolov, 57–75.

Chukovskii, Kornei. *Leonid Andreev: Bol'shoi i malen'kii.* St Petersburg: Izdatel'skoe biuro, 1908.

—— 'Iz vospominanii o L.N. Andreeve.' *Vestnik literatury,* 11 (1919): 2–5.

—— Vospominanii. In *Kniga o Leonide Andreeve,* 73–92.

Chulkov, Georgii. Vospominanii. In *Kniga o Leonide Andreeve,* 105–24.

Chunosov, M. [I. Iasinskii]. 'Hevyskazannoe. (L. Andreev. Rasskazy. SPb. 1901).' *Ezhemesiachnye sochineniia,* 12 (1901): 377–84.

Chuvakov, V., ed. 'Iz pisem L. Andreeva – K.P. Piatnitskomu.' *Voprosy literatury,* 8 (1971): 160–84.

——, ed. 'L.N. Andreev: Pis'ma k A.P. Alekseevskomu.' In *Ezhegodnik rukopisnogo otdela Pushkinskogo Doma na 1977 god.* Edited by A. Khramtsova, 178–92.

——, ed. 'Leonid Andreev. Pis'ma A.A. Kipenu.' *De Visu*, 3/4 (1994): 8–22.

——, comp. *Leonid Nikolaevich Andreev: Bibliografiia, vypusk 1; Sochineniia i teksty.* Edited by M. Koz'menko. Moscow: Nasledie, 1995.

—— *Leonid Nikolaevich Andreev: Bibliografiia, vypusk 2; Literatura 1900–1919.* Edited by M. Koz'menko. Moscow: Nasledie, 1998.

—— 'Perepiska L. Andreeva i E.Chirikova.' In *Leonid Andreev: Materialy i issledovaniia.* Edited by V. Keldysh and M. Koz'menko, 32–86.

Clark, Hilary, ed. *Depression and Narrative: Telling the Dark.* New York: SUNY Press, 2008.

Clowes, Edith W. *The Revolution of Moral Consciousness: Nietzsche in Russian Literature, 1890–1914.* DeKalb: Northern Illinois University Press, 1988.

Cohen, Stanley and Andrew Scull, eds. *Social Control and the State.* [1983] Reprint. Oxford: Basil Blackwell, 1986.

Costa e Silva, Jorge Alberto and Giovanni DeGirolamo. 'Neurasthenia: History of a Concept.' In *Psychological Disorders in General Medical Settings.* Edited by Norman Sartoriua et al., 69–81.

Couser, G. Thomas. 'Critical Conditions: Teaching Illness Narrative.' In *Teaching Literature and Medicine.* Edited by Anne Hunsaker Hawkins and Marilyn Chandler McEntyre, 282–8.

Davies, Richard. *Leonid Andreyev: Photographs by a Russian Writer. An Undiscovered Portrait of Pre-Revolutionary Russia.* London: Thames and Hudson, 1989.

de Man, Paul. 'Autobiography as De-Facement.' *MLN*, 94, 5 (December 1979): 919–30.

Dijkstra, Bram. *Idols of Perversity. Fantasies of Feminine Evil in Fin-de-Siècle Culture.* Oxford: Oxford University Press, 1986.

Dix, Kenneth Steven. 'Madness in Russia, 1775–1864: Official Attitudes and Institutions for Its Care.' Ph.D. dissertation, University of California, Los Angeles, 1977.

Dryzhakova, Elena. 'Madness as an Act of Defense of Personality in Dostoevsky's *The Double*.' In *Madness and the Mad in Russian Culture.* Edited by Angela Brintlinger and Ilya Vinitsky, 59–74.

Eakin, Paul. *How Our Lives Become Stories: Making Selves.* Ithaca, London: Cornell University Press, 1999.

Eichenbaúm, Boris. 'Tolstoi i Shopengauer' (K voprosu o sozdanii «Anny Kareninoi»). *Literaturnyi sovremenik*, 11 (1935): 134–49.

Eksteins, Modris. 'History and Degeneration: Of Birds and Cages.' In *Degeneration: The Dark Side of Progress.* Edited by J. Edward Chamberlin and Sander L. Gilman, 1–23.

Elbaz, Robert. 'Autobiography, Ideology and Genre Theory.' *Orbis Litterarum: International Review of Literary Studies*, 38, 3 (1983): 187–204.

Elpat'evskii, S. 'Leonid Nikolaevich Andreev: Iz vospominaniia.' *Byloe*, 27–8 (1925): 275–81.

Engelstein, Laura. *The Keys to Happiness: Sex and the Search for Modernity in Fin-de-Siècle Russia.* Ithaca: Cornell University Press, 1992.

Evreinov, N. 'O «Krivom Zerkale». Kak Leonid Andreev smeialsia v borodu.' *Novyi zhurnal*, 35 (1953): 190–207.

Fatov, N. *Molodye gody Leonida Andreeva*. Moscow: Zemlia i Fabrika, 1924.

—— ed. 'Pis'ma Leonida Adreeva k A.S. Serafimovichu.' In *Moskovskii al'manakh*, 271–310.

Fee, Dwight. 'The Broken Dialogue: Mental Illness as Discourse and Experience.' In *Pathology and the Postmodern*, 1–17.

—— *Pathology and the Postmodern: Mental Illness as Discourse and Experience*. London: Sage Publications, 2000.

Foucault, Michel. *Madness and Civilization: A History of Madness in the Age of Reason*. Translated by Richard Howard. [1989] Reprint. London: Routledge Classics, 2001.

Frank, Arthur W. *At the Will of the Body: Reflections on Illness*. Boston: Houghton Mifflin Company, 1991.

—— 'Reclaiming an Orphan Genre: The First-Person Narrative of Illness.' *Literature and Medicine* (Narrative and Medical Knowledge), 13, 1 (Spring 1994): 1–21.

—— *The Wounded Storyteller: Body, Illness, and Ethics*. Chicago: The University of Chicago Press, 1995.

Friche, V. *Leonid Andreev. Opyt kharakteristiki*. Moscow, 1909.

Fridlender, G., ed. *Dostoevskii. Materialy i issledovaniia*, vol. 11. St Petersburg: Nauka, 1994.

Galant, I. 'Psikhopatologicheskii obraz Leonida Andreeva. Leonid Andreev isteronevrastenicheskii genii.' *Klinicheskii arkhiv genial'nosti i odarennosti*, 3, 2 (1927): 147– 65.

—— 'Evroendokrinologiia velikikh russkikh pisatelei i poetov. L. N. Andreev.' *Klinicheskii arkhiv genial'nosti i odarennosti*, 3, 3 (1927): 223–38.

Galich, Leonid. 'O chernykh maskakh.' *Teatr i iskusstvo*, 51(21 December 1908): 911–14.

Ganzhulevich, T. *Russkaia zhizn' i ee techeniia v tvorchestve L. Andreeva*. Second edition. St Petersburg: M.O. Vol'f, 1908.

Garro, Linda C. and Cheryl Mattingly. 'Narrative as Construct and Construction.' In *Narrative and the Cultural Construction of Illness and Healing*. Edited by Linda C. Garro and Cheryl Mattingly, 1–49.

—— eds. *Narrative and the Cultural Construction of Illness and Healing*. Berkeley: University of California Press, 2000.

Gatrall, Jefferson J.A. 'The Paradox of Melancholy Insight: Reading the Medical Subtext in Chekhov's "A Boring Story".' *Slavic Review* 62, no. 2 (2003): 258–77.

Gekker, N. *Leonid Andreev i ego proizvedenie*. Odessa: M.S. Kozman, 1903.

Generalova, N. '«Moi zapiski» Leonida Andreeva. (K voprosu ob ideinoi problematiki povesti).' *Russkaia literatura*, 4 (1986): 172–85.

—— 'Dnevnik Leonida Andreeva.' In *Literaturnyi arkhiv: Materialy po istorii russkoi literatury i obshchestvennoi mysli*. Edited by K. Grigor'ian, 1994, 247–94.

—— 'Leonid Andreev, Dnevnik 1891–1892.' In *Ezhegodnik rukopisnogo otdela Pushkinskogo doma na 1991 god*. Edited by T. Tsar'kova, 81–141.

Gilbert, Elliot L. '"Tumult of Images": Wilde, Beardsley, and *Salome*.' *Victorian Studies*, 26 (Winter 1983): 133–59.

Gilman, Sander L. *Difference and Pathology: Stereotypes of Sexuality, Race, and Madness.* Ithaca: Cornell University Press, 1985.

—— *Disease and Representation: Images of Illness from Madness to AIDS.* Ithaca: Cornell University Press, 1988.

Gilman, Stuart C. 'Political Theory and Degeneration.' In *Degeneration. The Dark Side of Progress.* Edited by J. Edward Chamberlin and Sander L. Gilman, 121–44.

Goering, Laura. '"Russian Nervousness": Neurasthenia and National Identity in Nineteenth-Century Russia.' *Medical History*, 47, 1 (2003): 23–46.

Gor'kii, Maksim. Vospominaniia. In *Kniga o Leonide Andreeve*, 5–72.

Grechnev, V. 'Pis'ma L.N. Andreeva k A.A. Izmailovu.' *Russkaia literatura*, 3 (1962): 193–201.

—— 'Rasskaz L. Andreeva «Prizraki».' *Russkaia literatura*, 2 (1997): 67–77.

Greenslade, William. 'Fitness and the *Fin de Siècle.*' In *Fin de Siècle/Fin du Globe.* Edited by John Stokes, 37–49.

—— *Degeneration, Culture and the Novel, 1880–1940.* Cambridge: Cambridge University Press, 1994.

Greenwood, E.B. 'Tolstoy, Wittgenstein, Schopenhauer: Some Connections.' In *Tolstoi and Britain.* Edited by W. Gareth Jones, 239–50.

Grigor'ian, K., ed. *Literaturnyi arkhiv: Materialy po istorii russkoi literatury i obshchestvennoi mysli.* St Petersburg: Nauka, 1994.

Grimm, E. and K. Sokolov, eds. *Russkie sborniki*, book 2. Sofia: Rossiisko-bolgarskoe izdatel'stvo, 1921.

Grossman, Joan Delaney. *Valery Bryusov and the Riddle of Russian Decadence.* Berkeley: University of California Press, 1985.

Hachten, Elizabeth A. 'In Service to Science and Society: Scientists and the Public in Late-Nineteenth-Century Russia.' *Osiris* (Science and Civil Society, 2nd Series) 17 (2002): 171–209.

Hawkins, Anne Hunsaker. *Reconstructing Illness: Studies in Pathography.* West Layfayette: Purdue University Press, 1993.

Hawkins, Anne Hunsaker and Marilyn Chandler McEntyre, eds. *Teaching Literature and Medicine.* New York: Modern Language Association, 2000.

Henze, Matthais. *The Madness of King Nebuchadnezzar: The Ancient Near Eastern Origins and Early History of Interpretation of Daniel 4.* Leiden: Brill 1999.

Hogan, Joseph and Rebecca Hogan. 'When the Subject Is Not the Self: Multiple Personality and Manic-Depression.' *a/b: Auto/Biography Studies*, 16, 1 (Summer 2001): 39–52.

Horwitz, Allan V. *The Social Control of Mental Illness.* New York: Academic Press, 1982.

Ianishevskii, A. 'Geroi rasskaza L. Andreeva «Mysl'»' s tochki zreniia vracha-psikhiatra: Publichnaia lektsiia, chitannaia v aktovom zale Kazanskogo universiteta 12 aprelia 1903 g. V pol'zu pansionata Obshchestva vzaimopo-moshchi sel'skikh i gorodskikh uchitelei i uchitel'nits.' *Nevrologicheskii vestnik*, II, 2, Kazan (Supplement 1903): 1–31.

Iasenskii, S. 'Iskusstvo psikhologicheskogo analiza v tvorchestve F.M. Dostoevskogo i L.N Andreeva.' In *Dostoevskii. Materialy i issledovaniia.* Edited by G. Fridlender, 156–87.

Iezuitova, L. 'Leonid Andreev i Vs. Garshin.' *Vestnik Leningradskogo universiteta*, 8 (1964): 97–109.
—— "Krasnyi smekh' ego literaturnoe okruzhenie, kritika, analiz.' In *Tvorchestvo Leonida Andreeva (1892– 1906)*, 151–86.
—— *Tvorchestvo Leonida Andreeva (1892–1906)*. Leningrad: Izdatel'stvo Leningradskogo universiteta, 1976.
—— 'Deviat' pisem Leonida Nikolaevicha Andreeva k Lidii Semenovne Ramenskoi.' *Russkaia literatura*, 3 (1992): 148–54.
Iudin, T. *Ocherki istorii otechestvennoi psikhiatrii*. Moscow: Medgiz, 1951.
Ivanov, I. 'Leonid Andreev na sude psikhiatrov.' *Birzhevye vedomosti*, 90 (20 February 1903): 3.
—— 'O g. Leonide Andreeve i ego kritikakh: Pis'mo v redaktsiiu.' *Birzhevye vedomosti*, 107, morning edition (1 March 1903): 2.
—— 'G-n' Leonid Andreev kak khudozhnik-psikhopatolog.' *Voprosy nervnopsikhiatricheskoi meditsiny*, 10, 1, Kiev (January–March 1905): 72–103.
Ivanov-Razumnik [Razumnik Vasilievich Ivanov]. *O smysle zhizni. F. Sologub, L. Andreev, L. Shestov*. [Second edition, St Petersburg: 1910]. Introduction by P.D. Rayfield. Letchworth: Bradda Books, 1971.
Ivanova, L. and L. Ken, eds.'Leonid Andreev. Pis'ma k Pavlu Nikolaevichu i Anne Ivanovne Andreevym.' *Russkaia literatura*, 1 (2003): 148–85.
Izmailov, A. 'Novaia povest' Leonida Andreeva.' *Berzhevye vedomosti*, 10741 (5 October 1908): 6.
—— "Chernye maski' v teatre Komissarzhevskoi.' *Russkoe slovo*, 282 (5 December 1908): 2.
—— 'Poeziia bol'nogo uma i proza zdorovogo cheloveka: («On» Leonida Andreeva).' *Novoe slovo*, 6 (1913): 127–8.
Jamison, Kay Redfield. *Touched with Fire: Manic-Depressive Illness and the Artistic Temperament*. New York: Free Press, 1993.
—— 'Manic-Depressive Illness and Creativity.' *Scientific American* (February 1995): 63–7.
Jones, W. Gareth, ed. *Tolstoi and Britain*. Oxford: Berg, 1995.
Kalb, Judith E. and J. Alexander Ogden, eds. *Dictionary of Literary Biography, Volume 295: Russian Writers of the Silver Age, 1890–1925*. Detroit: Thomas Gale, 2004.
Kannabikh, Iu. *Istoriia psikhiatrii*. Moscow: Gosudarstvennoe meditsinskoe izdatel'stvo, 1929.
Karanchi, L. 'Leonid Andreev o psikhologicheskom izobrazhenii.' *Studia Slavica Hungarica*, 12 (1972): 91–104.
Katonina, V. 'Moi vospominaniia o Leonide Andreeve.' *Krasnii student*, 7–8 (1923): 14–25.
Kaufman, A. 'Andreev v zhizni i v svoikh proizvedeniiakh.' *Vestnik literatury*, 9 (1920): 2–4.
Kaun, Alexander. *Leonid Andreyev: A Critical Study*. [1924] Reprint. New York: AMS Press, 1970.
Keldysh, V., and M. Koz'menko, eds. *Leonid Andreev: Materialy i issledovaniia*. Moscow: Nasledie, 2000.
Ken, Liudmila and Leonid Rogov. *Zhizn' Leonida Andreeva, rasskazanna im samim i ego sovremenikami*. St Petersburg: OOO 'Izdatel'sko-poligraficheskaia kompaniia "KOSTA", 2010.

Khodotov, Nikolai. *Blizkoe-dalekoe*. Leningrad: Iskusstvo, 1962.

Khramtsova, A., ed. *Ezhegodnik rukopisnogo otdela Pushkinskogo Doma na 1977 god*. Leningrad: Nauka, 1979.

Kleinbort, L. 'Vstrechi. L. Andreev.' *Byloe*, 24 (1924): 163–82.

Kleinman, Arthur. *The Illness Narratives: Suffering, Healing and the Human Condition*. New York: Basic Books, 1988.

Kniga o Leonide Andreeve, Vospominaniia M. Gor'kogo, K. Chukovskogo, A. Bloka, Georgiia Chulkova, Bor[isa] Zaitseva, N. Teleshova, Evg[eniia] Zamiatina, A. Belogo. 2nd edn. Berlin, St Petersburg, Moscow: Izdatel'stvo Z.I. Grzhebin, 1922.

Kohout, Pavel. *Poor Murderer*. Translated by Herbert Berghof and Laurence Luckinbill. New York: Viking Press, 1977.

Koonen, Alisa. *Stranitsy zhizni*. Moscow: Kukushka, 2003.

Korsakov, Sergei. *Kurs psikhiatrii.* 2nd edn. Vols. 1 and 2. Moscow: I. Rikhter, 1901.

Koz'menko, Mikhail. 'Psikhokhronika Leonida Andreeva: rannie dnevniki kak protoformy poetiki pisatelia.' In *Russkaia literatura kontsa XIX – nachala XX veka v zerkale sovremennoi nauki*. Edited by V. Polonskii, 204–18.

Krafft-Ebing, Richard von. *Psychopathia Sexualis*. Translated by Franklin Flaf. New York: Stein and Day, 1965.

Krasnov, Pl. 'Koshmarnyi pisatel'. Literaturnaia kharakteristika Leonida Andreeva.' In *Literaturnye vechera* Novogo Mira. *1903 god*. St Petersburg: M.O. Vol'f, 1903, 38– 44.

Kube, Ol'ga. *Koshmary zhizni: Kriticheski-psikhologicheskii ocherk o L. Andreeve, Pshebyshevskom, i dr. sovremennykh pisateliakh*. St Petersburg, 1909.

Kurliandskaia, G., ed. *Tvorchestvo Leonida Andreeva: Issledovaniia i materialy*. Kursk: Kurskii gos. ped. institut, 1983.

Linden, Simeon. 'Leonidas Andreieff.' *Independent Review* (February 1906): 216–17.

Liubatovich, N., ed. 'Pis'ma k bratu. Andreiu Nikolaevichu Andreevu, unterofitseru vol'noopradelaiushchemusia deistvuiushchei armii.' *Zalp*, 1 (1933): 68–74.

Lodge, Kirsten, ed. *The Dedalus Book of Russian Decadence. Peversity, Despair and Collapse*. Cambridge: Dedalus, 2007.

Lukhmanova, Nadezhda. 'Iz chustva spravedlivosti.' *Birzhevye vedomosti*, no. 105, morning edition (28 February 1903): 2.

Lunacharskii, A. 'T'ma.' In *Literaturnyi raspad*: 153–78.

—— *Literaturnyi raspad: Kriticheskii sbornik*, issue 1 St Petersburg: Zerno, 1908.

Lutz, Tom. *American Nervousness, 1903: An Anecdotal History*. Ithaca: Cornell University Press, 1991.

L'vov-Rogachevskii, Vasilii. *Dve pravdy. Kniga o Leonide Andreeve*. St Petersburg: Protemei, 1914.

McClelland, James C. *Autocrats and Academics: Education, Culture and Society in Tsarist Russia*. Chicago: University of Chicago Press, 1979.

MacLeod, Kirsten. *Fictions of British Decadence. High Art, Popular Writing, and the Fin de Siècle*. New York: Palgrave MacMillan, 2006.

Manasein, M.P. 'V meditsinskom tumane.('V tumane', rasskaz Leonida Andreeva).' *Novyi put'*, 8 (1903): 227.

Matich, Olga. 'Gender Trouble in the Amazonian Kingdom: Turn-of-the-Century Representations of Women in Russia.' In *Amazons of the Avant-garde*. Edited by John E. Bowlt and Matthew Drutt, 75–95.

—— *Erotic Utopia. The Decadent Imagination in Russia's* Fin de Siècle. Madison: University of Wisconsin Press, 2005.

Meier, Franz. 'Oscar Wilde and the Myth of the *Femme Fatale* in *Fin-de-Siècle* Culture.' In *The Importance of Reinventing Oscar*. Edited by Uwe Böker, Richard Corballis and Julie A. Hibbard, 117–34.

Menchikova, Elena. 'Psikhopatologiia v proizvedeniiakh Dostoevskogo i L. Andreeva.' *Vestnik vospitaniia*, 4, 1 (1910): 172–212.

Meve, E. *Meditsina v tvorchstve i zhini A.P. Chekhova*. Kiev: Gosmedizdat, 1961.

Micale, Mark S. and Roy Porter, eds. *Discovering the History of Psychiatry*. Oxford: Oxford University Press, 1994.

Miller, Martin A. *Freud and the Bolsheviks: Psychoanalysis in Imperial Russia and the Soviet Union*. New Haven: Yale University Press, 1998.

Møller, Peter Ulf. *Postlude to the Kreutzer Sonata: Tolstoj and the Debate on Sexual Morality in Russian Literature in the 1890s*. Translated by John Kendal. Leiden: E.J. Brill, 1988.

Morris, David B. *The Culture of Pain*. Berkeley; Los Angeles; London: University of California Press, 1991.

—— 'Narrative, Ethics, and Pain: Thinking *With* Stories.' *Narrative*, 9, 1 (January 2001): 55–77.

Moskovskii al'manakh, book 1, Moskovskii rabochii: Moscow, 1926.

Mumortsev, Aleksandr. *Psikhopaticheskie cherty v geroiakh Leonida Andreeva*. St Petersburg: Otedl'nye ottiski 'Literaturno-meditsinskogo zhurnala,' 1910.

Muratova, K., ed. *Literaturnyi arkhiv. Materialy po istorii literatury i* obshchestvennogo dvizheniia. Institut russkoi literatury (Pushkinskii Dom), issue 5, Moscow: AN SSSR, 1960.

N/A. 'Leonid Andreev na sude psikhitatrov.' *Birzhevye vedomosti*, 90, morning edition (20 February 1903): 3.

N/A. 'Bolezn' pisatelia.' *Nash ponedel'nik*, 3 (3 December 1907): 3.

N/A. 'Literaturnyi kalendar': L.N. Andreev.' *Literaturnaia ucheba*, 11 (1939): 87–90.

Newcombe, Josephine M. *Leonid Andreyev*. New York: Frederick Ungar, 1973.

Nietzsche, Friedrich. *The Portable Nietzsche*. Edited and translated by Walter Kaufmann. New York: Penguin Books, 1976.

Nordau, Max. *Degeneration*. Translated and with an introduction by George L. Mosse. New York: Howard Fertig, 1968.

Odesskaya, Margarita. '"Let Them Go Crazy": Madness in the Works of Chekhov.' In *Madness and the Mad in Russian Culture*. Edited by Angela Brintlinger and Ilya Vinitsky, 192–207.

Orlov, V. ed. *Aleksandr Blok v vospominaniiakh sovremennikov v dvukh tomakh*. Vol. 1. Moscow: Khudozhestvennaia literatura, 1980.

Orlovskii, P. [V. Vorovskii]. 'V noch' posle bitvy: L. Andreev, F. Sologub.' In *O veianiiakh vremeni*. St Petersburg: Tvorchestvo, 1908: 3–17.

Orwin, Donna. *Tolstoy's Art and Thought 1847–1880*. New Jersey: Princeton University Press, 1993.

Pek [V.A. Ashkinnazi]. 'Kstati.' *Novosti dnia*, 7088 (2 March 1903): 4.

Pick, Daniel. *Faces of Degeneration: A European Disorder, c. 1848–c. 1918*.

Cambridge: Cambridge University Press, 1989.

Platonov, K. *'Ekaterina Ivanovna' L. Andreeva. (Sudebno-psikhopatologicheskii etiud).* Kharkov: 'Utro' Zhmudskogo, 1913.

Podarskii, V. [N.S. Rusanov]. 'Nash tekushchaia zhizn': («Mysl'»).' *Russkoe bogatstvo,* 9 (September 1902): 133– 43.

Polonskii, V. *Russkaia literatura kontsa XIX – nachala XX veka v zerkale sovremennoi nauki.* Moscow: IMLI RAN, 2008.

Porter, Roy. *Madness: A Brief History.* Oxford: Oxford University Press, 2002.

—— 'Introduction.' In Porter and Wright. *The Confinement of the Insane,* 1–18.

—— *Madmen: A Social History of Madhouses, Mad-Doctors & Lunatics.* Stroud: Tempus, 2004.

—— 'Madness and Creativity: Communication and Excommunication.' In *Madness and Creativity in Literature and Culture.* Edited by Saunders and Macnaughton, 19–34.

Porter, Roy and David Wright. *The Confinement of the Insane. International Perspectives, 1800–1965.* Cambridge: Cambridge University Press, 2003.

Prendergast, Catherine. 'On the Rhetorics of Mental Disability.' In *Embodied Rhetorics.* Edited by James C. Wilson and Cynthia Lewiecki-Wilson, 45–60.

Pyman, Avril. *A History of Russian Symbolism.* [1994] Reprint. New York: Cambridge University Press, 1996.

Rancour-Laferriere, Daniel. *Tolstoy on the Couch: Misogyny, Masochism and the Absent Mother.* New York: New York University Press, 1998.

Rehder, Peter, ed. *Die Welt Der Slaven. Halbjahresschriften für Slavistik.* Munich: Verlag Otto Sagner, 1979.

Rice, James L. *Dostoevsky and the Healing Art: An Essay in Literary and Medical History.* Ann Arbor: Ardis, 1985.

Rimmon-Kenan, Shlomith. 'The Story of "I": Illness and Narrative Identity.' *Narrative,* 10, 1 (January 2002): 9–27.

Rosenthal, Bernice Glatzer, ed. *Nietzsche in Russia.* Princeton: Princeton University Press, 1986.

—— *New Myth, New World: From Nietzsche to Stalinism.* University Park: Pennsylvania State University Press, 2002.

Ruddick, Nicholas. 'The Ripper Naturalized: Gynecidal Mania in Tolstoy's *The Kreutzer Sonata* and Zola's *La Bête Humaine.*' *Excavatio,* 14, 1–2 (2001): 181–93.

Rudnev, V. *Kharaktery i rasstroistva lichnosti. Patografiia i metapsikhologiia.* Moscow: Klass, 2002.

Rybakov, Feodor. *Sovremennye pisateli i bol'nye nervy: Psikhiatricheskii etiud.* Moscow: V. Rikhter, 1908.

Rylkova, Galina. *The Archeology of Anxiety: The Russian Silver Age and its Legacy.* Pittsburgh: University of Pittsburgh Press, 2008.

Sack, Ronald. *Images of Nebuchadnezzar: The Emergence of a Legend.* London: Associated University Presses, 1991.

Sartoriua, Norman, et al., eds. *Psychological Disorders in General Medical Settings.* Toronto: Hogrefe & Huber, 1990.

Saunders, Corinne and Jane Macnaughton, eds. *Madness and Creativity in Literature and Culture.* New York: Palgrave Macmillan, 2005.

Schiller, Francis. *A Möbius Strip:* Fin-de-siècle *Neuropsychiatry and Paul Möbius.* Berkeley: University of California Press, 1982.

Schneck, Jerome M. 'Pseudo-malingering and Leonid Andreyev's "The Dilemma".' *Psychiatric Quarterly*, 44, 1 (December 1970): 49–54.

Schopenhauer, Arthur. *The Philosophy of Schopenhauer*. Edited by Irwin Edman. New York: Modern Library, 1956.

Shaikevich, M. 'Psikhologicheskaia storona v proizvedeniiakh Leonida Andreeva.' *Vestnik psikhologii, kriminal'noi atropologii i gipnotizma*, 6, 1, St Petersburg. (1909): 25–55.

—— *Psikhopatologiia i literatura*. St Petersburg, 1910.

Showalter, Elaine. *Sexual Anarchy: Gender and Culture at the* Fin de Siècle. New York: Viking, 1990.

Silard, Lena. 'K voprosu o tolstovskikh traditsiiakh v russkoi proze nachala XX. veka.' *Acta Litteraria Academiae Scientiarrum Hungaricae*, 20 (1978): 215–30.

Sirotkina, Irina. *Diagnosing Literary Genius: A Cultural History of Psychiatry in Russia, 1880–1930*. Baltimore: Johns Hopkins University Press, 2002.

Skabichevskii, Aleksandr. 'Degeneraty v nashei sovremennoi bellestristike.' *Russkaia mysl'*, 9 (1904): 90–101.

Skitalets [S.G. Petrov]. 'Vstrechi. L. Andreev.' *Krasnaia nov'*, 10 (1934): 159–75.

Smirnov, Igor'. *Psikhodiakhronologika. Psikhoistoriia russkoi literatury ot ronantizma do nashikh dnei*. Moscow: Novoe literaturnoe obozrenie, 1994.

Smith, Susan Harris. 'Ironic Distance and the Theatre of Feigned Madness.' *Theatre Journal* (Theatrical Perception: Decay of the Aura), 39, 1 (March 1987): 51–64.

Smolenskii, Nikolai. *Zashchitnikam Leonida Andreeva!* Second edition. Moscow: V.I. Logachev, 1910.

Still, Arthur and Irving Velody, eds. *Rewriting the history of madness. Studies in Foucault's Histoire de la folie*. London: Routledge, 1992.

Stokes, John, ed. *Fin de siècle/Fin du Globe: Fears and Fantasies of the Late Nineteenth Century*. London: Macmillan, 1992.

Strutinskaia, E. 'Legenda o Salome.' *Russkoe isskustvo*, 1 (2004): 140–9.

Swift, Mark Stanley. 'Chekhov's "Ariadna": A Portrait of Psychopathy and Sin.' *Slavonic and East European Review*, 68, 1 (January 2008): 26–57.

Tchekhoff, Anton. *The Black Monk and Other Stories*. Translated by R.E.C. Long. [1903] Reprint. New York: Books for Library Press, 1970.

Teleshov, Nikolai. *A Writer Remembers: Reminiscences*. Translated by Lionel Erskine Britton. London: Hutchinson, c. 1945.

—— *Zapiski pisatelia: Vospominaniia i rasskazy o proshlom*. Moscow: Moskovskii rabochi, 1966.

Terras, Victor. *A History of Russian Literature*. New Haven: Yale University Press, 1991.

Thiher, Allen. *Revels in Madness: Insanity in Medicine and Literature*. Ann Arbor: University of Michigan Press, 1999.

Tkachev, T. *Patologicheskoe tvorchestvo: (Leonid Andreev)*. Kharkov: Mirnyi trud, 1913.

Tolstoi, Lev. 'Kreitserova sonata.' In *Sobranie sochinenii v dvadtsati dvukh tomakh*, vol. 12. Moscow: Khudozhestvennaia literatura, 1982, 123–96.

Tripp, Edward. *The Meridian Handbook of Classical Mythology (Formerly Titled: Crowell's Handbook of Classical Mythology)*. New York: New American Library, 1970.

Tsar'kova, T., ed. *Ezhegodnik rukopisnogo otdela Pushkinskogo doma na 1991 god.* St Petersburg: Akademicheskii proekt, 1994.

Urusov, [A.I.] *Bezsil'nye liudi v izobrazhenii Leonida Andreeva (Kriticheskii etiud).* St Petersburg: Obshchestvennaia pol'za, 1903.

Veresaev, V. 'Leonid Andreev.' In *Sobranie sochinenii v piati tomakh*, vol. 5, 395–421.

—— *Sobranie sochinenii v piati tomakh.* Moscow: Pravda, 1961.

Voitolovskii, Lev. 'Sotsial'no-psikhologicheskie tipy v rasskazakh Leonida Andreeva.' *Pravda*, 8 (August 1905): 123–40.

Vucinich, Alexander. *Science in Russian Culture, 1861–1917.* Stanford: Stanford University Press, 1970.

Wanner, Adrian. *Baudelaire in Russia.* Gainesville: University Press of Florida, 1996.

Weir, David. *Decadence and the Making of Modernism.* Amherst: University of Massachusetts Press, 1995.

Wessling, Robert D. 'Vsevolod Garshin, the Russian Intelligentsia, and Fan Hysteria.' In *Madness and the Mad in Russian Culture.* Edited by Angela Brintlinger and Ilya Vinitsky, 75–89.

White, Frederick H. 'Leonid Andreev: Litsedestvo i obman.' *Novoe literaturnoe obozrenie*, 69 (2004): 130–43.

—— '«Tainaia zhizn'»' Leonida Andreeva: Istoriia bolezni.' *Voprosy literatury*, 1 (2005): 323–39.

—— *Memoirs and Madness: Leonid Andreev through the Prism of the Literary Portrait.* Montreal: McGill-Queen's University Press, 2006.

—— 'Tak byl li bolen L. Andreev? (O pravde, pravdopodobnosti, i prave na literaturnuiu diagnostiku).' *Russkaia literatura*, 4 (2006): 152–60.

—— 'Leonid Andreev's Release from Prison and the Codification of Mental Illness.' *New Zealand Slavonic Journal*, 41 (2007): 19–42.

—— 'Peering into the Abyss: Andreev's rejoinder to Tolstoi's *Kreutzer Sonata*.' *Canadian Slavonic Papers* L, nos. 3–4 (September–December 2008): 471–86.

—— 'Ekaterina Ivanovna and Salomé: Cultural Signposts of Degenerative Illness.' *Slavic and East European Journal* 52, 4 (Winter 2008): 499–512.

—— 'Leonid Andreev's Construction of Melancholy.' In *Depression and Narrative: Telling the Dark.* Edited by Hilary Clark, 67–79.

—— 'The Role of the Scholar in the Consecration of Leonid Andreev (1950s to present).' *New Zealand Slavonic Journal*, 44 (2010): 85–110.

—— 'Marketing Strategies: Vadim Andreev in Dialogue with the Soviet Union.' *Russian Review*, 70, 2 (April 2011): 185–97.

White, Hayden. *Metahistory, The Historical Imagination in 19th Century Europe.* Baltimore: Johns Hopkins University Press, 1973.

—— 'The Historical Text as Literary Artifact.' In Hayden White. *Tropics of Discourse*, 81–100.

—— *Tropics of Discourse: Essays in Cultural Criticism.* Baltimore: Johns Hopkins University Press, 1978.

Wilson, James C. and Cynthia Lewiecki-Wilson, eds. *Embodied Rhetorics: Disability in Language and Culture.* Carbondale: Southern Illinois University Press, 2001.

Woodward, James B. *Leonid Andreyev: A Study.* Oxford: Clarendon Press, 1969.

Zaitsev, Boris. *Vospominanii.* In *Kniga o Leonide Andreeve*, 125–46.

—— 'Molodost'' Leonida Andreeva.' *Vozrozhdenie*, 1362 (24 February 1929): 3.

Index